The British Monarchy For Dummies®

D1490214

Rulers of England 1066 to th...

The table gives birth dates, the dates when each monarc... ...curred after the end of the reign.

Monarch	Birth Date	Dates When Ruled/ Date of Death If after Reign	Monarch	Birth Date	Dates When Ruled/ Date of Death If after Reign
William I	b c. 1027–8	r 1066–87	Mary I	b 1516	r 1553–8
William II	b c. 1056–60	r 1087–1100	Elizabeth I	b 1533	r 1558–1603
Henry I	b 1068	r 1100–35	James I	b 1566	r 1603–25
Stephen	b c. 1097	r 1135–54	Charles I	b 1600	r 1625–49
Henry II	b 1133	r 1154–89	Oliver Cromwell	b 1599	r 1649–58
Richard I	b 1157	r 1189–99	Richard Cromwell	b 1626	r 1658–9 (abdicated; d 1712)
John	b 1166	r 1199–1216	Charles II	b 1630	r 1660–85
Henry III	b 1207	r 1216–72	James II	b 1633	r 1685–8 (deemed to have abdicated; d 1701)
Edward I	b 1239	r 1272–1307	William III	b 1650	r 1689–1702
Edward II	b 1284	r 1307–27	Mary II	b 1662	r 1689–94
Edward III	b 1312	r 1327–77	Anne	b 1665	r 1702–14
Richard II	b 1367	r 1377–99 (deposed; d 1400)	George I	b 1660	r 1714–27
Henry IV	b 1367	r 1399–1413	George II	b 1683	r 1727–60
Henry V	b 1387	r 1413–22	George III	b 1738	r 1760–1820
Henry VI	b 1421	r 1422–61, restored to throne, 1471 (d 1471)	George IV	b 1762	r 1820–30
Edward IV	b 1442	r 1461–83 (briefly deposed during 1471)	William IV	b 1765	r 1830–7
Edward V	b 1470	r 1483	Victoria	b 1819	r 1837–1901
Richard III	b 1452	r 1483–5	Edward VII	b 1841	r 1901–10
Henry VII	b 1457	r 1485–1509	George V	b 1865	r 1910–36
Henry VIII	b 1491	r 1509–47	Edward VIII	b 1894	r 1936 (abdicated; d 1972)
Edward VI	b 1537	r 1547–53	George VI	b 1895	r 1936–52
Jane	b 1537	r 1553 (deposed; d 1554)	Elizabeth II	b 1926	r 1952–

For Dummies: Bestselling Book Series for Beginners

The British Monarchy For Dummies®

Cheat Sheet

English Princes of Wales

The table shows the dates on which the princes were made Prince of Wales.

Monarch	Date Made Prince of Wales*	Monarch	Date Made Prince of Wales*
Edward (later Edward II)	1301	Charles (later Charles I)	1616
Edward the Black Prince, son of Edward III	1343	Charles (later Charles II)	c. 1638
Richard (later Richard II)	1376	James, son of James II	1688
Henry (later Henry V)	1399	George (later George II)	1714
Edward, son of Henry VI	1454	Frederick, son of George II	1729
Edward (later Edward V)	1471	George (later George III)	1751
Edward, son of Richard III	1483	George (later George IV)	1762
Arthur, son of Henry VII	1489	Edward (later Edward VII)	1841
Henry (later Henry VIII)	1504	George (later George V)	1901
Henry Frederick, son of James I	1610	Edward (later Edward VIII)	1910
		Charles, son of Elizabeth II	1958

*Dates of formal investiture were sometimes later.

Rulers of Scotland, 1034–1625

Monarch	Birth Date	Dates When Ruled/ Date of Death If after Reign	Monarch	Birth Date	Dates When Ruled/ Date of Death If after Reign
Duncan I	b c. 1001	r 1034–40	Margaret	b 1283	r 1286–90
Macbeth	b c. 1005	r 1040–57	John	b 1240 or 1249–50	r 1292–6 (abdicated; d 1313 or 1314)
Lulach	b c. 1029–32	r 1057–8	Robert I	b 1274	r 1306–29
Malcolm III	b c. 1031	r 1058–93	David II	b 1324	r 1329–71
Donald III	b c. 1033	r 1093–7 (deposed; d 1099)	Robert II	b 1316	r 1371–90
Edmund		r 1094–7 (deposed)	Robert III	b c. 1337–40	r 1390–1406
Duncan II	b c. 1060	r 1094	James I	b 1394	r 1406–37
Edgar	b c. 1072	r 1097–1107	James II	b 1430	r 1437–60
Alexander I	b c. 1077	r 1107–24	James III	b 1452	r 1460–88
David I	b c. 1080–5	r 1124–53	James IV	b 1473	r 1488–1513
Malcolm IV	b c. 1141–2	r 1153–65	James V	b 1512	r 1513–42
William	b c. 1142–3	r 1165–1214	Mary	b 1542	r 1542–67 (abdicated; d 1587)
Alexander II	b c. 1198	r 1214–49	James VI*	b 1566	r 1567–1625
Alexander III	b 1241	r 1249–86			

*Also reigned England as James I, 1603–25.

For Dummies: Bestselling Book Series for Beginners

The British Monarchy

FOR

DUMMIES®

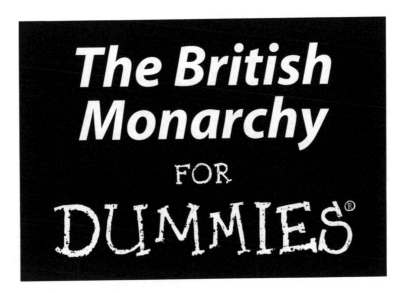

The British Monarchy

FOR

DUMMIES®

by Philip Wilkinson

BICENTENNIAL
1807
WILEY
2007
BICENTENNIAL

John Wiley & Sons, Ltd

The British Monarchy For Dummies®

Published by
John Wiley & Sons, Ltd
The Atrium
Southern Gate
Chichester
West Sussex
PO19 8SQ
England

Email (for orders and customer service enquires): cs-books@wiley.co.uk

Visit our Home Page on www.wiley.co.uk or www.wiley.com

British Library Cataloguing in Publication Data

A catalogue record for this book is available from the British Library

ISBN-13: 978-0-470-05681-3

ISBN-10: 0-470-05681-9

Printed and bound in Great Britain by Bell & Bain, Ltd, Glasgow

10 9 8 7 6 5 4 3 2 1

WILEY

About the Author

Philip Wilkinson was educated at Oxford University, after which he worked as an editor for various publishers in Britain. For the last 15 years or so, he has been a full-time writer specializing in history, the arts, and heritage. He has written books on these subjects for adults and for children, and his titles include *What the Romans Did For Us,* which accompanied the BBC television series presented by Adam Hart-Davis, the award-winning *Amazing Buildings,* and *The English Buildings Book.* He lives in the Cotswolds with his wife and son.

Author's Acknowledgements

I would like to thank Philip Hughes, David Boardman, and Michael Fisher for their advice, Zoë Brooks for her encouragement, my literary agent Isabel Atherton for her help, and the editorial team at John Wiley (especially Samantha Clapp, Rachael Chilvers, and Kelly Ewing) for their hard work on my text.

Publisher's Acknowledgements

We're proud of this book; please send us your comments through our Dummies online registration form located at www.dummies.com/register/.

Some of the people who helped bring this book to market include the following:

Acquisitions, Editorial, and Media Development

Development Editor: Kelly Ewing

Project Editor: Rachael Chilvers

Content Editor: Steve Edwards

Commissioning Editor: Samantha Clapp

Proofreader: Anne O'Rorke

Technical Reviewer: Sean Lang

Executive Project Editor: Martin Tribe

Executive Editor: Jason Dunne

Cartoons: Rich Tennant
  (www.the5thwave.com)

Composition Services

Project Coordinator: Jennifer Theriot

Layout and Graphics: Lavonne Cook, Stephanie D. Jumper

Proofreaders: Jessica Kramer, Susan Moritz

Indexer: Techbooks

Publishing and Editorial for Consumer Dummies

  Diane Graves Steele, Vice President and Publisher, Consumer Dummies

  Joyce Pepple, Acquisitions Director, Consumer Dummies

  Kristin A Cocks, Product Development Director, Consumer Dummies

  Michael Spring, Vice President and Publisher, Travel

  Kelly Regan, Editorial Director, Travel

Publishing for Technology Dummies

  Andy Cummings, Vice President and Publisher, Dummies Technology/General User

Composition Services

  Gerry Fahey, Vice President of Production Services

  Debbie Stailey, Director of Composition Services

Contents at a Glance

Table of Contents

Introduction

· ·

*B*ritain is one of a number of countries today that is a *monarchy* – in other words, the head of state isn't elected like the Presidents of the United States or France, but inherits the job from their parents. It sounds like an old-fashioned system, and it is – kings and queens have ruled in Britain for around 1600 years.

Everywhere you go in Britain, you find evidence of this long history. When you visit a stately home, the guide will tell you that 'Queen Elizabeth slept here'. If you travel around the country, you'll see the castles that monarchs built as strongholds and the sites of battles where kings fought for power. And you'll find towns and villages with royal names like King's Norton, Charlton Kings, and, of all things, Queen Camel.

And the royals are still very much around. The British press and TV news reports often feature items about Queen Elizabeth meeting foreign heads of state or Prince Charles extending his organic farm or speaking out about architecture or the natural environment. British soldiers still fight 'for queen and country', people who talk about the language sometimes refer to 'the queen's English', and in courts of justice, the senior barristers are called 'Queen's Counsel'.

The monarchy is still at the heart of British life.

About This Book

This book tells the colourful story of Britain's monarchy, from the earliest times to the present day. It explains how the monarch's role developed from that of warrior-king who had absolute power over his subjects and owned all the land in his kingdom to that of constitutional monarch with limited powers but considerable influence. It's a story that features great personalities like King Edward I and Queen Victoria, national heroes such as Robert Bruce and Owain Glyndwr, and characters like Kings Stephen and Edward II, who were disastrous as rulers and whose reigns saw their country undergo strife and upheavals that changed the course of history.

The story of the monarchy is interesting enough for these characters alone. But it's also the tale of how Britain has been governed – how rulers have worked with the people – nobles, Members of Parliament, and everyone else – and has sometimes tried to ignore the people's wishes and needs. And it's the story of how Britain gradually got more democratic, but managed to hang on to an inherited monarchy, too.

Of course, not everyone likes the monarchy. It's a bastion of privilege and doesn't seem right in the modern age. There have been some very able kings and queens, but no matter how good they are, you can't throw them out by voting for someone else, so they fail the ultimate test of democracy. But there they still are: They've lasted for 1,600 years or so with only one short break in the 17th century when there was an experiment with republicanism. If you're going to understand Britain, you need to understand their story.

Conventions Used in This Book

People – even British people – get confused about the terms used to talk about the country of Britain. Or is it England, Great Britain, or the United Kingdom? Well, actually, it's all three. The whole country is called the United Kingdom, or, to give it its more long-winded name, the United Kingdom of Great Britain and Northern Ireland. That mouthful means the nation is made up of the separate former states of England, Scotland, and Wales, plus Northern Ireland and all the islands around the British coast from the Isle of Wight to Shetland. That's the country over which the monarch reigns.

But it hasn't always been like this. For much of Britain's history, the various 'component countries' had separate rulers. Many of the characters in this book were rulers of England or Scotland. England conquered Wales in the Middle Ages, so you see a few princes of independent Wales, too. So in the early part of this book, the text talks about kings of England or Scotland, not of Britain or the United Kingdom.

In 1603, King James IV of Scotland became James I of England as well. From this point on, England and Scotland have had the same ruler. But only with the formal Act of Union in 1707 did the two countries come fully together – only after this date does it make sense to talk about kings and queens 'of Britain'.

Northern Ireland has been part of the United Kingdom for still less time and the earlier history of Ireland, a complex subject that deserves a volume of its own, lies outside the scope of this book. Even so, this book touches on the history of Ireland in a few places – when the rulers of England tried to dominate Ireland in the 16th and 17th centuries, for example, by encouraging

English settlers to live there. British monarchs ruled Ireland in the 18th and 19th centuries, just as they ruled all kinds of other countries that made up their huge worldwide empire. But in the 20th century, the southern portion of Ireland became independent, and only the North remained as part of the United Kingdom.

In addition, the dates I normally give for kings are the dates when they reigned. To discover the dates they were born and died, see the Cheat Sheet at the front of this book.

What You're Not to Read

In this book, you'll see many paragraphs accompanied by a small icon in the margin with the phrase Technical Stuff. The text next to this icon gives you interesting bits of technical information that will fill out the background of the main story. You don't have to read these paragraphs in order to understand the rest of the text. But if you do read them, you'll find out some interesting stuff about how the monarchy worked at different points in history.

Foolish Assumptions

It's a funny job being an author, having to write books with readers in mind, but with no idea who those readers are or what they know. So writers make assumptions about their readers. When writing this book, I assumed that you're vaguely familiar with the British monarchy, but don't know that much about it. You know that Britain still has a royal family, and you know some of their names, but you're not too clear about what they actually do all day or how much power they really have.

In the words of the old song, you probably 'don't know much about history', either. But you've likely come across some of the historical sites linked with the monarchy – places like Buckingham Palace or Windsor Castle. You may even have visited them or seen pictures of them on the Web.

How This Book Is Organised

This book is arranged chronologically, starting with the first kings and queens in Britain and ending with the present day. I've divided the book into parts. Part I gives you basic information about what the monarchy is and how it works. Each subsequent part deals with one period of history. Within the parts, the text is further split up into chapters. Most chapters tell the story of one ruling dynasty or family – for example, you'll find chapters on the Normans, who ruled in the 11th and 12th centuries, and on the Tudors, who came to power in 1485 and stayed on the throne until 1603.

You can read this book in one go, from start to finish, to get a broad history of the British monarchy. Or you can read just the chapters on the eras or monarchs you're especially interested in. The following sections give a quick summary of the information you can find in each part.

Part 1: All About the Monarchy

What do kings and queens actually do? And how much power do they really have? This part answers these questions. It tells you how, in the early centuries of the British monarchy, rulers had lots of power. They made the laws and everyone had to obey them. Partly because kings and queens were so powerful, lots of people wanted the job, and rulers often had to fight for power – and to fight some more to hang on to it. They also had to plan for the future, by making sure that they had a suitable heir to carry on their work when they died.

But nowadays, things are different, so this part of the book also looks at how the modern monarchy works. Today Britain's ruling family has nothing like the power it used to have. Laws are made by the democratically elected Parliament, and the queen simply advises the government and approves the new laws. But the ruler still has a busy time doing all kinds of work, from representing the nation as a ceremonial figurehead to supporting the activities of countless charities. Being monarch is certainly a full-time job.

Part 11: Early Rulers

This part tells you about the first monarchs to rule in England during the period after the Romans, who'd been ruling Britain as part of their huge empire, got fed up, and left in the early fifth century. Most of these rulers were Anglo-Saxons and came over from northern Europe to fill the power-vacuum left by the departing Romans. Loads of these Anglo-Saxon monarchs ruled mostly quite small areas of the country, and they came and went quite quickly.

Part II covers the most important and famous monarchs, especially those who were able to extend their territory and rule over a large region – or even, now and then, all of England. They were alive a long time ago, but some of them had an amazing influence that lasted for centuries – King Edgar, for example, spearheaded a revival of monasteries that transformed England's religion, while King Alfred promoted the English language, commissioning books and translations into English – and more or less inventing English literature.

Part III: The Middle Ages

In 1066, a dramatic change happened to the monarchy in England. William I, from Normandy in northern France, crossed the Channel, invaded, and became king. This part of the book looks at the 400-plus years that followed; the period known as the Middle Ages or medieval period. It was the time of knights and castles, which were the tools that medieval kings used to stay in power. It was a time when the Christian church became extremely influential, partly by playing a key role in king-making ceremonies, such as inaugurations and coronations, and effectively giving monarchs spiritual, as well as worldly, power.

And it was a period when England had a special, but stormy, relationship with France – English kings either ruled large chunks of France at this time or spent much of their lives fighting to win power there. Many of the most famous medieval kings were warriors – William I who conquered England, Edward I who won control of Wales, Henry V who beat the stuffing out of France. It all sounds disreputable today, but in the Middle Ages, if you were a successful fighter, you became a hero.

Part IV: The Kings of Scotland

This part looks at Scotland, which was a totally separate country from England before the 17th century. Just like England, Scotland began divided into a number of miniature kingdoms until some rulers eventually lost power to their neighbours, and a united country emerged.

But it wasn't all plain sailing because the Scots had to protect their southern border from the English. Border scrapping occurred all through the Middle Ages. Some of it was just local trouble – local families stealing each other's sheep and cattle. But sometimes the fighting was on a much larger scale – English kings Edward I and Edward II tried unsuccessfully to take over Scotland, and Edward III got involved in the dynastic trouble between two of Scotland's most powerful families, the Bruces and the Balliols. Eventually one dynasty, the Stewarts, became Scotland's most successful royal family, reigning from the late 14th to the early 17th century.

Part V: Kingdoms United: Tudors, Stuarts, and Hanoverians

I cover three of the most influential royal dynasties – the Houses of Tudor, Stuart, and Hanover – in this part, which follows the history of the monarchy from 1485 all the way to 1901. This was a time of huge change, seeing England and Scotland united and the English crown playing a major part in the government of Ireland, too.

It was also the period in which Britain's influence spread all around the world – a process that began with voyages of exploration under the Tudors in the 16th century and came to a climax with the growth of a huge British empire, which, in the 19th century, stretched from Canada to India.

The rulers who presided over these changes were some of the most outsize personalities in the history of the monarchy – Henry VIII, who divorced and even beheaded his wives in his desperation to get a male heir; Elizabeth I, who was a multitalented Renaissance woman; Charles I who lost a war with Parliament, making his country a republic for a while; George III, who had an illness that affected his sanity but was much loved; and Victoria, Britain's longest-reigning monarch.

Part VI: Modern Royals: The House of Windsor

The monarchs of the 20th and 21st centuries have had to adjust to the most rapid period of change in the history of the planet. Two World Wars, economic upheavals, the loss of the empire, and a more democratic system of government have brought huge changes for everyone in Britain – and huge challenges for the monarchy. This part tells the story of how the country's rulers have coped with these challenges.

It's a story of the shrinking of royal power. But this shrinkage hasn't meant that the monarchs have a less prominent part in the life of the nation – far from it. The monarchs of the 20th century gradually reinvented themselves, as advisers to their Prime Ministers, as national symbols and figureheads, and even as media personalities.

The British monarchy is still highly traditional – it respects titles, old wealth, old-fashioned courtesies, and privileges rooted in centuries of history. But it's also active in more ways, and in more corners of people's lives, than ever before.

Part VII: The Part of Tens

Here are some fascinating bits of royal trivia. This part covers royal homes and other places with links to royal history. They're mostly places you can visit, so the story of the monarchy comes alive here. You also find out about groups of royals who don't always get their time in the spotlight of history – the consorts (wives and husbands) of some of the rulers and the Princes of Wales. Some fascinating characters – some of whom are famous for eccentricities or special interests, some of whom were real 'powers behind the throne', men and women who influenced British history in their own right – reside in this part.

Icons Used in This Book

As you read this book, you'll see little icons in the margin, symbols that highlight some paragraphs in the text. Text that's accompanied by an icon gives you something extra to think about. Get used to icon-spotting, and you can see what kind of information is coming up as you read.

The history of the monarchy is full of interesting stories about the kings and queens who've ruled in Britain – but not all of them are actually true! This icon highlights the myths. The text tells the stories, warns you that they're false – and, where possible, explains why such tall tales came to be told in the first place.

Many kings and queens are quite complicated characters, and history is full of twists and turns. So it's not surprising that over the years, historians – most of whom like nothing more than a good argument – disagree about events and personalities. This icon highlights some of the main disagreements, and the text tells both sides of the story.

This icon points to text that's especially important because it helps you understand ideas and upcoming events. It helps to take special note of the text next to the Remember icon – and the icon can help you find the place in the text where you can find these explanations if you want to refer to them.

This text explains all kinds of out-of-the-way facts and details about the role and work of the British monarchs. You don't have to read this stuff if you're in a hurry, but it will help you understand some of the background to the monarchy and how it works if you do read it.

Where to Go from Here

Wherever you open this book, you'll find it's divided into small sections that are designed to be easy to find and give you access to information about separate topics. So you don't have to read the whole book.

If you're interested in the recent history of the monarchy, read Part VI. If you want to find out about the Tudors, you can just read Chapter 13. But whichever bit of British royal history grabs your attention, it's not a bad idea to read Part I first. This part gives you a brief low-down on the background to monarchy, how the system has worked over the years, and what being a king or a queen actually entails. After that, read what you want – if you want to know the whole story, you can even read the whole book!

Part I
All About the Monarchy

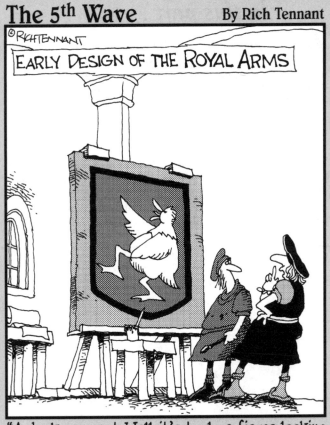

The 5th Wave   By Rich Tennant

EARLY DESIGN OF THE ROYAL ARMS

"A duck rampant. Well, it's truly a fierce looking duck, indeed. But I think His Majesty had another animal in mind. What about a swan rampant?"

In this part . . .

For hundreds of years, Britain's head of state has been a monarch – in other words, a king or a queen. But what does the monarch and the royal family actually do? Well, the role of the monarch has changed a lot over the years. The first kings wielded total power – they made all the laws, owned most of the land, and nearly everyone obeyed them unthinkingly.

The situation of today's queen is very different. She has a lot of influence, but very little real power. This part looks at how the job of the monarch has changed, what kings' and queens' priorities were in the early days, and how they differ from those of the ruler today.

Chapter 1

Ruling Principles

The British monarchy has existed continuously since the seventh century, with only one short break when the country was a republic in the mid-17th century. That's around 1,400 years, during which the monarchy changed a lot. But a number of important concerns and principles have remained at the heart of the monarchy for most of this 1,400-year period.

From the very beginning of the British monarchy, the island's rulers had to fight to gain control, to keep their kingdom united, and to stay in power, facing challenges both from local rivals and invaders from beyond Britain's shores. Many rulers became known as military leaders as a result. Once safe on the throne, they had to make sure that they had a suitable heir to take over after they died to carry on this leadership role.

But the struggles faced by a ruler weren't just military ones – paying for the monarchy became a challenge, too. To raise taxes, kings and queens had to secure the approval of at least some of their people. The people, in turn, realised that their taxability gave them some bargaining power with the monarch. They traded power for taxes, gradually curbing the authority of the monarchy and slowly tipping the balance of power in favour of the people. Eventually, the people gained power more formally through *Parliament* (the national assembly that eventually evolved into the country's legislative body), which, by the 18th century, had taken over many of the monarch's traditional powers.

Nowadays, the power of the monarch is strictly limited by the various rules, both written and unwritten, that make up the British Constitution. In other words, Britain has what is called a *constitutional monarchy,* one in which the real power is in the hands of Parliament, but in which the monarch can still advise his or her government.

How the United Kingdom Came to Be United

Today, when you talk about Elizabeth II being queen of the United Kingdom, you know roughly the size of her domain. Elizabeth is queen of the island of Britain (which includes England, Wales, and Scotland), plus Northern Ireland and various surrounding islands. She's also head of state of various lands around the world, from Canada to Bermuda.

For hundreds of years, national boundaries weren't very well defined, and rulers were nearly always under threat of attack. Plenty of rivals wanted a slice of the royal action, either by taking over the whole kingdom or by grabbing part of it. These rivals came from overseas or even from the ruler's own backyard. Monarchs had to be able to defend themselves and often had to fight to show that they were in charge.

Enemies within

The story of the British monarchy begins back in the fifth century. A few hundred years earlier, Britain had been part of the Roman empire, but in the early fifth century, the Romans pulled out. They left behind a power vacuum that was filled by seven or so regional rulers, each of whom reigned over a chunk of Britain. These local kings fought with each other to try to gain control of more territory, until one ruler, the king of Wessex, became the dominant power throughout England (see Chapter 4).

The eras of monarchy

For convenience, historians divide the huge time span of British history into broad periods. This division is especially useful in the early centuries of British history, when kings and queens changed quite frequently, and remembering where you are in the big picture is sometimes hard. One of the most useful period labels is the *Middle Ages,* or medieval period, which runs roughly from 500 until 1500 – that is, from the time of the first kings and queens until the beginning of the Tudor dynasty. The early bit of this period, from about 500 until 1066, is known as the *Anglo-Saxon* (or just Saxon) *period,* after the Saxon sovereigns who ruled at that time.

After the Middle Ages, historical periods are most commonly named for the reigning dynasties of the time. The most useful of these labels are the Tudor period (1485–1603), the Stuart period (1603–1714), and the Hanoverian period (1714–1901).

For hundreds of years afterwards, monarchs had to fight to keep their thrones, and the challenge often came from inside Britain itself. No wonder the Saxon kings, who ruled from the departure of the Romans in the fifth century until 1066, gained a reputation as warriors.

Monarchs have had to fight for power on their own soil at several points during British history. Here are a few examples:

✔ Between 1135 and 1153, Stephen, grandson of William I, fought Matilda, daughter of Henry I, and her son Henry for the English throne (see Chapter 6).

✔ Between 1455 and 1485, the rival families of Lancaster and York fought the Wars of the Roses (see Chapter 9).

✔ Between 1642 and 1649, Charles I fought the army of Parliament. When Charles was defeated, England became a republic (see Chapter 14).

So these battles over the monarchy ended up being serious stuff. As a result of these conflicts, one ruler, Charles I, was executed, and countless subjects lost their lives.

Ruling the waves

Challenges to royal power also came from outside. Britain, protected from the rest of Europe by miles of rough seas, hasn't been successfully invaded that often. But the first Saxon kings arrived as invaders, and William I invaded from Normandy in 1066 (see Chapter 6).

Because William came from what is now France, his family had lands there, too. This situation began a tradition that lasted throughout the Middle Ages: English rulers also ruled portions of mainland Europe, and some kings and queens spent more time overseas than in England.

Even if many English rulers were actually French, Britain was still dear to them, and they did everything they could to defend it and hang on to it. Although attacks and invasion attempts sometimes occurred, the British navy, often combined with the changeable weather in the English Channel and North Sea, kept most challengers at bay. British sea power had another effect, too, which has changed world history and vastly increased the power of the monarchy – it helped create the British empire.

The British empire

The growth of the British empire happened over a long period, as Britain's ships travelled further across the globe. The empire at its height in the 19th century was enormous, taking in vast countries and tiny islands all over the world (see Chapter 15), but Britain's monarchs ruled four major areas:

- **North America:** The British empire established lasting English settlements from the 17th century onward, eventually spreading all over North America. Although Britain lost its power over a large chunk of this territory when the United States was created in 1776, the British remained in Canada.

- **India:** English traders set up links with India in the 17th century, and the British governed much of the subcontinent by the early 19th century. Britain ruled through a series of officials called *Viceroys,* and Queen Victoria took the title Empress of India in 1876.

- **Australia:** Explorers were followed by convicts when penal colonies were set up in Australia in the 18th century. Other settlers followed, coming to farm or mine for gold.

- **Africa:** Britain was one of several European powers that grabbed large chunks of land in Africa in the 19th century.

Being a British monarch between the 17th and 19th centuries wasn't just about ruling Britain – it was also about being the sovereign over a diverse collection of states dotted around the world.

The road to independence

Today, the monarch's worldwide connections continue. A British empire no longer exists. Most places that Britain conquered between the 17th and 19th centuries are now independent. But many of them keep their links with the monarch. They do so in two main ways:

- **Dominion status:** Some of Britain's former colonies govern themselves, but hang on to the British ruler as their own head of state. This curious state of affairs is called *dominion status.* Several of Britain's largest former colonies became dominions. Canada was the first to be given dominion status, in 1867. Australia followed in 1900, New Zealand in 1907, and South Africa in 1910. South Africa now has its own elected President, but the other three nations still recognise the British sovereign as their head of state.

- **The Commonwealth:** Other former British colonies may have their own heads of state, but remain part of the *Commonwealth* – the family of allied nations that has replaced the empire. The Commonwealth was a concept that evolved gradually during the first half of the 20th century. It wasn't founded on a specific day, but developed as many of Britain's colonies began to leave the empire after World War II. In 1958, the Commonwealth was recognised nationally when Empire Day became Commonwealth Day. The Commonwealth is held together by regular meetings between the ministers and leaders of its countries, and by the enthusiasm of the royal family, who value this extended world 'family' greatly. Britain and the countries of the Commonwealth also shared close trade ties, but these ties have been less strong since Britain joined the European Union.

Uniting the kingdom

Today Queen Elizabeth II is the head of a state called the United Kingdom of Great Britain and Northern Ireland. For short, she's known as the queen of Britain. But monarchs haven't always ruled the whole of Britain. The Saxon kings mostly ruled small mini-kingdoms that often added up to just one English region each. Later, some of the more ambitious kings united England. But Scotland, Wales, and Ireland had separate rulers:

✔ **Wales:** England and Wales were joined fairly early. Numerous English kings ruled Wales, or at least parts of it, in the Middle Ages (see Chapter 8). They often gave their eldest sons the title Prince of Wales (a title previously held by native Welsh princes) to remind the Welsh that they were under the English thumb. The English Parliament put England's government of Wales on a formal footing in 1536 and 1543, when the Principality was divided into administrative counties and justices of the peace were appointed.

✔ **Scotland:** England and Scotland began to come together in a lasting union in the early 17th century, when James VI of Scotland also became King James I of England. But even then, although they had one monarch, the kingdoms of England and Scotland still had separate Parliaments and privy councils. Real union didn't come until the Act of Union was passed in 1707 (see Chapter 14).

✔ **Ireland:** Union of Britain and Ireland arrived with an act of Parliament that came into force on 1 January 1801, after centuries during which Britain's rulers had tried to dominate the island. But a strong nationalist movement in Ireland developed, and Irish nationalists and Ireland's British rulers had a series of disputes. In 1922, there was an attempt to patch up these differences by dividing Ireland in two. The Irish Free State consisted of the southern part of Ireland, a Dominion of Britain owing an oath of allegiance to the British crown; Northern Ireland was made up of the six northern counties and remained part of the United Kingdom. Eventually, the Free State became independent and is now known as the Irish Republic.

Searching for an Heir

The monarchy has always been bigger than any individual king or queen. Being part of a continuous succession of rulers is what gives monarchs their power. Kings and queens benefit from the accumulated experience (and accumulated conquests!) of those who went before them, and it's in the interests of the institution of monarch to pass the throne on to a competent heir.

As a result, having an heir has always been one of the top priorities of any ruler. In the early years, a successor was essential. Kings were usually military leaders, and a king could be killed in battle at any time. Even if times were peaceful, people didn't live as long in the Saxon and medieval periods as they do today. A ruler had to be prepared with an heir – and often a 'spare' as well, for good measure.

Keeping the monarchy in the family

Most monarchies are family affairs, and the British one is no exception. Today, the crown passes from ruler to eldest son, through a clearly defined line of succession. Everyone in the royal family knows where they stand in the line to the throne.

It hasn't always been like this. The Saxons and Norman rulers usually chose their own heir and announced the lucky candidate publicly, so no one was in any doubt. But even then, the heir was usually a close family member – someone the king or queen could trust – and someone who would be good at the job. The monarch usually chose a successor from amongst their most able relatives. Later, the custom developed of handing the crown to the ruler's eldest male child, the first daughter if he had no sons, or to another close relative if he had no children at all. The girls got a bad deal in this process, and in the early centuries of British history there were very few queens. The reason girls didn't usually get to rule was because in early societies, it was the men who were expected to be the leaders – they may have to lead an army into battle, after all.

This need for an heir has meant that when historians talk about the *British monarchy,* they don't usually mean just the king or queen. They mean the whole royal family – sons, daughters, cousins, uncles, aunts, the lot. As well as a seemingly endless source of heirs, the royal family also makes up a big support network for the monarch. In the Middle Ages, the king's sons might go into battle on behalf of their father, act as ambassadors, or occupy different royal castles to spread the family's power around the kingdom. Even today, although kings no longer go into battle, 'minor royals' do all sorts of duties, from representing the country oversees to giving out awards.

The importance of this working family has meant that kings and queens have nearly always been keen to have lots of children. A medieval king sighed with relief when his queen produced a son and heir. Having a son was best, because in the Middle Ages men were seen as having the dominant role – women didn't usually get a look when it came to positions of power.

Several British rulers have hit problems, both personal and political, because they found it difficult to produce an heir:

- **Henry I** (1100–1135) was a powerful and successful medieval king who had a reputation as a just ruler. But he ran into trouble when both of his sons were killed in a shipwreck in 1120. His wife, Queen Matilda, was already dead, and when Henry remarried, he had no more children. The result? After Henry died, two rival claimants to the throne (Henry's daughter Matilda and his nephew Stephen) came forth, and a civil war ensured between the two (see Chapter 6).

- **Henry VIII** (1509–47) and his first wife, Catherine of Aragon, could not produce a male heir, so he divorced her (which caused a religious crisis) and remarried. But his second wife, Anne Boleyn, gave birth to a daughter, too. Henry didn't get a son until he married his third wife, Jane Seymour (see Chapter 13).

- **Queen Anne** (1702–14) spent much of her life pregnant, but suffered a series of miscarriages and stillbirths. Her one surviving son only lived until age 11. The queen had a terrible time, and when she died, her German relatives, the Hanoverians, had to be invited to take over the throne (see Chapter 14).

So the succession was a big issue that sometimes dominated the entire reign.

Preparing the heir

Just having an heir was never enough. You had to train for the job of ruler, just like any other. Royal princes usually had plenty of work to do. Back in the Middle Ages, their jobs included leading the royal army in times of war. In more peaceful times, a medieval prince might learn about leadership by running his own dukedom – in other words, becoming overlord (or boss) of a chunk of the kingdom. Being a feudal overlord meant dealing with tenants, overseeing the regional economy, settling disputes in a local court, and turning out with your men in times of war. Running a dukedom was like being a king on a small scale and was good preparation for becoming ruler.

Another way medieval kings had of preparing their eldest sons for the job of monarch was to make them Prince of Wales. Edward I invented this title in the Middle Ages for his son Edward (see Chapter 7). Since the first prince, there have been another 20 Princes of Wales, all of whom have used the role in different ways – from acquiring leadership skills to ceremonial duties – to prepare for kingship (see Chapter 19).

Today, with the monarch playing a more symbolic part in government, the heir to the throne needs different skills. The heir still deputises for the sovereign and still keeps in touch with affairs of state. But the tasks he performs are more likely to be going on official visits or reading government briefings than going into battle. Some royals, such as the queen's second son Prince Andrew, have seen active service in war, but today's royal family would not allow the heir to the throne to risk his life on the battlefield.

Paying for the Monarchy

Everyone knows that royal families are some of the richest people in the world, but where does their wealth come from? In the medieval period, the ruling king or queen owned all the land in the country. Land was the biggest kind of wealth you could have in those days, because you could enjoy the benefits of all the produce grown on the land. If you didn't want the produce, you could allocate the land to tenants and collect rents in the form of either money or services.

If a medieval ruler needed to go to war, he expected his tenants to turn out and fight for him. One of the main services that tenants gave in return for land was fighting for their sovereign. An early king's tenants were usually members of the aristocracy, and these nobles were extremely important to medieval rulers.

The aristocracy

The British aristocracy began as the high-ranking class of men and women who were close to the royal family, held land and castles as direct tenants of the sovereign, and played a major part in running the country. In the Middle Ages, these nobles did everything from raising and leading royal armies to keeping the peace in their local area. They were the ruling class and stuck together.

A whole hierarchy of aristocrats developed, with titles and property inherited from one generation to the next, like the crown itself. The nobles at the top of the hierarchy were second only to the ruler in power and prestige. The various ranks that developed are, from top to bottom, Duke, Marquis, Earl, Viscount, and Baron. These ranks still exist today, and still include people with a lot of money and property. But hereditary nobles no longer play a central part in government.

But even medieval kings sometimes needed extra help – perhaps to hire more soldiers in a difficult war – so they had to resort to raising taxes. And that sometimes meant trouble.

The power of Parliament

The main way for an early ruler to raise taxes was to call a meeting of *Parliament* – the representatives of the people – and persuade them to cough up money. Parliament evolved in the Middle Ages and from early on had two chambers:

- ✔ **The Lords,** made up of members of the nobility plus senior churchmen (archbishops and bishops).
- ✔ **The Commons,** consisting of representatives of the people of the country.

To begin with, Parliament advised the king and carried out various administrative functions. But from the 14th century onward, Parliament developed into the forum where laws were passed, petitions from the people were heard, and taxes were raised.

Getting Parliament to approve taxes wasn't always easy, because people didn't like giving up their own wealth, so Parliament often used its power to get something out of the king in return. A number of rulers had a particularly torrid time with Parliament:

- ✔ **Richard II** (1377–99) had a series of disputes with Parliament over raising money for his wars with France and his lavish lifestyle at court. Parliament ended up appointing a special committee of advisers who had the power to control pretty much everything the king did (see Chapter 8).
- ✔ **James I** (king of England 1603–25) believed that he ruled by divine right, and that Parliament had no business interfering in his decisions. He ignored Parliament as much as he could, but fell foul of them when he had to ask them to raise taxes (see Chapter 14).
- ✔ **Charles I** (1625–49) had the biggest problem of all with Parliament. Eventually, the supporters of Parliament and those on the king's side went to war to decide who should rule the country. The Parliamentarians won this civil war, and for a few years, the country was a republic (see Chapter 14).

Parliament could become a useful brake on royal power – 'we'll give you the money if you agree to reduce your power or let us pass such-and-such a law'. But Parliament could also be the total undoing of a monarch who didn't know how to manage it properly.

The taxman cometh

As time went by, taxes became more regularised. Rulers hung on to specific kinds of taxes so that they could have a regular income. Two examples were the duties that were charged on goods that were traded and the taxes that were charged on people's income. Neither one was very popular – surprise, surprise!

- ✔ **Excise duties:** *Excise duties* – charges on goods that were bought and sold – became a common way of raising money in the 17th century. By this period, the feudal system of land in return for services had disappeared, and royal feudal rights were finally abolished in 1660. The rulers of the 17th century seized on excise duties as a way of raising money. All kinds of goods were taxed – for example, salt, candles, beer, and coal. Because most of these items were necessities, ordinary people hated the taxes and feared the excise men who collected them. But in the 18th century, up to half of government income came from these kinds of taxes.

- ✔ **Income tax:** The other important kind of tax was tax on peoples' income. *Income tax* was first introduced in 1798 and was collected frequently in the 19th century. In the 20th century, it came to be seen as a way of achieving social equality, by taxing the rich to help the poor. But 19th-century rulers and governments saw it more simply as a way of paying for crises, such as the Crimean War.

Sinister ministers

By the 17th century, government was paid for by taxes, and taxes were raised by Parliament. The most powerful people in Parliament were, and still are, the *government ministers,* the senior politicians of the political party that has the majority in Parliament. The ministers formulate policies and devise new laws. Monarchs sometimes found them hard to work with because they wielded power in the way that the crown once did.

Not surprisingly, one minister usually took the lead, and as time went by, this leader was recognised and given a title – the *Prime Minister.* The first Prime Minister was Robert Walpole, a politician who entered Parliament in 1700 and was Prime Minister from 1721 to 1742 during the reigns of George I and George II.

The Prime Minister became the person who formed the link between Parliament and the monarch. From the 18th century until today, rulers and Prime Ministers have had regular meetings, during which the Prime Minister outlines policies, new laws, and political issues, and the monarch offers advice.

Being Good to the People

The monarchy has never simply been about grabbing power, keeping hold of it, and squeezing the people for taxes. In all historical eras, Britain has had kings and queens who have tried to bring benefits to their people and their realm.

Holy kings!

Being a king has always meant being closely connected to religion. The earliest ceremonies in which a person was made a monarch usually took place in church and involved a senior priest anointing the new ruler with holy oils. In the Middle Ages, new rulers started to have coronation ceremonies, in which the process of becoming king or queen was marked by putting on the crown. But coronations still took place in church and usually involved anointing, too.

These sacred rituals still form part of the coronation, and they indicate that being a king isn't just about worldly power. It's also about being virtuous, worshipping God, and trying to do good by your people.

Of course, the sacred coronation rites didn't mean that every king or queen was a paragon of virtue. Far from it. But good behaviour was expected, and the bishops – who were powerful men in their own right in the Middle Ages – had something to say if a king stepped off the straight and narrow.

I serve

Today, monarchs are still expected to bring benefits to their realm and not just to use power for its own sake or for the good life it brings. In the 20th century, rulers such as George VI and Elizabeth II took this obligation very seriously, doing charitable work and using their position to help people in need. Elizabeth II continues charity work into the 21st century.

Modern monarchs see the charitable side of their role as a public duty, and this attitude seems set to continue into the near future. The current Prince of Wales is very well aware of the tradition that he has inherited from all the previous Princes of Wales. In a curious twist of irony, this rich and privileged prince has two words in Old German inscribed beneath his coat of arms. They are *Ich dien,* meaning I serve.

Chapter 2

How the Monarchy Works

*Y*ou're used to seeing Britain's queen on the television and in the newspapers. But what does she actually do? What is the role of a monarch in 21st-century society? The ruler of Britain actually has several roles – some are to do with being head of state, some are to do with a position as national figurehead. The sovereign also has a special position as head of the Church of England, not to mention roles in the armed services and the justice system.

If that all sounds like a long list of duties, it is. A British monarch has a very full diary. Luckily, the sovereign isn't the only person who fulfils all these duties. Other members of the royal family help, too, not just by standing in for the monarch when she's busy, but also by pursuing their own specialised parts of the royal agenda, whether helping others through charitable works or going on state visits to represent Britain overseas.

Understanding a Constitutional Monarchy

People often think of kings and queens behaving like dictators. It seems that monarchs aren't accountable to anyone for their power; you can't vote them out of office if you don't like them, and they can do virtually anything they like in their kingdom. They're rich, powerful, and privileged, and their subjects have to obey them, no matter what.

The monarchy in Britain used to be like that description. It was an *executive monarchy* in which rulers made laws. Some kings claimed that they ruled by *divine right* – in other words, they were God's representatives, and what they said went.

These days, the British monarchy's not like that. It's what is called a *constitutional monarchy,* where the king or queen governs according to a constitution or set of rules. In Britain, these rules make it very clear exactly how much power the monarch has and how he or she can act in virtually any situation.

So where's the constitution, then?

One of the oddest things about Britain's constitutional monarchy is that, unlike the United States, Britain has no one written document that forms the constitution. The British constitution consists of a set of rules, some unwritten, some written down in laws passed in Parliament, and some forming documents such as the Magna Carta (see Chapter 7). These rules have been established over a long period of time. The constitutional monarchy has evolved since 1689, the year after William III and Queen Mary came to the throne as joint monarchs (see Chapter 14).

The Bill of Rights of 1689 started the ball rolling. It set down some key principles to protect the rights of Parliament and limit the power of the ruler, including:

- ✔ The law should be free from royal interference.
- ✔ People can petition the ruler.
- ✔ The ruler can't levy taxes by royal prerogative alone.
- ✔ Elections of Members of Parliament should take place without royal interference.

In addition, many more rules have developed that limit the power of the monarch. For example, the monarch:

- ✔ Can't make or pass legislation.
- ✔ Must always be neutral politically.
- ✔ Doesn't vote in elections.
- ✔ In matters of government, always acts on the advice of his or her ministers and may not enter the House of Commons.

The monarch in Parliament

In Britain, new laws are made by *the monarch in Parliament* – in other words, by the three-headed creature made up of the two houses of Parliament – the House of Commons and House of Lords – plus the sovereign. The most powerful of these three parts is the *House of Commons,* the elected chamber of Parliament where new laws are made and debated. The *House of Lords* revises and debates the new laws. The monarch merely approves new laws on the advice of his or her ministers, who themselves are members of the House of Commons or Lords.

Because the ministers come up with the new laws in the first place, and these laws are passed by a majority in Parliament, it stands to reason that the ministers advise the monarch to give her assent to them. And the sovereign hasn't refused his or her assent for more than 200 years. It sounds as if the king or queen's role is purely formal.

So is the monarch just a rubber stamp? Well, not quite. The British king or queen still has the right to advise the ministers. Monarch and ministers meet regularly, and the sovereign may encourage or warn them about any new law they're thinking of passing. Generations of Prime Ministers have said how helpful it is to get the advice of monarchs, who after all are often people who have been around far longer than they have. The Prime Minister and ruler meet regularly, and even if the ruler doesn't have any tangible power, he or she has a lot of influence.

The monarch also has two formal roles in relation to Parliament. These roles are more symbolic, but they show that the ruler is still very much at the forefront of government. These roles relate to the opening and closing of Parliament:

- ✔ The monarch opens each session of Parliament personally, and a key part of the opening ceremony is the Queen's or King's Speech, which outlines the programme of new laws to be debated during the coming session. Of course, the queen doesn't write this speech herself. It's put together by her ministers. But this ceremony still shows that the queen is at the heart of government.

- ✔ When the time comes for Parliament to be closed – when an election is due – the Prime Minister travels to Buckingham Palace and asks the monarch for permission to close Parliament. Again, the sovereign is at the heart of things, even if his or her role is ceremonial.

One thing a reigning British monarch never does is cast a vote in an election. In theory, nothing stops the king or queen from voting. But in practice, casting a vote would be unconstitutional, because the sovereign is outside politics and able to function whatever the political colour of the government. The same goes for the heir to the throne, who will one day have to play the same politically neutral role. Other members of the royal family, such as the Duke of Edinburgh, are theoretically able to vote, but they don't. For them to put their weight behind a political party would compromise the neutrality of the monarch. And as far as the monarchy is concerned, whatever the personal political views of the members of the royal family, neutrality is all.

The power: Ruler and Prime Minister

One of the monarch's jobs is to appoint the Prime Minister. In practice, of course, the senior member of the government has to work with Parliament, and so the Prime Minister is the leader of the party that holds the majority in Parliament. The real power is with Parliament.

The monarch and Prime Minister meet once a week (or speak on the telephone, if they're not within easy travelling distance of one another). During these meetings, as in other dealings with Parliament, the sovereign's duty is to 'encourage or warn', but, ultimately, to respect the advice of the minister of the day.

The current queen, Elizabeth II, has reigned during the governments of ten Prime Ministers. The discussions she's had with these varied political figures (seven Conservative and three Labour leaders), together with her wide experience of talking to political leaders around the world, makes her one of the best-informed people in the country. Prime Ministers value her opinions, which are given in the strictest confidence.

The advantages

The constitutional monarchy puts Britain's kings and queens in a strange position – they seem to have lots of influence, and they certainly have a lot of privileges, but they don't have very much real power. To the citizens of many of the world's republics, where you can vote for the head of state you want and kick them out if they don't do their job properly, the British system seems archaic and unfair.

So what's so special about the constitutional monarchy? It does have a few advantages:

✔ **Continuity:** Elected governments come and go, but the king or queen remains. This continuity makes for a more stable regime.

✔ **Political neutrality:** There are benefits from keeping the head of state out of party politics – the crown is above the temporary squabbles of the political parties.

✔ **Experience:** A monarch who's reigned for more than a few years can have a valuable perspective and deeper knowledge of affairs than a politician who's only been in power for months.

✔ **Overview:** Both the continuity of the monarchy, and its involvement in the world outside Britain, gives it a valuable overview that is often lacking with other kinds of government.

Of course, there are drawbacks, too. Any monarchy relies on the accidents of birth, and while some kings and queens have excelled at their role, just as many would never have made it in a democratic system. And there's the ultimate drawback – however good or bad a hereditary ruler, you're stuck with him. Other than a revolution, you have no way of deposing a hereditary monarch.

Figuring Out the Monarch's Duties

Apart from talking to ministers and approving new legislation, what does the monarch actually *do*? British sovereigns have a wide range of duties. Most important is the work they do as head of state – all the official duties through which they represent Britain. But monarchs have a second group of duties, the less formal ones, through which the king or queen becomes a national figurehead for Britain.

Head of state

First and foremost, the monarch is the head of the British state and has to fulfil all the functions, ceremonial and governmental, that go with the job. Monarchs have many *in-house,* jobs, including:

✔ Opening Parliament and giving the monarch's speech.

✔ Approving Acts of Parliament and other government measures.

✔ Reading briefing papers on all kinds of government business.

✔ Meeting with the Prime Minister.

The monarch also has to perform other kinds of duties when representing Britain to other nations, such as:

- Holding receptions for the ambassadors and other officials of foreign countries.
- Receiving overseas heads of state.
- Going on state visits to other countries.

It's an impressive list of activities, and the receptions, state visits, and similar functions are major events that are meticulously planned with the help of a large staff and – when the ruler is playing host to foreign dignitaries – the backdrop of the sovereign's large official residences. Britain, with all her history as a great power and heritage of ceremony and protocol, likes to do this kind of thing well.

National figurehead

The monarch has another heap of duties that are less easy to define, but represent the side of the monarchy that provides a *national figurehead* – a person who acts as a focus for the nation. Once upon a time, in the plays of Shakespeare, for example, kings used to refer to each other as if they were named for their countries: 'My brother France,' 'My cousin England,' and so on. Kings and queens don't talk in this way today, but they still seem to embody their realms.

A modern monarch can still stand for his or her country in a number of ways:

- Rewarding special achievements or successes by handing out awards and honours.
- Supporting the needy and less well-off by all kinds of voluntary and charitable work.
- Leading the nation in showing grief or compassion after bad news or tragedy or when commemorating those who have died in war.
- Making contact with people through visits to different areas, *walkabouts* during which the sovereign meets ordinary people, and other occasions.

Each of these jobs is the tip of a very large iceberg. For example, giving out honours means a long and careful selection process and many investiture ceremonies for the monarch; the present queen's charitable work involves being patron of more than 600 different organizations; and the visits and walkabouts may be the culmination of months of planning.

Exploring the Royal Family's Responsibilities

With the British monarchy, you don't just get one royal; you get a whole bunch of them – the spouse of the ruler, their children, and very often a number of cousins, aunts, and others, who are all part of the deal. Antimonarchists often pillory the royal family. The monarch's children and the minor royals are criticised as hangers-in who contribute little while taking a lot in terms of privilege and money. In fact, the situation isn't quite as simple as the critics say.

The royal family has several roles in helping the ruler in their work. They can also take the effectiveness of the ruler into new directions. As the 19th-century writer Walter Bagehot put it, 'A family on the throne is an interesting idea also. It brings down the pride of sovereignty to the level of petty life.'

Helping the monarch

The other members of the royal family help the monarch in all sorts of ways, official and unofficial. The *senior royals,* the sovereign's closest family members, help on official duties, from state visits to award presentations. The rest of the family – and the senior royals, too – supplement the monarch's work with all kinds of extra activities of their own.

Official duties

The British monarch has to cope with a vast and expanding diary of engagements. As well as the events that are a regular part of the royal calendar, these engagements include all sorts of functions to which the sovereign is invited every year. One person can't handle them all, so close family members often step in. Under the present queen, Elizabeth II, close family means the queen's children, their spouses, and the queen's cousins. Here are some official palace figures that give you an idea of the workload the royals undertake:

- Attending 2,000 official engagements per year.
- Entertaining 70,000 people per year at royal parties, dinners, lunches, and receptions.
- Answering 100,000 letters per year.

These jobs vary a lot in size and complexity. Some engagements are state visits that take years of planning, while some are brief ceremonies – such as opening a hospital or visiting a factory – that still have to be done with care and dignity. Having a large family back-up team to do some of this work makes sense.

The family can help in emergencies, too. Heads of state sometimes have to attend events that can't be scheduled in advance – funerals of other rulers, for example. If the monarch is busy – perhaps tied up on a state visit on the other side of the world – another family member can go instead.

Extra duties

One way the monarch leads the country is in support of charities and voluntary organizations. The royal family helps, too, with each member supporting specific charities. Thousands of charities would like a member of the royal family to be their patron or president, and all together the royals play this role for about 2,000 charities in Britain.

The current Prince of Wales is particularly known for his charitable work, taking a lead by setting up his own charities in fields in which he has a special interest, from education to the environment. (For more information, see Chapter 18.) Other royal family members have also set up charities. The Duke of Edinburgh's Award Scheme and the Princess Royal Trust for Carers are among the best known.

Family benefits

Activities like these duties spread the work of the royal family into all kinds of areas and therefore make the monarchy still more effective as a symbol of the nation. A lot of the work – both with charities and with engagements – takes the family all over the country and enables people to see the monarchy and its activities first hand. And there's also an opposite, but equally beneficial effect. Travelling around allows the sovereign and her relatives to meet many different people, making the royal family less remote and more understanding of the country and its diverse population.

Bonding with the Church

The British monarchy is unusual in that the monarch has a religious role as well as a governmental one. In 1521, the Pope gave Henry VIII the title Defender of the Faith. When Henry broke with Rome, the Pope took away this title, but Henry persuaded Parliament to vote it to him and his successors in 1543, as defender of the English church. Henry was also styled Supreme Head of the English church, and his daughter, Elizabeth I, took the title Supreme Governor of the Church of England. Since then, all monarchs (even the Catholic James II) have held the title. This title has had important consequences for both the Church and the sovereign.

The Church of England

The link between the monarch and the Church means that the Church of England is the official, or *established,* church in England, and a number of other connections between the Church and state have evolved:

- ✔ The archbishops and senior bishops sit in the House of Lords, the second chamber of the British Parliament. This group is known as the *Lords Spiritual,* and they take part alongside the other lords in the debates about new legislation.
- ✔ The Lords Spiritual swear an oath of allegiance to the monarch.
- ✔ Parish priests also swear an oath of allegiance.
- ✔ Bishops and Archbishops may not resign without the permission of the sovereign.

Defender of the Faith

So, what does this religious connection mean for the monarch? It doesn't mean that the sovereign is an active church leader or a priest. The Church of England is effectively led by its *General Synod,* a Church body that includes bishops, representatives of the clergy, and lay church members. But the monarch's role does come with several duties and requirements:

- ✔ Appoints bishops and archbishops. The monarch makes appointments based on the advice of the Prime Minister, who in turn bases his advice on lists of candidates supplied by the Church. The Church actually has a big say in the choice of leaders, but the monarch has the final say.
- ✔ Opens the General Synod every five years.
- ✔ Gives assent to measures passed by the Synod, in the same way that assent is given to laws passed by Parliament (see the preceding section).
- ✔ Promises to *maintain* (or ensure the survival of) the Church.
- ✔ Is a full member of the Church of England who has been confirmed and who takes Holy Communion.

In addition to these duties, the sovereign also has several obligations to the Church of Scotland, promising to preserve it. But the monarch isn't head of the Church of Scotland. The special relationship of Defender of the Faith is the one between ruler and Church of England.

Conflicts with the Church

The role of the ruler in the Church of England has brought some complications in the personal lives of kings and princes. In the past, trouble occurred when the Prince of Wales, the future George IV, wanted to marry a Catholic. In the 20th century, even more trouble happened when Edward VIII wished to marry Wallis Simpson, who had been twice divorced.

Edward's marriage, which was against the principles of the Church, cost him his crown. The current Prince of Wales, whose wife the Duchess of Cornwall was divorced, has been allowed to marry with the blessing of his mother. The church and monarchy have moved slowly with the times.

Checking Out Other Royal Roles

The modern monarch, concerned with everything from opening buildings to doing charitable work, from state visits to royal garden parties, seems a far cry from the rulers of old. Back in the Middle Ages, and even in the Tudor period, the crown had much simpler priorities. In those days, much of the king's time was taken up with two very basic activities: dispensing justice and going to war. Even today, the monarchy still has a role to play in the justice system and the armed services.

The monarch and the courts

Once upon a time, the phrase *the royal court* meant two things: the circle of people around the monarch and the court of justice where the ruler sat as judge. Kings and queens were justices for centuries, from the Anglo-Saxon period until the time of the Stuarts. Rulers became known as *founts of justice,* and if they didn't sit in court themselves, their judges were closely identified with the ruler.

In 1689, with the beginning of constitutional monarchy, this setup changed. Rulers were no longer allowed to sit on the bench and dole out justice. That responsibility became the job of the specialists; the judges, magistrates, and similar officials who still preside over courts today.

Even so, the monarch is still closely identified with the justice system. When crowned, a king or queen swears to uphold the law and justice, and to see that justice is administered to all. And the sovereign is involved directly in the system in various ways, such as appointing senior judges – as usual, in response to the advice of ministers. The sovereign is also expected to be merciful and can grant pardons to convicted criminals, again with the advice of ministers.

Today, the ruler is still closely identified with the justice system, a fact that can be seen through the kind of language that is used to describe the courts, the cases tried there, and the prisons:

- Many courts are called *Crown Courts,* and the judges are known as *Her Majesty's Judges.*
- The prisons are known as *Her Majesty's Prisons.*
- Criminal prosecutions are brought in the name of the crown, and when cases are referred to, they're given the name *Regina (Latin: the Queen) v X,* where X is the name of the defendant.

There's a twist in the tail, though. As fount of justice and head of the justice system, the monarch can't actually be prosecuted in either a civil or a criminal case. It's just as well that the current monarch is careful to keep on the right side of the law!

The monarch and the military

Monarchs no longer lead their troops into battle as they used to. The last British ruler to do so was George II, who led his forces to victory against the French in 1743. But the sovereign is still the head of the armed forces, and the British royal family has a long tradition of involvement with the Army, Navy, and Royal Air Force.

Many modern royals have been active soldiers, sailors, or airmen. The Duke of Edinburgh had a distinguished career as a naval officer when he was a young man, and the Prince of Wales followed his father into the Navy after a brief period in the Royal Air Force. Whereas Prince Charles's time in the Navy was seen primarily as part of his preparation for his other roles in the royal family, his brother, Prince Andrew, had a long career in the Royal Navy, spending 20 years as an officer and seeing active service in the Falklands War in 1982. And the tradition continues, with both of Prince Charles's sons, Princes William and Harry, training as Army officers at Sandhurst. In addition, many members of the royal family hold appointments and honorary ranks in various military units.

However, the British sovereign no longer has the power to raise an army. This ancient right was removed when the constitutional monarchy came into being in 1689 and now Parliament raises and maintains armies.

But just as the monarch keeps close links to government through regular briefings from ministers, so she keeps up to speed with the country's military forces. The ruler's Defence Services Secretary (who is both a member of the royal household and an officer in one of the services) acts as the liaison person between the ruler and the government minister responsible for defence.

To ordinary servicemen and women, the monarch is more than someone keeping a remote but benevolent eye on their progress. Members of the Army and Royal Air Force swear an oath of allegiance to the sovereign when they join up. (Traditionally, this oath doesn't happen in the Navy, but it's called the Royal Navy, so sailors are always reminded of the importance of the monarch.) And all soldiers know that if they have to go into battle, they're fighting 'for queen and country,' not for any specific government or political party.

Part II
Early Rulers

The 5th Wave By Rich Tennant

"They call me Aethelred, the 'Unready', but I like to think of myself as Aethelred, the 'Fashionably Late.'"

In this part . . .

The early years of the monarchy, from the centuries after the Roman empire until the Normans invaded England in 1066, saw more kings and queens than ever before or since – because often several were ruling at once. The country was divided into a number of different regions, each with its own ruler. But gradually the more powerful kingdoms conquered their neighbours until England was united.

The rulers of this period were mostly Anglo-Saxons, people who originally came from northern Europe. But these foreign rulers played a huge part in defining many aspects of Englishness – from English literature to the English church.

Chapter 3

Mini-Kingdoms

. . . .

. . . .

*H*istorians know very little about who ruled Britain before the island became part of the Roman empire in the first century A.D. To begin with, the Romans allowed some of the local English kings and queens to keep certain powers, but this situation did not last long. However, after the Romans left Britain in the early fifth century, royal rulers reappeared in the form of the Anglo-Saxons.

When the Anglo-Saxons arrived, they established a number of small kingdoms across England. Some kingdoms were tiny – one corresponded roughly to the modern county of Kent in the far southeast of England. But some Anglo-Saxon kings controlled quite large parts of the country and were ambitious to extend their power. So the early Anglo-Saxon period, from the fifth to the ninth century, saw these rulers fighting each other to gain more territory, until, by the beginning of the ninth century, they claimed to rule all of England.

The Romans in Britain

Between the first and fourth centuries, Britain was part of the vast Roman empire. The Romans conquered the country in A.D. 43, largely because they wanted to get hold of its valuable resources. They had already been trading with Britain, buying commodities such as grain and tin, and ruling the country would give them even easier access to what it had to offer.

During their time in Britain, the Romans built roads to enable their soldiers, and later their merchants, to travel, and founded many towns that acted as centres of trade and administration. They also brought with them many new ideas – from houses with under-floor heating to their famous baths, from theatre-going to gladiatorial combat. These inventions transformed life for some Britons, although for most working people, life went on very much as it had before.

Rule Britannia!

The part of Britain ruled by the Romans included nearly all of England and sizeable parts of Wales. The Romans called this area the province of Britannia. Its overall ruler was the Roman Emperor, based in Italy, so the provincial government took care of the day-to-day running of the area.

To run Britain, the Romans relied partly on the native British rulers who were already there when they arrived. The Romans softened up these local rulers by giving them access to all the most luxurious trappings of Roman life. Historians don't know much about these British rulers, known as *client- kings,* but archaeologists have excavated some of their probable homes. One example is the vast Roman palace at Fishbourne in Sussex, which was probably the residence of the client-king Cogidubnus.

Cogidubnus seems to have been king of a tribe called the Atrebates, who lived in central southern England. Judging by the enormous size of his palace and its lavish mosaic decorations, Cogidubnus must have been fabulously rich, and the Romans probably let him have a lot of power locally. But if he ever stepped out of line, the Roman army would have turned up on his doorstep and deposed him. It was kingship, but not as you know it.

Romanization

The process of *Romanization* was the way the Romans made the benefits of Roman life available to the people they conquered. To get the British upper classes on their side, they encouraged them to adopt a Roman lifestyle, helping them to build lavish houses with all the best Roman features – under-floor heating, colourful mosaic floors, suites of bathrooms, painted walls, and so on. The Romans gave the British tribal leaders access to all sorts of products from the empire, such as different foods, and encouraged them to wear Roman clothes. Innovations in livestock breeding and crop growing made their farms more efficient, which benefited both the Romans and the British. So the British bigwigs were more comfortable, lived a more lavish lifestyle, and were richer than they were before. The Romans hoped that this improved lifestyle would make them more likely to accept Roman rule. Judging by the length of time the Romans ruled Britain, the tactic of Romanization seems to have worked.

Royal rebellion

The client-kingdom system worked well for the Romans when locals and Romans lived in harmony, but sometimes things went wrong. This is what happened with the kingdom of the Iceni, a people who lived in eastern England, in the area of the modern counties of Norfolk and northern Suffolk.

Soon after the Romans arrived, they gave the Iceni's ruler, Prasutagus, the status of client-king. But in the year A.D. 60, Prasutagus died leaving a widow, Boudicca (also known as Boadicea) and their daughters, who were brutally treated by the Romans. The Romans expected to take over Prasutagus's kingdom, whereas Boudicca believed that her daughters should inherit at least part of their father's power.

The Romans took away the lands of Boudicca's family, assaulted some of the women, and imprisoned others. But they didn't reckon on the spirit of Boudicca herself. By A.D. 61, the queen of the Iceni was leading a rebellion against Roman rule. The Iceni were joined by their neighbours the Trinovantes, who resented the fact that the Romans had taken over their area (southern Suffolk and Essex). The combined rebel forces travelled south, taking the important city of Colchester.

Then the rebels swept across southern England, destroying major centres such as St Albans and doing major damage to London. The Roman governor, Suetonius Paulinus, was away trying to conquer the Welsh at the time, which accounted for the rebels' early success. But eventually news reached Suetonius of what was happening, and he turned away from his campaign in Wales and ruthlessly put down the rebellion.

Much bloodshed occurred, and Boudicca herself died soon afterwards – unable to accept having her queenly power removed by the Romans, she probably committed suicide by poisoning herself. In spite of her dramatic revolt, the Romans had triumphed by sheer military power and what had happened was a dire warning to any others who felt like rebelling.

Eventually, as a result of episodes such as Boudicca's revolt, the Romans phased out the system of client-kingdoms. Direct rule by a Roman governor, backed up by the might of the Roman army, was the best way for them to keep control. So from the second to the fourth centuries, local tribal leaders had little power. The Romans called all the shots.

Enter the Saxons

By the early fifth century, the Roman empire had become so big that it was difficult to hold together and it began to break apart. Whole books have been written about why this collapse happened, with answers ranging from barbarian invasions to economic pressures. But one immediate effect was that the Romans began to pull out of some of their conquered lands.

The Romans left Britain in 410 when the emperor Honorius decreed that the Britons should henceforth govern themselves. But Britain's people weren't left alone for long. Between the fifth and seventh centuries, people from the mainland of northern Europe launched a series of invasions.

The new invaders were actually three different peoples – the Saxons from northern Germany, the Angles from the southern part of the Danish peninsula and the nearby islands, and the Jutes from Jutland, the main part of the Danish peninsula. For convenience, these people are now known collectively as the Anglo-Saxons (or sometimes simply as the Saxons).

The Anglo-Saxons set up a number of kingdoms in England. Each Saxon kingdom was made up of one region, so there were a number of monarchs in England at any one time. From the fifth to the end of the eighth century, these mini-kingdoms fought against one another for dominance, and eventually one of these kingdoms, Wessex, became so strong that its rulers claimed kingship of the entire country.

Vanishing Celts

Historians know very little about what happened to the native British people when the Anglo-Saxons invaded; they used to say that these Celtic people were pushed back into Wales, Scotland, and Cornwall by the waves of invaders. But it's also possible that the locals lived alongside the invaders, under their rule, just as they had with the Romans. Historians simply don't know for sure because there aren't many surviving records.

Putting up a fight

It's likely that the Britons put up a fight when the invaders first arrived. But historians know about this struggle only because of the writings of some early historians, who aren't very precise about things. One of these historians was a sixth-century writer called Gildas, who tells of a Roman leader called Ambrosius Aurelianus who stayed on and helped the Britons fight the invaders.

Early historians also mention another resistance leader, named by some writers as Vortigern, a Celtic ruler living in the west of England, who defended his country against invaders in several battles in the fifth or early sixth century. For a while, probably in the first half of the sixth century, the Saxons seem to have been thwarted in their invasion plans as a result of these shadowy resistance leaders.

Archaeologists investigating the hill fort at South Cadbury, Somerset, have found that it was refortified in the sixth century and was the site of a large hall, the equivalent of a royal palace or at least a nobleman's seat. Such a site was likely the home of one of the local leaders who was involved in fighting off the first waves of Saxon invasions. But historians have no way of knowing who actually lived there.

Once and future myth

Much later, by the 12th century, writers were naming the man who led the struggle against the invaders as King Arthur. Stories abounded about Arthur. He was said to have fought many bloody battles against the invaders. Famous tales described his kingly court, where his chosen elite group of knights sat in state around a famous round table. There were even stories about him becoming a European conqueror.

Arthur was also said to be 'the once and future king' – in other words, he would return one day, when Britain was in its hour of deepest need. So any king of England would be proud to have Arthur as his ancestor, and it's no wonder that stories of this superhero were popular for hundreds of years. There's no evidence that an early king called Arthur really existed. There were Saxon invasions, some of which were repulsed by a ruler in western England. But as to the character of the 'real' King Arthur, evidence of his personality has vanished like so much of the evidence about the people who lived in Britain in the sixth century.

Seven kings for seven kingdoms

By the seventh century, the Saxon invaders had returned, fought off any remaining resistance, and settled down. They established a number of kingdoms stretching from Northumbria in the far north to Kent in the south. How many kingdoms? Well, if you read about Saxon England, different books give different numbers, because the numbers changed over time. This fluctuation in numbers tells historians something about how Saxon kings saw their job.

Conquering kings

Part of the job of a Saxon king was warfare. The Saxons were warriors who continuously fought to extend their territories. Extra territory brought extra power, respect, and wealth, because the spoils of war can be of huge value. And if you had an army, you needed to keep them fed, and helping yourself to your enemy's food was one way of doing it.

Warfare also helped the Saxons show off. From the surviving remains, it's obvious that Saxon kings liked luxury. They had fine swords, elaborate jewellery such as belt buckles, and clasps for their cloaks made of precious metals and coloured jewels. And they liked to give such items as rewards for heroism or loyalty.

The kingdoms

The Saxon warriors carved out seven main kingdoms in England. Here's a list, with a note about the location of each one, starting in the north and working southward:

- **Northumbria:** Most of northern England from the Scottish border to the River Humber. Northumbria eventually incorporated the smaller kingdoms of Bernicia (in the far north) and Deira (Yorkshire).

- **Mercia:** The Midlands, sometimes incorporating the kingdom of Hwicce, in the area of the River Severn.

- **East Anglia:** The modern counties of Norfolk and Suffolk.

- **Essex:** To the south of East Anglia.

- **Kent:** In the far southeast, covering roughly the same area as the modern county of Kent.

- **Sussex:** Again, based in an area similar to the modern southeastern county.

- **Wessex:** In the southwest of England, but excluding Cornwall, which, like Wales, remained a stronghold of the Britons.

So there were a lot of kingdoms, and a lot of kings to go with them. What's more, even when one king gained supremacy over a neighbouring kingdom, it didn't necessarily mean that he deposed his neighbour. In the Saxon period, when communications were difficult and government was still developing, it wasn't always easy for one king to rule over a large area. So it was sometimes easier to let a conquered neighbour go on ruling, as a sort of dependent, or *subking*.

Struggles for Supremacy

With seven main kingdoms and a number of smaller subkingdoms, it is no surprise that some of the more powerful ones became dominant. Eventually three kingdoms, Northumbria, Mercia, and Wessex, ended up with the most power. But before this dominance happened, a lot of fighting took place.

Sutton who?

Of the seven main Saxon kingdoms, East Anglia was one of the smaller ones. But even a small kingdom can be seriously rich. And the riches of the rulers of East Anglia were brought stunningly to light in 1939 when buried treasure was discovered at Sutton Hoo in Suffolk. The awesome treasure – jewelled buckles and clasps, plates and vessels made of precious metals – turned out to have been buried inside a complete wooden ship, recalling the Viking ship burials of Scandinavia. But no body was discovered with the lavish finds.

Whose treasure was inside the Sutton Hoo ship? The most likely candidate is an East Anglian king called Raedwald, who died around A.D. 625. Raedwald was a powerful warrior who won a notable battle against the king of Bernicia. The battle came about because the Bernicians had asked Raedwald to hand over a man called Eadwine, a prince from Deira who had been exiled and was serving as a warrior at Raedwald's court.

Raedwald, apparently on the advice of his wife, refused to hand over Eadwine and instead waged a war against the Bernicians and won. After the battle, Raedwald saw to it that his friend Eadwine was placed on the throne of Deira. This move effectively extended Raedwald's power into northern England. A king of little East Anglia held power over a huge tract of England.

No wonder Raedwald was able to amass such a rich collection of treasure. But the power of East Anglia didn't last long after his death. His son, Eorpwald, was a Christian who was killed by his non-Christian subjects, and later East Anglian kings were slaughtered in battles with an ambitious king from the Midlands, Penda of Mercia. Further north, the kings of Northumbria were also becoming more powerful.

Northumbria versus Mercia

Up north, there were two kingdoms, Bernicia (by the Scottish border) and Deira (based in and around modern Yorkshire). The Bernicians were generally the more powerful of the two, and a strong early king, Aethelfrith (A.D. 593–617) carved out a big kingdom that included a large chunk of southern Scotland. There was an interlude in Bernician power when Eadwine ruled the north with the backing of the East Anglians (see preceding section), but in A.D. 634, one of the most powerful northern kings, Oswald, came to the throne.

Oswald was an interesting ruler because he combined success on the battlefield with a commitment to the up-and-coming religion of Europe, Christianity. Having beaten his Welsh enemy Cadwallon of Gwynedd in battle, he turned to quieter pursuits and invited the monk Aidan to build a monastery on the island of Lindisfarne and begin a mission to convert the north to Christianity.

The first monasteries were immensely important for England and its rulers. Today, people think of monasteries as places where very religious people go to devote their lives to God. But in the Anglo-Saxon period, they were far more than just places of worship because they made an enormous contribution to culture. The monasteries taught their monks and nuns to read and write, and they produced beautiful illuminated manuscripts, which are still among the treasures of western art. The literate monks and nuns who produced these books also developed links with monasteries in other parts of Europe, creating connections with other countries. Some monks travelled widely, and their royal benefactors used them to carry messages and to find out what was going on in other parts of England or Europe.

Oswald did not devote himself entirely to Christian good works. The king had a long-running dispute with the powerful Mercian king, Penda, who was an ally of Cadwallon. Less than ten years after coming to the throne, Oswald was killed in a battle with Penda, and the northern kingdom passed to his brother, Oswiu. King Oswiu was an important figure in both political and religious terms.

Oswiu and Penda

King Penda of Mercia wanted either to conquer the north or at least increase his influence there. In 654–5, Penda and Oswiu came to blows when Penda marched northwards and besieged Oswui's castle at Giudi, probably an early name for Stirling in Scotland. Penda had a formidable army, and it was said that he managed to assemble 30 kings to lead it – an indication of the number of kingdoms that were around if you roped in the various divisions of Wales and England.

Oswiu was forced to give in and persuaded Penda to withdraw by buying him off with most of the royal treasury. A huge redistribution of royal wealth took place when Penda shared out much of the booty to his kingly followers before retreating back towards the Midlands. But he didn't bank on Oswiu, who, peeved at his lost fortune, was soon pursuing Penda. Oswiu caught up with his foe near a river called the Winwaed, somewhere in south Yorkshire, and a battle ensued. The tables were turned, Penda's army was annihilated, and Mercian power was curtailed. For the moment.

Which way for the church?

The other dispute in Oswiu's reign was more peaceful. It was a disagreement between the two branches of the English church, one influenced by Celtic missionaries from Iona, the other under the sway of Roman churchmen from the south. Although their core beliefs were the same, they had different ways of working out the date of Easter and were organised differently.

The two churches

The English church was split in two during the early Anglo-Saxon period because of the way the country had converted to Christianity. Southern England had been converted by missionaries, such as St Augustine of Canterbury, who had the direct backing of the pope and so followed the Roman Catholic faith. But the missionaries who worked in northern England were influenced heavily by the Irish church, which at that time had grown apart from Rome on some issues. Irish monks set up a monastery on the Scottish island of Iona and another at Lindisfarne in Northumbria. From here, men like St Aidan preached in northern England and converted people to the Celtic branch of Christianity.

In 664, things came to a head. The two dates for Easter were especially far apart that year and as a result Lent, the period of fasting and austerity, was nearly twice as long as it usually was. Bad news all round. So a church meeting or synod was called at Whitby, where there was an important monastery, to sort out the controversy. After a big debate, Oswiu threw his weight behind the Roman church. As a result, the entire English church now looked to Rome for its leadership, and England would remain Catholic for nearly 900 years.

Keep Offa the Dyke

Mercia had been dealt a heavy blow when northern king Oswiu defeated rampaging Mercian ruler Penda. (See the preceding section on Oswiu and Penda.) But the Mercians were far from finished. Penda's son Wulfhere (658–c. 675) was an aggressive king, but after Penda's drubbing in the north, Wulfhere expanded southwards, scoring victories in the southeast and getting the South Saxons – the people of Sussex – under his thumb. The kings who ruled Mercia in the decades after Wulfhere – men such as Wulfhere's brother Aethelred (674–704) and Penda's descendant Aethelbald (716–57) – ruled in a similar way, dominating various subkingdoms such as the region of the Hwicce (Gloucestershire and Worcestershire) and even penetrating into distant areas such as Kent.

By the time of the Mercian ruler Offa (757–96), the Midland kings were claiming to be rulers of all England. Offa went further than most, dramatically reducing the power of his subkings so that his own power was concentrated and centralised.

Warring with Wales

Offa's greatest enemies were the Welsh, especially the king of Powys, Eliseg, who tried to move into the western parts of Mercia, along what is now the border between England and Wales. Offa's response was to build an enormous fortification, the earth rampart and ditch now known as *Offa's Dyke*.

Offa's Dyke is an amazing structure. Its bank is up to 20 ft (6 m) in height, and it runs for miles from Sedbury, near the River Severn, northwards along the border between England and Wales. Gaps occur in the dyke, sometimes where natural barriers (such as the gorge of the River Wye) make an artificial fortification unnecessary. Offa's Dyke was essentially a political boundary, its course agreed after discussions between Offa and his Welsh counterparts during the second half of Offa's reign, which was fairly peaceful.

The dyke was a big symbol of Offa's power. No other Saxon king had built such an enormous structure. And Offa's influence was not just military. In 794, he made an agreement with the great Frankish emperor Charlemagne, the most powerful man in Europe, to encourage trade between England and the European mainland.

But even Offa's power and influence could not guarantee peace between Mercia and Wales. In 796, the Mercian king was fighting the Welsh again. Offa died in battle, after a long and successful reign.

More Mercians

When the great Mercian king Offa died in 796, some regions over which he had reigned, such as East Anglia and Kent, broke free of Mercian rule and set up their own independent kings. The next few Mercian kings had to work and fight hard to re-establish their power. Some of them also tried to push westward and conquer parts of Wales.

Several of these later Mercian kings were shadowy figures who only reigned for a few years each. Among the more long-lived and successful were:

- ✔ **Coenwulf (796–821)** took Kent and East Anglia back from their local leaders and invaded North Wales.

- ✔ **Coelwulf (821–3)** made further conquests in Wales.

- ✔ **Burgred (852–74)** made an alliance with the king of Wessex and again attacked the Welsh. But he was attacked in turn by invading Vikings. In the end, he gave up his crown to go on a pilgrimage to Rome.

- ✔ **Aethelred (879–911)** suffered several defeats in Wales. He married Aethelflaed, daughter of Alfred, king of Wessex, and after his death his kingdom passed into the hands of the rulers of Wessex.

So Aethelred was the last of the independent kings of Mercia. Continuous wars, and the increasing strength of Wessex, had brought an end to Mercia's power.

Wessex Rules

The southwestern part of England was known as the kingdom of the West Saxons, or Wessex. Its heartland stretched along the valley of the River Thames and eventually included all the counties along the south coast of England from Devon in the south west to Hampshire. This area was quite large, but nowhere near the size of the Midland kingdom of Mercia or the vast realm of Northumbria in the north of England.

Compared with these larger kingdoms, Wessex didn't seem a likely bet to take over the whole of England, especially when Mercia was so powerful, but that is what happened. By a combination of conquest, alliances, and judicious use of family ties to place people in positions of power, the kings of Wessex gradually increased their influence until they became rulers of England.

Small beginnings

To begin with, Wessex wasn't a unified kingdom. It was more like a federation of tiny states, each with its own king. This was the situation in the seventh century, when the people of the Thames valley took a pounding from the powerful Mercian king Penda and his son Wulfhere. In around 660, the important town of Dorchester on Thames fell to the Mercians, and the former rulers of the Thames valley moved their headquarters, including their *bishopric* (the headquarters of their bishop), southward to Winchester.

From this base in the south of England, the West Saxon rulers began to take over the small kingdoms of their neighbours and to expand into territory in the far west (such as Devon) that had not previously been conquered by the Saxons. By the end of the seventh century, it made sense to talk about a unified Wessex. Here are some of the kings, mostly rather shadowy characters, who made this unification a reality:

- **Caedwalla (685–8)** killed off most of his rivals for power in Wessex and also took control of the Isle of Wight.
- **Ine (688–726)** brought Devon under Wessex rule, supported the Christian church, and issued the first law code in Wessex.
- **Cynewulf (757–86)** made peace with the powerful Mercian king, Offa.
- **Beorhtric (786–802)** strengthened the alliance between Wessex and Mercia by marrying Offa's daughter, Eadburh.

Poor Beorhtric was one of the first English kings to become the victim of a royal scandal. He died in 802, as the result of poisoning. The rumour was that the deadly dose had been administered by his wife, Eadburh. So much for royal alliances. It was said that the poison was actually intended for someone else, but the cruel mistake sent Eadburh on the run. She ran off to mainland Europe and threw herself on the mercy of the Frankish emperor, Charlemagne, who used his influence to make her an abbess. But Eadburh couldn't stay out of trouble. She broke her vow of chastity, was found out, and ended her life in obscurity in Italy.

When Beorhtric met his untimely end, the kingdom of Wessex was strong but still confined to the south of England. But in the next 30 years or so, it expanded to become the most influential of all the Saxon kingdoms, with its rulers claiming power over the whole of England.

Ecgbert, king of England

The next king of Wessex was Ecgbert (802–39). Ecgbert was a Saxon prince, but as with many rulers in this period, historians know little about his background. He may have been the son of one Ealhmund, who had ruled Kent for a short while. What we do know is that Ecgbert had had his eye on the throne of Wessex for a while. The previous king, Beorhtric, had fought him off, and Ecgbert had been forced to live in mainland Europe, at the court of the Franks.

When Beorhtric died, Ecgbert returned to claim the crown of Wessex. Ecgbert was a warrior, but he also had some good ideas about government, which he may have picked up during his time in exile with the Franks.

Ecgbert probably divided his kingdom up into small units called *shires,* the origin of modern British counties that still form part of the country's local government system today. Each of these convenient administrative units was headed up by a man who was appointed by the king and who was usually based in the most important town in the shire. It was a simple way of spreading royal power throughout the kingdom.

In 825, Ecgbert's power was challenged when an army of the Mercian king Beornwulf pushed south into Wessex territory in Wiltshire. Warrior Ecgbert rose to the challenge and fought the invaders at a place called Ellandun, probably near the modern village of Wroughton near Swindon.

The result was a resounding victory for Ecgbert and Wessex. The Mercian forces were scattered, and Ecgbert took over Kent, Surrey, Sussex, and Essex. These areas had been under Mercian lordship, but Ecgbert appointed his son Aethelwulf to rule them as subking.

In 829, Ecgbert continued his assault against Mercia, evicting the new king, Wiglaf, from his throne. In the same year, the Northumbrians submitted to Ecgbert's lordship, and the ruler of Wessex became king of all England.

This all-embracing power didn't last, though. Wiglaf got his throne back only a year after Ecgbert's victory. But Wessex was still strong in the south, and Ecgbert consolidated this strength by conquering a combined force of Cornish and Vikings at the Battle of Hingston Down in 838. The following year, 839, Ecgbert died.

So Ecgbert's grip on the kingdom of England was loose. But that wasn't what really mattered. Ecgbert was successful because he strengthened Wessex and built the foundations for a powerful future. But first, the kingdom had to face up to further troubles both inside and outside the royal family.

Aethel-this, Aethel-that

After the death of Ecgbert, Ecgbert's son Aethelwulf took over the throne of Wessex. For just more than 30 years, the crowns of Wessex and its subking-doms passed through the hands of Ecgbert's various descendents, nearly all of whom had weird-sounding names beginning with Aethel-. Sorting out all these Aethel-kings is all very confusing for the modern reader, and the upshot was that Wessex remained a strong southern-English kingdom throughout the period. But just to allay the confusion, here's a brief low-down on the most important Aethels:

- ✔ **Aethelwulf:** Aethelwulf (839–58) was Ecgbert's son. He was threatened by the Vikings, whom his father had defeated just before he died, and made a treaty with the kings of Mercia for mutual protection against marauding Norsemen. Aethelwulf then went on a pilgrimage to Rome, handing out his lands to two of his sons. Aethelbald became ruler of the South West. Aethelbert became king of the South East. When Aethelwulf returned from his pilgrimage, a dispute broke out because one of his sons, Aethelbald, would not hand back his crown to his father. Aethelwulf wouldn't fight his son, so he let Aethelbald rule on in Wessex while he took control of the rest of southeast England. But by 860, both Aethelwulf and Aethelbald were dead.

- ✔ **Aethelbert:** Eventually, after the crown-swaps of the previous decade, Aethelbert (860–5) became king of a reunited Wessex. Like his father, he had to face Viking attacks, notably when a big Viking host attacked Winchester and killed many of the inhabitants before Aethelbert fought them off.

✔ **Aethelred:** Another brother of Aethelbert, Aethelred (865–71), also had to contend with Viking invaders. This time they came from the north, and it was serious. The Norsemen had formed a great army and meant business. First, in 866, they landed in East Anglia. By sheer force of numbers, they were quickly able to persuade the king of East Anglia to make peace. They then took all his horses and rode north, taking over York and slaughtering any Northumbrians who tried to defend the area.

Then the Viking host rode south to Mercia, taking Nottingham. The West Saxons marched northwards to help their allies in Mercia put up a resistance. But they were unable to defeat the Vikings who then returned to York. In 870, they were back in the east, charging through East Anglia, defeating its defenders, and putting the local ruler to death.

By 870, the Vikings controlled Northumbria and East Anglia – the whole of the north and east of England. Mercia was hanging on by a thread, and Wessex had so far been left relatively unscathed. But 870 was the year the Vikings went for Wessex. This move was a pivotal moment in English history, because the invaders were attacking the strongest of the English kingdoms. Wessex was the key to power in England – especially in the southern part of the country.

When the Vikings began their assault on Wessex, Aethelred was joined in the field of battle by his surviving brother, Alfred. The pair had to face a formidable assault and fought several battles including, in the year 871:

✔ **Englefield:** A force from Berkshire scored another blow against the invaders, killing one of their commanders.

✔ **Reading:** The Wessex force attacked Reading, a Viking stronghold, but were defeated.

✔ **Ashdown:** Wessex counterattacked. A Wessex defeat was narrowly avoided because Aethelred was attending Mass and would not leave until the priest had finished, but Alfred fought fiercely and his men sent the Vikings running.

In 871, Aethelred died, leaving the war against the Vikings still in the balance and leaving his brother Alfred with the crown. It was a decisive moment for Wessex, with the kingdom's future poised on a knife-edge and a young, fairly inexperienced man about to take over as king. The forces of Wessex had kept the invaders at bay, but the Vikings had not been decisively defeated. It could have gone either way.

Chapter 4

England United

*B*efore the late-ninth century, England was made up of a group of small kingdoms that were constantly vying to be top dog. On one or two occasions, a ruler was so successful in adding to his territories that he claimed kingship of all England. But in the last three decades of the ninth century, one kingdom above all became dominant: Wessex.

The success of Wessex was due above all to King Alfred, a gifted leader who not only dealt with persistent Norse invaders but also presided over a flowering of culture. More than any previous king, Alfred earned himself the right to call himself king of England. And his enthusiasm for learning and writing meant that he nurtured English literature, encouraging writers to help create England's identity as a nation through their words.

One later ruler, Aethelstan, claimed to be even more powerful than Alfred, giving himself the title King of All Britain. He wanted to be famous and respected all over Europe. But most of the later Saxon kings did not live up to Alfred's high standards. As the tenth century went on, Norse raiders and invaders launched more attacks. These attacks became increasingly serious until, by the beginning of the 11th century, it looked as if England would soon have a Danish king on the throne.

Beware, Vikings!

When the Wessex king Aethelred died in A.D. 871 (see Chapter 3), he left his younger brother Alfred to take on the job of ruling his kingdom. Alfred was well placed to take on the kingship. He was quite young – probably in his early to mid 20s, though historians don't know his precise birth date – healthy, and intelligent. And he had a special political strength, too. He had married a princess, Ealhswith, who was the granddaughter of a king of Mercia. A marriage tie between the royal families of Wessex and Mercia would help bring the two kingdoms together.

Alfred was an exceptional character. He had already proved himself in the way that every Anglo-Saxon could understand – he was a brave, decisive war leader. The new king also quickly got a reputation for being fair and for listening to advice when necessary. He needed these qualities, because he faced a big challenge as soon as his reign began. This challenge can be summed up in one word: Vikings.

The people now called Vikings were the invaders from Denmark and Scandinavia who attacked England's shores between the eighth and 11th centuries in search of either plunder to steal or land to settle. Some of these attackers came in small bands and plundered in a fairly disorganised way, but occasionally, the Vikings banded together in a large army and made concerted attacks on Britain and its rulers.

Alfred's first and most urgent job was to deal with the constant attacks from the Scandinavian invaders who, at the end of his brother Aethelred's reign, were making a sustained attempt to take over England.

Alfred had already been fighting the invaders as a commander under his brother, Aethelred. He had proved himself as a brave and decisive warrior, and he may have been expected to fight the Vikings straightaway. But Alfred knew that his army was exhausted. It made more sense to make peace and buy some time.

Raid or trade?

Alfred negotiated a peace treaty with the invaders, who marched off to their lands in northern England. Under their leader, Halfdan, they created a northern capital at Jorvik (modern York). Here the restless Danes settled down and became traders rather than the raiders they used to be.

The Vikings also dug in at a group of towns around the east Midlands – Lincoln, Stamford, Derby, Nottingham, and Leicester – so that they could keep a tight grip on a large chunk of what had been the Saxon Midland kingdom of Mercia.

With their long history of warfare and territorial gain, the Vikings were unlikely to stay in the north. They began assembling a large fleet, roping in some of their relatives, a group who had settled in France. Soon 120 ships were heading straight toward England carrying maybe 10,000 men armed to the teeth.

For once, the English had a bit of luck with the weather. A storm blew up and pushed the invasion fleet off course. The Vikings were in disarray, and now they were forced to negotiate a treaty with Alfred. The resulting agreement, the Treaty of Exeter, allowed the invaders to cross Wessex and march northwards to friendly territory in Mercia, provided that they didn't attack Wessex on the way.

It was now January 878. Because the Danes had agreed to this truce and winter was not a good time for campaigning, Alfred told his military leaders to go back to their homes and spend the time with their families. Winter wasn't the time for warfare. But the Vikings didn't keep their word. At Chippenham in Wiltshire, they broke the treaty and made a shock attack on Alfred.

It was nearly the end for the English king. He had to run. Quickly. Taking with him just a small group of supporters, Alfred beat it to the Somerset Levels, the lonely wetland area around Glastonbury, in those days a region of islands and lagoons only known well by the locals. It was a good place to go if you didn't want people to find you, and Alfred went into hiding on one of the islands in the marshlands, the Isle of Athelney.

The one thing that almost everyone knows about Alfred is that 'he burned the cakes'. In fact, the story of Alfred and the cakes is probably a myth, but it's supposed to have happened when the king was in hiding on the Isle of Athelney. Alfred was taking refuge in the home of one of his cowherds, but the cowherd's wife didn't know who he was. One day, when the woman was baking cakes, she had to go to fetch water from the spring and asked Alfred to keep an eye on the oven. But the king, daydreaming about getting back his power, let the cakes burn. When the cowherd's wife returned, she lost her temper with Alfred and was mortified when her husband told her who Alfred really was. But Alfred forgave the woman, telling her she had been right, and he should have been minding the cakes. This story is a good example of a myth that has been repeatedly retold because it establishes Alfred's character as gentle and forgiving. To be a successful king, though, he must have had a ruthless side, too.

With the king in hiding, it looked for a while as if the glory of Wessex had come to an end. A Saxon leader counted for very little if he couldn't behave like a warrior – he was expected to enjoy getting on to the battlefield, knocking the stuffing out of his enemies, and then spending a happy evening carousing with his men in his hall. But Alfred was a thoughtful character who knew very well that being a man of action meant next to nothing if you did not know how to time your actions. He knew that he maybe able to turn things around if he waited and struck at the right time.

The only answer – fight!

When spring came, English fortunes began to change. Oda, Ealdorman of Devon, met the Viking leader Ubba (sole survivor of three brothers who began the serious Viking attempt at conquest in 865) on the battlefield and beat him. When Alfred heard the news, he realised that it was time for him to get ready to fight again.

Oda, and a whole bunch of other bigwigs in Anglo-Saxon England, held the rank of *ealdorman*. This Old English word means literally 'senior man' and was used by the Anglo-Saxons to refer to the most important noblemen in the country. In Alfred's time, an ealdorman was responsible for a single shire or county of Wessex. Later, kings used the term to refer to magnates who held power over an entire region – almost a subkingdom – such as Mercia or Northumbria.

Alfred gathered his army together and attacked the Viking horde at Edington in Wiltshire. He beat the invaders on the battlefield and then, when the Danish survivors retreated behind their defences, he surrounded them and laid siege. Alfred waited for 14 days before his enemies gave in.

Alfred made it clear that he meant business and wanted to send the Vikings back to their homes in the north and east by setting the following terms:

- ✔ The Vikings gave hostages to Alfred.
- ✔ Their leader, Guthrum, became a Christian and took a new baptismal name, Aethelstan.
- ✔ Aethelstan and his men retreated immediately to Mercia.
- ✔ In 880, Aethelstan was allowed to become king of East Anglia.
- ✔ An invading army based near London was ordered to leave England.

Alfred in Control

With the Danes out of the way, Alfred set about tightening his control over his kingdom and extending his influence across a wider area. He achieved this goal in various ways. As well as further military conquests, he also changed how his kingdom was run.

Alfred put in place a raft of measures, both military and administrative, that made it easier both to fight and to rule. His new ideas included:

- ✔ **Changing the way men were called to fight.** From now on, only half of the *fyrd* – the fighting force that the king could call on – would be made to fight at any one time. This change kept the other half in reserve and fresh, ready to relieve the first half.

- ✔ **Setting up a network of fortified towns, called *burhs*.** These burhs were evenly spaced around southern England and were all protected by earth ramparts. They provided strongholds to protect the surrounding countryside from future invasions. Later, they became homes to markets and centres of coin-minting.

- ✔ **Building a navy.** Alfred brought ship-builders over the sea from Frisia, and craftsmen built a fleet to fight the Vikings, who had previously enjoyed supremacy on the sea.

These measures show Alfred as Mr Efficiency. It must have taken planning, and a degree of ruthlessness, to set up all the burhs across southern England, let alone build up the navy from scratch and reorganise the fyrd.

The reforms put in place by Alfred seriously strengthened his rule. But Alfred's ambition didn't stop there. He had his eye on a prize in southeastern England: London. London and the lands to the north of the River Thames weren't traditional Wessex territory. Before the great army of Vikings arrived, they had been Mercian. Now the Danes were occupying the area. Alfred wanted them out.

Alfred didn't necessarily want to rule London and the territory on the north bank of the Thames directly, but he wanted to exercise his power there. So in 886, the king and his army laid siege to London and captured the city. Straight away, Alfred called for Aethelred of Mercia. Aethelred could be king of the territories conquered by Alfred – provided that the Mercian recognised him as overlord.

This system was attractive to both sides. Alfred wielded the real power, but Aethelred could still call himself king and rule his people. Interestingly, a number of Welsh princes also offered themselves to Alfred, recognizing his lordship in return for protection.

So by the end of the 880s, Alfred was overall ruler of a large part of England and much of southern Wales, too. He was more powerful than any of his predecessors in Wessex, and he had earned the title by which he now liked to be known – King of the Anglo-Saxons. In later years, he earned a nickname, too. Alfred is the only English king to be widely known as 'the Great'.

Learning and Law-Giving

Alfred's conquests and military achievements are well known, but the king had another side. He learned to read and write when he was a teenager, giving him a deep love of learning. He even told his biographer, Asser, that he wished he had been taught his letters when he was a young child. And when he grew to adulthood, his love of learning was certainly strengthened. As may be expected of such a dynamic character, Alfred put his interest in scholarship to active use when he became king. He encouraged the foundation of monasteries – the places where writing and learning flourished in the days before schools or universities.

Not only that, but Alfred was an accomplished writer himself and liked his top servants to be literate, too. The king's love of literacy was very unusual in this period. In the ninth century, monks and priests were usually the only people who can read or write. Kings were expected to be men of action who would not have time for book-learning. They employed *scribes* – men who had been educated in the monasteries – to take care of the business of drawing up treaties and charters.

The literary king

Alfred not only encouraged the monks in the English monasteries to do literary work; he was an able writer himself – with a difference. In the ninth century, the language of scholarship in Europe was Latin. The monks used a Latin translation of the Bible, sang their services in Latin, and wrote their religious books in Latin.

Few people outside the church understood Latin, and Alfred saw that it was also important to have books in English. So he commissioned a series of translations of some of the most important Latin books and, amazingly, given that he was already busy running his kingdom, Alfred actually translated some of these works himself. He was one of the few British monarchs to be a writer and the only one to produce work of lasting importance.

It's not always certain which of the translations of Alfred's reign were done by the king himself. But people who study Anglo-Saxon literature say that the ones that are definitely Alfred's work show a distinctive, lively way of writing Old English that stands out as something special. Here's a list of the main texts that the king translated:

- The *Cura Pastoralis* (Pastoral Care), a manual for the clergy written by Pope Gregory I.
- The *Historia Adversus Paganos* (History Against the Pagans: a history and geography of the world), written by the Spanish priest Orosius.

> ✔ The *Soliloquia* (Soliloquies) of the great theologian of the Roman period, St Augustine.
>
> ✔ The *De Consolatione Philosophiae* (Consolation of Philosophy) written by the Roman writer Boethius.

These texts were serious, heavy tomes, but Alfred knew that they would also be useful in their English versions. He wrote a preface to his translation of Gregory's *Pastoral Care*, in which he lamented how learning had decayed in England and said that he was determined that this situation should change. Alfred sent a copy of the translation to every bishop in England.

Alfred was not above adding extra bits to his translations, to improve on the originals. He did this with his version of Orosius's *History Against the Pagans*. This book was full of geographical information, but since it was originally written in the early fifth century, explorers had discovered quite a lot about the world. So Alfred inserted accounts by Scandinavian explorers about regions such as the Baltic, to bring the book up to date.

History and law

It wasn't just Alfred who was busy at his desk. As well as doing his own translations, the king commissioned scholars to make others. One important work that was translated in Alfred's reign was the *Ecclesiastical History of the English People*, by the monk Bede (673–735). This key historical work covers the history of Britain, with a special emphasis on church history, from the Roman invasion up to 731.

As well as translations like Bede's *History*, Alfred's scribes also produced new works of their own. The most important was another work of history, the compilation called the *Anglo-Saxon Chronicle*.

Laying down the law

The other big literary work of Alfred's reign was the writing of the king's law code. Because the king's realm was made up of areas that had previously been separate kingdoms, it was immensely important for Alfred to have a unified set of laws to which everyone can refer.

Drawing up a universal set of laws could have been fraught with problems. People from one part of the kingdom might easily have objected if they were made to obey a set of harsher laws imposed by another of the former kingdoms. And yet it must have been tempting to Alfred to just write the laws of Wessex and force everyone in his kingdom to obey them.

The Anglo-Saxon Chronicle

The most famous work produced by the circle of scholars encouraged by King Alfred was a new book, a history of events in England from the start of the Christian period onward. This work, which continued after Alfred's death, is now known as the *Anglo-Saxon Chronicle*, and it has become the main source of knowledge about the entire Anglo-Saxon period.

Monks had been making notes about past events before Alfred's reign. But most of these notes were brief jottings made in Latin. Alfred was probably the person who asked the monks to start making a more detailed record and to write it down in English. The *Chronicle* certainly gives a lengthy account of Alfred's own reign, especially his last wars against the Danes.

After Alfred's death, the monks continued with the *Chronicle*, writing down details of events in England until 1154. These records have survived in seven different handwritten versions, precious manuscripts that are a unique window on the world of the Anglo-Saxons.

But Alfred didn't just keep to the laws of Wessex. He took the opportunity to take a good, hard look at all the English laws and tried to pick the ones he thought worked best. In his preface to his laws, Alfred explained that he took the advice of his councillors when he was choosing which measures to include – and that he took advice again, getting the approval of the councillors, once the whole list had been written out.

By taking advice and saying that he'd done so, Alfred was ensuring that the laws would meet with widespread approval. He also hoped that later generations would obey them because, like all conscientious kings, Alfred was interested in his legacy. He didn't want everything he'd achieved to fall apart as soon as he died.

A royal life

One of the scholars at Alfred's court was a Welsh monk called Asser. Asser came from St David's in southwest Wales, spent up to six months each year at the king's court, and was eventually appointed Bishop of Sherborne. Historians know about Asser today because he wrote a biography of Alfred, which is the first full-scale, detailed account of the life of an English king.

Asser's *Life of Alfred* is not like today's scandal-filled royal exposés. It's written in Latin, for a start, which is ironic given the king's love of the English language. It's also very respectful. Asser clearly admired Alfred and painted a portrait of him as a model king and a good man. So can historians actually believe the bishop's dutiful account of Alfred as a model king? It's probably a bit too favourable to Alfred – it doesn't say anything about the king's hard, ruthless streak. And some historians have suggested that it isn't a genuine life at all but a medieval forgery. But the balance of opinion accepts Asser's *Life* as a genuine, if biased, biography.

The bishop put down his quill pen in 893. Alfred died six years later in 899, having insisted that his heir should be his son Edward, not one of his nephews who had an eye on the throne.

In this period, it wasn't automatic that the king's eldest son got the crown. Other brothers or cousins could inherit instead. So a wise king made a clear announcement about the identity of his royal heir.

After Alfred

After the death of King Alfred, the two big issues of his reign – keeping the Danish invaders at bay and running England as a united kingdom – came back to haunt the kings who followed him. Although Alfred had laid strong foundations for a united English realm, keeping the nation together as he had done required strength of character, intelligence – and a certain amount of good luck. Some of the rulers of the tenth century managed to keep the country together; others were less successful. On balance, they failed, leaving England vulnerable to Danish domination by the early-11th century.

Marriages and marauders: Edward

The first king to rule after Alfred was his son, Edward, who was probably around 29 years old when he came to the throne in 899. Alfred wanted his son to succeed him and had probably prepared Edward well for the throne. One document describes him as a king before his father's death, which probably indicates that Edward held some sort of subkingship – an ideal way in which the young man could learn the ropes of ruling before taking on the big task of governing the whole country.

Take your partners

Edward married three times, but no one knows for sure why he swapped partners so often. The records are silent about the fate of the first wife, Ecgwynn, but it's certain that the second, Aelfflaed, left the court for a nunnery. What was going on? Here's a brief low-down on Edward's wives:

✔ **Wife No. 1: Ecgwynn:** Edward's first partner was Ecgwynn. Historians don't know much about her background, but Edward was married to her before he became king, and she produced one son, Aethelstan.

✔ **Wife No. 2: Aelfflaed:** Edward married her at around the time he became king. She was the daughter of Aethelhelm, Ealdorman of Wiltshire, and it may be that the reason for the marriage was to give Edward his father-in-law's support as king of Wessex. Aelfflaed bore eight of Edward's children.

✔ **Wife No. 3: Eadgifu:** Edward ditched Aelfflaed toward the end of his reign. She went to live in the nunnery at Wilton, and Edward married Eadgifu, daughter of another Ealdorman, this time from Kent. Eadgifu was the mother of two sons and two daughters.

So while the reason for Edward's first wife-swap was probably political, the second is a bit of a mystery. Some historians think it may have been a religious decision. Toward the end of Edward's reign, the church brought in a number of religious reforms, including new restrictions on who could marry whom. It may be that Edward and his second queen were distantly related, and such was the importance of the opinion of the church that they thought it unwise to stay together. This theory would tie in with Aelfflaed's decision to spend her last years in a nunnery.

Power struggle

King Alfred died in 899, but Edward was not formally inaugurated as king until June of the following year. This large gap probably had something to do with the fact that Edward had a rival for the throne. The rival was Aethelwold, who was a son of Aethelred, the man who had been king before Alfred and Alfred's brother. Aethelwold meant trouble for Edward – and for several of those around him.

Aethelwold made his move soon after Alfred's death. His first step sounds rather odd. He broke into a nunnery, carried off one of the nuns, and married her. Historians don't know who this nun was, but she was probably somebody well-connected – nuns were often women from the upper classes and frequently members of the royal family. It's a good bet that Aethelwold's victim was Alfred's daughter, Aethelgifu, who had taken the veil. Probably he thought that if he married the old king's daughter, he'd have an even better claim to the throne.

Aethelwold grabbed the mystery nun and set himself up in the Dorset town of Wimborne, letting it be known that he was making a bid for the crown. Edward arrived with an army, captured Wimborne, and rescued the nun. But Aethelwold escaped. It was first blood to Edward, but the trouble wasn't over.

The usurper returned in 902. This time Aethelwold had the backing of the most formidable ally – England's old enemy, the Danes, in the person of the Danish ruler of East Anglia, a man called Eohric. Edward made a decisive move. The Danes had no right to go rampaging over his kingdom, and he pursued them back to East Anglia. The two sides fought at Holme, and Edward scored a decisive victory. Both Aethelwold and Eohric lost their lives.

Expanding royal power

After the Battle of Holme, Edward was fairly safe on the throne, but he still wasn't finished with the Vikings. There were Danish rulers around the edges of his kingdom in East Anglia and the eastern part of Mercia, as well as farther north in Northumbria, and sometimes they threatened Edward's rule. The king dealt with them at various stages:

- Edward defeated an attempted invasion of the English-ruled part of Mercia in 910.

- Between 911 and 916, Edward got back most of eastern Mercia and East Anglia by a combination of purchase and conquest.

- In 917, Edward was formally accepted as king in East Anglia.

- In 920, a clutch of northern rulers, including the kings of Northumbria and the Scots, formally recognised Edward.

- After his takeover of eastern Mercia, Edward followed the methods of his father, setting up burhs and establishing shires to foster security and aid government.

Edward had to work hard to achieve the sort of domination won by his father, but when he died, he had a large sphere of influence across England and into Scotland. But his serial marriages and profusion of sons meant that when he died in 924, the future of the crown was uncertain.

Crowning glories: Aethelstan

Aethelstan was lucky. He was the eldest son of King Edward, who died in 924, and his first wife. But Edward, who had married three times, had several sons and one of them looked a more likely ruler than Aethelstan: Aethelweard, Edward's eldest son by his second wife, who had been chosen to succeed his father as ruler of Wessex. Aethelstan, on the other hand, was the favoured candidate of the Mercians. England looked set for a bitter civil war.

But sometimes fate steps in and changes things decisively, which is what happened in 924. Aethelweard died a couple of weeks after Edward, leaving the way clear for Aethelstan. Now Mercia and Wessex, the two main parts of southern England, could rally behind the new king.

King of all Britain

Aethelstan picked up where his father and grandfather, Edward and Alfred, had left off, claiming to be overall ruler of a large chunk of Britain. As with these previous rulers, he received the submission of various northern rulers, including kings from Scotland. Even many of the Welsh accepted him as overlord.

Aethelstan seized the opportunities given him when rulers from various parts of Britain offered him their submission. Aethelstan and his advisers were quick to take advantage of these acts of homage by giving the king grandiose titles, such as the impressive-sounding Rex totius Britanniae (king of all Britain) and King of Albion. These titles weren't necessarily very meaningful, but they did mean that the king was seen as a seriously big cheese. Aethelstan was known and recognised everywhere – even on the European mainland.

A challenge from the North

When Aethelstan had been on the throne for ten years, a crisis developed in the north. A local northern ruler, Ealdred of Bamburgh, died, and Constantine, king of the Scots, tried to muscle in on his territory. Aethelstan led a large army northwards and tracked down Constantine, who was holed up at Dunottar, near Aberdeen. The English king laid siege to Dunottar and forced Constantine to give himself up.

Constantine must have been miffed by this defeat and seriously worried by Aethelstan's expansionist ambitions in the north. So three years later, in 937, the Scotsman planned his revenge. He gathered together a group of allies, including the Norseman Olaf Guthfrithsson, who was king of Dublin and also Constantine's son-in-law, and moved south toward Mercia.

Aethelstan and his army moved northwards to meet the invaders. They confronted each other at a place called Brunanburh. Historians don't know exactly where Brunanburh was, but it must have been somewhere in the East Midlands. When the two sides engaged in battle, it was a vicious and bloody fight. Both sides suffered heavy losses, but Aethelstan was the victor.

Aethelstan ruled for two more years before dying in 939. He had never married, so his crown passed to his half-brother Edmund, son of King Edward and his third wife, Eadgifu.

King and victim: Edmund

Like most of the Saxon kings, Edmund, who came to the throne in 939, had to face invasion attempts from the old Danish enemy. He had only a short, seven-year reign and much of that time was taken up with losing and regaining territory from the Danes. But Edmund also had time to start a movement that would bear very different, more peaceful, fruit after his death – he began a revival of monasticism and learning in England.

A barrel Olafs

Edmund had hardly settled on his throne when the Norse leader Olaf Guthfrithsson, who had made trouble for his half-brother Aethelstan, started war-mongering in northern England. A lot of to-ing and fro-ing occurred between England and the Danes. To cut a long story short:

- ✔ In 940, Olaf Guthfrithsson invaded Mercia.

- ✔ Olaf and Edmund came to an agreement whereby Olaf took control of the north and east of England – all the territory to the north of the old Roman road, Watling Street.

- ✔ In 941, Olaf died. He was succeeded by Olaf Sihtricsson, but the second Olaf could not hold on to his lands when a power struggled erupted amongst the Danes.

- ✔ Edmund seized the moment and muscled in on Mercia and East Anglia when the Danes were distracted by their own internal squabble.

- ✔ In 944, Edmund seized control of Northumbria, too.

So it was the classic tussle between Saxon and Dane, with the Saxon king winning in the end. Things were looking up for Edmund.

Monastic-drastic

The other side of Edmund's career was his encouragement of England's monasteries. Since the Danes had started raiding England, the monasteries had had a hard time. The *Anglo-Saxon Chronicle* includes a number of mentions of monasteries being destroyed and plundered by the non-Christian invaders. In fact, things may not have been quite as bad as the chroniclers say. The people who wrote the *Chronicle* were monks themselves, and they may have exaggerated the damage. But however bad things were, the monasteries had certainly suffered since Alfred's time. King Edmund felt that the time was ripe for a monastic revival.

Edmund's main move toward reviving the monasteries was to promote the appointment of an intelligent and energetic churchman called Dunstan as abbot of Glastonbury, one of England's most important abbeys, in 940. Dunstan was one of the king's key advisers, one of the churchmen who regularly attended the royal court to give the king the benefit of their learning and experience.

Dunstan was both a churchman and a royal adviser. This dual role seems strange in today's secular society, but in Anglo-Saxon England, it was quite normal. Churchmen became advisers because they were educated – they had to be able to read and write so that they could understand the Bible and pass on this understanding. Few other people in this period could read and write, so men like Dunstan often had double careers. Their education made them good royal advisers and ambassadors, while they could often put their political contacts to work when it came to gathering support and funding for the church.

With Dunstan at the helm, Glastonbury Abbey flourished. Dunstan had a number of associates who would also become leaders of important English monasteries, but any move toward a general monastic reform depended for its success on royal support and political stability. In other words, no one would want to join a monastery if they thought there was a good chance that it would be sacked by invading Danes in a year or two's time.

So all the hopes for the monasteries were dashed when Edmund met an early death in 946. Somehow the king got involved with a fight. One of his servants was being assaulted, and Edmund did the worthy thing and went to defend his man. In the struggle, the king was murdered, and the promise he had showed in both the political and religious spheres was cut short with the stroke of a knife.

More Saxons

After Edmund was murdered, England was ruled by a succession of kings, most of whom did not reign for very long. These short reigns were unfortunate, in a way, because they meant instability and uncertainty for everyone from the royal family down. Here's a short summary of the next four Saxon kings:

- **Eadred (946–55):** Edmund's brother Eadred spent much of his reign trying to dominate the Northumbrians and remove their Norse rulers. He died, after a long illness, without any children.

- **Eadwig All-Fair (955–9):** Eadwig, Edmund's son, was famous for his lax morals and for splitting up his kingdom so that his brother Edgar ruled in Mercia and Northumbria. When Abbot Dunstan of Glastonbury criticised his morals, the churchman found himself thrown out of the country.

- **Edgar (957–975):** When Eadwig died, his brother Edgar took over the whole kingdom. He enjoyed a longer reign than his two predecessors and seems to have been able to protect his kingdom from outside attacks. He brought Dunstan back from exile and encouraged the monastic revival.

- **Edward (975–8):** Edward's short reign was ended when he was murdered, probably by supporters of his rival, his brother Aethelred, for the throne.

By the time Edward met his death, England was in dire need of stability, of a long-reigning monarch who could pull his kingdom together. It got what it needed with the next ruler, Aethelred.

Eadric Streona

Eadric Streona was Ealdorman of Mercia when he became Aethelred's chief advisor in 1007. It is probably Eadric who earned the king his later nickname, the Unready, or ill-advised, because Eadric was something of a dead loss as an adviser. His second name, Streona, means acquisitor. In other words he was Eadric the Grabber – he was probably helping himself to money from the royal taxes.

But his greed wasn't the worst thing about him. He was also Eadric the Traitor. In 1015, with Aethelred's star falling, Eadric decided to forsake the king's cause and back his son, Edmund. But his support for Edmund didn't last long. Later the same year, he changed his allegiance to the Danish leader, Cnut, and his treachery helped give Cnut the upper hand.

The unready king: Aethelred

Aethelred, who came to the throne in 978, was the younger brother of the previous king, Edward, and son of King Edgar. The new king was only 12 years old and had to rely on experienced advisers, who included his mother, Aelfthryth, and a senior churchman, Aethelwold, Bishop of Winchester.

Ever since the 12th century, Aethelred has been known as 'the Unready'. The nickname comes from the Old English word *unraed,* which means badly advised. It points to the fact that by the end of his long reign, Aethelred had lost most of his kingdom to the Danes. But it is difficult to be sure, more than a thousand years after his death, whether the king's loss of his lands was actually due to poor advice.

Trouble from the North

The new Viking raids on Britain began in the 980s. They were mostly attacks from Norse warriors who had left Scandinavia because of trouble at home. To begin with, the attackers arrived in fairly small bands, but the bands got larger and more aggressive in the 990s.

Aethelred decided to persuade the attackers to leave by buying them off. To begin with, it worked. The Norse peoples had a highly developed sense of justice, and many of those who received payments, which came to be known as Danegeld, sailed back home and did not return. But some were less scrupulous and started to regard England as a cash-cow to be milked at every opportunity. Through the 990s, the attacks increased.

In 1002, Aethelred changed policy and launched a violent attack on the Danes, an assault that came to be known as the massacre of St Brice's Day. The people Aethelred attacked were those who had already settled in

England and who, for the most part, were people of peace. So, in effect, the English committed an act of racial war on innocent people. Worse still, one of the victims was the sister of Svein Fork-Beard, King of Denmark. And Svein was a formidable warrior who could not let the outrage go unpunished.

The Danes invade

Svein invaded England in 1003, and a long and bitter war began. It seems to have been a particularly dirty war, with commanders changing sides more than once. In part, this disloyalty was due to Aethelred, who had a good idea but then spoiled it by having a bad one.

- **The king's good idea:** It was blindingly obvious that the Norsemen were Europe's most accomplished sailors. They dominated the seas around Britain, which gave them a huge advantage because they could launch attacks anywhere on the English coast. So a few years into the war, Aethelred decided to build an English fleet to stop the Vikings in their tracks. A special tax was levied to pay for it, and boat-building was soon underway.

- **The king's bad idea:** But Aethelred decided to man his ships with Vikings! On the face of it, the idea had a certain logic: they were the best seamen, after all. But he chose as their leader a character called Thorkel the Tall who had not long ago been implicated in the murder of the archbishop of Canterbury. No wonder people were soon changing sides.

The war was a disaster for Aelthelred. By 1013, he had to flee from England and ended up in exile in Normandy. Meanwhile, things were looking grim for his cause in England, when his adviser Eadric Streona changed sides.

As a result of Aethelred's absence and Eadric's treachery, Svein took control of the kingdom of England, but he lived only another year, so his son, Cnut, took over. When Aethelred himself died in 1016, his son Edmund, known as Edmund Ironside, fought Cnut for the crown, and Cnut was the victor in the battle. Edmund then did the sensible thing and made a bargain with Cnut – the two men agreed to split the country between them. But the bargain didn't last. In November 1016, Edmund died. The rest of his family, unwilling to start the dispute all over again, fled the country, and Cnut was ruler of England.

Chapter 5

Danes versus Saxons

. . . .

In This Chapter

▶ Introducing King Cnut

▶ Describing the squabbles of Cnut's sons

▶ Restoring Saxon rule under the pious King Edward the Confessor

▶ Battling to succeed Edward

. . . .

After years of attacks in which Vikings had raided and invaded parts of England, the most powerful Danish king to date, Cnut, conquered England in 1016. Many Britons, fearful of the Danes' violent reputation, probably quaked in their shoes when Cnut became king. But once he was king, Cnut wasn't too bad. He dealt ruthlessly with traitors, but with good reason. He wanted England to be stable and therefore safely under his rule.

Cnut was absent from England a lot of the time because he also had lands in Scandinavia to rule. But he tried to lay down a framework so that England would run smoothly in his absence, dividing up the kingdom under powerful nobles called earls and putting together an influential law code.

Cnut ruled for 19 years, but he did not leave a clear line of succession when he died. For this reason, his reign was followed by several years of dispute and fighting between his sons before the Saxon Edward the Confessor, son of Aethelred the Unready and a man with strong connections with Normandy, came to the throne. Edward's reign followed a curiously similar pattern to Cnut's – a period of relative stability followed by a disputed succession. But Edward's reign was also troubled by internal bickering – especially a conflict between Earl Godwine and Edward's Norman advisers and associates. By the time the king died, in 1066, the Normans were eyeing England and planning to take over completely.

There Is Nothing Like a Dane

The Danish prince Cnut became king of England when he conquered the country in 1016 (see Chapter 4). His triumph came at the end of a long war that had occupied the last 14 years of the reign of King Aethelred and a few months in 1016 when Aethelred's son, Edmund, claimed the throne. As a result of the long struggle, the upper classes of England were ready to accept the rule of a foreigner, in spite of the fact that Cnut was a Norseman, and Norsemen had a reputation for cruelty and ruthlessness.

But Cnut was a Christian king. The Danes had been converted to Christianity in the 960s by Cnut's grandfather, the memorably named King Harald Bluetooth. So although the Danes still had a reputation for cruelty and violence, they were no longer likely to make marauding attacks on churches and monasteries, as their ancestors had done (see Chapter 4). King Cnut did have a cruel streak, but he presided over a period of relative peace in England.

Change your partners

One of the most surprising things about Cnut was his married life. He had two wives. That wasn't all that unusual for an English king. But Cnut was different because he seems to have had two wives *at the same time*. His two marriage partners were both highly influential women, but they came from rather different backgrounds:

- ✔ **Royal wife No. 1 – Aelfgifu:** Cnut married his first wife in 1013, three years before he became king of England. Aelfgifu, sometimes known as Aelfgifu of Northampton, was from an upper-class English family. She bore Cnut two sons. The first was Svein, who his father made ruler of Norway, but who died before Cnut in 1034. The second was Harold, known by the curious nickname of Harold Harefoot. Aelfgifu remained powerful after her husband's second marriage and stood in for Svein in Norway for some time.

- ✔ **Royal wife No. 2 – Emma:** After Cnut became king, he married Emma, who was the widow of King Aethelred. Emma was an astute choice politically, because marrying her stressed continuity with the regime of King Aethelred. But Emma, who originally came from Normandy, at this period an area settled by the Vikings, had Norse ancestors, so she strengthened Cnut's ties with Scandinavia, too. Emma bore the king one son, Harthacnut.

When kings remarried, the first wife usually got thrown out. A 'retired' royal wife was a focus of resentment and could become a rallying point for the king's enemies who might want to depose him. But things seem to have been different between Cnut and Aelfgifu. Perhaps because of her son's power in Norway, she was already too powerful to cast aside. Historians don't know for sure. Contemporaries were confused, too, especially when it came to sorting out who was Cnut's legitimate heir.

Cnut and the Saxons

When he became king of England, Cnut knew all too well that he hadn't got there by the 'natural' route. He had had to fight for the crown, and he'd won partly because some high-ranking supporters of the Saxon king Aethelstan had changed sides during the war (see Chapter 4). Cnut owed his crown to a bunch of traitors, especially Ealdorman Eadric Streona, who had actually changed sides twice. Cnut knew that anything he could do to strengthen his position with the English nobles would help him hang on to power.

Getting the nobles on-side

After the death of Edmund, Cnut assembled the leading men of the country – both Ealdormen and bishops – and persuaded them to give their support to his kingship. They swore to obey him, that they would pay their taxes to support his army, and that they would not support any of the descendants of Aethelred and Edmund if they made a challenge for the throne.

Cnut also asked them all whether the dying Edmund had earmarked any of his brothers or sons to succeed him. They replied that he had not and furthermore that Edmund would have wished Cnut to be the 'protector' of Edmund's descendants.

 In the Anglo-Saxon period, when the crown did not automatically pass from father to son, it was important for kings that their claim to the throne was acceptable and had some sort of formal legitimacy. This support was even more important for a king like Cnut, who had won his throne by military might. By extracting these affirmations out of the English nobles, Cnut gave his kingship legality. He had been officially rubber-stamped by the English, and it would now be more difficult for them to make trouble.

Removing the rivals

Cnut also knew that there were potential rivals to the throne and that at least one of Aethelred's old supporters, Eadric Streona, had the ability to break his promises. So Cnut started to show his ruthless side. He took these measures to deal with potential rivals and traitors:

- ✔ He sent Edmund's two sons to the king of Sweden with a message that they should be put to death. The Swedes were merciful, however, and saved the princes, who went to live at the court of the king of Hungary.

- ✔ He ensured that two other potential rivals, the sons of Aethelred's queen, Emma of Normandy, stayed in Normandy, well away from the English throne.

- ✔ He ordered that Eadric Streona should be put to death.

Cnut made one other move to make his position more secure. In 1017, the same year that Eadric met his death, the king married Aethelred's widow, Emma. This liaison helped cement his links with the previous rulers, making him seem more like a king from the Saxon tradition. Cnut also retained some of the more trustworthy and intelligent of the advisers from Aethelred's court, including the powerful churchman Wulstan, the archbishop of York. Once more, King Cnut was showing that there was some continuity between his regime and the previous one.

Cnut the astute: England prospers

Even with traitors like Eadric out of the way, it was a tall order for a foreign king to rule England – especially as Cnut had lots of territory in Denmark, ruled much of Norway, and also conquered part of Sweden. These responsibilities meant that he had to spend a lot of time away from England and he knew he had to leave his new realm in the hands of others. He needed a good team of nobles to run things in his absence, and clear laws that they could enforce.

Like the Saxons before him, Cnut divided up his kingdom, putting leading associates in charge of the four divisions. Under Cnut, high-ranking nobles ran Northumbria, Mercia, and East Anglia, while Cnut kept Wessex (still the senior division, as it had been since Alfred's time) for himself.

Cnut gave the leaders of these separate chunks of his realm a Scandinavian title, *earl.* The new title made the division of the kingdom look like something new, but in fact it had existed under the Saxons. The usual Saxon name for the local deputies had been *Ealdormen,* but the title of Ealdorman was also used for lesser bigwigs, men who had control of one shire or county, so the picture looked more confusing. Under Cnut, the divisions were clearer, with the king at the top of the hierarchy, the earls immediately below him, and the Ealdormen lower still.

Cnut's other key achievement in government was to produce a new law code. Like many law codes, Cnut's did not contain much that was new. It was a collection of laws that mostly already existed. But it was the longest law code of the Saxon period and would be referred to by lawyers in just the same way as the law code of King Alfred had been.

Cnut's laws tried to accommodate both English and Danish legal opinion. But they gave ultimate precedence to the law of God, because Cnut was a Christian and wanted to stress that he was not like some of his violent, non-Christian forbears who had so terrified the locals when they raided England's shores.

Cnut in Europe

In some ways, Cnut was the most powerful and influential king of England to date. He had a large empire and wanted recognition as one of the major Christian kings of Europe. In 1027, the opportunity for this recognition came. A new Holy Roman Emperor – the ruler of lands based in Germany – was to be crowned by the pope in Rome, and Cnut was invited to attend.

It's hard today to understand what a big deal attending the imperial corona-tion was for Cnut. The Emperor and the Pope were the two most powerful men in Europe, and up to this point, England had been a small kingdom on the edge of Europe, little regarded by more powerful monarchs on the main-land. But now Cnut was being invited to meet the Pope and the Emperor as an equal. No previous English king had had this double privilege, and it was a feather in England's cap, as well as Cnut's.

When he got to Rome, Cnut was impressed. He met the crowned heads of Europe and was showered with costly gifts, such as jewels, gold and silver vessels, and robes of precious silk – the kind of things with which monarchs impressed each other in those days. It was a diplomatic triumph.

Cnut made a speech to them all, asking that his subjects, English and Danish alike, should be granted free and unhindered passage when they travelled across Europe to Rome, whether they were making the journey as a religious pilgrimage or whether they were merchants carrying goods.

Both the Emperor and King Rudolf of Burgundy, who ruled much of the terri-tory Cnut's subjects had to pass through to get from England to Rome, agreed to Cnut's request. This deal gave the king a lot of pleasure and a lot of pres-tige. He was now truly a ruler of international consequence who could hold his head high amongst the most powerful men on the continent.

Not only that, but the king's diplomatic triumph was good for England, too. It meant that English traders would be expected in mainland Europe and would be given a welcome. England felt less on the edge of Europe, more a part of the continent as a whole.

An all-powerful king?

After his famous trip to Rome, Cnut's image was that of a supercharged monarch with incredible power. After all, he had a northern empire that was one of the biggest in Europe. It's not really a surprise that his courtiers, awed by his power, took to fawning and trying to flatter him. Cnut, though, was a very level-headed character. And as a Christian, he believed that his power was nothing compared to God's.

Cnut and the waves

The most famous story about Cnut came about because of the flattery of his courtiers. Some people at Cnut's court were supposed to have told him that he was so powerful, he could turn back the waves. Cnut, so it's said, dragged his whole court down to the beach and ordered the waves to turn back. He knew they wouldn't, but he wanted to teach the courtiers a lesson – which they duly got when the waves continued up the beach, giving everyone a good soaking.

It's unlikely that the story of Cnut and the waves really happened. It first appears in a chronicle written in the 12th century, quite a while after the king's lifetime, and it's probably a myth. But the tale does have an underlying truth, which is that the king probably did suffer from sycophants and probably did see through them. The fable of the waves was a good way of telling the story, especially as Cnut came from a culture where mastery of the seas – in a longboat – was expected of any ruler.

Cnut backed up his assertion of God's power by showing that he could be good to the church. He was a generous benefactor to churches and monasteries and gave lands to the Old Minster at Winchester and to the abbeys at Sherborne and Bury St Edmunds. He also encouraged others to make gifts to the church – monasteries at Abingdon, Canterbury, and Evesham benefited as a result. And Cnut is said to have founded the monasteries at St Benet Holme and Bury St Edmunds, although no firm documentary evidence supports this theory.

An iron fist

In a way, Cnut was a bit of a contradiction. He was a diplomat, but was also much feared; he respected the church, but he was also ruthless. His English subjects probably saw enough of the ruthless side. The English at one time or another had to suffer because of Cnut's rule in several ways:

- ✔ He taxed the English very heavily, especially at the beginning of his reign.
- ✔ He bumped off political rivals who posed a threat to his power.
- ✔ He installed many Danish families on British lands, levering locals out in the process.

Even his marriage to Queen Emma, who was herself of Norse ancestry, looked like another example of Danish influence over a conquered people.

But Cnut's 'iron fist in a velvet glove' approach to kingship worked, in that England was relatively stable and relatively powerful on the European stage. Cnut's main problem was that he did not secure the succession. When Cnut died in 1035, he had two sons. One, Harold, known as Harold Harefoot, was the son of Cnut's English wife, Aelfgifu. The other, Harthacnut, was the son of the king's second wife, Emma of Normandy. Given Cnut's unorthodox married life, a dispute occurred as to who was the legitimate heir, and the Danish king's empire began to break apart.

A cruel legacy: Cnut's sons

The death of King Cnut in 1035 led to a dispute between his two surviving sons, Harold Harefoot and Harthacnut, over who should rule. Confusion abounded because Harold was Cnut's son with his first wife Aelfgifu, but he hadn't renounced Aelfgifu when he married his second wife, Emma of Normandy, the mother of Harthacnut. So for a start, there were arguments about who was legitimate.

In these circumstances, it mattered a lot who got backing from the country's senior earls and highest-ranking churchmen. But the earls were split, too. Godwine, Earl of Wessex, came out in favour of Harthacnut. Leofric, Earl of Mercia, said Harold (whose grandfather, after all, had been a Mercian) should be king. Stalemate again.

Another factor was who was available to grab hold of the crown – often when a dispute like this one arose, the successful claimant was the person who was ready to persuade the church to crown him. By this measure, Harold should have become king, because Harthacnut was away in the North, fighting a war with Magnus of Norway. But for some reason, the Archbishop of Canterbury seemed unwilling to crown Harold. Still no decision.

Emma intervenes

At last, the backers of this pair of princes came up with a compromise: split the kingdom between the two. But even this solution couldn't work without Harthacnut coming back from Scandinavia to claim his side of the bargain. The problem began to drag on for months. Emma of Normandy, who was anxious to hang on to some power for her family, decided to intervene.

Harthacnut was still fighting his Norwegian war in 1036. But he wasn't Emma's only son. She still had two sons, Edward and Alfred, by her first husband, the Saxon king Aethelred. These two power-hungry princes were holed up in Normandy and didn't take a lot of persuading to cross the Channel and muscle in on behalf of their mother's side of the family.

So in 1036, the pair launched a two-pronged attack. Alfred met up with his mother and Earl Godwine of Wessex, who had backed Harthacnut's claim and so should have been on the side of Emma and her sons. Meanwhile, Edward started rampaging violently around the south of England, showing everyone that Emma's boys meant business.

It should have led to a takeover, but there was a spanner in the works: Earl Godwine. Godwine, with an eye for the main chance, decided that he wasn't on Emma's side after all and promptly took Alfred into custody and handed him over to Harold Harefoot. Before the poor prince knew what was happening, he was carted off to prison in Ely and blinded. It was not long before the hapless Alfred died. Harold took control in southern England and forced Emma to leave the country. She settled in Bruges and waited for her next opportunity to make a play for power in England.

Emma intervenes – again

It wasn't very long before Emma seized the chance to win power for her family once more. This time, she teamed up with her long-absent son, Harthacnut, who by 1039 had left his Scandinavian war, assembled a large fleet of longships, and sailed southwards to Flanders where he met up with his mother.

While Emma and son were preparing to invade England, things turned dramatically in their favour. Harold died without an heir, leaving a power vacuum, and Emma and Harthacnut arrived in England in 1040 eager to fill it. Soon Emma's other son, Edward, also turned up, and in 1041, both men were crowned as joint kings. After all the fighting and plotting, the joint kingship lasted less than a year. Harthacnut died in 1042. He had no sons, so Edward was left as sole ruler of England.

Pious Potentate: Edward the Confessor

In 1042, England's King Harthacnut died, and his half-brother Edward became king of England. After years of Danish domination of the country under Cnut and the subsequent squabble for the throne between his sons Harold and Harthacnut, Edward was something different. For a start, he was the son of King Aethelred and his wife Emma of Normandy, so he wasn't a Dane. For another thing, he had been brought up in Normandy and had spent most of his first 35 years with his mother there.

So was Edward a Frenchman? Not really. His connection with Normandy meant that he had close ties with the Vikings who had settled there in the previous century. In a way, Edward was England's first Norman king, 20 years before the famous Norman Conquest that was to bring William I to the throne in 1066.

Like most people in western Europe by this date, Edward was a Christian. But Edward was a particularly pious one. He acquired the nickname Edward the Confessor because he was said to go to church to confess his sins *every day*. Very virtuous. But did he have the right stuff to be a king? Some people had their doubts.

Normandy and the Vikings

In the year 911, a Viking leader called Rollo had settled in northern France, and as a result of this move, Normandy (the name comes from the same root as Norse) became a Viking outpost. Both Svein Forkbeard, the Viking leader who had raided England, and his son Cnut, who had conquered the country, had used harbours in Normandy for their ships. By the time Edward the Confessor was born around 1003, Normandy had its own identity, influenced both by its people's Viking heritage and by its neighbour France. Since his birth, Edward had been surrounded by Norman nobles and Norman churchmen. He spoke the same language as the Normans and was much more familiar with Normandy than with England.

Earls and nobles

When Harthacnut died, Edward himself wondered whether he should become king. So he asked Godwine, Earl of Wessex, England's most powerful noble and the man who had backed Harthacnut in his bid for the throne. Godwine saw this request for advice and backing as a chance to carve himself a position of power as Edward's right-hand man. Before long, Godwine was the most influential person at Edward's court, and the problems that resulted from Godwine's power dogged the first part of Edward's reign.

Earl Godwine said he would back Edward as king provided that Edward did him some favours in exchange. Godwine wanted several things out of Edward:

- Edward should appoint Godwine to an important office of state.
- Edward should marry Godwine's daughter Edith.
- Edward's mother Emma, who might be too influential on the king, should have her wealth taken away and be put under house arrest in Winchester.
- Princess Gunnhild of Poland, a potential bride for Edward and rival to Edith, should be expelled from the country.

These demands are big, especially the one about Queen Emma. It seems amazing that Edward should agree to his mother being placed under house arrest. But Edward was so convinced that he needed Godwine's backing, he agreed to the earl's demands and was crowned king. The coronation took place at Winchester, which as capital of Wessex had a special place in the history of Anglo-Saxon England. Holding the ceremony there reminded people that Edward was the descendant of the Anglo-Saxon kings Aethelred and Alfred.

With Edward safely crowned and married, things looked good for the monarchy. But the king's concessions to Godwine caused a problem. It wasn't just Godwine who made trouble for Edward, but also Godwine's son, Swein, who had been made Earl of Southwest Mercia. Swein turned out to be the kind of character who must have made the pious Edward see red. Here's the low-down on his catalogue of sins:

- ✔ He kidnapped the abbess of Leominster and kept her as a concubine.
- ✔ He ditched the hapless abbess.
- ✔ He had Earl Beorn Estridsson, who had advised Edward not to make peace with Swein, killed.

Edward outlawed Swein and removed his earldom, but Godwine stuck up for his obnoxious son. By 1050, Godwine found himself and the rest of his family outlawed, too. Even poor Edith was condemned to go and live in a nunnery.

By now, fighting had broken out, and Godwine and his other son Harold mounted a naval attack on England, causing mayhem along the south coast and sailing up the Thames toward London. Edward was compelled to give in to Godwine. Within months, Godwine's earldom was restored, and when he died a short while later, his title passed to Harold.

There's a good story about the death of Godwine. It's probably a fabrication by medieval chroniclers who wanted to see him get his just desserts, but it's interesting anyway. The story goes that the king and Godwine had a banquet together shortly after the earl returned from exile. Edward asked whether Godwine really had his brother Alfred blinded, killing him shortly afterwards. 'May God strike me dead if I did,' replied Godwine. Instantly, the earl choked on a piece of meat and died.

After Godwine's death, Queen Edith was allowed to leave the nunnery and return to Edward's side. As for the dreadful Swein, he went on pilgrimage to Jerusalem as a penance for his misdemeanours, but he soon died, too.

Trouble in bed

After the trouble with Earl Godwine, Edward and Edith settled down again. Things should have gone well. They were an intelligent couple, and Edward, a pious Christian, seems to have been faithful to his wife. But they did not manage to produce a family, which must have been upsetting personally. It was certainly a problem politically, because it meant that the succession would be in dispute when Edward died.

Medieval writers, who were mostly monks and who revered Edward for his piety, came up with a special reason for the lack of young princes or princesses around the royal court. They said that Edward was so holy that he was immune from physical passion – Edward and Edith simply didn't have sex. The idea is interesting, but on the whole, it's unlikely. Medieval kings and queens saw it as their *duty* to go to bed together and produce children, even if they didn't want to. The lack of a son and heir made things uncertain, and the royal family has always preferred certainty.

In the Anglo-Saxon and Norman periods, it was customary for a king to nominate an heir before he died. In theory, the king could choose anyone, including a brother or cousin, to do the job. This custom of naming an heir was especially strong among the Normans, who influenced Edward greatly. But even so, having a son you could train to step into your shoes was the safest way to go. So Edward and Edith would have wanted children. The probability is that they just couldn't conceive.

In search of an heir

In 1054, with the king now well into his 50s, the issue of an heir was becoming urgent. Edward's favourite choice seems to have been another man called Edward, known as Edward the Exile because he was living in Kiev, Russia. Edward the Exile was a grandson of King Aethelred and so a nephew of Edward the Confessor.

The king sent one of his trusted advisers, Bishop Ealdred of Worcester, off to Kiev to track down his exiled nephew in 1054. By 1057, Edward the Exile was back – but also dead. No one knows quite how he died, but his end seems to have been sudden and suspicious. This event left King Edward with several choices when it came to an heir:

- ✔ **Potential heir No. 1 – Edgar the Aetheling:** Edward the Ex-exile had a son called Edgar. Edgar was known as Edgar the Aetheling. Aetheling was a word that originally meant 'young nobleman' (*aethele* meant noble in Old English), but had come to mean a prince. The young Prince Edgar would probably have been Edward's favoured choice as heir, but for one thing – he was young. In fact, when the king died in 1066, Edgar the Aetheling was probably about 14 years old, which was just too young to be king in his own right.

- ✔ **Potential heir No. 2 – William, Duke of Normandy:** Back in the early 1050s, before Edgar the Aetheling appeared on the scene, the king apparently offered England to his cousin William of Normandy. William, as a Norman, would obviously have appealed to Edward as an heir. But the circumstances of the offer were rather murky, and the deal was struck a long time ago. So William became an outsider in the race to be the next king.

✔ **Potential heir No. 3 – Harold Godwinsson:** On his deathbed, Edward ignored his earlier preferences and declared that Harold, son of Earl Godwine of Wessex, should have the crown. Why did Edward choose a relative of Godwine, who had caused him so much trouble? Harold had done a lot to win favour with the king. He had fought with distinction on the royal side against the Welsh. He had shown that he was a just man when, in a dispute between some Northumbrian nobles and his brother, Tostig, Harold came out against Tostig. And he was the brother of Edith, Edward's queen.

When making an important decision, an Anglo-Saxon king was expected to listen to the advice of the nobles around him, a body called the *witan* or *witenagemot*. This group didn't have a standard membership in the way that a modern parliament or cabinet does; it was just made up of the earls or Ealdormen who were currently with the monarch. Most kings respected the advice of the witan and took what was said seriously.

Edward consulted his nobles, and together they came down in favour of Harold. Harold wasn't a member of the royal family, but most royal advisers agreed that he was a practical choice. As the country's most powerful earl, he and his family controlled much of England anyway, and they were well placed to defend it against aggressors from outside. The only member of the witan who may have opposed Harold was the earl who controlled Mercia, the main area of the country not in the control of the Godwine family. Fortunately for Harold, the current earl had recently died, so the Witan unanimously approved Edward's choice of heir (see Chapter 6).

Part III
The Middle Ages

The 5th Wave By Rich Tennant

Oh for gosh sake, Richard! It's a couple of mice in the basement stealing grain. Quit making a crusade out of everything!

In this part . . .

Historians have different ways of defining the Middle Ages, but this book uses the term for the years 1066–1485. This period was a time when monarchs were incredibly powerful – as well as lording it over England, most kings in this period also ruled lands in France. Having such a large kingdom made them rich and strong. But in an era when fast communications usually meant galloping for days on horseback, keeping control of such vast territory was hard, and many rulers of the Middle Ages had to fight for their thrones – and fight on to keep their crowns. So the Middle Ages was a period when kings were occupied with warfare, often for decades at a time.

Chapter 6

Conquering Kings

· ·

In This Chapter

▶ Discovering how the Normans took over England

▶ Checking out their use of the feudal system to keep the peace and provide help in wartime

▶ Understanding how they invented ways of raising and accounting for royal revenue

▶ Revealing dynastic squabbles

· ·

*I*n 1066, a new ruling family arrived in England: the Normans. As their name suggests, the Normans came from Normandy, in northern France. But the Normans were originally Norsemen – their ancestors were Vikings, Scandinavians from northern Europe, who had settled in France in the early tenth century. When they took over England, the Normans kept their long history of links with France, so for hundreds of years, kings of England also ruled territories across the Channel.

The kings of the Norman dynasty ruled from 1066, when William of Normandy conquered England and became William I, for nearly a century until the death of King Stephen in 1154. The 11th and 12th centuries seem remote, but historians can still find their legacy today. Several cathedrals and many castles were built by Norman churchmen and knights who owed their power to England's rulers from northern France.

Conqueror: William I

William I was born in 1027 or 1028 in Falaise, northern France, the illegitimate son of Robert, Duke of Normandy, and he had to go through his early life putting up with the nickname William the Bastard. His mother was a woman called Herleva. Not much is known about Herleva, but she came of a lowly family – she was probably the daughter of a tradesman, perhaps a tanner or an undertaker, from Falaise.

In most ducal or royal families, not much more would have been heard of the duke's illegitimate son born of a woman from the lower classes. But William was lucky. There was no hooray Henry in the ducal castle to kick him out – he was his father's only son. William was helped by Norman custom, too. The Dukedom did not automatically pass through the legitimate family. Dukes of Normandy usually made a formal announcement naming their chosen heir.

So when in 1035, Duke Robert went off on pilgrimage to Jerusalem, he announced that young William would be the next duke. And then, while on pilgrimage, Robert died, leaving young William as ruler of one of the most powerful dukedoms in northern Europe.

One in the eye: The Battle of Hastings

William grew up tall, strong, and powerful – but also greedy for more power. And from 1051, he had his eye firmly on England. What seems to have happened in 1051 was that the English king, Edward the Confessor, promised that William should take over England when Edward died. But the trouble was that just before Edward's actual death in January 1066, he named his brother-in-law Harold Godwinson as his heir, putting the kibosh on William's chances. (See Chapter 5 for the scoop.)

William decided he had reason enough to sail to England and fight for 'his' kingdom. But he also knew that Harold had a good claim to be king of England, too. William felt the need of a powerful ally, one who could claim the moral high ground. He sent a mission off to the Pope, asking for the church's backing for his assault on England. He got God on his side, and the moral ground doesn't get any higher than that.

Battle royal

In the summer of 1066, William gathered a fleet of ships, an army, and supplies, and on the night of 27 September, they crossed the Channel and landed the following morning at Pevensey. William's timing was perfect. Harold was up north, at Stamford Bridge, fighting another invader, Harald Hardrada of Norway. The Englishman came out on top in this battle of the Harolds, but his army was exhausted by the time it had marched south to confront William.

The two forces lined up in Sussex near the site of the modern town imaginatively known as Battle and slogged it out for a whole day. By the afternoon, Harold's troops were looking the worse for wear. He had rushed down from Stamford Bridge with only infantrymen, and William's Norman archers were proving too much for them. Then one of the Norman bowmen took the biggest prize – he landed an arrow right in Harold's eye.

With their leader gone and their spirits flagging, the English were soon defeated, and William took off on a march around the South East. As he went, most of the local nobles pledged their loyalty. The churchmen, remembering that the Pope was on William's side, gave their support, too.

Coronation conflagration

On Christmas Day 1066, William was crowned king in Westminster Abbey. William obviously had an eye for a good date. He liked ceremonies and symbols, and a Christmas coronation must have been a symbol of the moral high ground he wanted to occupy.

But everything nearly went pear-shaped. When the people in the abbey began to shout in triumph, the guards outside thought the noisy nobles were trying to start a rebellion. In panic, the guards started setting fire to the houses near the abbey, and when the church started to fill up with smoke, most of the congregation dashed outside to see what was happening. Only a few churchmen stayed inside with William, and they got the crown on the new king's head as quickly as they could. Riot or no riot, William was crowned.

The feudal system

William controlled his new kingdom by using the *feudal system,* a method of allocating power through the occupation of land. It worked in a social hierarchy with the king at the top and was really quite simple:

- ✔ As king, William owned all the land in England. Some of it he kept for himself, but most he allocated to noblemen (his *tenants-in-chief*).

- ✔ The tenants-in-chief held their portion of land in return for providing men to fight for the king in times of war. The tenants-in-chief could in turn allocate some of their land to subtenants.

- ✔ The subtenants were lesser lords who contributed their share of men to fight for the king. And these lesser lords could parcel out much of their land to peasants.

- ✔ The peasants farmed the land and gave their lord produce and services as rent.

The feudal system helped William spread his power across the whole country – any trouble, and a tenant could be booted off his land. The system also helped keep the peace, because each lord was supposed to maintain law and order throughout the land he held. Conversely, the system also gave the king access to an army when he needed it. The lords built castles where they could live and where their soldiers could be based. These castles could then become royal bases in times of war or trouble.

It was a clever system, and, as far as the king was concerned, it worked, provided that the nobles did not get too powerful and challenge royal power. William guarded against this fear by giving each noble scattered portions of land in different parts of the country, to stop them from building up big local power bases that could challenge the king.

Jobs for the boys

Not everyone took William's domination lying down. By turning up with his archers, castles, and feudal rule, William had made enemies, big time, amongst some of the English nobles, especially those in the North and Midlands, away from the conqueror's heartland around London. Some of these lords staged revolts, and in the first few years of his reign, William was busy putting down rebels.

Two prominent nobles who wanted William removed from the throne were Morcar, Earl of Northumbria, and his brother, Edwin, Earl of Mercia. They staged a revolt, which William ruthlessly put down. After the defeat, William took away the lands belonging to their families and gave them to new Norman tenants who would stay loyal. Soon, most of England was occupied by Norman tenants-in-chief. The English aristocracy was becoming more and more Norman.

Putting your friends in high places was one way of keeping control. William had two other tactics for bolstering his power.

Power tactic No. 1: Scorch the earth

William kept up the pressure on would-be rebels and their supporters. He had a cruel streak, and putting on pressure came naturally to him. In 1069–70, some people in Northumbria staged a rebellion, so William moved quickly to put it down.

But just defeating the rebels wasn't enough for this conquering king. William embarked on a ruthless, scorched-earth campaign in northern England. It was enough to make the Northumbrians squirm. He destroyed villages, ransacked farms, killed anyone in his path, and left most of the survivors as refugees. Large parts of the North became waste land, and some estimates put the deaths as high as 100,000. In modern terms, William's policy of murder and pillaging looks like a serious war crime. But the Normans didn't see things in modern terms. William was simply showing who was in charge.

William had other military campaigns, too. He put down rebels in the West of England, on the border of Wales, and in East Anglia, where a lord known as Hereward the Wake put up a strong resistance to William but was finally crushed in 1071.

Power tactic No. 2: Work with the church

Ever since he got the Pope's backing for his English invasion, William had understood the importance and power of the church. So he used his influence to get Norman abbots and bishops appointed to English monasteries and cathedrals.

Hereward the Wake

Hereward (no one knows why he became known as 'the Wake') became an English hero, but he was no saint. A Lincolnshire lord with a hatred of the Normans, he robbed the abbey at Peterborough to pay for a military campaign against William in the low-lying fenlands of eastern England. Many of his friends soon threw in the towel and accepted William's kingship, but Hereward and a few followers refused to give in and holed up amongst the marshes on the Isle of Ely. The Normans surrounded the island, but Hereward would not surrender, even when his food ran out and he had to grub around for roots to eat. Finally, William forced his way on to the island via a secret route shown to him by some local monks, and one more rebellion was defeated.

William's most powerful friend in the church was not actually a Norman at all, but an Italian with Norman connections. The churchman Lanfranc had been abbot of a monastery that William had founded at Caen in Normandy. He became Archbishop of Canterbury in 1070. At that time, England's two archbishops – York and Canterbury – were seen as equals, but Lanfranc quickly turned Canterbury into the headquarters of the English church. Lanfranc transformed the church in England:

- ✔ He oversaw the appointment of many Normans and Frenchmen as bishops and abbots in England.
- ✔ He reorganised the bishoprics, moving some of them to more important towns.
- ✔ He presided over a period of frantic church- and cathedral-building.

These changes to the church added up to increased Norman influence and another success in the conquering king's search for power.

Domesday Book

By the 1080s, William was a success. He had grabbed control of England, and with plenty of Normans in high places, things seemed likely to stay that way. But William wasn't finished yet. He was in power, but, in the days before fast communications and detailed record-keeping, William didn't know exactly who held which land – which was a problem when it came to knowing who to tax.

When William's court met at Gloucester to celebrate Christmas in 1085, William did something no European ruler had done before. He commissioned a thorough survey of the whole country, sending officials to check out every manor in detail. The result was Domesday Book, an extraordinary account of England in 1086.

Domesday Book was not perfect. Some counties weren't covered, and some were recorded in more detail than others. But it included a huge amount of information, showing:

- ✔ Who had held each manor before the conquest
- ✔ Who held it now
- ✔ How much income it would bring in
- ✔ How many animals or ploughs were there
- ✔ Whether it included pasture or woodland
- ✔ Where the mills and fishponds were

Domesday Book was an awesome tool for government and taxation and shows that William's rule was not simply ruthless and violent – it was efficient as well.

A sticky end

By 1086, William had a good grip on his kingdom and had cause to be pleased with his achievements. But in the following years, trouble developed in Normandy. French king Philip I had invaded the southern part of the Duchy, and William, by now older and fatter than he had been when he conquered England some 20 years before, dashed across the Channel to defend his lands.

William threw himself into the fighting at a town called Mantes, but was hurled forward on to the pommel of his saddle. Badly wounded, he realised that he might be dying and quickly announced that if he perished, his son Robert should be Duke of Normandy while his second son, William, should take the English throne. It was a wise move, because William I died of his wounds shortly afterward.

William's funeral was a bizarre affair. The king's body, now seriously over-weight, could hardly be squeezed into the coffin, and by the time of the burial, it had burst open, causing an appalling stench in the church. It was a sad end for such an ambitious ruler.

Ruthless Rufus: William II

William I was survived by three sons. The eldest, Robert Curthose (the medieval equivalent of Robert Short-Arse), inherited the Duchy of Normandy, while the second, William, became king of England. The youngest, Henry, was given a small fortune of £5,000 and told to make his own way, which he did by buying some lands in Normandy from Robert and settling down as his brother's neighbour and ally.

By dividing his lands between Robert and William in this way, the Conqueror was doing the usual Norman thing. According to Norman custom, you left your first son the main family lands, but if you conquered any extra land, it went to your other male offspring. In 1087, a second William was on the English throne.

This second William was very different from his father. He looked different, being short and rather podgy, and had a red face and red hair that turned blond as he got older, plus a fiery temper to go with it. Because of his appearance and temper, a famous 12th-century historian, Orderic Vitalis, gave him the nickname Rufus, which has stuck.

William's character was as colourful as his complexion. He loved chivalry and was always rushing around recruiting knights. He was addicted to the latest fashions and had a pair of rams-horn shoes that narrowed and curved into such a long point that it was hard to put one foot in front of another. His language was extreme, too. If the royal court had had a swear box, it would always have been full during Rufus's reign, and the king was continuously shocking visiting churchmen with his foul language and love of blaspheming. Some clerics talked of loose morals at William's court, too. Rufus never married and may have been gay, although historians have no way of knowing for sure.

Money-making schemes

William's love of show did not stop with fine clothes. He was also a great builder. Two of his pet projects were Westminster Hall (a vast chamber at the heart of the Palace of Westminster), which was used for royal court sittings and ceremonies. Although much altered, this awesome hall still survives as part of London's Houses of Parliament. The king's other architectural achievement was to finish off the White Tower, the big keep in the middle of the Tower of London, a project begun by his father.

All this building cost money, as did the king's military exploits. William had to put down a rebellion in the South East of England before embarking on a series of campaigns designed to strengthen his borders with Wales and Scotland. It was an expensive business, and William, together with his hated justiciar, Ranulf Flambard, came up with some cunning schemes to swell the royal treasury:

✔ **Money-maker No. 1 – The church:** According to Norman law, the crown could take income from vacant church posts, so when Lanfranc, the old Archbishop of Canterbury, died, William used his influence to keep the post unfilled so that he could siphon off church revenue into the royal treasury. William was merciless in milking the church. Some accounts tell of churches that had to give up their precious altar candlesticks and chalices so that they could pay up.

✔ **Money-maker No. 2 – The barons:** William squeezed the barons, too. Under the feudal system, a kind of inheritance tax was paid on the death of the king's tenants-in-chief. William the Conqueror had only taken this tax if it was clear that the baron concerned had plenty of cash. But William Rufus and Ranulf Flambard extorted it mercilessly.

✔ **Money-maker No. 3 – Royal wards:** Children and young people who were left as orphans often became wards of the king. He was meant to look after their interests and manage their estates until they came of age. William saw this responsibility as an opportunity to grab more cash for his coffers. Many was the royal ward who came of age to find his estate gone to rack and ruin, with assets sold off. Young heiresses could have an even worse time, married off to William's cronies into the bargain. It was a bad time to be young and unprotected.

✔ **Money-maker No. 4 – Spongeing:** William Rufus had a large court, made up of hundreds of people who travelled around the country with him. When the king travelled, he expected his tenants-in-chief to put up the entire court for the night – another money-making scheme, in a way, because when they were staying with one of the barons, William didn't have to pay the fat food bill. Needless to say, the barons didn't like this expectation very much. If the king stayed more than a day or two, he could make a baron bankrupt. William's unruly court also had a reputation for trashing your house. Stories abound of barons trembling with fear or even going into hiding when William was in their area, in case the king turned up on the doorstep demanding hospitality.

In medieval times, communications were poor, and it was hard for kings to keep tabs on the whole country from their base in the south. So kings travelled constantly, calling in on different areas to keep an eye on every corner of the kingdom. They travelled with a big retinue of knights and servants, known as the *royal court,* together with most of their furniture and belongings.

Beastly bishops

By the spring of 1093, William had been milking the revenues of the archbishopric of Canterbury for four years. Although it was William's right under feudal law to do so, his conscience was far from clear about it. Then, in March 1093, William fell seriously ill. Not wanting to die without this wrong put right, William acted fast and promoted the appointment of the best candidate as archbishop: Anselm, the abbot of Lanfranc's old abbey at Bec in Normandy.

But there was a problem. Anselm didn't want the job. Think about it. Anselm was a saintly 60-year-old abbot, who was content to run his abbey in Normandy surrounded by monks who respected and obeyed him. If he came to England, he would have to defend the English church against the notorious money-grabber and blasphemer William. The pair would be fighting every week, and Anselm had no stomach for a fight. As Anselm said, it would be like tethering a tired old sheep to a headstrong young bull.

But something made Anselm give in and come to England. According to one story, the king was so insistent that he should take the job that he picked up the archbishop's ring of office and forced it on to Anselm's finger. Whatever really happened, Anselm became head of the church in England, and the arguments began:

- ✔ Anselm wanted to hold ecclesiastical councils; William would not give permission.
- ✔ Anselm wanted the king to recognise Urban II as Pope; William refused.
- ✔ William demanded money from the church for his military campaigns against the Welsh; Anselm refused.
- ✔ William's disrespect and licentiousness continued to offend Anselm.

In the end, Anselm insisted that only the Pope had the authority to settle the arguments between them. William responded by threatening to take Anselm to court, whereupon Anselm fled to Rome. William must have been relieved to get the intrepid Anselm out of his hair. What was more, with the churchman in Rome, he could claim that the post of archbishop was in effect vacant, so he could start tapping the church's money again. Ker-ching!

Was he murdered?

William Rufus was good at making enemies. Many barons hated him because of his money-grabbing. Churchmen were appalled by his loose lifestyle, much of it paid for by money that rightly belonged to the church. William even had a difficult relationship with his brother Robert Curthose, whose lands in Normandy William envied, although the pair had patched it up. So when in August 1100 William was felled by an arrow in a hunting accident, some people were suspicious that the king had been murdered.

It was an ugly story. The king and his courtiers, including his younger brother Henry, were out in the New Forest hunting. An arrow, as if from nowhere, hit William and brought him down. Then things started to happen very quickly:

- ✔ The king was dead within minutes.
- ✔ A Norman baron called Walter Tirel, who was suspected of shooting the fateful arrow, rode off immediately and was soon on a ship to Normandy.
- ✔ Henry and most of the hunting party immediately rode off to nearby Winchester, where the royal treasury was kept, leaving the king's body in an undignified heap.
- ✔ A local charcoal burner, a man called Purkess, lifted the body on to a cart and pushed it to Winchester himself.

As soon as he arrived in Winchester, Henry hot-footed it to the royal treasury and took control. An old Saxon custom dictated that whoever held the treasury could, with the backing of the nobility, be crowned. So Henry roped in some local nobles, got them to hail him as king, and was crowned three days after William's death, before Robert Curthose could come from Normandy and stake his claim to the throne.

Henry won the race to be king, and William Rufus was buried under the tower in Winchester Cathedral with the minimum of ceremony. A few months later, the tower collapsed. People took this as a sign that God was angry with the way William had lived and reigned.

And since then, tongues have wagged. Did Henry kill his brother or have him killed by Walter Tirel? The most likely answer is no. The rumours did not start immediately, and the timing wasn't ideal for Henry, who would probably have preferred to confront Robert Curthose fairly and squarely rather than beat his supporters to the treasury in an unseemly race. Henry was probably taking advantage of a terrible accident and seizing the opportunity as best he could. Henry certainly knew that he could rely on support from the many nobles who had feared and hated his brother William.

Lion of Justice: Henry 1

Henry I leapt into the power vacuum left after the sudden death of his brother, William II, in August 1100, when he was 33 years old. Henry was witty, well educated, and good company. He also had a way with the ladies – a serial adulterer, he fathered more than 20 illegitimate children, more than any other English king. He also had four children by his first wife.

Henry found a country in which the monarchy was all powerful, but also, thanks to William I's cruelty and William II's ruthlessness, much feared. Henry knew that he could benefit from the immense power in his hands, but also that it would be to his advantage to rule in a fairer way than his brother.

Having grabbed hold of the royal treasury and got himself crowned in record time, Henry looked for ways to make sure that he kept the power he had seized. Several actions sent signals that were very different from the actions of ruthless Rufus:

✔ He published a Coronation Charter, promising to rule in a more moderate way than Rufus had done.

✔ He imprisoned William II's hated money-grabbing justiciar, Ranulf Flambard.

> ✔ He recalled Archbishop Anselm from exile in Rome, signalling a more conciliatory standpoint toward the church.
>
> ✔ He married Edith, who was daughter of Scottish king Malcolm III and sister of Edgar the Aetheling, of the line of Saxon royals (see Chapter 5), indicating a desire to unify Norman, Scottish, and Saxon interests.

It looked as if Henry would be a more thoughtful and diplomatic ruler than William, and England must have breathed a collective sigh of relief.

Curthose curtailed

In 1101, Henry faced the first big challenge to his rule – the arrival from the Holy Land of his brother, Robert Curthose, with an army behind him. For a moment, it must have looked as if things were about to go back to the unsettled days of William Rufus. But Henry preferred diplomacy to war, and Robert, still sore from his efforts in the Holy Land, probably didn't feel like fighting either. So the pair came to an agreement under which Robert recognised Henry as king of England.

During the next few years, wily Henry turned the tables on Robert by nibbling away at Curthose's power base in Normandy. He could do so because some of Robert's most powerful barons also held lands in England. Henry kicked these barons off their English lands, making them poorer and less able to throw their weight around in Normandy. Henry then needed one decisive battle against Robert, at Tinchebrai, southwestern Normandy, in 1106, to defeat his brother, who was bundled off to Cardiff Castle to spend the last 28 years of his life a prisoner.

Henry could claim to be effective ruler of Normandy, even though his rule was frequently interrupted by attacks from his neighbours, such as the king of France and the Count of Anjou. Land-grabbing and scheming were not so straightforward as Henry had hoped, and one chronicler said that each of his victories only made Henry more nervous that he would lose what he had gained.

Well advised?

Education, education, education. Rulers didn't go in for it much in the Middle Ages. It was more important to be able to fight for your rights than to be able to write. Henry had a reputation for being quite well educated and even had a nickname, Beauclerc, which means 'good writer'. But this ability didn't mean a lot in medieval times. You could get a reputation as a 'clerk' by being able to write your own name, and that was probably as much writing as Henry did.

Where Henry scored, though, was that he was able to find intelligent men to help him govern. One of the most important was Bishop Roger of Salisbury. Henry liked Roger because he could get through mass faster than any other priest. But the king also liked Roger's managerial skills and appointed him to run, and probably revamp, the administrative side of the government.

When Roger arrived in government service, he found that no one had much idea about where all the money was going. Counting and calculating were really difficult – western Europeans hadn't even worked out that they needed the number zero. So Roger came up with a couple of bright ideas to keep track of the royal finances.

- ✔ **Bright idea No. 1 – The Exchequer:** The *Exchequer* was a large cloth divided into squares like a chequer board (hence the name), and it worked rather like an abacus, with counters that were moved from one square to another to represent money being added or subtracted. It was Roger's cleverest innovation and still gives its name to the financial department of the British government.

- ✔ **Bright idea No. 2 – The pipe roll:** The transactions were written down on long strips of parchment, which may have been another innovation of Roger, though no one is really sure. When they were rolled up for storage, these parchments looked like pipes, so they're now known as *pipe rolls.* From them, historians know the wages – paid in a combination of cash and food – of many of the court officials. Roger himself got five shillings a day, a fixed allowance of flour to make bread, cake, and wine, plus a generous supply of candles. Whether or not he actually invented this form of record-keeping, Roger was certainly methodical and was a good adviser to Henry, making his government more efficient.

Henry was also keen on the law. He had a reputation as a fair and just man, and was nicknamed Lion of Justice. The king was famous for sending royal justices around the country to hear cases. Some important books of law were also written in his reign. These books were actually compilations of laws that had existed since the Saxon period and suggest that many of Henry's laws had been in force since before the Norman conquest. Henry was a Norman through and through, but he still wanted people to realise that he was upholding the same justice as his Saxon forebears.

Shipwrecked succession

Over a long reign, Henry won a reputation as a good and fair king. His kingdom was at peace, and his court was well run and less unruly than William Rufus's rambunctious rabble. Everything looked set for a long, peaceful future in England. But in 1120, disaster struck the royal family.

Roger of Salisbury

Roger was a priest from Caen in Normandy who rose through the ranks of the church to become bishop of Salisbury, where he remodelled the cathedral (although the cathedral that stands in Salisbury today is a more recent building, dating from around 150 years later). In the Middle Ages, when few people outside the church could read or write, talented priests like Roger often combined their 'day job' in the church with work in the royal service. Roger was outstanding at his second career, starting as royal steward before becoming Henry's chancellor or senior minister.

The royal court was always on the move around Henry's domains, and these moves included regular trips across the Channel between England and Henry's territory in Normandy. In November 1120, most of the court was crossing the sea back to England after a long stay in Normandy when their vessel, known simply as the White Ship, ran into trouble. The drunken pilot who was supposed to be guiding the ship led it on to the rocks, and the vessel went down, taking with it Henry's two sons, William, the heir to the throne, and Richard.

Henry was distraught. Onlookers reported that when he heard the news, he let out a great cry and fell to the floor. Some said the king never smiled again. But the loss was more than a personal tragedy – England was left without a male heir to the throne, and Henry's wife, Matilda, had died two years previously. Henry took a second wife, a young woman who was the daughter of the Count of Louvain and who was variously known as Adeliza, Adela, or Adelaide. The king obviously hoped for another son and heir, but the couple did not have any children.

By 1126, Henry was resigned to the fact that he would not have another legitimate son. So he named his daughter Matilda as his heir, and Henry's barons duly swore allegiance to her. Matilda had married the emperor Henry V of Germany and was by now a widow. She kept the title of empress and was obviously well connected. But England's alpha-male barons were not used to the idea of being ruled by a woman. Many hoped that a male relative of Henry's would emerge and seize the crown. It looked as if trouble was brewing for the succession.

In 1135, Henry died. The cause of death was said to be that he ate a supersize meal of lampreys, a rich and indigestible kind of fish to which he was partial. The Norman love of fine and fattening foods had finally done in Henry. With a big question mark over the succession, things looked grim for England.

Scramble for the Crown: Stephen

When Henry I died in 1135, the heiress he had named, the empress Matilda, was at home in Anjou. When Matilda heard the news that the king was dead, she prepared to set off for England to be crowned. But in Normandy, another of the dead king's relatives had also been told what had happened. It was Stephen, son of Henry I's sister Adela and thus the old king's nephew. As a close male relative, Stephen felt he had a good claim to the English throne and, like his uncle before him, he acted quickly.

Luckily for Stephen, he was in Boulogne when he learned of Henry's death, so he crossed the Channel at top speed and, like his uncle before him, made straight for Winchester to get hold of the royal treasury. He was soon arguing that the oath of allegiance he had sworn to the empress Matilda had been forced out of him under duress and that Henry had changed his mind about the succession on his deathbed.

Stephen took a gamble. He thought that the English barons would object to two things about Matilda – they wouldn't want to be ruled by a woman, and they wouldn't much like being governed by someone from Anjou, an old enemy of Normandy. Stephen was right. As soon as he turned up in London, he got backing from:

✔ Most of the barons.

✔ Many of the merchants.

✔ Roger of Salisbury, Henry I's right-hand man, who brought most of the administrative service with him.

✔ Stephen's brother, Henry, Bishop of Winchester, who brought the backing of the church.

The Archibishop of Canterbury crowned Stephen in December 1135.

Too good by half: The chivalrous king

The English found themselves with an energetic, chivalrous king, a man who really wanted to succeed. Stephen was also brave in battle, a figure who had all the knightly virtues loved by William Rufus but without the posturing or cruelty. He seemed to embody the manly virtues that the barons found so attractive. He would soon need all his soldierly skills.

On 30 September 1139, the trouble started. The empress Matilda, together with her half-brother and supporter Earl Robert of Gloucester, landed at Arundel in Sussex to make her claim for the English throne. This move meant war.

Stephen was too chivalrous to attack a lady as soon as she landed on his soil. He graciously gave Matilda and her men permission to march across the country to Bristol. Big mistake. Bristol became a key stronghold of the empress.

Stephen had probably hoped to confine Matilda's supporters in the South West and pick them off when he was ready, but the king was too generous to his barons in hoping that they would all fight for him. One of the most powerful, Earl Ranulph of Chester, decided to go over to the empress's side in revenge against Stephen, who had taken away some of his lands in northern England. Ranulph immediately grabbed himself a major stronghold in the East by taking over Lincoln Castle. Stephen galloped off to Lincoln to sort out rebellious Ranulph.

The earl put up a tough fight, and everyone said that Stephen fought him with great bravery and persistence. But it wasn't enough. The brave king was captured and carted off to Bristol. The king was in prison and the country was in chaos.

So did Matilda then depose Stephen or have him killed? Curiously enough, no. Stephen was a king who had gone through the religious ritual of the coronation. He had been anointed with holy oils. In some sense, even though Matilda felt that he was not the rightful ruler, he had God on his side. To depose Stephen would have been sinful in the extreme. As a result, Stephen was held in Bristol, in a kind of royal limbo.

Warring Matildas: Queen versus empress

Eventually, Stephen was saved by his wife, who was called, of all things, Matilda. In September 1141, a showdown occurred between the Matildas, queen and empress. The empress, with all her support in the South West, was trying to extend her power in the South East. But in London, she got everyone's back up. She started by doling out gifts to win loyalty, but the next moment, she was slagging everyone off and refusing to cut taxes. Eventually, the people of the capital had enough of her, started a riot, and threw her out of the city in the middle of dinner.

The empress rode off in a huff and attacked Winchester, the city where Stephen's brother was bishop. At this point, the battle of the Matildas took place. The queen turned up with an army and began to attack the empress and her troops. In the melee, the queen's forces captured Earl Robert of Gloucester, a big enough fish to swap with the imprisoned Stephen, and soon the king was free again.

Political ping-pong

By this time, many of the barons who had declared their loyalty to Stephen had gone over to the empress's side. Their political ping-pong had everything to do with self-interest. Most had extensive lands on both sides of the Channel and wanted to hold on to them. Increasingly, they looked to support the side that was most likely to win.

Revolts broke out continuously, and England had to put up with a state of civil war for nearly 15 years. Stephen continued to fight bravely, but could not make enough gains to impose his will on the whole country. In addition, his generous nature meant that he was usually lenient with rebels, which meant that his enemies were all too often allowed to fight another day. Stephen came closest to sending Matilda packing deep in the winter of 1142. She was holed up in the castle at Oxford, and Stephen's forces surrounded her. But Matilda made a daring escape across the snow.

By the late 1140s, hostilities started to die down. Earl Robert of Gloucester died in 1147, and the following year, Matilda left for Normandy. She did not come back, although she sent her son Henry to fight Stephen, and the tensions between king and empress smouldered on.

On the last two occasions when Henry and Stephen confronted each other on the battlefield, something extraordinary happened. The armies simply refused to fight. They had had enough of civil war, and the two leaders were forced to sit down and work out some kind of peace agreement. In 1153, they reached an agreement that Stephen could remain as king for his lifetime but that Henry should become king after his death (see Chapter 7). Stephen had just under a year to live.

Chapter 7

Plantagenet Power Struggles

● ●

In This Chapter

▶ Recovering from civil war

▶ Ruling a huge European empire

▶ Taking steps to limit royal power

▶ Developing the system of common law

● ●

*I*n 1154, King Stephen died with England still scarred by a lengthy civil war. The country needed a period of stronger, more decisive rule to recover from the war, and strong rule was exactly what the kings of the Plantagenet dynasty aimed for. Henry II, the first of these rulers, displayed his strength by successfully asserting his own power and developing a better legal system.

But ruling England became more and more complicated during the 12th and 13th centuries, because the country was part of a much larger empire that also included an enormous chunk of France. More than ever, kings were on the move across their domains, defending their borders. And more than ever, these borders were under threat. There were enemies within, too – nobles who resented having to fight or pay excessive taxes to the king and wanted to limit royal power. The period saw a number of attempts to put legal brakes on the king. The most famous, the document called Magna Carta, is still quoted today.

Succession Sorted: Henry II

After decades of civil war and the unsteady rule of King Stephen, the country needed firmer control and more just rule. Under the new king, Henry II, England got these qualities in spades. Henry was one of the most outstanding and able monarchs ever to rule in Britain.

From the start, Henry had luck on his side. Henry was born not with a silver spoon in his mouth, but with an umpteen-carat, extra-heavy, solid gold spoon. He had been named and accepted as king of England; through his mother, the empress Matilda, he had a legal claim to Normandy; through his father, Geoffrey of Anjou, he inherited a further large chunk of France, notably Anjou (the area around Angers) and Touraine (the bit around Tours).

What was more, Henry was intelligent and able. Unlike many previous kings, he was well educated, and not only could read and write, but actually *enjoyed* reading. He had a voracious appetite for learning, picking up new developments in law and philosophy, and keeping his mind alert enough to stay one step ahead of most of his rivals.

But Henry wasn't a mere intellectual. He was a man of action, famous for travelling restlessly around his domains to see what things were like first hand. People said his strong but bowed legs were the result of spending hours on end in the saddle, and this observation was probably true.

Unlike some of his Norman predecessors, Henry wasn't interested in fine clothes or showy possessions; he just wanted to get things done. And when things didn't get done the way he wanted them, he had a fearsome temper. According to one story, when things got really tough he would fall to the ground and bite the rushes that covered the floor in a rage. Fiery? Volcanic!

Marrying well: Queen Eleanor of Aquitaine

Even before he became king of England, Henry held huge power as Duke of Normandy and Count of Anjou and Touraine. But in 1152, Henry increased his territory still further, by marrying the most powerful woman in Europe, Eleanor of Aquitaine. Eleanor had inherited a vast chunk of France, stretching from Poitou in the middle of the country down to Gascony in the south.

Eleanor was just as strong a character as her husband – a powerful ruler, a great patron of literature, and a woman of passion who would bear her husband eight children. Her temper was as hot as Henry's, and the couple argued a lot. But in political terms, Henry could not have done better. Even before he came to the English throne, Henry had more French land than the king of France himself.

Enter the Plantagenets

The royal dynasty that Henry built on these foundations is sometimes called the Angevin Dynasty, because of Henry's inheritance in Anjou. It's a useful label, because it reminds everyone that the family had vital connections in France and that, in Henry's time at least, England was part of a major empire. But Henry's sons could not hold on to these large possessions, and the Angevin label later fell out of use.

So another family name, *Plantagenet,* was coined. This mouthful was a name that was adopted in the 15th century and has been widely used for the family ever since. It comes from the Latin name for the flowering broom plant, *Planta genista,* and refers to the broom badge that Geoffrey of Anjou used to wear. Apparently, Geoffrey first wore the broom after his hat fell off when he was hunting – when he scooped it up, some of the flowers were stuck to it. So Plantagenet is a rather accidental name, but it will do.

Demolition job

The first Plantagenet, Henry was 21 years old when he came to the throne in 1154 – old enough to see that his kingdom needed sorting out after the civil war and young enough to get on quickly and do something about it. He began with a dramatic action to show who was boss. In the Middle Ages, you had to ask the king if you wanted to build a castle, but during the war, more than a thousand illegal castles had sprung up across the country. These so-called *adulterine castles* were a big threat to royal power, so Henry embarked on a massive demolition job, pulling down all the illegal castles. While he was at it, the king also sent packing the various bands of mercenaries that Stephen had employed in the war (see Chapter 6). No way was he going to let his barons hire them and launch an attack on his power.

Border business

Then Henry turned to England's borders with Wales and Scotland. If his kingdom was to be secure, Henry had to make sure that the Welsh would not invade while his back was turned when he was looking after his possessions in France. Henry strengthened the Welsh frontier by bringing English lords back to the border regions. He soon had many of the Welsh lords indicating that they would stay friendly by paying homage to him. Even the bishops in Wales agreed that they would come under the control of the archbishop of Canterbury. Henry also received homage from King Malcolm IV of Scotland.

Turbulent times

In 1162, Henry's troubled relationship with the church came to a head. Henry's able chancellor was a churchman called Thomas Becket. Thomas was one of those intelligent, worldly clergymen who often did well in government service during the Middle Ages. He looked every inch the part, and people said Thomas was more ostentatious that the king. According to one story, the pair were together one day when they met a beggar who stood shivering without a coat. The king got Thomas to admit that the poor man needed some warm clothes, but couldn't persuade Thomas to give up his own fine fur-lined cloak. Finally, the king pulled the cloak from Thomas's back and threw it to the thankful beggar.

Thomas had already helped the king gain extra power over the church by insisting that royal taxes were payable on church lands. Henry, who wanted to extend his power over the church still further, decided to appoint Thomas as archbishop of Canterbury. With 'his' man in the top church job, Henry thought, he'd have the church under his thumb.

Thomas saw it differently, though. Thomas warned Henry that if he took the post of archbishop, his first responsibility would be to God; Henry would have to come second. But Henry ignored the warnings, and Thomas became archbishop.

In the 12th century, the church had its own law courts, and churchmen who committed crimes were tried there. Many lay people resented these courts because they thought the church looked after its own and did not punish wrongdoers properly. What was more, the church courts also tried cases involving people with some slight connection to the church. All kinds of criminals could claim a church connection and escape proper punishment. This setup was a sore point with Henry II, and with anyone who wanted to see the legal system on a level playing field.

The trouble between the king and the archbishop started with these church trials. Henry wanted to reform church law so that clergy who committed crimes were tried not only in church courts, but also in the royal courts. Thomas dug in his heels: It was wrong for a criminal to be tried twice, and the church should be allowed to punish its own as it saw fit. And Henry was soon adding other restrictions on church power to his wish list. Here are some examples of his demands:

- Convicted churchmen should be tried in royal courts.
- Priests must have the king's permission to travel outside England.
- Church land disputes and debt cases were to be settled in royal courts.
- Appeals to the Pope could only be made with Henry's permission.

Although the English bishops eventually agreed to these demands, Becket refused, and the more Henry tried to bully him into submission, the deeper he dug in his heels. Eventually, Thomas left for Rome in disgust and stayed out of the country for six years. When he returned, relations between king and archbishop got even worse when Thomas excommunicated everyone involved in an important royal ceremony, the crowning of Henry's eldest son, another Henry, as king to be.

Excommunication

Excommunication was the most serious punishment the medieval church could inflict on someone. It was a total ban from church. This ban doesn't sound too bad to modern ears, but it had huge implications for a devout medieval Christian. It meant that you could not go to Mass, and you were banned from confession, which meant that you would die 'unshriven' and without the last rites. As a result, you'd probably go to hell. Excommunication was about as serious as things could get.

It was all too much for Henry. On Christmas Day 1170, the king was trying to enjoy a seasonal feast in Normandy. Then someone announced that the Pope had come out on Thomas's side as well. In one of his famous temper tantrums, Henry let fly at the barons around him. He is supposed to have shouted, 'Who will rid me of this turbulent priest?'

His actual words may have been a bit more long winded, but a group of barons took the king at his word. Before the goose was cleared away from the table, four barons set off on a journey to England with one thing on their minds: punishing the man who they saw as a traitor. On 29 December 1170, the fateful four followed Thomas into his cathedral, accused him of treachery, and stabbed him to death in front of the high altar as he was about to hear Mass.

When Henry heard the news, he was overcome with grief. He hadn't meant his words literally. And he certainly hadn't wanted the murder of a defenceless churchman, in cold blood, at the high altar of a church. The king reacted immediately by putting on sackcloth and ashes and fasting for three days. Henry wanted to show that he was repentant.

A legal mind

Henry's education gave him the edge over other rulers when it came to understanding the law. Although he wasn't a lawyer himself, Henry understood how the law worked, and, just as importantly, had clear ideas about how it *ought* to work. Henry's new ideas about the law were really influential. Some historians see him as the father of English law.

Most importantly, it was established in Henry's reign that there was one common law, which was effective throughout England and which was more important than all the minor local laws that had developed in different parts of the country. Henry made a number of other, more detailed reforms:

- ✔ The system of travelling justices was improved, with six defined *circuits* on which they travelled.
- ✔ He required regular court sittings in every county.
- ✔ The Court of Common Pleas dealt with civil matters nationwide.
- ✔ The Court of the King's Bench heard criminal cases.
- ✔ The principle of trial by jury was reasserted.
- ✔ Reliance on old-fashioned forms of justice, such as *trial by battle,* where opponents fought it out to determine who was in the right, was reduced.
- ✔ The role of the coroner, or investigator of suspicious deaths, was established.

Fortunately for historians, details of Henry's legal reforms were written down in a book called *De legibus et consuetudinibus regni Angliae* – in other words, On the Laws and Customs of the Kingdom of England. Not exactly a snappy title, so the book is usually known, after its author, as *Glanvill*. It shows that under Henry England had a fairer and better organised legal system than at any time since the Norman conquest.

Family fortunes

Henry was a hugely powerful and important king, who achieved a lot for his country during his 35-year reign. But it wasn't all plain sailing. By the early 1170s, Henry and Eleanor were estranged. These two strong characters had gone their separate ways, with Eleanor left in Aquitaine, more or less ruling it in her own right, while Henry ran the rest of his empire and took solace with his mistress, a woman from the Welsh borders called Rosamund Clifford, who has gone down in history as Fair Rosamund.

However, in 1173, a dispute broke out between Henry and his sons about who should inherit which parts of Henry's empire. Before Henry knew it, war broke out, and he found himself fighting his sons and his wife for control of his empire.

By the end of 1174, Henry had won. He had captured Eleanor and threw her in prison, while he agreed to peace terms with his sons. To be on the safe side, Henry kept Eleanor locked up, and the proud Aquitainian queen spent 15 years in confinement. But if the most powerful threat was out of the way, Henry's trouble didn't end. In 1183, his eldest son, Henry, known as the Young King because he had already been crowned in anticipation of inheriting the English throne, died. Then just three years later, the king's son Geoffrey also died, trampled to death in a tournament.

Henry II was left with two sons, Richard, who had spent much of his life with his mother in Aquitaine, and John, a younger son who had not originally expected to inherit a major title but was now second to Richard in line to the throne. Having fewer sons meant more trouble for Henry because he now had to replan the succession. Richard expected to inherit Aquitaine, a land that he loved, and refused to give up, so Henry hoped to hand England and his other French lands to John. The king refused to name Richard as heir to the English crown, which alienated Richard, who joined with the French king Philip Augustus and started a war against his father.

By now, Henry was sick of a fever, and Richard and Philip pushed him into signing a treaty that made Richard his heir and forced John into second place. A few days later, Henry died, a sad and disappointed man. He felt defeated, and his last words were said to have been, 'Shame, shame on a conquered king'.

Henry's reign had a sorry end, but he had achieved a great deal. He passed on to his son an empire that was the biggest in Europe. His legal reforms meant that society was fairer than when he became king. He had protected his interests in Britain with shrewd diplomacy. England was in better shape than during the war-torn reign of Stephen. But would it last?

Missing Monarch: Richard 1

When Richard came to the English throne in 1189, he had spent much of his life in his mother's homeland of Aquitaine, in far southwestern France. His mother, Eleanor of Aquitaine, was a fiercely independent woman who had brought her son up to be independent, too. And he had to be. After Eleanor was involved in a rebellion against her husband, Henry II, she was imprisoned. Richard was left to run Aquitaine on his own from 1174 until Henry's death in 1189.

Richard was tall – at about 6 foot 4 inches, he towered above the people around him. He cut a fine figure on the battlefield and was brave too, earning his nickname Lionheart. Richard also had a more cultivated side. Because his real home was Aquitaine, he loved the culture of southern Europe, especially the songs of the troubadours, and he even wrote some song lyrics himself.

The absentee king

Richard had longed to take over his father's kingdom, but at his coronation in 1189, his reign got off to a decidedly shaky start. To begin with, all went well, with lots of guests bringing lavish gifts for the new king. But when a group of Jews arrived to give their presents, part of the crowd went berserk with anti-Semitism and viciously attacked the visitors.

Before the coronation, Richard was already embroiled in the affairs of the Middle East. He had promised to go on a crusade, and when the old king died, he was raising money to take an army to the eastern Mediterranean to defend the tiny Christian territory in the Holy Land. By selling charters to towns, and by accepting cash for jobs in both the state and the church, Richard soon had enough money, and before the end of the year, he was off on his expedition to the Holy Land.

In the East, Richard the Lionheart showed himself worthy of his famous nickname. He won an important victory over the famed Muslim leader Saladin, captured the city of Acre for the Christians, and showed himself to be both a brave fighter and an intelligent military tactician. He stopped short of trying to take the city of Jerusalem, the goal of many Crusaders. Instead, Richard negotiated a deal with Saladin that allowed Christian pilgrims to visit the city safely.

In 1192, Richard began his return journey to England, conscious that his duty now lay with his new kingdom. But Richard, who had dodged danger in battle in the Holy Land, now fell foul of fate. He was captured by an enemy, Duke Leopold of Austria, who sold him to a more powerful enemy, the German emperor Henry VI. Henry put an enormous price on the king's head: 100,000 marks would secure his release. But if the English refused to pay up, Richard would be handed over to his arch-enemy, Philip of France, who was itching to break up Richard's empire and get his hands on the former Crusader's French territory.

Back in England, Queen Eleanor started fundraising to free her son. The church's arm was twisted, and sacred vessels were melted down for the precious metals. A year's wool production from the northern Cistercian abbeys – virtually all of Yorkshire's fleeces – was donated. Even so, all this booty wasn't enough to pay the whole of the emperor's enormous ransom demand. But Henry decided to let Richard go anyway, on the condition that the English king paid homage to the emperor. The power Henry exerted over Richard by holding and then releasing him was a signal that the English king was below the emperor in the European pecking order and, in theory, gave Henry the excuse to grab control of the country if Richard ever stepped out of line. In practice, however, Henry's power over Richard didn't mean a lot once he'd been released, except that Richard returned home to England, and disaster, for the moment, was averted.

Richard couldn't relax, though. When he was in England, Philip Augustus threatened his French lands. No sooner had Richard got home when he set out again for France to protect his domains there. He spent his last five years in France and never saw England again.

Hero or villain?

Richard cut a fine figure, dashing around the world fighting battles. He was brave on the battlefield, and his soldierly qualities made him both feared by his enemies and admired by his friends. In the Middle Ages, people *expected* kings to spend a lot of time on the battlefield defending their kingdoms or carving out new ones. And Europeans also saw crusading – which people today see as European land-grabbing in the East – as a noble occupation. But there *was* a problem. All this fighting meant that Richard hardly spent any time at all in England. Did this make him a bad king?

Well, Richard had good staff – some of them inherited from his efficient father, Henry II – so the country was not badly governed. It wasn't so much Richard's absenteeism that was the problem as his war-mongering. War has always cost a lot of money, and Richard fought on a grand scale. He employed more and more mercenaries, built big castles, and shelled out loads of cash to various nobles in Germany and the Netherlands to bribe them to stay on England's side against France. And his English nobles got royally fed up when Richard tried to make them provide fighting men for longer than previous monarchs had done.

The Crusades

The Crusades were a series of wars fought from 1095 to 1291 between Christian and Muslim forces for control of the sites in the eastern Mediterranean that were, and are, sacred to Jews, Christians, and Muslims. They began as an attempt by Westerners to protect the rights of Christian pilgrims in the East, but soon deteriorated into a sorry catalogue of attempted Western conquests of the Holy Land. Although most people now look on the European involvement in the Crusades as wrong, it is important to understand that many of the actual Crusaders saw the enterprise as a worthy attempt to protect pious Christian pilgrims.

The truth was that Richard, who had been brought up in Aquitaine, in the south of France, cared more about France than England. Fittingly enough, he died fighting in the middle of his beloved Aquitaine. When besieging the castle at Chalus in 1199, one of the defenders fired a crossbow at the king. The bolt hit Richard in the chest. The surgeon who was sent to tend the king made a mess of trying to remove the missile, and Richard, in a typical fit of impatience, tried to pull the thing out himself. Between the two of them, Richard and the incompetent surgeon infected the wound, and the king died of the infection.

Missing Land, Missing Treasure: John

Henry II's youngest surviving son, John, came to the throne in 1199, after his brother Richard I named him as his successor. He had always hoped to be king, but with a hale and hearty Richard on the throne, he didn't expect to inherit the crown. His nickname, Lackland, rubbed salt into the wound. Richard had no sons to inherit his titles, but even when he died, many expected the late king's nephew, Arthur, to become king (see the next section). Arthur had a good claim to the throne as son of Richard's brother, Geoffrey, but when Richard named his heir, Arthur was only 10 years old and probably thought too young to succeed. Richard named John his heir in 1197, but before then, John had thought he was more likely to get the crown by deposing his brother and had spent years of his early life plotting against Richard.

In fact, John was a habitual schemer – for example, he was always on the lookout to find ways of squeezing more taxes out of his barons and the church. Adding to this downfall was the fact that he had no glamour. He was not a brave soldier like his brother, but was seen as a bookish character, educated by churchmen, with little charisma.

In a way, the education helped John. He got to grips with the administrative side of government better than Richard ever did and regularly presided over court sittings dispensing justice. But the biggest disaster of John's reign had nothing to do with justice.

Royal murderer?

The greatest disaster of John's career began with a royal marriage scandal. John was fed up with his wife, Isabella of Gloucester, who had failed to bear him any children. He wanted to chuck her and marry a well-connected French princess, another Isabella, Isabella of Angoulême. But this second Isabella was already betrothed to a French baron, Hugh de Lusignan. When John grabbed his young fiancée from under his nose, Hugh went to the French ruler Philip Augustus, who still had his greedy eye on the English king's lands in France. Philip saw this request as an opportunity to help himself to a large chunk of France. The wily Frenchman supported Arthur's claim to rule in central France, while preparing to move his army to Normandy with the hope of taking over there himself.

John suddenly found himself with two enemies in France and decided to attack the weaker, younger Arthur. John defeated Arthur, clapped him in prison, and, after a while, Arthur's death was announced.

The rumour spread quickly that the young prince had been murdered. And there were stories that John himself had done the deed, visiting Arthur's cell late at night, and flying into a fearful temper. Whatever the truth, John was responsible for Arthur, and the young man had been killed. The year of 1204 was a black one for the monarchy.

Meanwhile, Philip Augustus had pushed John out of Normandy and made it virtually impossible for him to hang on to his territory further south. The dispute between John and Philip rumbled on for most of the rest of the reign, but in 1214, England and France fought the decisive battle of Bouvines. Philip was the winner, and John lost all his French lands north of the River Loire. The king's old nickname Lackland had come back to haunt him.

King versus barons

Things weren't much better at home. Like his brother before him, John was overtaxing his barons. He had also tried to interfere in the business of the church. In 1215, he faced a baronial revolt, but it was a revolt with a difference. Usually revolts involved a rival claimant to the throne, but with Arthur dead, no obvious candidate existed. Instead of promoting a rival to the king, the nobles produced one of the most famous documents in English history: Magna Carta.

The idea behind *Magna Carta* (the name means Great Charter) was to restrict the king's power and to protect others, especially the barons and the church, from misuses of royal power. It was a long document with 63 clauses covering many different aspects of royal responsibility. Key provisions included:

- ✔ No free man would be punished or imprisoned without prior judgement according to the law of the land.
- ✔ Free men should have the right to judgement by their peers.
- ✔ Justice would not be denied, delayed, or sold.
- ✔ Certain taxes should be levied only with the common consent of the country.
- ✔ The freedom of the church was to be upheld.
- ✔ A committee of 25 barons should monitor the king's actions and bring him to book if he broke any of the provisions of the charter.

In addition, Magna Carta contained many clauses designed to protect specific rights of the barons. But the document was addressed to all free men and their heirs, 'for ever', and so took on the character of a great declaration of human liberty. As a result, Magna Carta has been quoted, and cited, and misquoted, ever since in discussions about human rights.

In June 1215, the barons met John at Runnymede, on the south bank of the Thames near Windsor, and twisted his arm. The rebels had swept through the country and taken over London, and John had little choice but to accept their demands. John put his seal to the document.

But anyone who knew John knew that he would not keep the promises contained in Magna Carta. As soon as he could, the cunning king appealed to the Pope, pleading that the head of the church should declare the charter illegal, and promising to go on Crusade as an extra inducement. The Pope complied, and soon John was on the rampage against his rebellious barons, heading swiftly north to one of the baronial strongholds, Lincoln.

During this campaign, John suffered his final humiliation. His march across eastern England took him along the damp coast around the Wash. When the tide came in suddenly and unexpectedly, all the royal treasure disappeared under the water. John's losses included the crown jewels, priceless gems that were also symbols of his royal authority.

In October 1216, the king ate a hearty supper, rounding it off with peaches and cider. The rich meal contained a dangerous bug, and John quickly caught a violent gastric upset and died. His son and heir, Henry, was just nine years old. In the end, the barons got their way. The senior noblemen of England would rule on the young Henry's behalf until he came of age.

Lord of Misrule: Henry III

When Henry III came to the throne in 1216, the country was in a mess. His father John had overspent fighting the barons and losing land in France, so funds were at rock bottom. Huge tensions existed between the barons and the royal family, again made worse by John. And Henry was only a boy, so incapable of ruling for himself.

Henry's youth turned out to be a blessing in disguise. Senior royal officials were selected as his guardians, and they ruled competently on his behalf. Foremost of these officials was William Marhsall, a man who had worked for all the previous Plantagenet kings and who commanded huge respect. William retired in 1219, and when he did so, a trio of regents was appointed.

Part of the deal for the regents was that they ruled with the consent of a larger group of barons known as the Great Council. If they wanted to levy taxes, the regents had to get the approval of the Council, who thereby acted as a sort of brake on the power of the regents. The Council were keen on this role and also insisted on reissuing Magna Carta, the document that had curtailed the power of King John, to remind everyone that kings, and those who rule on their behalf, are not above the law. The barons were flexing their muscles and doing everything they could to limit royal power.

The art of making enemies

Henry himself did not take kindly to the restraints put on royal power by the barons, especially as the barons held on to power long after he was old enough to rule. They'd lost a lot of their trust in royalty after the rough way King John had treated them. Henry wanted to rule in his own right, even if his rule was restricted by the law. In 1232, when he was in his mid-twenties, the young king finally lost patience, threw out the regents, and started to govern. To begin with, things went well. Henry respected Magna Carta and ruled in relative peace until 1258.

Then the problems began. In 1236, Henry had married Eleanor of Provence, a princess with a lot of powerful relations in Europe. Henry hoped that these people would help him gain more power in France, so he started to shower expensive gifts on them and give them important positions at court. A number of other foreigners, including Henry's half-brothers, the children of his mother Isabella and her second husband Hugh of Lusignan, also got powerful jobs in England. At the same time, Henry began an expensive scheme to conquer Sicily.

Simon de Montfort

Simon de Montfort, Earl of Leicester, was one of Henry III's key servants. He married the king's youngest sister, Eleanor, and was appointed Henry's deputy in Gascony, where he put down local rebels. But when he returned to England, de Montfort became leader of the barons in their revolt against Henry's capricious rule. The rebel leader presided over Parliament in 1265, showing the way to limitations on royal power in the future.

The English barons were appalled. They were losing their power to foreigners and losing their money to the king's madcap schemes. Before he knew where he was, Henry had a clutch of baronial enemies at court. These enemies were peeved, and they were in no mood to be messed around. In 1258, the barons confronted Henry with their demands.

In a weird twist of irony, the man who emerged as leader of the rebel barons was a Frenchman, Simon de Montfort (see sidebar). It was de Montfort who realised that if they were to get further with Henry, they would need to do more than throw a few French lords out of the country. They would have to be more organised. He began to draw up lists of demands to limit royal power.

Royal power reduced

Simon de Montfort and his friends got serious about government in a document called the Provisions of Oxford. For the first time, this document drew up proper guidelines for selecting the people who were to advise the king. It also laid down the law about parliament. Key points of the Provisions of Oxford included:

- A committee of 24 men (12 chosen by the king, 12 by the nobility) were to oversee the reforms.
- A group of 15 (selected by representatives of the 24) should make up the king's Council or advisers.
- Parliament should meet at set times, not just when the king wanted it to meet.
- The king's officers should be appointed for specific year-long terms and were to be answerable to the Council, as well as the monarch.

The Provisions truly tied Henry's hands. He could hardly move without baronial approval. For a couple of years, the barons had him cornered, and he had to play by the rules. Henry was still king, but a huge chunk of the power was, if not with the people, at least with the upper classes.

It couldn't last, though. Henry was too headstrong, and the members of the Council could not always reach agreement on decisions. Soon England found itself embroiled in civil war. De Montfort defeated Henry, captured his son, Prince Edward, and forced the king into another agreement to abide by the Provisions of Oxford – and to forgive him and the other rebels for their treacherous behaviour.

This victory made de Montfort into the effective ruler of England, a state of affairs that lasted for around a year until Edward escaped, attacked de Montfort, and defeated him at the Battle of Evesham in 1265. It was a total triumph for Edward, and he sealed his victory by having de Montfort's body torn apart and put on show in all its bloody bits. With de Montfort out of the way, Henry's rule was secure, and for the last seven years of his reign, his power went unchallenged.

Henry gained added brownie points by rebuilding Westminster Abbey, which endeared him to the church. He also claimed to have healing powers, allegedly being able to cure the disease scrofula (known as 'the king's evil') by touching sufferers. Churchmen interpreted this supernatural power – which was also claimed by many later rulers – as God-given, lending Henry greater credibility with believers. The king went to his grave in 1272, a confident monarch with a powerful platform, both worldly and religious, on which his son and heir, Edward, would be able to build.

Chapter 8

More Plantagenets

*T*he Plantagenet dynasty (see Chapter 7) continued with the reign of Edward I. Edward was a strong, impressive-looking king in the traditional mould of the medieval warrior-ruler. He believed in going for what he wanted by conquest and spent one fortune conquering Wales and building some of the country's finest castles to defend it, and another fortune on a failed attempt to take control of Scotland, too. Edward I used to be seen as a great king, and his legal reforms – introducing local justices of the peace and giving communities the power to police their local areas – were effective. But his bully-boy tactics against the Welsh and the Scots made him a villain rather than a hero for all but die-hard English patriots.

Edward was followed by two more Edwards; his son Edward II and grandson Edward III. Edward II was a promising king, intelligent and loyal. But his reliance on a succession of favourites caused mishap and rebellion in his kingdom, and after a 20-year reign, he was forced off the throne and almost certainly murdered. His son and successor Edward III was a very different character. He embraced the traditional virtues of chivalry and founded the famous Order of the Garter. He also claimed to be rightful ruler of France and began the Hundred Years War to try to take over the country. The war lasted long after the end of Edward III's 50-year reign.

The last Plantagenet king was Edward III's son Richard II. Like his father, Richard loved chivalry, and he began his reign by successfully defeating the popular uprising now known as the Peasants' Revolt. But in his later years, saddened by the death of his first queen, Anne, he became both tyrannical and unpredictable. His fights with his senior barons finally got too much and Richard was deposed, the first Lancastrian king, Henry IV taking over.

Longshanks: Edward 1

The eldest son of Henry III and his queen, Eleanor of Provence, was born in 1239 and was in his 30s before he came to the throne in 1272. By this time, Edward I already had a reputation for being a man of action who was used to playing a key role in the affairs of the nation.

Edward had sided with the barons, led by Simon de Montfort, who wanted to reform the monarchy and limit the power of his father, but he turned against de Montfort when the rebellious baron seemed to be posing too great a threat to royal power. Edward even led the royal forces when they defeated de Montfort in 1265 at the Battle of Evesham.

Edward I must have cut an impressive figure on the battlefield. He was tall – a head taller than most other men at the royal court – and his stature earned him the nickname Longshanks. His arms were long, too, which meant he usually had the advantage over his opponent in a sword fight. The king's awesome stature, combined with bravery and a quick temper, made him a fearsome figure.

When Edward was away from the battlefield, his family sometimes had to bear the brunt of his temper. He once had a row with his daughter Elizabeth and threw her coronet into the fire, and on another occasion he is said to have grabbed his son Edward and started to tear out his hair in rage.

But Edward had a more peaceful side, too. He loved chess and falconry, was an enthusiast for the courtly virtues of chivalry, and was a pious Christian. The religious and soldierly sides of his character came together in 1270 when Edward went off to the Holy Land to join one of the numerous Crusades, ostensibly to win back territory in the eastern Mediterranean for the Christians.

It didn't work out that way. Edward didn't do a lot of fighting in the East, the Crusade's leader, Louis IX of France, died, and the expedition fizzled out. Travelling across France on his way home in 1272, Edward heard that his father, Henry III, had died, too, and he was now king of England.

A devoted couple

Edward is famous as one of the most devoted husbands in the history of the English monarchy. He married his wife, the Spanish princess Eleanor of Castile, in 1254, and the handsome prince and dark-haired princess, one of the beauties of her age, seem to have been deeply in love. Eleanor bore Edward 16 children, many of whom died young, and she even went with him on Crusade.

According to one chronicle, Eleanor once saved Edward's life. The prince was stabbed during an assassination attempt while he was in the East. The assassin had dipped his dagger in poison, and Eleanor is said to have sucked the poison from the prince's wound. The story is almost certainly a chronicler's myth, but it points to the closeness of the couple and how their fates were intertwined.

The queen was an educated young woman who employed her own scribes to copy books for her. She also liked making tapestries and longed for the exotic fruits of her native Spain. When a Spanish ship docked in England, she sent her staff straight to the quay to buy up any oranges, figs, or pomegranates on board. Sadly, Eleanor was only in her mid-50s when she died, at a village called Harby in Nottinghamshire, and the king was heartbroken. Edward did eventually find a new wife, Margaret of France. But there was a gap of nine years between Eleanor's death and Edward's second marriage.

At two villages in the English Midlands, Geddington and Hardingstone, stand beautiful carved memorials called *Eleanor Crosses*. Edward I ordered that these stunning stone crosses should be erected at each of the stopping places of the queen's funeral procession as it made its way from Harby to London. The Eleanor Crosses, encrusted with intricate carving and statues, were erected at all 12 stops and were among the wonders of the age. As well as the original survivors, a reproduction also exists: London's famous Charing Cross.

Moving in on Wales

When Edward I got back home from the Crusade, the new king soon made it clear that he meant business. For generations, the kings of England had had their eye on Wales, and Edward's gaze was fixed there more firmly than most. In the 13th century, Wales was ruled by a number of Welsh princes. By the time Edward came to the throne, one of these princes, Llewelyn ap Gruffydd (see Chapter 21), the ruler of Gwynedd, had taken the overall title of Prince of Wales. Henry III had recognised Llewelyn, but when the Welshman refused to pay homage to the new English king, Edward acted.

The English king launched a military campaign in 1277 to bring Wales to heel. To begin with, Edward didn't want to conquer Wales, just to force Llewelyn into submission so that it was clear who was boss at the top of the British feudal pecking order. When Edward beat the Welsh in battle, it seemed as if he had succeeded. Edward took over a chunk of northwest Wales but let the Welshman keep his title, and an uneasy peace followed.

But there was a problem: Llewelyn's brother, Daffydd. In 1282, Daffydd staged a rebellion against the English, and Edward was furious. The Englishman began a campaign to conquer Wales outright. The campaign lasted for years:

✔ After a series of struggles, Llewelyn was ambushed and killed near Builth in November 1282.

- In June 1283, the English captured Daffydd and executed him as a traitor.

- In 1284, a law called the Statute of Wales was passed, putting the principality under the direct rule of the English king.

- The Welsh rebelled again in 1287 and 1294, and Edward crushed these uprisings.

- Throughout this period, Edward built a series of castles in North Wales as English bases; castles such as Conwy, Caernarfon, Beaumaris, and Harlech remain some of the most impressive built in the Middle Ages.

In addition to all his military measures, Edward made one still more far-reaching move. In 1301, he made his eldest son Prince of Wales, beginning a tradition of English Princes of Wales that has lasted to this day.

An old story speculates that the king was playing a cunning trick on the Welsh by giving this title to his young son Edward. He is supposed to have held the baby boy up as a kind of offering to a bunch of Welsh nobles, saying, 'Here is your new prince of Wales,' and pointing out that the tiny child could speak no English. The idea was meant to suggest that the king was pretending to offer them a prince who, knowing no English, could grow up a Welshman.

The story is a myth, though. Young Edward was born in 1284, so he was already 7 years old and presumably very talkative when he was made Prince of Wales. And although the boy had been born in his father's Welsh castle at Caernarfon, he was English through and through.

The Hammer of the Scots

Before he conquered Wales, Edward was launching a still grander scheme of conquest – he wanted to take over Scotland and bring the whole of Britain under English rule. In 1286, he saw a golden opportunity to increase his influence in Scotland. The Scottish king, Alexander III, died, leaving a little girl, Princess Margaret, as his heir. Edward did a deal with the Scots in which they planned that Edward's son would marry Margaret and become ruler of Scotland.

In 1290, however, all these plans fell apart because little Margaret died. Edward found himself drawn into the political wrangle over who should be her successor and then into a military campaign north of the border. The consequences were very different from those in Wales. The Scots objected to Edward meddling in their succession crisis, and Edward marched north with an army, hoping to bring them to their knees:

- Edward marched through Scotland in 1297 and stole the famed Stone of Destiny, symbol of Scots royal power, from the town of Scone.

✔ He made the new king, John Balliol, resign, making Scotland a *dependency* (in other words, a subordinate country) of the English crown.

✔ The Scots, under William Wallace, fought back, defeating the English under the Earl of Surrey in 1298. A series of battles followed.

✔ In 1305, Wallace was caught and put to death, and Edward claimed sovereignty over Scotland.

✔ The next year, a new Scottish claimant, Robert Bruce, came to the fore to question Edward's power (see Chapter 11).

In 1307, Edward died, with his business in Scotland unfinished. His repeated campaigns had earned him the nickname Hammer of the Scots, but his hammering had got him nowhere.

New laws, model parliaments

Edward did not spend all his time rampaging around the country trying to conquer his neighbours. He also found time to improve the English legal system, building on the work of his Plantagenet predecessors (see Chapter 7) to make the operation of the courts fairer and to make Parliament more relevant to the needs of the people.

What was Edward's interest in legal reforms? Well, from one point of view, Edward probably didn't make these reforms solely out of a desire to be fair to his subjects. His military campaigns, as ever, cost a lot of money, and big Welsh castles didn't come cheap. Some, but not all, of his reforms were to do with how taxes were negotiated. The king and his ministers had a sense of justice, too, and the other reforms were to make life safer and fairer for many people.

The following reforms to the laws and Parliament made Edward popular in England, and the English have usually seen Edward as a good king. But opinions in Wales and Scotland are different – here he is usually seen as a bully who poked his nose, and his armies, into places where they should not have been.

As for Edward himself, he was probably proud of his achievements in England and Wales, but disappointed with his failure to conquer Scotland. His personal life was a mixture of happiness and sadness, too. After Queen Eleanor died, Edward took a second wife, Margaret, daughter of the King of France. But although she bore him three children, she was no replacement for his beloved Eleanor.

Law reforms

Early on in his reign, Edward faced up to a number of problems to do with crime and punishment. Keeping the peace was good for everyone, king and subjects alike:

- Edward passed the laws allowing the appointment of the first Justices of the Peace.
- The king gave local communities the responsibility for policing.
- He laid out clearly the rights held by the nobility when it came to dispensing justice on behalf of the crown.
- He dealt with the problems that arose when sheriffs did not carry out their duties properly.
- He passed a range of statutes tightening up issues such as land law and the law relating to debt.

Edward's reforms made English law faster, more efficient, and on the whole fairer. They also gave more power to the king to bring cases in royal courts, providing him with much-needed revenue in the shape of fines.

Model Parliaments

Edward also made changes to the way Parliament operated. He made it more relevant to the people by encouraging subjects to come to Parliament to ask for royal help if they had been wronged. To make this system work, Edward promised that all petitions brought to Parliament would be answered.

Parliament became more relevant in another way, too. Individuals from both the counties and towns were asked to come to Parliament whenever the king was discussing the raising of taxes. A medieval Parliament was a far cry from the modern institution, but it was starting to become representative of the people. The 1295 Parliament included elected burgesses from the towns and members of the clergy, and well as nobles and knights. It covered such a broad spectrum that this sitting became known as the Model Parliament.

Cruel Fate: Edward II

Edward I died in 1207, on his way north to make another attack on his enemies, the Scots. He was succeeded by his son, also called Edward. Young Edward had had a difficult upbringing. His mother, Eleanor of Castile, died when he was 6 years old, and he saw little of his father, who was often away fighting.

As a result, Edward had a difficult youth and grew up with a reputation for eccentricity. Although he was good-looking and tall like his father, Edward did not have much passion for the kind of horsey activities that royal sons usually went in for. Young Edward preferred swimming and was said to like rural crafts, such as hedge-laying – something that other royals and nobles would have seen as way below their dignity.

Living apart from his family, Edward's main emotional attachments were to his aristocratic friends. The trouble was that no one else liked Edward's friends very much, a situation that more than once brought the kingdom to crisis-point.

King and favourite

Before he became king, Prince Edward's closest friend was a young lord from Gascony called Piers Gaveston. Gaveston had come to England to find his fortune, and young Edward soon became attached to him. Just before old king Edward died, the prince asked his father to confer a title on his friend. The prince wanted Gaveston to be made either Count of Ponthieu (one of England's possessions in France) or Earl of Cornwall (one of the most important English earldoms). Edward I would have nothing of either idea and sent Gaveston packing off to France. You didn't just turn up from France and start expecting earldoms – it wasn't done.

A few months later, the old king died, and Edward II was on the throne. Edward quickly took the opportunity to bring back his friend:

- ✔ Edward recalled Gaveston back from exile.
- ✔ Gaveston was made Earl of Cornwall.
- ✔ The earl was given the place of honour – right next to the king, where the queen would normally expect to sit – at the royal coronation banquet.
- ✔ Gaveston began to act like an assistant king, influencing all Edward's decisions.

All these favours offended people at court. The king's favourite seemed to have far more power than he deserved. People began to wonder exactly what was going on.

Discussing royal sexuality in public was taboo in the Middle Ages. But some people probably thought that Edward was gay, and that Gaveston was his lover. Writers at the time certainly talked about the king's love for his favourite, but they may have been talking about brotherly love.

Edward certainly fathered children by his queen, Isabella, and, in addition, had at least one illegitimate son. Historians just don't know for sure the details of his personal life, although rumours abounded.

The important thing, though, was that the English nobles felt that Gaveston had too much power, and that the time was ripe for some more curbs on the crown. In 1311, a royal commission drew up the New Ordinances, a list of restrictions designed to put Edward in a straitjacket. The king had to seek the consent of the barons in Parliament for the following:

- ✔ Dishing out major titles and privileges.
- ✔ Declaring war.
- ✔ Drawing up peace terms after a war.

In addition, the barons insisted that Gaveston should be sent back into exile again. The pampered favourite was out on his ear.

An unseemly few years followed in which the royal favourite was exiled, brought back by Edward, and hidden away in the castle at Scarborough, where Gaveston hoped he would be able to defend himself against any baronial attack.

But Gaveston didn't reckon on the determination of the barons. In 1312, they pursued him to Scarborough, forced him to give himself up, and marched him off to Warwick. After a mock trial, it was a case of 'Off with his head': the hapless favourite was put to death as a traitor.

Defeat in Scotland

The death of Gaveston did Edward some good, in a way. Some of the barons who had withheld their support from the crown when he was carrying on with his favourite returned to the king's side. And this support was just as well because hapless Edward was about to face a formidable enemy. In 1314, Edward tried to pick up the pieces of his father's war with the Scots.

Up to this point, England still had a chance of muscling in on Scotland. But hardly had the campaign begun than they suffered a major defeat. Robert Bruce and his army routed them at the Battle of Bannockburn (see Chapter 11).

Scots patriots still celebrate the Battle of Bannockburn, but the battle wasn't a big deal on its own. So why was it so important? The main reason was that Robert Bruce used it as a key lever in his case to be undisputed Scottish king. He got approval of his position from the Pope, and by 1323, Edward had made a truce with Bruce. The Scots rejoiced – and Edward slunk away, leaving the people of the far north of England unprotected from Scottish border raids.

Dispensers of power

The death of Edward's favourite, Piers Gaveston, should have meant a better time for those who feared that power would be arbitrarily wielded in Edward's reign, but not a bit of it. By 1318, Edward had two new favourites, Hugh Despenser and his son, also called Hugh. Both men threw their weight about in distressing ways.

Here's the dirt on how they, ahem, dispensed their power:

- **Chamberlain:** Hugh the Younger was given the job of royal Chamberlain. This office was important because young Hugh controlled who had access to the king, and therefore who had influence over the decisions he made about policy and about who else, if anyone, he would favour. It was a key position for depriving other barons of power over the king.

- **Lord of Glamorgan:** Hugh the Elder stacked up a huge portfolio of lands along the borders of England and Wales, which gave him vast power and enormous revenues from all the lands. An indication of the kind of power he could wield can be seen at his key fortress, Caerphilly Castle, with its miles of stone walls, tons of towers, and acres of water defences.

Some of the other barons soon started a campaign of armed struggle against the Despensers. Chief amongst these opponents was the king's cousin, Thomas, Earl of Lancaster, who had been prominent in the campaign to get rid of Gaveston. Soon revolts popped up all over the kingdom – in the south east at Leeds Castle, in southwest England, in South Wales (no surprise there with Hugh the Elder so powerful), and up north in Lancaster's territory. Altogether, they added up to a civil war. Could the king survive?

Well, yes, for a while. The Despensers and Edward rounded ruthlessly on the rebels:

- In March 1322, Lancaster was caught and killed.

- Shortly afterward, six of his key followers were murdered.

- The king abolished earlier curbs on his power.

- The Despensers were given more titles and lands.

It seemed as if the king and his two friends could do what they wanted to do – and that the strings on the whole were being pulled by the Despensers, while Edward danced to their tune. The early 1320s weren't a great time to be English unless your surname was Despenser.

A gruesome end

The end of the oppressive regime of the Despensers came in the most unlikely way. The main player was, of all people, Edward's queen, Isabella. She had gone to France to help negotiate peace terms between Edward and her brother, the French king Charles IV, in a dispute over who should hold power over part of Aquitaine. While she was in France, Isabella, who probably felt frozen out of her marriage because Edward was so close to his favourites, found an ally in Roger Mortimer, a nobleman and opponent of the Despensers who had left England after the defeat of Lancaster and his rebels a couple of years earlier.

Mortimer and Isabella plotted to end the tyranny of the Despensers once and for all – even if it meant deposing Edward, too. Strong rumours circulated that the pair did a lot of their plotting in bed. Be that as it may, their plans were in place by September 1326, and they landed on the coast of Essex before making swiftly for London. Edward was nowhere to be found. He had fled to the Despenser lands in Wales, and Mortimer, Isabella, and the teenage Prince Edward were soon hot-footing it westward in pursuit.

Because no kingly presence was found, Mortimer and Isabella declared the prince Keeper of the Realm, indicating that he was effective ruler in the king's absence. This tactic was a way of assuming authority that looked legitimate. The prince became a sort of honorary ruler without actually taking the title of king – but in reality, the power lay with Isabella and Mortimer.

Mortimer then set about rounding up the Despensers and their followers. Soon after, the Despensers were executed for treason, and the king himself was found at Llantrisant and imprisoned. Young prince Edward was declared king.

It was the end of the road for Edward II. In September 1327, a few months after his son had been put on the throne, Edward's death was announced from his prison at Berkeley Castle. No one witnessed the death, and rumours began immediately. Some said the king had escaped and was in hiding. But the most persistent story was that he had been murdered, on the orders of Mortimer, by the insertion of a red-hot poker into his rectum.

Chivalry Rules: Edward III

Edward III was thrust into public life before his time. In 1326, Edward II was on the throne, but his queen, Isabella of France, and her lover, Roger Mortimer, staged a coup ousting the king, who had alienated the English barons by concentrating power in the hands of his favourites. As a result of this coup, Edward and Isabella's 14-year-old son, also called Edward, found himself king in January 1327.

For the first three years of the reign, Isabella and Mortimer effectively ruled on young Edward's behalf. The barons weren't amused. Instead of Edward II and his favourites, they now had to cope with Isabella and her lover exercising power just as arbitrarily. Things looked bleak.

Showing who's boss

The year after he became king, Edward III married. His wife, Philippa of Hainault, daughter of William, Count of Hainault and Holland, was an attractive, intelligent girl in her teens, and the couple got on well from the start. But there was a problem. Isabella and Mortimer would not allow Philippa to be properly crowned. Isabella didn't want a young woman ousting her from her powerful position as queen of the English hive.

Edward and Philippa must have felt pushed to one side, but in 1330, things changed when Philippa got pregnant. Now she *had* to be made queen, to ensure that her child would be the offspring of a king and queen of England and undisputed heir to the throne. In 1330, Edward and Philippa went off to Westminster Abbey for Philippa to be crowned queen. A few months later, she gave birth to a bouncing boy – yet another English prince called Edward.

Mortimer cornered

But even with his queen at his side, Edward couldn't rule independently. Isabella and, especially, Mortimer, were still calling the shots. They even sent letters to other rulers on Edward's behalf. Edward had to send a message to the Pope saying that only letters that included the words 'Holy father' in the king's own hand genuinely came from him.

But with his queen on the throne beside him, a healthy heir in the cradle, and many barons resentful of Mortimer's power, things were on Edward's side. In late 1330 he and some baronial allies sought out Mortimer at Nottingham Castle, entered the castle through a secret passage by night, dragged him from his bed, and carted him away.

Mortimer was found guilty of treason and hanged. Isabella was sent for a quiet retirement, and Edward announced that from now on he would rule in his own right.

Damage repair

Getting to a position where he was properly in charge was only half the battle for Edward. After the disastrous reign of his father and the dodgy episode with Isabella and Mortimer, the reputation of the crown had taken a nose-dive. Edward knew that he would have to make a huge effort to turn things around.

One of his biggest challenges was foreign relations. Like his grandfather Edward I, Edward was a supporter of the Balliol family for the Scottish throne. England fought bravely in Scotland, and the England-Balliol alliance eventually sent the Bruce candidate for the Scottish throne scuttling across the sea to his allies in France. The French king, Philip VI, backed the Bruce dynasty, and Philip let it be known that if Edward kept his weight behind the Balliols, his lands in France would be under threat.

War with France looked likely, so Edward set about getting the English people, especially the nobles, firmly on his side. One thing that Edward did appealed directly to the medieval idea that a king had God-given powers that verged on the miraculous. For example, people believed that a king was able to heal the disease *scrofula* (a form of tuberculosis affecting the lymphatic glands) by touching the sufferer. In 1340–1, Edward carried out a staggering 355 healings. Over half of these healings were done in Westminster and would have impressed both the court and the people of the capital. Historians have no way of knowing how real the king's healing powers were. But the important thing for Edward was that people believed in them.

Even more important were the political moves Edward made to generate support for his planned war with France. In particular, the king:

- ✔ Moved troops across the Channel.

- ✔ Garnered more support in England by appointing six new earls and a duke.

- ✔ Began to buy alliances with rulers in Holland and Germany.

- ✔ Gave himself the title of King of France. (He had a claim to the French throne because his mother was the sister of a French king.)

By 1340, England was ready for war with France. No one could have guessed how long the conflict would last.

The Hundred Years War

Edward III and Philip VI of France began the longest war in the history of their two nations in 1340. The conflict actually lasted more than 100 years, because it wasn't really over until 1453, when England finally lost all its French possessions except Calais.

The long war was a tale of woe for both England and France because both countries lost thousands of men, and the people had to put up with years of fighting, together with all the looting and pillage that went with medieval warfare. But during Edward III's reign, things went well for England. Here are some of the highlights:

- ✔ **1340 Battle of Sluys:** England's first sea battle gave Edward domination of the Channel, although he failed to invade France.

- ✔ **1346 Battle of Crécy:** A major victory for the English, who defeated the French in spite of being outnumbered by more than two to one.

- **1347 Siege of Calais:** This strategic town surrendered to the English.

- **1356 Battle of Poitiers:** Another victory for the English army, led by Edward's son, Edward the Black Prince, who took the French king prisoner.

- **1360 Treaty of Brétigny:** Edward gave up his claim to the French crown, but retained lands in Calais, Gascony, Guienne, and Poitou; he was paid big ransoms for the French king and David of Scotland, who was also his prisoner.

Although he had to give up his claim to be king of France, Edward made huge territorial gains as a result of 20 years of fighting. What was more, the English army he had assembled had more than proved their skill. England was a force to be reckoned with on the battlefield, and this recognition undoubtedly meant a lot to Edward. The English achieved this with two not-so-secret weapons:

- **Not-so-secret weapon No. 1, the longbow:** Medieval armies had various weapons at their disposal, from the sword and lance of the horse-riding knight to the powerful crossbow. But the English perfected a still more impressive weapon, the longbow. The *longbow* was a powerful weapon – its sharpest arrowheads could even pierce armour – and it was light and quick to shoot. While a crossbowman was spending valuable seconds loading his weapon and getting ready to aim, a longbowman just grabbed an arrow, lifted his weapon and fired in one swift movement. Showers of arrows from hundreds of English bows did in the French at Crécy and terrified enemies until accurate guns became available.

- **Not-so-secret weapon No. 2, The Black Prince:** Edward's eldest son was just 16 years old when he fought at the Battle of Crécy. His father gave him a kind of honorary command of part of the force at this battle, and he impressed those around him. The prince was a natural on the battle-field, both brave and tactically astute, so he was quickly promoted to a full commanding role. His most famous success in the Hundred Years War was at Poitiers, where he turned a near-defeat into a resounding vic-tory. Oh – his nickname? No one knows for sure why he was called the Black Prince, but it was probably because he wore black armour.

With the Black Prince's powerful presence on the field of battle and the all-important Treaty of Brétigny, it seemed as if England had won the war. Almost a decade of uneasy peace between England and France followed. The Black Prince was made ruler of Aquitaine, and the king already had some interesting projects on hand back home in England.

The Order of the Garter

When he was not gallivanting around France trying to win back territory, Edward had another passionate interest – the cult of chivalry. In fact, warfare and chivalry are closely linked, because *chivalry* means the etiquette and tra-ditions surrounding the role of the knight.

Being a knight

The *knight* was the upper-class elite fighting man of the Middle Ages. Knights wore armour, rode into battle on horseback, and used the sword, the weapon of the aristocracy. To be a knight was very prestigious.

Only the king could appoint you as a knight, and the knightly way of life required a long training period. But once you were a knight, you were given great respect – you might become a military leader and would certainly have a lot of influence at home, probably becoming lord of a castle or large manor house, and enjoying considerable wealth.

In return, though, you were expected to abide by a code of behaviour, called the *code of chivalry*, that required you to be courteous and civil. You were meant to be especially respectful to your womenfolk and merciful to your enemies. It didn't always work out like this in practice – knights were energetic, often boisterous men who could be a handful, especially when they were young. But that was the theory: chivalry, at all times.

In his love of chivalry and knightly pursuits, Edward was following in the footsteps of his grandfather, Edward I. But whereas the earlier Edward was above all a ruthless conqueror whose main interest in knights and castles was their power to subdue his neighbours, Edward III was more taken with the trappings of chivalry. He liked tournaments with elaborate costumes and lots of pageantry, and he rebuilt Windsor Castle in lavish style, taking more than 20 years and most of the craft workers and masons in the country to do so.

Edward harked back to the days of his grandfather in other ways, too. Edward I had been one of those English kings who had looked back with nostalgia to the golden days of King Arthur. To historians, Arthur is a mythical figure, but to the Plantagenets, he was a real king who presided over a chivalric court in which knights went off on valiant quests and returned to sit around the famous round table, where every knight was meant to be equal in status and equal in virtue. Edward was fascinated with the story of Arthur and even had a search made for the body of Joseph of Arimathea, the biblical character who was said to be the ancestor of the mythical king.

New order

In 1348, to celebrate the great English victory at the Battle of Crécy, Edward III founded a new order of knights who were inspired by the ideals of Arthur's round table. They were called the *Knights of the Garter,* and to be chosen as one of their number was one of the greatest honours the king could bestow.

According to an old and enduring story, the *Order of the Garter* got its weird name in a peculiar way. One night at a party at Windsor Castle, the king noticed that a garter belonging to the Countess of Salisbury had fallen to the floor. When the courtiers started to snigger at this courtly piece of underwear, the king picked it up and tied it around his own leg (or in some versions of the story, his arm). Then he ticked the giggling courtiers off: 'Honi soit qui mal y pense,' said Edward (Shame on him who thinks evil of it), demonstrating the courteous, chivalric values he prized so much.

The king's one-liner became the motto of the new Order of the Garter. It was – and still is – a highly exclusive order. Edward would admit only 24 people, plus himself and the Black Prince, and the members were all high-ranking men chosen specifically by the king.

A lasting influence

As part of his rebuilding work at Windsor Castle, Edward had the castle chapel made over. The chapel, formerly St Edward's chapel, was rededicated to the knightly figure St George, and became the religious headquarters of the Order of the Garter. The members still meet there every year for a commemorative service, and to be made a Knight of the Garter is still one of the highest honours the monarch can convey.

Since Edward founded the Order of the Garter, several later monarchs have founded other orders of knights, such as the *Order of the Bath,* which was set up in the 15th century. Such orders show how Edward's interest in chivalry has continued down through the ages and are still a way of honouring people.

Edward was very good at using pageantry and ceremony to impress his subjects and produce an aura of glory. If he was alive today, the king would be seen as an image-conscious ruler who created a powerful chivalric brand for the monarchy. Other examples of Edward's canny use of image-manipulation include:

- Presenting gold model ships to important pilgrimage churches.
- Having a new gold coin called the noble minted, bearing the image of the king on board a warship.

Both of these striking images helped to promote the idea of Edward as a leader who could rule the waves.

Parliamentary questions

Edward III's reign was outstandingly successful in many ways. He scored victories in France, promoted good relations with his aristocracy, had a happy married life, and produced a bunch of healthy sons to secure the succession. But his last years were clouded with sadness. His beloved Philippa died in 1369, and many of his friends were dying, too. He placed great hope in his eldest son, Edward, but the Black Prince contracted an illness on military campaign in Spain in 1367 and spent the next few years a shadow of his former self. The prince died in 1376, a year before his father.

The king also saw some of his power ebbing away. This loss of power was partly the result of some devious courtiers, who gathered in a circle that may have been centred on Edward's mistress, Alice Perrers. But it was also due to Parliament. It was in this period that Parliament made two innovations that would become important in the future.

Parliament in Edward's reign was very different from a modern parliament, but was beginning to show its muscle. By the 14th century, the Commons was made up of representatives from the *shires* and *boroughs* (in other words, the countryside and town) and met separately from the Lords (the representatives of the nobility). Two key innovations of Edward's reign changed the way Parliament worked.

- ✔ **Parliamentary innovation No. 1 – The Speaker:** In 1376, Parliament appointed the first known Speaker. It was his job to take Parliamentary complaints to the king and do something about getting them addressed. Today, the role of Speaker is that of chairman – the Speaker is the person who watches the members' behaviour and doesn't actually 'speak' very much at all, apart from shouting 'Order, order' to bring everyone into line. But the Speaker in Edward III's time had a slightly different role – he was another of Parliament's attempts to curb the excesses of the crown.

- ✔ **Parliamentary innovation No. 2 – Impeachment:** The 1376 Parliament used the Speaker to bring charges against key officials and courtiers who were abusing their power. In other words, they were impeaching officials. Again, it was a way of using Parliament to stop courtiers from throwing their weight around. No wonder the 1376 Parliament went down in history as the Good Parliament.

These reforms were all well and good, but they didn't have much effect in Edward's reign. By 1377, the old king was dead and lying with his ancestors in Westminster Abbey. His crown was to pass to his grandson Richard, the oldest surviving son of the Black Prince.

Sad, not Bad: Richard II

Richard II, son of the Black Prince and grandson of the previous king, Edward III, came to the throne in 1377 at the tender age of ten. To run the country while the king was a boy, councils of noblemen were appointed. There was naturally a lot of jockeying for position amongst nobles who wanted to be included in these influential councils, and amongst those who supported the various candidates.

One person who was not selected for the councils was Richard's uncle, John of Gaunt, who as a son of the previous king and had some claim to the throne himself. No doubt Richard's advisers wanted to keep this powerful member of the royal family away, in case he tried to take over the crown himself. And as a close relative of the king, John of Gaunt probably already had a powerful influence. Richard's reign certainly started with uncertainty, as so often happened in the Middle Ages when a child ascended to the throne. But these troubles with the aristocracy were nothing compared with what happened when the lower classes started to make trouble for the young king.

Revolting peasants

In previous centuries, when objections were raised against the way a king ruled, the objectors were usually members of the upper classes – especially nobles who thought they or their friends could do a better job of ruling than whoever was on the throne. But in 1381, things were different. Ordinary people – farmers from the English countryside – led a rebellion. The Peasants' Revolt was under way.

Why did the peasants finally lose their temper in 1381? There were several reasons, and together they meant that for the first time ordinary people not only felt hard done by but could also see a way of doing something about it.

- **Villeinage:** Most of the revolting peasants were *villeins*. In other words they were unfree tenants, who held their land in return for paying onerous rents and services to their landlords. They were right at the bottom of the feudal system, with no way out, and it hurt.

- **Radicalism:** A new movement, on the fringes of the church, spoke out against the iniquities of church and state. Men like religious reformer John Wyclif stressed that all people, not just priests, should have access to the Bible. The implication was that all good people were equally worthy, and out-of-date feudal customs shouldn't stand in the way of people's rights.

- **Taxes:** The authorities had ordered that every male over the age of 15 should pay a poll tax – the same amount would be due from everyone, irrespective of whether they were rich or poor.

Taken together, the situation was too bad for the peasants. They found a charismatic leader, a craftsman called Wat Tyler (that's Tyler as in roof tiles), who led them across Kent, collecting more supporters on the way, and into the capital, winding them up to fever pitch with his oratory. Very quickly, people in London realised that Wat and his friends were serious.

From revolution to confrontation

Wat led a large army of peasants into London. The rebels, armed only with farming tools like axes and billhooks, overwhelmed the city guards, started fires in Southwark, killed the archbishop of Canterbury, and started a blaze in John of Gaunt's London palace that sent the whole building tumbling to the ground.

Meanwhile, Richard's advisers started to panic. They'd never seen a popular uprising before and were at sea when it came to dealing with it. It was left to the young king and his mother Joan to cope with the crisis. While his advisers flapped around, Richard and Joan, together with London's Lord Mayor, William Walworth, met the rebels face to face. Many of them respected Joan, who came from Kent, the home of many of the rioters; the young king seemed sympathetic, too.

Things were starting to calm down when Tyler rested his hand on the king's bridle. Walworth, who didn't trust the rebels (they'd burned half his city down, after all), misinterpreted the gesture, thinking Tyler was about to attack the king. So Walworth drew his sword and instantly ran Tyler through.

Now the peasants' leader was dead, and the 2,000 other rebels had their bows and arrows trained on the king. With only Walworth and Joan to defend him, it seemed that Richard didn't stand a chance. But thinking quickly, the young king spoke to the rebels. He offered to take up their cause himself and assured them, 'I will be your captain now.'

Picking up the pieces

Richard diffused the wrath of the peasants by promising to pardon them for the revolt and agreeing to abolish villeinage. But he went back on his promises, executing some of the more prominent rebels and using violence to put down rebellions in other parts of the country. The rebels had been tricked by a plausible teenaged king.

But it wasn't all bad news for the peasants. In early 1382, Richard married Anne of Bohemia, a princess from central Europe. Anne, pious and thoughtful, begged her new husband to pardon the remaining rebels, and Richard agreed.

In addition, many landlords abolished tenancies under the old restrictions of villeinage and introduced tenancy agreements that were more favourable to peasant farmers. Less labour was available since the great plague, known as the Black Death, had swept across the country in 1348. Suddenly, small farmers were more valuable than before, and landlords had to agree to some of their demands. So life was better after all for many at the sharp end of the feudal system.

Protesting Parliaments

Richard had made a seriously good start as a ruler. He had diffused the Peasants' Revolt, got rid of the ringleaders, and, thanks to his clement queen, done something to help the plight of the poor peasants, too. But he also had more complicated work to do. England was still embroiled in the on-and-off conflict with France and her ally, Scotland, which had started in Edward III's reign and is now called the Hundred Years War.

The dispute over money-raising to pay for the war (and for Richard's lavish court) led to a series of interventions by Parliament:

- In 1386, Richard's chancellor, Michael de la Pole, made a really heavy tax demand.
- Parliament met and sent a deputation to see Richard and demand that de la Pole be sacked.
- Richard at first refused, but then relented and removed de la Pole.
- Parliament appointed a commission of top barons to run the administration for a year and to sort out any royal abuses of power.

Not surprisingly, Richard didn't take kindly to having his power snatched away. He insisted on being advised by his own favourites, not men appointed by Parliament. Before long, the king was locked in a battle of wills with Parliament over who had the power to govern. Royalists and barons took up arms and, in December 1387, fought the battle of Radcot Bridge, where the king was captured and imprisoned in his own castle, the Tower of London.

Then another Parliament met to discuss once more what to do about royal power. This meeting was known as the Merciless Parliament, and no wonder:

- A group of lords accused the royal favourites of treason.
- Two of the traitors, Robert Tresilian and Nicholas Brembre, were executed.
- The Commons then accused and executed four other courtiers.
- Parliament made the king accept another group of advisers, the Lords Appellant, who were to have the power to control all his actions.

Richard was in an impossible position, but he was fortunate that several of the advisers made peace with the royalist group and together king and advisers were able to rule in an uneasy alliance. The king bolstered his position by currying favour with the gentry and by making peace for a while in France.

A broken-hearted king?

In 1394, Richard's queen, Anne of Bohemia, died of the plague. The king was said to be heartbroken. Richard was so distraught that he started to lose control of his actions. He had the couple's favourite home demolished and walloped the Earl of Arundel in the face for being late for Anne's funeral.

But two years later, Richard made the best of things and got married again – to a Frenchwoman! Improbable as it seemed, he got hitched to Isabella, daughter of Charles VI, king of the old enemy, France. It was a shrewd diplomatic move, of course, because it cemented, for the moment, peace between the two countries.

By now, Richard was more confident holding the reins of power – in fact, for many he was too confident and more and more was unpredictable and ill-tempered. Finally, in 1397, Richard had his revenge on the Lords Appellant, arresting the three key Lords. One, the hated Earl of Arundel, was tried and beheaded for treason. Another, the Duke of Gloucester, was killed in Calais, while the third, the Earl of Warwick, was heavily fined.

Another former Appellant, Richard's cousin Henry Bolingbroke, initially did rather better. He was made Earl of Hereford and promised the Duchy of Lancaster on the death of John of Gaunt. But when John died, Richard, fearful of making Bolingbroke too powerful, went back on his promise and kept the Duchy of Lancaster in royal hands.

The revenge on the Lords Appellant, the incident at the funeral of Anne, the willingness to take offence, the way he surrounded himself with bodyguards – it is difficult to see what lay behind these actions except some kind of mental breakdown. Some thought that the cause of the trouble was the king's grief at the death of gentle Queen Anne. Others argued that it was a sign of deeper derangement.

Whatever the cause, the effect was a kind of tyrannical whimsy that was unjust, arbitrary, and hard to bear – so hard that Richard's support ebbed away. Bolingbroke saw his chance to act and returned to England to lean on Richard and persuade him to abdicate. Parliament supported Bolingbroke's claim to the throne, and Richard found himself in prison in Pontefract Castle. Here, a broken man (if not actually broken-hearted), Richard died. Bolingbroke's supporters said he had starved himself to death, but he was probably murdered.

Chapter 9

Lancaster and York: Fighting Families

. . . .

In This Chapter

▶ Revealing how the throne changed hands between rival ruling families

▶ Finding out about the Wars of the Roses

▶ Exploring England's troubled relationship with France

▶ Uncovering a suspected royal murder

. . . .

*W*hen Henry Bolingbroke arrived in England in 1399, he found a power vacuum. The current king, Richard II, was ill – he seemed to have lost his mind and had spent the last few years of his reign falling out with his advisers and showing himself unfit to rule. Bolingbroke took over decisively and ruled as Henry IV, dealing with a number of challenges to his power and showing himself to be a dynamic king.

His son, Henry V, was even more of a man of action, entering the old war with France and winning some of the most famous battles in history. His victories, such as the Battle of Agincourt, were immortalised in Shakespeare's play *Henry V*, turning the king into a kind of superhero who licked the French and then married their princess. The reality wasn't so straightforward, though, especially as Henry died young, before making sure of his gains.

After Henry V died, his baby son became King Henry VI. The boy king had to rule through advisers, and when he did finally take responsibility for the realm himself, he proved unsuited to the job. Although kind and pious, he lacked the ability to govern shrewdly. While his military leaders were losing the lands England had conquered in France, Henry lost his grip on power in England. A civil war began, and the crown passed back and forth between Henry and his rivals of the House of York, Edward IV, Edward V, and Richard III. This conflict, the Wars of the Roses, lasted from 1455 to 1485 and ended when a leader from a different family, the Welsh Tudors, defeated Richard III in battle and claimed the throne through his connection with the Lancastrians.

Strongman: Henry IV

The new king who forced Richard II from the throne in 1399 (see Chapter 8) was a much more attractive individual than his predecessor. Henry IV was a dynamic character, already in his early 30s, who had proved himself as a man of action. He wasn't a giant of a man like Edward I (see Chapter 8 for him, too), but was athletic, liking sports such as jousting, and had been on Crusade and on pilgrimage to Jerusalem. The people who met him – and on his travels he gained many friends in the royal and noble houses of Europe – were impressed by his character, seeing him as strong, courteous, and knightly. Henry seemed to be a good leader of men, too. In other words, he seemed the ideal kingly figure.

But Henry also had a more reflective side. He could read and write and was a patron of poets and musicians. One contemporary said that the king was a good musician himself, perhaps playing the recorder or flute. He was also highly religious, making regular offerings to the church and seeking out the most learned clergymen as his advisers.

The two sides of Henry's character came together in an ambition he had to bring Europe together and lead a European force on a Crusade to Jerusalem. Many rulers in the Middle Ages shared this dream, but for Henry, it seemed more real than for most – after all, he had already been to the Holy Land, and he had heard a prophecy that he would die in Jerusalem. Henry was a good all-rounder, which made him a leader that people wanted to follow.

Henry was a widower when he came to the throne. His late wife, Mary de Bohun, had had two daughters and five sons. Four of the boys survived infancy, so he had plenty of heirs already waiting to take over when he died. In fact, Henry had no difficulty producing children. He also had several off-spring from his second wife, Joan of Navarre.

As you would expect from his character, Henry's rule was stronger and more decisive than that of Richard II. But his reign was dogged by the fact that others had a better claim to the throne, and Henry had to deal with various rebellions and uprisings.

Grabbing the throne

In 1399, Henry Bolingbroke was a man with a grievance. His cousin, King Richard II, had banished him and prevented him from taking up his rightful inheritance and becoming Duke of Lancaster. This title went with big estates, so it meant riches as well as status, but with the lands in royal hands, Henry could access none of what was rightly his.

So in 1399, Henry crossed the Channel to sort out his inheritance. He did not plan to make a bid for the crown. After all, his cousin Richard was on the throne. Richard had no children, but if he died, another cousin, the Earl of March, had a better claim to the throne than Henry.

But when he arrived in England, Henry realised that he had overwhelming support for his cause. The people, especially the members of Parliament, were fed up with Richard II's capricious rule and wanted him out. Suddenly, Henry looked like an attractive replacement.

Soon the unfortunate Richard was imprisoned and persuaded to give up the throne. Henry stepped into his shoes, Parliament declared its approval, and just two months after Richard's imprisonment, the new king was crowned. England seemed pleased with its decisive new king.

Making Henry's case

Henry knew he was on dodgy ground. He had grabbed the throne, but there were other potential claimants and he had to have a good legal case up his sleeve to justify the path he had taken. Henry made his case in several ways:

- ✔ He stressed that he was a blood relation of Henry III, thereby tracing his line back to the early Plantagenets and, through them, to the Normans.
- ✔ He argued that royal rule in England was breaking down under Richard II – something had to be done.
- ✔ He claimed that God was on his side and had sent him to sort out the kingdom.

A good effort. But it didn't alter the fact that the Earl of March had a better claim to the crown than Henry. There was going to be trouble ahead.

A raft of risings

Several people challenged Henry's claim to the throne and took up arms to make their point. The trouble began a mere three months after the king's coronation:

- ✔ **The old king's men:** In January 1400, a bunch of Richard II's old courtiers rebelled against Henry. The king quickly put down the revolt, and soon after the imprisoned Richard died under suspicious circumstances.
- ✔ **The Welsh:** In September of the same year, an uprising occurred in Wales. Welsh leader Owain Glyndwr (see Chapter 21) started the movement, which was so successful that English forces were pushed back to the borders; fighting went on for nine years.

- **Harry Hotspur:** Sir Henry Percy, known as Hotspur, was the son of the Earl of Northumberland, originally one of Henry's allies. In 1403, Hotspur upheld the Earl of March's claim to the throne; Henry defeated him at the Battle of Shrewsbury.

- **Northumberland:** In 1405, the Earl of Northumberland himself rebelled, this time in alliance with Glyndwr and, of all people, the archbishop of York Richard Scrope, the second most powerful churchman in the land. Defeated by Henry, the earl fled to Scotland. Scrope was captured and executed in 1407.

- **Northumberland – again:** In 1408, the Earl of Northumberland returned to launch yet another rebellion, but this time Henry defeated him, and the earl was killed in the battle – an end to the pesky Percy problem.

Henry needed all his skills in warfare and decision-making to cope with this lot. And to make matters worse, he had another problem. England's old enemies, the French, muscled in on the act, too. They made more trouble for Henry by supporting Glyndwr, attacking English lands in France, and launching raids on English coastal towns, such as Plymouth and Dartmouth.

The taxes to support Henry's wars against his rivals stretched Parliament to the limit. In 1404, at the height of the fighting, Parliament demanded the appointment of special treasurers who oversaw expenditure on the war. Parliament put the brakes on Henry's household spending, too, sharply cutting the accounts for the *great wardrobe,* which supplied robes and clothes for the king, court, officers, and so on, and the *chamber,* which kept funds for the king's personal use.

It was only because Henry was so forceful – and well backed up by powerful allies in the nobility – that he was able to carry on with his expensive wars – and also perhaps because, unlike Richard II, he was a good politician who knew how to negotiate with Parliament.

The ailing king

In 1406, after nearly seven years of dynamic, hands-on kingship, Henry IV got sick. Because medical diagnosis wasn't exactly very sophisticated in the 15th century, no one knows for sure what the trouble was. Some said that Henry had been struck down by leprosy and that the disease was God's punishment for the execution of the rebellious Archbishop Scrope. But modern historians think leprosy was unlikely.

The most likely theory is that Henry had a number of strokes and that these left him incapacitated. Whatever the trouble was, it meant that the king had to take a back seat. For such a dynamic king, this step back must have gone against the grain.

The rule of the Council

With the king unwell, the Council took over the day-to-day government. To begin with, the king's main adviser, Thomas Arundel, the archbishop of Canterbury, dominated the Council. Arundel was a powerful figure, the third son of an earl who had been made Bishop of Ely at age 21, and by his early 40s, he had the top job in the English church.

Arundel made it his priority to sort out the royal finances. The fact that the royal wars were petering out made this task easier as there was less of a drain on the treasury. And the French were making less trouble in the Channel, so trade picked up, too. Things were looking rosy, except for one thing: Prince Henry, heir to the throne, was flexing his muscles. He wanted more influence in government.

Court in a struggle

Prince Henry was in his early 20s and keen to take a bigger part in the affairs of the realm. He had some powerful allies in the Beaufort family. The most powerful was Henry Beaufort, another formidable churchman, who was Bishop of Winchester and had been Henry IV's Chancellor.

With the Beauforts on his side, Henry wrested power from Arundel and ran the Council from 1409 to 1411. Young Henry, who already had his own household as Prince of Wales, took on more of the trappings of power, creating what amounted to a royal court to rival his father's. Ailing Henry IV was under threat from his nearest and dearest.

Tired and ill, Henry decided to rope in his younger son, Thomas, Duke of Clarence, as a counterweight to Prince Henry. The two factions clashed over English policy in France. This issue was important because a civil war was raging across the Channel between the French royal family and the Duke of Burgundy. The two English factions had opposing views on this policy:

- ✔ **View No. 1 – Batter the Burgundians:** Thomas, working with the king's trusted servant Arundel, thought England's best chance of success in France was to make an alliance with the French king, who would be likely to let England keep its interests in the South of France. But this move would mean sacrificing any English claim to lands in Normandy.

- ✔ **View No. 2 – Fight France:** Prince Henry could not stomach giving up the English claims in northern France. He wanted to join up with the Duke of Burgundy, sworn enemy of the French king, and recover England's old lands in Normandy – which would mean fighting the French.

Arundel and Thomas won the argument initially, but in 1413, the sick king finally gave up the ghost. Henry IV had pinned his hopes on the old prophecy that he would die in Jerusalem, on Crusade. He longed to get back to fighting strength. But the king passed away in his palace, ironically in a room called the Jerusalem Chamber. Now Prince Henry would be able to get his way at last.

Superking: Henry V

Henry V was well schooled for the role of soldier-king. By the age of ten, he could ride and use both bow and sword. He could also swim and was a keen huntsman. He looked the part, too. Chroniclers described him as handsome, and he was tall, slim, with a long neck, and a lean face. He gave the impression of a rather solemn, withdrawn character – some people even thought he was like a priest – but under the austere exterior was a man who used his intelligence to act decisively.

Henry was both a generous and loyal friend. Occasionally, his loyalty went slightly too far – when a young man, Henry struck the Lord Chief Justice in the face because the judge had been unfair to one of his servants. Henry was a good man to have on your side.

As a young man, Prince Henry was restless. Shakespeare, in his plays, portrayed him as a madcap teenager, always getting into scrapes and getting drunk with dissolute friends. Not a lot of evidence supports this view of Henry. He was restless in a different way, itching to pick up the reins of power while his father, Henry IV, lay ill in bed.

With old Henry's death, the prince had his chance, and he did not hang around. The young king was soon on campaign across the Channel, beating the stuffing out of France. He seemed even more than his father the true man of action, the ruler who got what he wanted by military force.

In a few years, Henry V had the prize within his reach. He negotiated a deal with the French whereby he would marry a French princess and become heir to the throne of France. Alas for Henry, he was to die before he could take up his inheritance.

Agincourt and all that

Even before he became king, Henry wanted to lead a military campaign in France. There was a civil war on there between the French royal family and the Duke of Burgundy over who should rule France. Henry figured that it would be a good time to move in on the action and resume the long conflict between England and her cross-Channel neighbour. With the French already fighting Burgundy, Henry thought they'd be sitting ducks against an English assault. At worst, England could make territorial gains in France. At best, Henry could even fight his way on to the French throne himself.

Prelude to war

The young king was a gifted leader who could inspire people to join him. Henry managed to persuade nearly all the English nobles to join him on his campaign in France. In fact, out of 17 senior English nobles, only three did not go with Henry to France. (Two of these were children, and one was blind.)

Before fighting, Henry made a show of negotiating with the French. But the demands the English king made were vast. Henry wanted:

- The whole of the old Angevin empire, as ruled by Henry II.
- The ransom money that should have been paid for King John.
- The hand in marriage of the French's king's daughter.
- A dowry of two million crowns.
- The throne of France.

Clearly, no French king would agree to this lot, so, as Henry well knew, the stage was set for war. He assembled an army and in August 1415 – shortly after Henry put down an abortive rebellion ordered by the family of the Earl of March, who had a claim to his throne – the force set sail for France.

Henry's triumph

Landing in France in mid-August 1415, Henry swiftly laid siege to the strategic town of Harfleur. The English had to sit it out for several weeks, but eventually one of Henry's commanders, the Earl of Huntingdon, got control of part of the fortifications, Henry stormed the town, and the defenders handed over the keys to the town gates.

Henry now held a key town in Normandy, and on 8 October, he led his army on a triumphal march through Normandy toward Calais, which was still in English hands. By 25 October, Henry's forces had reached Agincourt, some 20 miles south of Calais, and the French, following the English as fast as they could, had caught them up. The Battle of Agincourt proved to be a decisive victory for the English.

The Battle of Agincourt was essentially a clash between around 9,000 English, mostly foot soldiers and archers, and a larger French force, mostly made up of cavalry. The key to Henry's success was his bowmen. Using a longbow, an archer can shoot several arrows a minute, and the English rained a continuous shower of deadly arrows on their enemy, felling knights and crippling their horses. The exact figures aren't known, but probably around 6,000 Frenchmen lost their lives, whereas England had only 400 casualties.

When Henry returned to England after the battle, a huge reception was organised, with a pageant in London as a tribute to the king. In the course of the pageant, Henry was compared to some of the greatest heroes from the Bible. Here are some of the key features of the celebration:

✔ Tall towers set up and decorated with the coat of arms of the city of London.

✔ A conduit that gushed wine instead of water.

✔ A performance of the biblical battle between the hero David and Goliath.

✔ Another performance designed to compare the king to the biblical patriarch Abraham.

✔ Figures representing the 12 Apostles and past English kings, all of whom gave their blessing on Henry's achievement.

A victory on the scale of Agincourt was overwhelming. The French ducked out of any more confrontations with Henry. But Henry took the war to the French, landing a large invasion force in 1417 and working his way around northern France. By 1419, when the major city of Rouen surrendered to English forces, Henry had Normandy under his control and was ready to make a peace settlement.

The result of Henry's negotiations was the 1420 Treaty of Troyes, which had these key provisions:

✔ Henry was given the hand in marriage of Catherine, the daughter of Charles VI, king of France.

✔ The English king was recognised as Regent of France, in effect ruling on behalf of his father-in-law.

✔ On the death of Charles, Henry would become king.

Incredibly, after a short military campaign, Henry was within a whisker of achieving the main goal of his demands of 1415. It had seemed outrageous then, but now Henry was almost there.

A big mistake: Dying young

Henry and France agreed on the Treaty of Troyes on 21 May 1420. Because one of its provisions could be fulfilled immediately, Henry didn't hang around. At Troyes Cathedral on 2 June, Henry and Princess Catherine were married. Before the end of the following year, they had a baby son and heir, another Henry. The future looked good.

But there were complications in France. In spite of the Treaty of Troyes, the French king's son, the Dauphin, was still putting up resistance against the English. Henry had left his brother, Thomas, Duke of Clarence, in charge of the English forces in France while he brought Catherine back to England to be crowned queen. Soon after the coronation in Westminster Abbey, Henry heard that his brother had been killed in a battle at Beaugé, near the River Loire in France. It turned out that Thomas had rashly begun to fight without waiting for his archers to arrive at the battlefield. Henry realised that he had to return to France to fight again.

Having gathered reinforcements, the king sailed to France and marched south. The Dauphin would not be drawn into pitched battle again. Henry was known as a fearsome opponent – and he had plenty of archers at his side. Without the prospect of a pitched battle, Henry settled for besieging a city that was in French hands in the hope of gaining territory. So he surrounded the town of Meaux, which surrendered in May 1421.

Henry stayed in France campaigning through the winter of 1421–22, but dysentery swept through the English forces, and the king fell victim. Ever a fighter, he spent the first half of 1422 trying to recover, but finally died on the last day of August at Vincennes near Paris. He was in his mid-30s.

If Henry had lived, he would probably have had further successes in France. A decisive battle would have brought the Dauphin to his knees and made the provisions of the Treaty of Troyes truly achievable. And the French king Charles VI himself died in October 1422, so the Englishman would have been able to claim his French crown. Instead, his baby son became king of England alone.

Musical Thrones: Henry VI and a Pair of Edwards

The years between 1422 and 1483 were some of the most fraught in the whole history of the English monarchy. They began with the accession of Henry VI, who was a nine-month-old baby and the only son of Henry V and his queen, Catherine of France. With an infant on the throne, the real power was in the hands of a Council of nobles, but when Henry eventually took power himself, he proved to be a poor leader who let faction flourish at his court.

The result was a series of squabbles between the nobles of England over who should rule, with the crown changing hands several times. To avoid confusion, here's a rundown of who reigned when:

- Henry VI, Lancastrian, 1422–61.
- Edward IV, Yorkist, 1461–1470.
- Henry VI, Lancastrian, restored to the throne, 1470–71.
- Edward IV, Yorkist, restored to the throne, 1471–83.
- Edward V, Yorkist, April–June 1483.

With monarchs jumping on and off the throne, there wasn't much stability, and for a lot of the time, the real power lay not with the king at all, but with the aristocracy.

Protection racket

When little Henry VI took the throne in 1422, a Council of nobles was established to govern on his behalf. The key person on this Council was Humphrey, Duke of Gloucester, who was the brother of Henry V and thus the young king Henry VI's uncle. Humphrey took the title of Protector of the Realm and became the most powerful man in England. Almost as important was John, Duke of Bedford, another of the king's uncles, who was made Regent of France. A third key member of the Council was Henry Beaufort, Bishop of Winchester.

The Council had quite a heavy agenda and didn't always see eye to eye on how to achieve their goals. Amongst other things, its members had to:

✔ Carry on fighting the war with France, which had been going on since 1337.

✔ Try to balance royal accounts at home.

✔ Maintain law and order in England.

✔ Secure England's border with Scotland.

✔ Not squabble between themselves so badly that the other aims would not be attainable.

Henry on the throne

On the whole, the Council that ruled on behalf of the young Henry VI did not do too badly, and when Henry assumed power in 1437 at age 16, the royal finances were in better shape than under Henry V, and England itself was peaceful, even if war still raged on in France.

But there was a problem. Henry himself seemed temperamentally unfit to rule. He was a complex character, and he certainly had his good side. But he did not work out very well at all as a king. Henry VI, unfortunately, had two sides to his personality:

✔ **Good points:** Henry was a model medieval man in one way – he was very religious. But his piety has been exaggerated because one contemporary account emphasised this quality in an attempt to portray the king as a saint. Henry was also a notable patron of education, founding both Eton and King's College, Cambridge. And he was loyal to his friends, although sometimes stubbornly so.

✔ **Weak points:** Henry didn't want to be a great war leader like his father, Henry V – a drawback in the Middle Ages when kings were expected to be soldiers. He wasn't much good at government – he was a weak, feeble character who nobles were soon wrapping around their little fingers. He vacillated and changed his mind a lot. He would pardon wrongdoers and dole out gifts at the drop of a hat and seems to have left a lot of the decision-making of government to his advisers.

Henry VI simply did not have the kingly ability of his predecessors, and his indecisiveness created just the kind of atmosphere into which power-hungry nobles could sink their teeth. And things got even worse when, in 1453–4, the king seems to have had some sort of mental breakdown. He could hardly move and became completely withdrawn, incapable even of the indecisive rule he'd managed to date. After hanging around for a few months hoping he'd get better, the Council appointed the king's cousin, Richard, Duke of York, as a new Protector of the Realm.

Richard was well connected and ambitious enough to have an eye on the throne himself. When Henry recovered and Richard lost his job as Protector, a power struggle developed. On one side were the followers of Richard (the Yorkists), many of whom hoped to put Richard on the throne in place of Henry. Opposing them were the men closest to the king, such as the Duke of Somerset and the Earl of Northumberland, men who wanted to keep the house of Lancaster on the throne.

These two sides came to blows at St Albans in 1455. The Yorkists killed both Somerset and Northumberland, and the long struggle between the House of York (symbol, the white rose) and the House of Lancaster (red rose) was on. The Wars of the Roses had begun.

The Wars of the Roses

The Wars of the Roses, between the rival royal houses of Lancaster and York, went on for 30 years, from 1455 to 1485. Like any wars, the Wars of the Roses caused a lot of pain and destabilised England. Here's a blow-by-blow account of the main stages:

✔ **1455, First Battle of St Albans:** Richard, Duke of York, seizes control of the government.

✔ **1459:** Parliament declares that Richard, Duke of York, is a traitor.

✔ **1460, Battle of Northampton:** Richard Neville, Earl of Warwick, defeats the Lancastrians; Henry VI is taken prisoner, but Queen Margaret (see Chapter 22) escapes to Scotland.

✔ **1460, Battle of Wakefield:** Margaret scores a victory for the Lancastrians; Richard of York is killed.

- ✔ **1461, Battle of Towton:** Warwick defeats Margaret, and Edward IV is declared king; Margaret rescues Henry and retreats to Scotland.

- ✔ **1464, Battle of Hexham:** Henry VI is captured.

- ✔ **1469, Battle of Edgecote:** Warwick turns on Edward IV and defeats him.

- ✔ **1470:** With Warwick on his side, Henry VI returns to the throne.

- ✔ **1471, Battle of Barnet:** Edward defeats Warwick, who is killed; Henry VI is murdered; and Edward resumes power.

- ✔ **1485, Battle of Bosworth:** Edward IV's brother, Richard III, is now on the throne, but he's defeated by the Lancastrian heir, Henry Tudor, bringing the Wars of the Roses to an end.

Complicated, huh? And that's just the major turning points. No wonder the monarchy was destabilised with all this to-ing and fro-ing.

Things were not quite as bad as they sound because, as with most medieval wars, the fighting in the Wars of the Roses was not continuous. And most English people were not involved in the fighting – the battles, for the most part, involved nobles, their retainers, and mercenaries. Ordinary people could go for years without seeing a sword drawn.

But the monarchy was in a mess, and in this state of affairs, who held the real power? Well, two people stand out as playing decisive parts in these events: Richard, Earl of Warwick, and Henry VI's queen, Margaret.

The She-wolf of France

Henry VI married French princess Margaret of Anjou in 1444. The wedding was part of a peace deal between England and France and so was like most medieval royal matches – a diplomatic marriage. Mild-mannered, indecisive Henry probably didn't realise what he was taking on. Margaret was a handful, and chroniclers referred to her as the She-wolf of France.

Actually, the chroniclers were probably exaggerating. They were writing history from a Yorkist point of view and wanted to find ways of attacking Henry and his family. The queen may not have been as bad as they say, but she was certainly formidable, and when the king had his breakdown in 1453–4, Margaret became a rallying point for the supporters of the Lancastrian cause.

In the 1460s, Margaret fought for the Lancastrian cause from bases in Scotland and northern England. She scored a notable victory at Wakefield where she led the army she had raised in the North against Richard of York, who met his death in the struggle.

In an era when women were usually expected to stay at home, Margaret was remarkable. Women did sometimes get involved in warfare in the Middle Ages – records recount women defending castles under siege when their husbands had fallen in battle, for example. But it was very rare indeed for a woman to lead an army on to the field of conflict.

The kings and the king-maker

The other leader who had a huge influence on the Wars of the Roses was Richard, Earl of Warwick. Warwick was a great soldier who played a major role in the warfare and politics of the Wars of the Roses. He fought bravely at the first Battle of St Albans and became a hero among the English when he defeated a fleet of Spanish ships off Calais in 1458.

In 1461, Warwick was instrumental in getting Edward IV declared king after the Battle of Towton. Nine years later, in 1470, he was the leader of the coup that put Henry VI briefly back on the throne.

These manoeuvres later gave Warwick his famous nickname, King-maker. The person who can put a king on the throne is almost as powerful as the king himself, and Warwick's power didn't stop there. During Henry VI's brief second rule in 1470–1, Warwick ruled on behalf of the king, who sat on the throne weak and bewildered while the power politics went on around him. His power only ended when he was killed by Edward IV at the Battle of Barnet in 1471.

Marrying a commoner: Edward IV

Edward IV came to the throne at age 19, and in the early part of his reign, much of the power was held by his backer and cousin, Richard, Earl of Warwick, the king-maker. But as he grew to maturity and took on the tasks of government, Edward, a tall, rather handsome young man, showed himself to be a hard worker who wrestled with the royal finances and tried to improve the justice system.

Edward was a conscientious monarch who realised the importance of those in society who produced the wealth – the peasants and merchants. He helped the peasants by introducing a new court, the Court of Requests, where peasants could bring problems with their landlords. He also encouraged a boom in trade, which pleased the merchants.

This trade boom was partly the result of improvements in continental Europe. It was also helped because Edward stamped down on piracy, making sea trade safer. And he gave the capital's merchants more power by allowing them to take part in the election of the mayor of London. The merchants were happy, and all the more so as exports rose steadily during Edward's reign.

But things were not so straightforward in Edward's relations with the aristocracy. At the beginning of his reign, the young king relied heavily on the Earl of Warwick as his chief adviser.

Warwick was now more than a royal counsellor – he was a serious power behind the throne. Having used his power to get Edward on the throne in the first place, Warwick now used his role as elder statesman to negotiate a new alliance with France, and in 1464, the talks had reached a turning point. The French king wanted Edward to marry his wife's sister, Bona of Savoy.

When Warwick told his king about the proposal, Edward took the wind out of his sails. The king announced that he was already married. He had secretly married Elizabeth Woodville, the widow of Lancastrian supporter Sir John Grey.

Elizabeth, still in her 20s when her first husband was killed, was one of the beauties of the English court. But although she was the daughter of a lord, she was not a member of the higher ranks of the aristocracy, and the wedding was a surprise to most English nobles, who would have expected Edward to marry a foreign princess, just as Warwick had planned. But Elizabeth seems to have captured the king's heart.

The couple were happy and had ten children, but politically the marriage led to a break between the king and his adviser Warwick, who was seriously miffed that his plans for the proposed diplomatic marriage with Bona of Savoy were to come to nought. The resulting row turned Warwick against the king. The earl led and promoted a series of rebellions that resulted in the former king, Henry VI, being brought briefly back to the throne in 1470–1, before Edward himself was restored to the throne, and Warwick was defeated. A royal marriage can have explosive consequences, as later rulers were to find out.

Once Edward was back on the throne in 1471, he was able to rule competently and relatively peacefully. He worked hard as a ruler, and England's prosperity continued. The king also had a reputation for enjoying himself – or for living a life of debauchery, as some churchmen put it. He certainly found time to father at least four illegitimate children by several different mothers.

Then, in 1483, Edward had a sudden stroke and died. Some of the churchmen who had criticised his love of loose living said it was a punishment for his conduct, but it was more likely to have been the result of hard work. As so often in the past, a young boy was left to claim the crown. This time, it was the king's son, Edward, who was just 12 years old.

Scandal! The princes in the Tower

Edward IV's eldest son Edward became king in April 1483. Not much is known about the 12-year-old Edward. He seems to have lived happily away from the royal court with his mother's family in Ludlow Castle, Shropshire. Here he was given a good education and was said to have been a good student. The old king had instructed that his brother, Richard, Duke of Gloucester, should act as Protector if young Edward had to become king before he came of age. Richard rushed to the new king's side, but just before the coronation, a bombshell was dropped: Edward was said to be illegitimate.

But Edward IV and his queen Elizabeth Woodville were married when the prince was born. What was the problem? The reasoning went like this: When Edward IV secretly married Elizabeth Woodville, he was actually officially betrothed to another woman, Lady Eleanor Butler. This betrothal amounted to a commitment that made Edward and Elizabeth's marriage void, so any children born to Elizabeth were illegitimate.

So who *was* the rightful heir to the throne? It will come as no surprise that the young king's opponents had that one worked out. They argued that the rightful king was the old king's brother, Richard, Duke of Gloucester. Richard, who in any case held most of the power, should get the real prize and be king in his own right.

It was a debatable point. The old king and queen had been married, after all. But Richard was ruthless and saw that if he moved quickly, he might be able to grab the crown for himself. Once he arrived in London for his coronation, the young king Edward V was bundled off to the Tower of London and kept securely there. His younger brother Richard was sent to the Tower as well, just to make sure that he wouldn't press his claim to the throne if anything untoward happened to Edward.

The two boys, who have gone down in history as the princes in the Tower, never left the Tower of London. They were seen in the summer of 1483, but after that, they vanished for good. In the 17th century, a pair of skeletons, thought to be of two boys, were unearthed in the Tower. No one knows whether these bones were the princes, but it is possible. The rumour was that Richard of Gloucester had had them killed, but no one knows for sure.

What is sure is this: Edward V's brief, uncrowned reign lasted only from 9 April to 25 June 1483. That June, Parliament declared Edward to be illegitimate, and Richard of Gloucester became king the next day after one of the shortest reigns in British history.

Much Maligned: Richard III

Richard III came to the throne in 1483 after the mysterious disappearance, and possibly murder, of Edward V. Although he reigned for only two years, Richard has left a big mark on English history – a big black mark as the most maligned of English monarchs.

Many people know about Richard III because of the drama by Shakespeare in which he plays the leading role. The Bard portrays Richard as a scheming, murderous hunchback. But was he really that evil?

Crook or crookback?

Crookback was the Tudor nickname for Richard III. The writers of the Tudor period described him as a hideous, deformed character, whose morality was as twisted as his body and who murdered rivals to the throne. But the fact is that the Tudors had it in for Richard. They wanted to destroy his reputation because he was an enemy of the Tudors. The reality was probably rather different. No hard-and-fast evidence supports the theory that Edward V was murdered. It also seems unlikely that Richard was even a hunchback – contemporaries commented on his good looks, though he seems to have been shorter and slighter than many of his ancestors.

Perhaps to distract people from his small stature, Richard became well known for his fine clothes. He was certainly well-dressed at his coronation. For this occasion, Richard wore

- A doublet of blue cloth-of-gold decorated with nets and pineapples.
- A gown of purple velvet and ermine adorned with 3,300 thin strips of lamb's fleece.
- Later in the day, a long gown of purple cloth-of-gold lined with white damask.

So Richard made a kingly impression. The quality went deeper than his clothes, too, because Richard did have some good character traits. When his brother, Edward IV, was on the throne, he was unflinchingly loyal to him. He was also valiant in battle, proving his bravery when he fought on the Yorkist side in battles such as Tewkesbury. Richard had other good personal qualities. He was brave, seems to have had a genuine Christian piety, and, with his queen, Anne, was interested in education and funded colleges at Cambridge.

So what went wrong? Well, some English nobles weren't happy when Richard seized the crown. In 1483, shortly after he was crowned, a rebellion was launched. Unlike in previous reigns, the rebels were not supporters of a rival dynasty; they were Yorkists. In other words, they should have been Richard's natural allies, being people who had supported Edward IV, but they objected to the way Richard grabbed power.

One of the leaders of the rebellion was Henry, Duke of Buckingham, one of the most prominent Yorkist nobles. Another was Henry Tudor, the son of a Welsh gentleman, but with enough royal blood in his veins to be a potential claimant to the throne. These men posed a serious threat to Richard.

The rebellion was a flop. Buckingham was captured, and Henry, who was arriving with a small fleet from France, was the victim of gales – only a couple of his ships actually landed in England. Most of the other rebels scattered, and Henry fled back to France. Richard had triumphed, and he hadn't even needed to fight very hard.

But the threat from Henry Tudor was a chink in Richard's armour. The Welshman was still at large. Richard punished many of the other rebels by taking away their lands. But this move left them disaffected and ready to rebel once more. Many people, especially in the south of England, waited eagerly for Henry Tudor to return.

My kingdom for a horse!

In August 1485, little more than two years after Richard had become king, Henry Tudor, the Welsh challenger for the throne, returned. Richard was astute enough to know that Henry would mount another challenge to his rule, and he was prepared with an army to meet the Welshman.

Henry landed at Milford Haven in South Wales. He had military backing from the French and, as he marched through England, it became clear that he had a formidable force of around 8,000 men. But Richard still had a good chance. He had gathered together an army of 12,000.

The two armies met at Bosworth in Leicestershire. Richard thought that if he sent Henry packing, this threat to his power would end. It didn't work out like that. A number of the king's key supporters went over to Henry's side or did not turn up to fight. In spite of this disappointment, Richard launched a brave, or perhaps foolhardy, attack against Henry. Richard fought bravely. In Shakespeare's account of the battle, Richard loses his horse, utters the despairing cry, 'My kingdom for a horse!' and fights Henry in single combat. In reality, Richard, desperately slashing his way through the battle, did not quite reach Henry before an opponent cut him down. The crown was left for Henry Tudor to claim, and the power of the Yorkist dynasty was brought to an end.

Part IV
The Kings of Scotland

In this part . . .

Scotland had its own royal family separate from England from the earliest times until the Scottish king James VI also become king of England (as James I) in 1603. During the Middle Ages, many of these rulers came from two or three dominant families – the Bruces, the Balliols, and, most long-lasting of all, the Stewarts. These ruling families faced similar challenges to their counterparts down south. They had to fight to keep their kingdom united – and they often had to fight the English to stop them invading their country. Because England was an enemy for much of the time, the Scottish kings formed alliances with countries in mainland Europe, especially France.

Chapter 10

Picts, Scots, and Others

. . . .

. . . .

*T*he early chroniclers describe Scotland as the home to a number of different tribes or peoples. They all had their own monarchs, who frequently fought each other to gain extra territory. This murky story of Scotland's early days is difficult to understand because few written sources exist and the records contain big gaps. Historians aren't even sure of the exact origins of some of the people involved.

The main players in the early history of Scotland are two peoples, the Picts, who seem to have occupied a large chunk of mainland Scotland, and the Scots, who came originally from Ireland and lived in a kingdom called Dalriada, in the west of Scotland and the Western Isles.

Both these groups were in turn made up of several smaller tribes. Each of these small, close-knit groups had its own ruler, who would owe allegiance to the overking of the Picts or Scots, so from the fifth to ninth centuries many kings ruled Scotland at once, and in many cases, historians don't know much about them.

From time to time, these diverse tribes were united under a single, dynamic leader who claimed to be king of the whole of Scotland. None of these periods of unity lasted for long until the mid-ninth century, when the Scots king Kenneth MacAlpin overcame the Picts and united the country for good.

Celtic Confusion

Picts from Scotland, Scots from Ireland, and shadowy war leaders with names like Gabran and Loarn – the early story of Scotland is a confusion of Celtic names about which historians know frustratingly little. But as time goes by, historians started to get a sense of what the Scots and Picts were like – both from their artistic remains that still lie scattered around Scotland, and from the surviving records of their rulers' activities, especially their battles.

Things start to become a little clearer during the period when the Romans ruled much of Britain. The broad picture is that the far west of the country was occupied by the Scots; the Picts occupied much of the north and east; the southwest was home to the kingdom of Strathclyde, home to Welsh-speaking Britons; and the southeast was settled by Angles from Northumbria. In addition, the far northeastern tip of Scotland, plus Shetland and Orkney, were home to Norsemen who had originally come on raiding expeditions but later made permanent settlements.

Strange but true: Scots from Ireland

Today people are used to thinking of Scots as people from Scotland. But back in the early centuries A.D., things weren't quite so simple. The Scots, believe it or not, originally came from Ireland (strange, but true). Actually, it's not quite so strange if you look at a map. The northeasternmost point on the island of Ireland is actually only about 16 miles across the sea from the Mull of Kintyre in far western Scotland, so anyone who wanted to make the crossing didn't have too far to go.

The first Scots to make that trip across the sea were probably raiders who travelled in search of plunder in the third century. By the fifth century, they were settling down in Scotland – initially in the western isles and the western highland region now known as Argyll. Around a hundred years after this settlement, they had formed a kingdom on this western region, and this kingdom was called Dalriada.

The people of Dalriada were not originally one coherent group, but a confederation of tribes. The key ones were

- The people of Óengus, who settled on the isle of Islay.
- The people of Loarn, who occupied Colonsay and Lorne.
- The people of Gabran, who were spread across Kintyre other parts of the mainland, and the islands of Arran and Bute.

The last group, the people of Gabran, were the most widespread, had the largest population, and controlled key areas such as the borders with the area of Strathclyde. As a result, they became the most powerful, and their leaders became overkings of Dalriada in the sixth and seventh centuries before being supplanted by the people of Loarn.

The kings of Gabran

Coming from Ireland, where Christian missionaries had been at work since St Patrick in the fifth century, the people of Dalriada were either Christians when they arrived or converted soon afterwards. A key figure in their history was St Columba (c 521–97). Columba was the son of an Irish royal family who had been driven out of Ireland and found himself among the islands of the Scottish coast.

On the island of Iona, Columba founded a monastery that became the centre of a network of other abbeys in Dalriada. From these monastic houses, monks left to convert the Picts, and missionaries such as St Aidan travelled southwards to convert the people of Northumbria in northern England.

The kings of Dalriada made full use of all the power and potency of the church in the sixth century. Whether they did so out of devout faith or because they realised it could make them look more powerful is not known. But it was certainly effective. In 573, Columba ordained Aedán mac Gabráin as overking of Dalriada, explaining that he was doing so on the instructions of an angel from heaven.

With the angels on his side, Aedán soon showed himself to be a powerful warrior. He set out to conquer the Picts and swept across their territory, reputedly travelling as far as Orkney in his zest for conquest. His men marched far eastwards, too, cutting their way through Pictish lands towards Edinburgh. According to the writer of the poem Berchan's Prophecy, Aedán fought the Picts for 16 years.

But Aedán's success did not last. He conceded several defeats at the very beginning of the seventh century – some in the eastern Scottish region of Angus, some in the south, near the border with the Angles of Northumbria. These defeats show both how far his armies had reached and how hard it was to keep power over such a far-flung area.

Under Aedán's grandson, Domnall Brec (the name means Spotty Donald), the decline continued. After a number of defeats, Domnall was killed in 642 in a battle with the king of Strathclyde. Soon, the leaders of other Scots tribes were challenging the rights of the kings of Gabran to be supreme rulers of Dalriada.

The kings of Loarn

Things weren't easy either for the next ruling dynasty of Dalriada kings, the kings of Loarn. Ferchar Fota ruled Dalriada from the 670s to 697 – although for some of that time, he was king only in name, since he was attacked by the people of Strathclyde and suffered a punishing defeat in 678.

Another king of Loarn, Selbach, was also harried by his neighbours in the 720s. This time it was the Picts who did the damage. And from this time onward, Dalriada was attacked again and again by its increasingly powerful Pictish neighbours. Through the eighth century and into the ninth, the Picts increasingly became the dominant people in Scotland.

The Britons of Strathclyde

Strathclyde was the kingdom based in the Clyde valley and immediately to the south of the major Scottish river, the River Clyde. Its people were Welsh in origin and were known to the Scots as Britons. The Scots later called the region Dumbarton, which means The fort of the Britons and is still the name of a town on the Clyde.

By the sixth century, the kings of Strathclyde were a powerful bunch, and they became a thorn in the side of the rulers of Dalriada, stopping them from expanding southwards into the lush lowlands. The numerous rulers of Strathclyde are known mainly for their military exploits and included:

- **Ywain,** who defeated the Scots ruler Domnall Brec in 642.
- **Elffin,** who helped his allies, the Picts, beat the Northumbrians in 685.
- **Tewdwr,** who fought the Picts in 750.
- **Arthgal,** who was beaten by the Vikings in 871.
- Another **Ywain,** who, allied with the Scots, was beaten by the forces of the English kingdom of Wessex in 934.
- **Owain the Bald,** the last king of Strathclyde, who died in battle in 1018.

The northern Picts

In the first century A.D., the Romans conquered what they called Britannia, or Britain. Britannia was their name for their new British province, but the name concealed a truth that was a pain for the Romans – they never managed to get the whole of the British Isles in their clutches. They certainly managed to dominate England, and they conquered a fair bit of Wales. But the people of the far north resisted Roman rule fiercely.

The Romans saw the inhabitants of Scotland as barbarians. The earliest document referring to the Picts by name is a Roman account of the year 297, and it makes clear that the Romans saw the Picts as war-painted warriors – the name *Pict* means painted. Some sources suggest that they were people who had come originally from mainland Europe, but their origins are shrouded in mystery.

But what historians can say is that in the Roman period, these painted warriors were well established north of the Roman fortification called the Antonine Wall, which in the second century ran across Scotland between the Rivers Forth and Clyde, fencing off the area of lowland (southern) Scotland that the Romans were trying to take over in the reign of the emperor Antoninus Pius (138–61).

Welcome to Pictland

After the Romans left Britain for good in 410, the Picts continued to gain strength. By the sixth century, they occupied the area from the Firth of Forth northwards, only excluding the far northeastern tip of Scotland (which was occupied by Norse peoples) and the far western land of Dalriada (occupied by the Scots). As a result, a vast tract of Scotland was in fact Pictland.

Modern historians can track the Picts by looking for their physical remains – stunning carved stones bearing relief carvings of beautiful abstract patterns and of battle scenes. The Picts can also be tracked by the place names they left behind. Names beginning with the syllable *Pit* belonged originally to Pictish places. Pitlochry, the town to the north east of Perth, is one of the best known, but many other smaller settlements with Pit names are scattered around Scotland showing where the Picts once were.

Pictish peoples

The people labelled Picts were actually members of several smaller tribes or subkingdoms. Historians discovered a little bit about these groups from Roman writers. Some of the tribes they mention are:

- ✔ **The Caledonii:** People who lived in the central Highlands and fought off invasion attempts by the Romans.
- ✔ **The Taexali:** A group who lived in the valley of the Dee, not far from Aberdeen.
- ✔ **The Venicomes:** A tribe who occupied the areas now known as Fife and Strathmore.

By the fourth century, all these people seem to have been thought of as Picts.

Pictish rulers

Long lists of Pictish kings survive, but they are just lists of names – and many of the same names are repeated, so it's even more confusing. The Northumbrian historian Bede, writing in the early eighth century, says that the Pictish rulers handed down their crowns through the maternal line. This succession is very unusual in the male-dominated world of the time – so unusual that some modern writers question whether it was actually the case. Certainly all kinds of cousins seem to have inherited the crown in Pictland –

it wasn't a question of one ruler passing the kingship on to his eldest son, as became the case in later centuries. But historians differ about whether a strict matrilineal system existed. On the one hand, Bede says it did, and some of the monarchs fit the pattern. On the other, some recent historians point out that kings may have been put forward as rulers because of their strength and their ability to rule. No one knows for sure.

Among the dozens of Pictish rulers mentioned in the king-lists, a handful stand out as important personalities about whom historians have been able to find out more. Here is the low-down on some of the better known kings of the Picts:

- **Bridei mac Máelchú (c 555–c 584):** He was around in the middle of the sixth century and defeated the people of Dalriada in battle towards the beginning of this period. He was a pagan king who received the Christian saint Columba, who visited the royal court to ask the king and his people to protect Christian missionaries.

- **Bridei mac Beli (672–693):** This second Bridei fought a war with the Northumbrians, who he eventually defeated.

- **Nechtan mac Derile (706–c 732):** Nechtan had a troubled reign, suffering defeat by the Northumbrians and a civil war amongst his own people. He was forced into 'early retirement' in 724, but returned to fight a number of rival contenders for the Pictish throne. He was finally defeated by Unuist, otherwise known as Óengus, a man from Fortriu, near the border with Dalriada.

- **Unuist mac Uurguist (c 732–61):** Unuist was a formidable war-leader who fought endless battles to broaden his power beyond Pictland. He wielded huge power throughout much of Scotland.

These powerful Picts saw themselves as warrior-leaders. It was their aim to dominate their neighbours by military might or to fight off neighbours who were trying to dominate them. When they defeated one of their neighbours, though, the Picts didn't usually move in as direct rulers. Instead, they forced the defeated ruler to accept the status of subking or installed some friendly relative as subking – and left for home with as much booty as they could carry.

A new kind of king

In the year 789, an event changed the pattern of kingship in Scotland. As usual, it began with a battle. A new challenger to Pictish power appeared from the west. His name was Castantín – or Constantine, as historians call him today – and he probably came originally from Dalriada. What happened in 789 was that he attacked the reigning king of the Picts, Conall, and defeated him in battle. Conall wasn't killed. In fact, he had enough support to carry on ruling, with restricted power, for a few more years. But in 807, he was killed, and Castantín became ruler of the Picts.

Castantín was a new kind of king because he ruled both Dalriada and Pictland directly, without subkings. In other words, Scotland was turning into a united kingdom, and a trend of overall kingship was beginning that would last for hundreds of years.

What was new about Castantín?

Ruling directly without subkings wasn't the only new thing about Castantín's rule. Another unusual thing about the king was his name. Its modern equivalent, Constantine, was the name of one of the most important Roman emperors. The original Roman Constantine was the leader who converted to Christianity. Before Constantine, being a Christian was illegal in the Roman empire – Christians were persecuted, and people were encouraged to worship the old gods of the Classical world or local pagan gods who were similar to the Classical ones. Constantine made Christianity legal. Later, when the Roman empire broke up, its eastern capital city was called Constantinople (it's Istanbul, Turkey, today) after the great Christian ruler. With its fine churches and shrines, Constantinople became the greatest Christian city in the world.

Like the Roman Constantine, Castantín learned to work with the church. He developed the city of St Andrews as both a centre of royal power and a centre of the church. St Andrews is one of Scotland's oldest Christian sites. It is said to have been founded in the fourth century by St Regulus, who was shipwrecked nearby when bringing the remains of St Andrew to Scotland from the Greek island of Patras. He buried the saint's remains there, and a monastery was established. By promoting this ancient Christian site, Castantín was identifying himself closely with the church. This identification was a political benefit, too, because giving himself a power base in St Andrews strengthened his influence in the eastern part of Scotland, helping to cement the unity of his kingdom.

Onward, Christian soldiers

To modern eyes, Castantín looks like a king with a split personality – a Christian who loved the monastery at St Andrews and a powerful warrior leader. But these two sides of his character came together because he fought off attacks from marauding Vikings, who in the early ninth century were focused on plundering the Scottish coast. Several attacks occurred, and on at least three occasions (in 795, 802, and 806), the raiders burned down the monastery of Iona, Scotland's premier religious site. By defending his lands against the Norsemen, Castantín could also claim to be striking blows for Christianity.

In 820, Castantín died, and his crown passed to his brother Óengus, who ruled until 834. Óengus continued his brother's work as a Christian king, founding a new monastery at Dunkeld. He used his Christian connections to send churchmen as ambassadors to Europe, maintaining good relations with the most powerful empire on the mainland, the Frankish realm of the great ruler Charlemagne, who had a great palace at Aachen (near the borders of what are now Germany and Belgium), and whose empire stretched across much of what are now France and Germany.

By the end of Óengus's reign in 834, much of Scotland was united under one ruler. The family of Óengus and Castantín seems to have come from Dalriada, so they were of Scots ancestry. But a large chunk of their kingdom was Pictish, and they seem to have tried to dominate the Picts, not simply by force but also by adopting some of their customs. For example, Castantín's younger son, who followed Óengus to the throne in 834, had a Pictish name, Drest.

Everything seemed set for a united Scotland to continue under this successful ruling family. But in 839, the raiding Vikings returned and slaughtered virtually all the male members of the royal family. As a result, a power vacuum occurred – and into this vacuum stepped a dynamic new leader who was to forge a greater and longer lasting ruling dynasty.

All Together Now

The early ninth-century kings Castantín and Óengus pulled off the achievement of uniting Scotland under their rule (see preceding section). But their dynasty didn't last. It took another ruler, Cináed mac Alpin (now known as Kenneth I), to unite Scotland and keep it united. Kenneth is often known as the first king to rule the whole country, which isn't quite true. But Kenneth is still a very important figure because his family ruled a united Scotland for more than 200 years.

Canny Ken: Keeping Scotland together

Kenneth I came to power in Scotland in around 840. At this time, he still faced a number of challengers for power, members of Castantín's family who probably ruled small territories in Perthshire and Angus. By 848 or 849, these rivals had gone, and Kenneth was virtually undisputed as king of Scotland.

How did Kenneth achieve his rise to power? Well, it probably wasn't as straightforward as it sounds. Scotland had been a collection of separate tribes and mini-states for most of its history, and many areas had more than one claimant to the throne. The biggest split was between the western lands and the northern and eastern territories that had been ruled by the Picts.

War and peace

In the west, Kenneth fell back on the old technique of bringing in a trusted colleague. He invited over a leader from Ireland, one Gofraid mac Fergusa, to western Scotland. Historians don't know a lot about Gofraid, but his name is a mixture of Norse and Celtic elements, so he could have been a compromise leader, able to please both the Scots and the Vikings who were in the habit of attacking Britain's shores at around this time.

Kenneth saved his own energies for eastern Scotland. Between about 842 and 848, he was busy in the east imposing his authority. Historians aren't sure how he ruled. Some people think he was a peaceful ruler who was accepted with little bloodshed. Others portray Kenneth as a war lord. Certainly, the early chroniclers stress his battles and military ruthlessness, so he probably had to conquer his way to power in the east.

Staying safe on the throne

However he achieved his victory, Kenneth was widely accepted as ruler of Scotland by the year 848. Once he was settled on the throne, Kenneth set about making sure of his power using one of the most popular methods open to early rulers – arranging favourable marriages for his children.

Kenneth was blessed with several daughters. Early medieval kings sometimes looked down on their womenfolk because girls weren't usually thought to have the right stuff to be rulers – for that, you had to be a macho warlord. But princesses were useful to early kings in another way. They could get married to your neighbours to create useful political alliances.

Canny Kenneth married his daughters to a bunch of influential rulers, including:

- **Rhun,** son of the king of Strathclyde.
- **Óláfr Hvitr,** king of Dublin and one of Ireland's Norse rulers.
- **Áed Findliath,** another ruler in Ireland.

Alliances with this lot must have bought Kenneth a great deal of security. Ireland would launch fewer attacks, and less trouble should occur in western Scotland, as a result.

But Kenneth's army was still busy making war with enemies who threatened to give him a pounding on several fronts at once. Kenneth's challenges included:

- Fighting off Viking raiders who were still turning up on Scotland's coast and making off with booty from villages and monasteries.
- Repelling challenges to his kingship from rebels who ignored his careful alliance-making in Strathclyde.
- Taking part in a series of battles against the Northumbrians in an attempt to extend his rule southwards.

All together, it sounds as if Kenneth had a busy time making war, and when he died in 858, he was probably still fighting to keep his kingdom secure. He had made important gestures of peace, such as the marriage alliances and building a new church at Dunkeld where St Columba's relics were housed. But his reign was mostly one of war.

Sons, brothers, nephews

After the death of Kenneth, the throne of Scotland passed through the ruling family, not generally from father to son as became the tradition later, but via other routes – for example, uncle to nephew, or brother to brother. Most of the late ninth century kings who inherited the throne in this way had quite short reigns, and their lives were dominated by family squabbles and war with the Vikings. In fact, sometimes these activities were linked because the Viking and Scottish royal families intermarried. The five rulers who followed Kenneth were:

- ✔ **Donald I (858–62):** Famous as a war leader, Donald continued the work of his brother, King Kenneth. He introduced a famous law code, confirming his authority as ruler of Scotland.

- ✔ **Constantine I (862–77):** Constantine was Donald's nephew. He fought off Norse attacks before making peace with the Norse king of Dublin. When a new king came to the throne in Ireland, the raids began again, and Constantine died fighting the Vikings.

- ✔ **Áed (877–8):** Constantine's younger brother, he was killed in battle by his rival Giric.

- ✔ **Giric (879–89):** The son of Donald II, Giric's position was insecure because he had taken the throne by violence from Áed.

- ✔ **Donald II (889–900):** This son of Constantine defeated Giric and spent the next few years in further battles against the Vikings.

King of Alba: Constantine II

After a succession of short-lived and briefly reigning kings, the next ruler, Constantine II, was a different proposition. He ruled from 900 to 943, long enough to set his own stamp on the kingdom. He was the cousin of the previous king, Donald II, and was known as a strong warrior lord.

In some ways, though, it was more of the same for Constantine. The Vikings were still raiding and posing a threat to security in Britain both north and south of the border. And by now, the Vikings had a strong foothold in Britain. They had settled in the area around York, and, although most of them just wanted to put down roots and live in peace, Viking York, or Jorvik as it was known then, was a potential base for any Norse leader who had ambitions to extend his power in England or Scotland.

That's what happened in 910, when a new batch of Vikings arrived, and their leader took over York. This ambitious Viking was called Ragnall, and his people were soon settling in eastern Northumbria. To Constantine, they looked like a dangerous threat both to his own power and to his own ambitions to take over

Northumbria. In 918, the Scots and Norse armies finally clashed at Corbridge, a town on the Tyne, on Hadrian's Wall, the old Roman wall that divided England and Scotland.

Constantine was the victor and took northern Northumbria under his rule. Ragnall made peace with Constantine so that the two communities could trade with each other and protect themselves from yet another potential aggressor, the up-and-coming power of the southern English kingdom of Wessex. In the following years, Constantine ironically found himself actually supporting the Vikings in York because they could shield him from potential attacks from Wessex.

In 937, the men of Wessex moved northwards, and the showdown came at the Battle of Brunanburh, an unknown site. The famous warrior Constantine was overwhelmed. The Scots were pushed back northwards, and the advance of Wessex as the most powerful of the English kingdoms was confirmed. (For more about Wessex, see Chapter 4.)

Constantine was a spent force after this defeat. A few years later, in 943, he gave up his throne. He went off to one of Scotland's most important monasteries and became a monk, leaving the complex and violent business of ruling Scotland to his heirs.

The kingdom of Constantine was, like that of his predecessors, a realm that embraced the whole of Scotland. But Constantine was a powerful enough character to stamp it with a new name – a new brand, almost. Instead of being known as the kingdom of the Picts and Scots, Constantine called it the Kingdom of Alba, a new name that stressed the unity of the realm. It was another step in the process of pulling Scotland together that had begun back in the previous century.

More Kens and Cons

The reign of Constantine II was a success in the terms of the day. The king was a successful general who held his kingdom together – and he was helped by the fact that fate allowed him to rule for more than 40 years. Life wasn't quite so kind to those who came after him. The period from the end of Constantine's reign in 943 to the accession of Malcolm II in 1005 saw more short-lived rulers. Here's a selection of them:

- ✔ **Malcolm I (943–54):** He agreed to a treaty with Edmund, king of the English, to cement Scottish power in southern Scotland.

- ✔ **Constantine III (954–62):** He was killed when fighting the Vikings.

- ✔ **Kenneth II (971–95):** Like Malcolm, he knew the importance of the English and agreed with King Edgar to keep the boundary between the two realms safe in return for recognition of his (Kenneth's) overlordship in Lothian.

✔ **Constantine III (995–7):** Known as Constantine the Bald, he was killed by his rival, Kenneth, who became Kenneth III.

✔ **Kenneth III (997–1005):** He had to fight continuously to keep his crown.

Well, if your eyes are glazing over at this swift procession of Kenneths, Constantines, and others, the main point is that many of these kings found it hard to hang on in there because they were always being challenged by rivals from inside and outside their own families. And as if this opposition wasn't enough, they also had to keep their eyes on what the English were doing south of the border.

Mighty Malcolm

Things took a turn for the better with Malcolm II (1005–34). At the start of his reign, it didn't look that way, though, because he launched an ambitious raid on England and ended up defeated and in disarray outside Durham. Looking over his shoulder, as it were, he saw that the Vikings were still threatening the northern parts of his kingdom.

Like the more able Scottish rulers of this period, Malcolm realised that success as warlord was best managed by using the art of diplomacy, as well as skill with the sword. Malcolm succeeded because he made a number of shrewd moves against his enemies. But there was no gain without pain for Malcolm – each of his shrewd moves was really a double-edged sword:

✔ **Shrewd move No. 1 – Make an alliance with the Vikings.** A year or two after coming to the throne, Malcolm married his daughter to a prominent Viking, Sigurd the Mighty. Sigurd controlled Shetland, Orkney, a big part of northern Scotland, and the Hebrides. He was an important person to keep sweet if Malcolm wanted his northern borders to be both secure and peaceful. Things looked a bit wobbly when Sigurd died in 1014, but Malcolm took advantage of what may have been a problem. His grandson, Thorfinn Sigurdsson, needed a powerful supporter to hang on to power after Sigurd died. Malcolm threw his weight behind Thorfinn and gained more power in the north in the process.

✔ **Shrewd move No. 2 – Defeat the Northumbrians.** To keep his southern borders safe, Malcolm needed to keep the Northumbrians from encroaching on his territory. He defeated them in battle in 1018, but his success attracted the gaze of another potential rival, the great Danish ruler of England, Cnut (see Chapter 5). Cnut was a busy man, with interests all over Europe, so it wasn't until 1031 that he led his forces northwards and threatened Malcolm. The Scot was forced to submit to Cnut, and Cnut's ally Siward of Northumbria policed the border region, preventing Malcolm from making further inroads in Northumbria.

✔ **Shrewd move No. 3 – Remove some rivals.** Kenneth III's family still included members who had strong claims to the Scottish throne, so Malcolm set about having some of them removed. That means murdered, basically. One hapless descendant of Kenneth was put to death in 1032, and at least one other followed him to an early grave. But Malcolm wasn't able to remove the entire family.

Malcolm II did enough to ensure that his preferred candidate as successor, his grandson Duncan, would take over the throne when he died in 1034. Thanks to mighty Malcolm, the new king took over a large, robust, and strong kingdom.

Delightful Duncan?

Malcolm was followed by his grandson, Duncan I, who ruled from 1034 to 1040. Now, if you've seen Shakespeare's *Macbeth*, you'll know about Duncan. In the play, he's the benevolent, nice, and rather doddery king who gives Macbeth all sorts of honours and titles – and is rewarded with treachery when Macbeth and his evil wife kill him to speed their path to the throne.

Was Duncan really such a goody? Well, historians don't know a lot about the personal lives of the early Scottish kings, so it will come as no surprise that Shakespeare had to make up quite a lot about Duncan. The king was probably quite young – maybe in his 20s – when he first wore the crown. He also had his grandfather's go-getting character, liked to raid Northumbria, and actually launched an attack on Macbeth, who was a member of Kenneth III's family that were rivals to the line of Malcolm and Duncan. The nice old king of Shakespeare's play is a bit of a myth.

Duncan's desire to get rid of Macbeth proved his undoing. When the two met in battle at a place called Pitgaveny near Elgin in 1040, Macbeth was the victor, and Duncan was dispatched. The king's young children were taken into exile, away from the dangerous Macbeth, and a power vacuum was left in Scotland. Macbeth was ready to step in.

Macbeth – villain or hero?

Yes, that's the Macbeth who's the main character in Shakespeare's famous play. In Shakespeare, Macbeth is a lord who, in cahoots with his wicked wife (whom the Bard doesn't even give a name – she's just Lady Macbeth), bumps off King Duncan and steps into his shoes.

Just as Duncan wasn't the white-haired old king portrayed by Shakespeare, the real Macbeth, as far as historians can tell, was a very different character, too, from Shakespeare's usurper. For a start, Macbeth went into battle against Duncan because he was forced to – Duncan attacked him. Second, no evidence supports the notion that the historical Macbeth was the kind of baddie who makes such a big impression in Shakespeare's great tragedy. Third, Lady Macbeth was probably not the fiend-like queen that the great playwright described.

But Macbeth did depend on his wife for his crown, not because she helped him kill Duncan but because of who she was. Mrs Macbeth was actually a woman called Gruoch, the granddaughter of Kenneth III and the vital link in the royal chain that gave Macbeth his claim to the Scottish throne. Malcolm II had killed off most of the male members of Kenneth's family, but Gruoch remained, and her husband had a good claim to the throne. In 1040, having killed Duncan in battle, Macbeth became king thanks to his well-connected wife.

Keeping the throne

Once Macbeth had won the throne, he had to work hard to hang on to it. Various people in Scotland and beyond wanted him out, to strengthen their own power bases. Sources of potential and real challenges to Macbeth's rule included:

- ✔ **Orkney,** the home of dead ex-king Duncan's cousin Thorfinn.
- ✔ **Atholl,** where others had their eyes on the throne.
- ✔ **England,** where Edward the Confessor supported an invasion by one Siward.

Siward was able to defeat Macbeth when he first invaded in 1046, but later Macbeth kicked him out. From that point on, Macbeth seems to have been much safer on the throne. The reign was fairly peaceful for a few years, and in 1050, Macbeth disappeared for a few months on pilgrimage to Rome. Shakespeare's character would never have done that, but Macbeth turns out to have been a notable patron of the church.

The Duncan family returns

After Macbeth beat Duncan in battle, the defeated king's children were taken into a safe exile, but when they grew up, they began to plan to take back Scotland from their enemy Macbeth. As had been the case earlier in the reign, the English got involved in the fight for the throne, too. The struggle was a game of two halves between Macbeth and Duncan's son Malcolm, with his English backers:

- ✔ **First half:** In 1054, Siward, a previous opponent of Macbeth, launched an invasion of Scotland. Siward hoped that if he beat the Scots, the English king Edward the Confessor would promote Malcolm as the new king. Siward won the battle, and Malcolm pushed his way into southern Scotland, but the victory wasn't conclusive. Siward's son was killed in the fighting.

> ✔ **Second half:** In 1057, Malcolm brought the fight to Macbeth once more, this time still more decisively. Macbeth was killed in a battle at Lumphanan. However, Malcolm was still not the undisputed king until he had disposed of Lulach the Simpleton, Gruoch's son by a previous husband. Lulach didn't last long. By 1058, he was killed, and Malcolm III was ruler of Scotland.

New Brooms: The Canmore Kings

In 1057 and 1058, Malcolm III disposed of Macbeth and Lulach, the last remaining rulers who were descended from Kenneth III, and set himself firmly on the throne of Scotland. His actions were typical of a time when countries were ruled by warrior kings who built their power through success in battle. Malcolm was known as *Ceann Mór,* which means great chief, and the Canmore dynasty that he founded was to be one of Scotland's most successful.

The Canmore kings achieved a lot in Scotland. They benefited from outside influences, developing Scottish culture so that it took on board some of the best of the Anglo-Saxons and later the Norman kings. They brought in better systems of government and helped reform the church, but toward the end of their period, they lost some of their territory and power.

Malcolm: War lord, new style

Malcolm III reigned from 1058 to 1093. On the face of it, he looked very much like the Scottish kings who had preceded him – he was a seasoned war lord who didn't hesitate to make treaties with his neighbours and then break them when their backs were turned.

Malcolm was a rather different character from his forbears. For one thing, he was more cosmopolitan. He had a good Scottish lineage, of course, and could trace his line back to Kenneth I. But he had spent a lot of time in England, at the home of Earl Siward in York, and there he absorbed the local Viking-based lifestyle. Later, after he became king, he married an Anglo-Saxon princess who introduced him to the highly sophisticated culture of the English. But at heart, Malcolm was an old-fashioned Scottish leader, keen to expand his territory and protect his borders.

Make peace, then war

One place where Scottish kings often had trouble was in the south, along the border with Northumbria. Malcolm, though, had made peace with Tostig, the Earl of Northumbria, so his border was secure. Peace reigned until in 1061 when Tostig decided to go off to Rome on a pilgrimage. Once Tostig had set off on his journey, Malcolm launched a major raid on Northumbrian territory. It was an indication that the Scottish king wanted to expand his power base – and was none too scrupulous about how he was going to do it.

Sometimes Malcolm had no choice but to make peace. In 1072, the formidable Norman king William I, who had come over from Normandy and conquered England in 1066 (see Chapter 6), decided he would invade Scotland, too. William turned up with both foot soldiers and sea-borne troops, looking typically scary. Sensibly, Malcolm decided he'd make peace with William. He did homage to the Norman king and promised to throw out the Anglo-Saxon exiles who had hidden in Scotland after William conquered England.

Malcolm obeyed the terms of his agreement with William until 1079, when he made another raid into Northumbria, intent on pushing his border southwards. When he heard what the Scots were up to, William sent his eldest son, Robert Curthose, to stop Malcolm in his tracks. Malcolm and Robert met and made another treaty, preventing further Scottish southwards expansion.

Was this latest attack a defeat for Malcolm? The Normans had prevented him from pushing on south, so in a way it was. And they built a castle at Newcastle to guard the border. But Newcastle was further south than Malcolm's original border, so the Scots *had* gained some ground. It wasn't a total defeat.

New queen, new culture

When Malcolm became king, he was married to Ingibjorg, a member of the Norse family that ruled Orkney. The pair had two children, Duncan and Donald, but around 1069, Ingibjorg died. Shortly afterwards, fate took a hand, and a group of Anglo-Saxon exiles, fleeing northwards from the ravages of William I, arrived in Scotland. Two members of the party were a pair of princesses, Margaret and Christina, sisters to Edgar, who was the Anglo-Saxon claimant to the English crown. Soon enough, Margaret and Malcolm got married.

The Anglo-Saxon court where Margaret had been brought up was a sophisticated place, which had strong connections with mainland Europe, with the learning of the church, and with the latest in modern manners. The Anglo-Saxon court was rather more sophisticated than the Scottish court, and before long, the new queen was introducing her husband and his court to the ways of the Anglo-Saxons. She accomplished this task in all sorts of ways:

✔ Margaret and Malcolm's children were given Anglo-Saxon names – Edward, Edmund, Aethelred, and Edgar. The couple may have thought that one day one or more of them might get the chance to become king of England.

✔ The court began to adopt Anglo-Saxon or European clothing, hair styles, and the like.

✔ Manners at the court improved, and at mealtimes, the court used the latest tableware – no more throwing the scraps on the floor. Well, not quite so much of this kind of behaviour anyway.

Margaret was interested above all in religion. She knew that the mainland European and Anglo-Saxon churches had brought in reforms to make priests more effective in their daily work with parishioners and to make monasteries stricter in their observance of the monastic rules. She hoped to introduce such changes in Scotland, too:

- ✔ A church assembly was called to discuss how to bring in new reforms.

- ✔ Monks were invited from down south to show the Scottish monks how to regulate their lives.

- ✔ Margaret had her sons instructed about the religious reforms so that they would able to continue her work.

The religious reforms were a starting point. But more lasting reforms would come later, building on the start the queen had made with the backing of Malcolm III.

More Norman troubles

At the end of his reign, Malcolm renewed his tussle with the Normans. Another of his raiding forays in 1091 was followed by a further treaty with William I – and by yet more fighting when neither side could resist provoking the other. Finally, in late 1093, Malcolm went all out for an invasion of Northumbria. The Normans ambushed Malcolm, killed him, and wounded his son Edward, who died soon afterwards. A few days later, Queen Margaret died, too.

Feudal kings

When Malcolm III died, together with his heir Edward, in 1093, confusion surrounded who should take over because in those days, the crown still didn't automatically pass from father to son. Several would-be kings, some with the backing of the English king William II, jumped on the royal bandwagon, and few of them ruled for long or made much of an impression on Scotland. Here's a little information on these men who reigned in Scotland at the turn of the 12th century:

- ✔ **Donald III (1094–97):** Malcolm III's brother, Donald was an old man by the time he became king and was known in Gaelic as Domnall Bàn, or Donald the White-haired.

- ✔ **Duncan II (1094):** Duncan was Malcolm III's son by his first wife, Ingibjorg. He had the backing of William II, beat Donald III in battle, but was murdered after a few months on the throne.

- ✔ **Edmund (1094–97):** Malcolm's eldest surviving son did a deal with Donald III and seems to have ruled in parallel with his uncle. But he had a power struggle with his younger brother, Edgar. Edgar captured him and let him live out his life quietly as a monk in England. Donald, meanwhile, was imprisoned and lived a only couple more years after he and Edmund were deposed in 1097.

✔ **Edgar (1097–1107):** Edgar cemented his bonds with England by having his sister marry English king Henry I. This tie kept the peace with England, and Edgar made a treaty with the Norwegians, allowing them control of the Hebrides. Edgar's rule was more peaceful and stable as a result.

✔ **Alexander I (1107–24):** Yet another of Malcolm's sons, Alexander was once more dependent on England for support – his wife, Sibylla, was the illegitimate daughter of Henry I of England. As a feudal dependent of Henry, Alexander fought on Henry's side in the English king's wars in Wales. But he protected the independence of the Scottish church, refusing to let Scottish churchmen swear to obey the English archbishops. His reign lasted for 17 years before he died in Stirling Castle.

Several of these Scottish kings actually relied on the English for their position. What they were doing was becoming part of the feudal system, the arrangement through which English kings wielded their power. Under the feudal system, the Scottish rulers became dependents, or vassals, of the English king. (For more about this system, see Chapter 6.) This arrangement meant that the English king gave them support, and in return, the Scottish ruler supported the English in politics and on the battlefield. It was an arrangement that put the Scottish kings on a lower rung of the political ladder than the English, but in difficult times, it gave them the support they needed.

David: Devout and determined

David I (1124–53) was a strong king who had a lasting influence on Scotland. He had close ties with England and got heavily involved with the civil war that raged in that country in 1130s and 1140s. But he was able to introduce church reforms and governmental improvements that meant that Scotland was better run and, on the whole, wealthier.

The English connection

David, the youngest son of Malcolm III, was an important man before he became king. He held vast lands in southern Scotland, and through his wife, Matilda of Senlis, was Earl of Huntingdon and thus one of the most important aristocrats in England.

When he became king of Scotland, David soon began bringing in English friends, senior nobles like Robert de Brus and Walter Fitz Alan, who became his key advisers. The English and Scots didn't exactly mix very well in the Middle Ages, so it sounds like a problem for the Scottish nobles. Some Scots did resent the English influx, and the newly arrived English were given extensive lands. But these territories were mostly in southern Scotland, so the incomers did not alienate the native Gaelic population, who were mainly concentrated in the north, too much.

The real problem with David's English connection came when English king Henry I died in 1135, and a dispute started over the English succession, leading to a civil war between the supporters of Henry's daughter, Matilda, and Stephen, the grandson of William I of England. (For more about this war, see Chapter 6.) David fought on the side of Matilda, to whom he had sworn allegiance. The darkest days of Scottish involvement in the war came in 1138, when a Scots force under David's nephew, William Fitz Duncan, brutalised parts of northern England, killing innocent people and carrying off women as slaves. They were defeated by an English force led, improbably, by the archbishop of York, at the Battle of the Standard, which was fought near Northallerton in August 1138.

The Battle of the Standard was a huge setback for David and Scotland, and any king involved in such a defeat would have to do a lot to redeem his reputation. Thankfully, David did not devote all his energies to the disastrous civil war. Several periods of peace enabled him to concentrate on his business in Scotland, and on his interest in the church, both areas where he was much more successful.

Church reforms

David's links with the English and Normans put him in touch with the latest developments in the church. Some especially interesting reforms were going on in the monasteries.

Many monks in England and on mainland Europe felt that the once-strict rules of monastic life had slackened too much. A reform movement began, with new monasteries observing more strictly enforced regulations, better organization, and a more austere lifestyle. Foremost amongst these new reformed monastic orders were the Cistericans, named after their mother monastery at Cîteaux in France, and the Tironensians, from Tiron, also in France. Both groups were to have a lasting impact in Scotland.

David encouraged the reformed monasteries in the best way he knew, by founding new monasteries and inviting monks who were well versed in the reforms to come to Scotland. His foundations included:

- **Selkirk Abbey,** home to Tironensian monks and the first reformed monastic house in Britain.
- **Melrose Abbey,** a Cistercian foundation.
- **Newbattle Abbey** and its two daughter-monasteries, **Kinloss** and **Holmcultram.**
- **Cambuskenneth**, a monastery of Augustinian canons.

It was an impressive record by any standards, but David knew what he was doing. It was partly pay-back time for the war-crimes committed by his men during the civil war in England, but the monasteries came with other, more worldly benefits, too. The Cistercians, especially, were large-scale farmers, and their activities brought better farming methods to Scotland.

Monasteries brought an increase in economic activity, and so developed trade. This process was enhanced as towns sprang up around many of David's castles, towns that soon played host to markets and the host of craft workers and merchants that urban populations attract. Scotland as a whole, not just the monks, began to benefit from the resulting rash of buying and selling. The country was becoming more prosperous under David I.

Better government

David's other improvements were to do with the way Scotland was ruled. Whereas most of his predecessors had been war lords, David was keen to be seen as something more – a just and fair king. He had a law code drawn up and made it known that he would hear petitions from all his subjects, even the humblest. A network of sheriffs ran the legal system in the regions, so the law, in theory at least, stretched its long arms right across the kingdom. The Scots must have seen a huge difference between their developing legal system and the situation in England, where the war dominated life at every level.

Ironically, though, many of David's improvements were influenced by what he saw happening in England. South of the border before the war, the royal court had developed in ways that David wanted to imitate. David introduced to Scotland the great offices of state that helped both court and country run more smoothly. The chancellor headed up the legal system, the chamberlain was the head of the royal finances, and the constable managed security. Even a steward supervised the running of the royal household.

David's other good idea about government wasn't very original. He encouraged his son Henry to take an active part in ruling the country, thereby preparing for the day when the young man would take over the country in his own right. But that succession couldn't happen because in 1152, while still in his 30s, Henry died. The king had no more sons, so he settled on his eldest grandson, Malcolm, as his heir. David began to prepare the young boy for kingship, but David died in 1153, when Malcolm was still only 11 or 12 years old.

The legacy: Malcolm IV

Coming to the throne as a boy, David's grandson Malcolm IV (1153–65) was seen as a soft touch to others who wanted to grab the throne or wield power in Scotland. He was hardly on the throne when a rebellion erupted in the west of the country. This revolt was quelled, but Malcolm also had to face a challenge from the south – in the shape of the strong English king Henry II (see Chapter 7). Henry snatched back the earldom of Northumberland from Scotland and forced Malcolm to become his vassal.

Malcolm was known as Malcolm the Maiden. This nickname doesn't mean that he was effeminate, simply that he never got around to marrying. He seems to have been in love with the idea of being a knight – especially the old-fashioned kind of knight who devoted his entire life to military pursuits. In 1159 Malcolm marched off to fight on the side of his overlord, Henry, in a war in France.

Malcolm's trip to France earned him his knighthood, but lost him the respect of many of the Scottish nobles, who felt he should have stayed at home and learned the business of ruling his country. The young king was still only a teenager, after all. But before Malcolm could do much to redeem himself, the young king got ill, and he suffered repeated bouts of illness until he died in 1165.

William the Lion sleeps tonight

Scotland's longest ruling medieval monarch was William I (1165–1214), brother of Malcolm IV and grandson of David I. He had been made Earl of Northumberland as a boy but had been forced to give up his earldom when Northumberland passed to the English king Henry II in the previous reign. William was preoccupied throughout much of his reign with getting this territory back, as well as with strengthening the power of the Scottish royal family more generally. His nickname, William the Lion, was given to him after his death and refers to his reputation as a Lion of Justice.

William's attempts to restore Scottish power in the south and win back Northumberland added up to a chapter of accidents. He began by asking Henry – and was promptly refused. Then he tried a range of ruses, military and diplomatic:

- ✔ William launched a series of military attacks on northern England, which ended in him being ambushed and taken prisoner in 1174.

- ✔ In 1175, he was humiliated by Henry and forced to do the Englishman homage – thus making William the feudal inferior of Henry.

- ✔ In 1189, a new English king, Richard I, was short of money and agreed to sell William his freedom – but still would not give him Northumberland.

✔ In 1194, William persuaded Richard to agree that William's daughter Margaret should marry Richard's nephew Otto, and that Northumberland should be part of the marriage settlement of the couple. But the marriage plans later fell through.

✔ In 1209, the next English king, John, forced William into another humiliation – William had to renounce his claims to the northern parts of England once more.

This sorry chain of events makes William look like an incompetent – a mangy lion, if ever there was one. But those defeats weren't all there was to William.

In spite of all his schemes to win back Northumberland, when it came to governing the territory that *was* in his hands, William made a better job of things. By the end of his long reign, the royal rule over the north was as strong as it ever had been. William achieved this in several ways:

✔ He built and strengthened the royal castles to provide a network of bases.

✔ He made sure that his most trusted lords were installed in these castles and in lordships throughout his kingdom, effectively bringing royal power to the remotest regions.

✔ He was shrewd in promoting loyal men to senior positions in the church.

William was not always a sleeping lion. Even in his last couple of years, when he was an old man and very frail, he kept an eye on the business of government, ably assisted, it seems, by his queen, Ermengarde, who was much younger than him, and his son Alexander. With his death clearly near, the court was well prepared for the hand-over of power, and Alexander was inaugurated as king the day after William died.

Chapter 11

Troublesome English, Troublesome Islanders

*I*n the 13th and 14th centuries, Scottish monarchs had to grapple with a host of problems – disloyal nobles, clashes with England and Norway, and money troubles, to name just three. Scotland's rulers varied in their ability to keep all the balls in the air, but the period produced two kings who have gone down in history as Scottish heroes: Alexander III, who presided over a period of prosperity, and Robert I, who was one of Scotland's most famous war leaders.

Attacking the Neighbours

For much of the 13th century, Scotland was ruled by two kings, Alexander II and Alexander III, who were preoccupied with relations with their neighbours – both the English and the people of the Western Isles who were still under the overall authority of the king of Norway. After many diplomatic wrangles and a fair bit of fighting, Scotland enjoyed a boom period under Alexander III. Its king gained power over the Hebrides, making the country bigger than it had ever been, and trade increased, bringing wealth at least to the upper classes. But all of these changes took time.

Qualified success – Alexander II

Alexander II (1214–49) was the son of the previous king, William, and was 16 years old when he came to the throne. Because his father had been ill the last couple of years of his reign, the young prince had been well schooled in kingly work – no doubt helped by his mother, Queen Ermengarde, who had helped her husband rule in his declining years and remained a major influence when her son came to the throne.

Scotland versus England

But it was events in England that were to have the most pressing effect on Alexander's first few years as king. Down in the south, the English king, John, was facing demands from his barons to limit royal power and impose basic rights to justice. These demands were formalised in 1215 as the famous document known as *Magna Carta* (the Great Charter), which John signed in 1215.

Magna Carta, an agreement between King John and his nobles, was mainly concerned with the English king's relations with his barons. Some of the barons were related to Alexander, and the charter also contained important material concerning Scotland – it promised that several issues to do with Alexander's rights would be resolved, including the return of some Scottish hostages held by John and the settlement of various disputes between the two royal houses.

The concessions in Magna Carta helped Alexander – but he was helped even more by John's weakness as a king. While John was busy in disputes with his barons, Alexander took the chance to march south and move into Northumberland. He received the homage of the barons there and took Carlisle, making the town's castle into his headquarters in northern England. It was a triumph, and when John died in late 1216, Alexander's position seemed even stronger (for more about King John and Magna Carta, see Chapter 7).

But the new English king, Henry III, didn't like the way Alexander had flexed his muscles. In a series of political moves, Henry clawed back his power in the north of England. The final straw came when the Pope took Henry's side and sent a papal representative from Rome to excommunicate Alexander, cutting him off from the church. The Scotsman knew it was time to concede and do homage to Henry for his lands south of the border.

In fact, though, the trouble between Scotland and England rumbled on through Alexander's reign. Things still weren't resolved when Alexander agreed in 1217 to give up his large claims to northern England in return for a smaller parcel of land in Cumberland and Northumberland. The tensions between England and Scotland would simmer away for centuries.

Coronation blues

While trying to sort out relations with England, Alexander was also trying to improve his standing at home. Like many Scottish kings, he was resentful that, while English kings got crowned and anointed by a priest, Scottish kings were merely inaugurated in a nonreligious ceremony. This difference was important because the process of anointing put the powerful church on your side and even, it was argued, gave the king a sacred status, as if approved by God himself.

Alexander wanted this kind of coronation and anointing ritual to take place in Scotland. He asked the Pope in 1221 and again in 1233, but the Pope was having none of it. The privilege of anointing was not something the church was going to hand out on a plate.

The king at home

Alexander had several women in his life, and they had varying influences on his kingship and behaviour. Historians don't know that much about the king's personal life, but several influential women stand out:

- ✔ **Ermengarde:** Alexander's mother seems to have been a huge influence, giving the king the benefit of her years of experience beside his father, William I.

- ✔ **Joanna:** Alexander's first queen was the sister of Henry III of England, and their marriage in 1221 promoted better relations between their two countries. Little is known about Joanna's character, and her power seems to have been slight compared with that of the dowager queen Ermengarde. Joanna died in 1238, leaving the king without a male heir.

- ✔ **Marie de Courcy:** After Joanna's death, Alexander swiftly married Marie, daughter of a French nobleman. She gave him a son, Alexander, that he so desperately wanted.

As well as his two wives, Alexander probably had a number of mistresses. In particular, he seems not to have cared much for Joanna. The queen died on a pilgrimage trip to England, and Alexander didn't even bother to have her remains brought back to Scotland for burial.

Mixed-up monarch?

It's tough to know what to make of Alexander. He played for high stakes against England but had to be content in the end with fairly meagre gains. He was unsuccessful in his attempts to increase the status of the Scottish monarchy by getting himself anointed. But he did have some good points:

- ✔ He was a generous patron of the church, founding several monasteries.
- ✔ He was the first to invite the *friars,* members of a new dynamic monastic movement, to Scotland.
- ✔ He controlled his noblemen carefully, rewarding good service.

Alexander also seemed on the verge of another triumph when he died. In 1249, he led his fleet to the Hebrides and seemed likely to impose his rule there. But he died suddenly before making the decisive move. People said that the Celtic saint, Columba, had protected the islands from his aggression. More importantly, he left behind an 8-year-old heir and all the uncertainty that came when a child had to take over the throne.

Golden age – Alexander III

Coming to the throne as a boy, the new king, Alexander III (1249–86), enjoyed a long reign. In his 37 years on the Scottish throne, he achieved a lot and presided over something of a boom time for Scotland. But his rule began with uncertainty because of a dispute between his barons and officials about who should control the kingdom during his minority (see the next section).

Once he began to rule in his own right, though, things got better for Scotland, with increased prosperity for the country and more power for the monarch. Alexander also gained a reputation as a *bon viveur*. He was said to have made illicit night-time visits to nunneries for very unholy liaisons with some of the nuns. And when he died, he left a big unpaid bill for claret. He seems to have worked hard and played hard.

Power politicians

Two factions tried to get control over young Alexander when he became king. One was led by Alan Durward, who had already become very powerful as Scotland's Justiciar under Alexander II. He was also married to the king's illegitimate sister, Margaret. The other contender for power was powerful baron Walter Comyn, Earl of Menteith. The years 1249 to 1260 saw a ding-dong battle between the two:

- Durward began in power, appointing key officers of state and winning a dispute over what form the king's inauguration should take.
- In 1251, Alexander, probably acting under the thumb of English king Henry III, sacked all his officials, and Monteith stepped into Durward's shoes.
- Durward staged a coup in 1255, grabbing control of the king and government again.
- In 1257, Monteith led a counter-coup, kidnapping the king.

None of this turmoil did any good for Scotland's stability or government, and in 1260, the king, now age 19, took over power himself.

Norse force – trouble in the Isles

Once he was securely in command, Alexander turned his attention to an area – the Hebrides – where he thought he could increase his power and secure the borders of his kingdom. Although the Hebrides was still officially under the rule of Norway, Scotland had more and more influence there.

Alexander began by sending ambassadors to Norway to bargain with the Norwegian king, Håkon IV. But Håkon was having none of Alexander's overtures and responded by sending a fleet to attack Scotland. So in 1263, Alexander found his western coasts under threat from a Norse army. It was as if the old Viking aggressors of the ninth century had returned.

Alexander was lucky, though. Storms wrecked a large part of the Norwegian fleet, and when the two sides clashed at the Battle of Largs, the result was inconclusive. The Norwegians withdrew to Orkney for the winter, where Håkon died. Norway's new king, Magnus, had his work cut out establishing his power at home and had little stomach for a fight, so Alexander was off the hook.

In 1264 and 1265, the Scottish king moved through the western isles and the Isle of Man imposing his power and receiving the submission of the local lords. And in 1266, Alexander's rule of the area was made official – the Treaty of Perth signed lordship of the isles over to Alexander. Scotland was now bigger and more powerful than ever.

Boom time – success in Scotland

Scotland was prosperous during Alexander's reign, and this prosperity bene-fited the country in a number of ways:

- ✔ Ports such as Berwick developed, enabling produce from Scotland to be sold on the European mainland.

- ✔ Cash flowed into the country as a result of sales of goods, such as wool and hides.

- ✔ Many monasteries and cathedrals were rebuilt or extended.

- ✔ Many nobles built large castles, partly for protection, partly to show off their great wealth.

Historians disagree about how much of this prosperity was due to Alexander himself. Those who are pro-Alexander point to the fact that much of his reign was peaceful and stable. Once he began to rule in his own right, the king was able to get the barons working well for him. And his military success in the isles, together with diplomatic success in England, made Scotland stronger. But the other view is that much of Alexander's success came about through good luck – even his triumph over Norway in the Hebrides was mainly due to the weather. So the best answer to the question is that Alexander helped the situation, but that he was also lucky.

Alexander probably didn't feel very lucky, though. His reign was clouded by a number of personal misfortunes that must have left him sad and frustrated. The first tragedy came in 1275, when his queen, Margaret, died. She was only 34 years old, and the king was said to have been close to her. Sadder still, all the children of the marriage died young – their daughter Margaret aged 20 in 1281, their son David aged 8 the same year, and their son Alexander, aged 20, in 1284.

This family history was not only sorry, but it left the king without a close descendant to whom to pass the throne. Shortly before his death in 1286, he remarried. But this second marriage, to the French noblewoman Yolande of Dreux, did not produce any children.

Alexander himself died in tragic circumstances. In March 1286, after a long meeting with his nobles in Edinburgh, the king decided to ride home to Yolande, who was at Kinghorn in Fife. A storm blew up, and Alexander got separated from his companions and rode on alone. The next day, he was found dead on the shore about a mile from the manor where Yolande was waiting for him. People originally thought he had ridden over a cliff in the darkness, but it seems his horse probably threw him, and he broke his neck when he landed. Either way, it was a tragic end.

All at Sea – Queen Margaret and John 1

In the aftermath of Alexander III's successful reign came a disastrous period for Scotland under the rule of Margaret (1286–90) and John Balliol (1292–96). Margaret's reign was problematic because she was an infant who never even saw Scotland. John Balliol was a weak king who succumbed to a powerful English opponent.

The lady of Scotland

Because all of Alexander III's children predeceased him, he named as his heir his granddaughter Margaret. In naming her as the next queen, he referred to Margaret as the 'illustrious girl', but, illustrious or not, she was only 3-years-old when Alexander died. So two earls, two barons, and two bishops were chosen to form a council of Guardians to look after Scotland on her behalf.

Much rivalry developed between the Scots nobles – and the English king Edward I – to try to get control over Margaret and, through her, dominate Scotland. In 1290, an agreement was reached that she would eventually marry Edward I's son (later to become King Edward II), uniting the two kingdoms. The little princess had spent her life in her father's home, Norway, so Edward I sent a fleet of ships to bring her to England. But the Norwegians had other ideas and sent her instead to Orkney (still Norwegian soil at this period). Here, she died of an illness aged only seven. Never crowned queen, poor Margaret was generally known simply as 'the lady of Scotland'.

John Balliol

With Margaret dead, a dispute raged in Scotland about who was the rightful ruler. John Balliol, an Anglo-Scottish lord related to William I of Scotland, had a strong claim. So did Robert Bruce of Annandale, who also traced his lineage back to William. A long legal enquiry in 1291–2 eventually came down on the side of John, who ruled from 1292 to 1296.

John was not bad at domestic government. He could appoint sheriffs, dispense justice, and hold parliaments quite effectively. And he made a promising start in foreign policy, by making an alliance with France. But he could not stand up to the repeated poundings being given to Scotland by the English king Edward I. When Edward attacked Berwick in 1296, John didn't even show up to lead his army. Instead, he became the victim of a series of humiliations:

- ✔ He fled to the northeast.
- ✔ He then gave himself up to Edward.
- ✔ The Englishman had him stripped of his royal robes and made him renounce the alliance he'd made with the French.
- ✔ He was forced to give up the title of king and ended up in prison in London.

Kicked off the throne, John Balliol was eventually released from prison and sent into exile in northern France. The Scottish throne was left to the English, and later to John's rival, Robert I.

Robert 1

Robert I (1306–29), sometimes known by his family name as Robert I Bruce or Robert Bruce, was a very different character from his predecessor, John I. He was resourceful, determined, and a good image-builder. He had to fight a die-hard struggle against the English to recover Scotland's independence, sometimes using tactics that were new or at least unusual in medieval warfare. Against the odds, he succeeded and established a new dynasty on the Scottish throne.

Know your enemy. It could have been the motto of Robert Bruce. As a young man, he lived in England and, on and off, served the aggressive English king Edward I in his attempts to conquer Scotland. But his heart was not with the English cause, and after a few years, he was quietly canvassing support for a revival of the independent Scottish monarchy.

By 1306, when Robert was 31, his plans were coming to fruition. But they went badly wrong when Robert met up with prominent Scottish noble John Comyn, probably to discuss his bid for the throne. At some point, perhaps because Robert thought Comyn had told the English about his ambitions, the two men came to blows. Robert struck Comyn with his sword and – after further fighting between Comyn's and Bruce's men – Comyn lay dead. Robert now knew he had to go all out for the kingship; Edward would be down on him like a ton of bricks for the murder of Comyn, whether or not he went for the throne.

Fighting for the throne

Robert was so anxious to stay on the Scottish throne that he had two inauguration ceremonies – the second perhaps gave him extra legitimacy because one of the key participants, the representative of the Earl of Fife, hadn't turned up for the first one. But just as important as the ceremonies was the fighting Robert had to do to hang on to the kingship. Robert's struggle involved:

✔ An English fight-back in which many of Robert's followers were captured and killed, and Edward locked up Robert's sister and the Countess of Buchan in iron cages.

✔ The execution of his brothers Thomas and Alexander by the English.

✔ A guerrilla war campaign against the English.

✔ A scorched-earth campaign in which Robert demolished enemy castles.

✔ The capture of a string of Scottish castles.

By 1314, Robert had a large body of support in Scotland, which he nurtured with generous gifts of land. But the English still had huge forces and sent an army of some 16,000 to retake the vast fortress of Stirling Castle. Robert met this force at Bannockburn and, by cutting off part of the English host, was able to take on his enemy and send them running away or drowning in the mud that stretched from the castle to the nearby Forth estuary. Robert's occupation of the Scottish throne was confirmed.

The decisive victory at Bannockburn enabled Robert to rescue his womenfolk from their iron cages and to boot out his Scottish opponents from their lands. He also carried on fighting the English – probably partly for revenge, partly to stop any thoughts they may have had of returning to attack Scotland. Robert made a series of ruthless raids in northern England and went all-out for an invasion of Ireland, which the English were then ruling from Dublin. The Irish campaign was a mistake. It gained Robert nothing because although he scored some victories, he didn't oust the English. And, worse still for the Bruce family, Robert's brother, Edward, was killed in the fighting.

The continued scraps between Scots and English after Bannockburn frustrated Robert and his allies. A victory on that scale ought to have been decisive. In 1320, many nobles and bishops from Scotland came together at a big meeting in Arbroath to discuss how to secure Scotland's future. They decided to write to the Pope, John XXII, demanding that he acknowledge the independence of their country. The document they sent, now called the Declaration of Arbroath, became a key statement of the Scots' view of their independence.

The Declaration said that as long as a hundred of the signatories were alive, they would not consent to rule from England, 'for it is not for glory we fight . . . but for freedom alone'.

Murmurs against the king

So was Robert safe on the throne? Not entirely, because some people in Scotland still supported other candidates. Robert was well aware of this support, and a law passed in the Scottish parliament that banned *murmuring against the king* seemed designed to help him nip such opponents in the bud. One plot, the *Soule conspiracy,* came to light in 1320. A group of Balliol supporters were discovered planning to remove Robert and were promptly punished. A number were executed.

Opposition from England was another danger. After an uneasy truce between the two countries, Robert agreed a treaty in 1328. The English agreed to recognise Robert as king, and plans were put in place for his young son David to marry Joan, the sister of the English king Edward III.

Robert achieved a great deal in his struggle to strengthen Scotland against its enemies both north and south of the border with England. But was he the great hero that many Scottish writers later claimed? He was certainly a formidable fighter, and this quality was what the later medieval Scottish writers so admired. But his lavish grants of land to supporters left the monarchy poorer than it had been for a long time. The Scottish superhero wasn't perfect.

William Wallace

William Wallace was a key leader in the Scottish struggle against English rule. Although of Welsh ancestry, this Scotsman had a reputation as one of the greatest Scottish patriots, and he certainly risked his life for his country. He led an uprising in 1297, when he defeated the English at the Battle of Stirling Bridge. But his triumph was short-lived, and the English defeated him at Falkirk the following year.

After this disappointment, Wallace first fled to France to get more support for Scottish independence and then led a guerrilla campaign against the English. He carried on the struggle until 1305, when supporters of the English finally caught up with him, carted him off to London, and finished him off by hanging, drawing, and quartering him. The four quarters of his body were sent to four different towns – Berwick, Newcastle, Stirling, and Perth – as gruesome reminders of what happens to those who rebelled against the English.

Dark and Drublie Days

After the triumphant reign of Robert I, the Scottish monarchy suffered a period of difficulty and decline under Robert's son, David II. David came to the throne as an infant, and the nobles who ruled on his behalf had to deal with a challenge to the throne from the rival Balliol family, who had been kicked out of Scotland at the end of the 13th century. The resulting period of power struggles and uncertainty was called by one contemporary Scotland's *dark and drublie days.*

David comes and goes

David II became king on the death of his father, Robert Bruce. The reference books will tell you that David ruled from 1329 to 1371, but in fact, this reign was interrupted by a long period of exile in France and a still longer spell as an English prisoner in the Tower of London. David had some strong personal qualities as a king – authority and political astuteness, for example – but tough circumstances often prevented him from exercising them.

As a child, David was brought up in the households of some of the loyal nobles of his father, Robert I. It was common in medieval royal households for children to be brought up away from the family home, and some even had noble foster parents, as David may have done. Certainly, when David's mother died in 1327, he spent time with a number of Scottish noble families. But he's also likely to have been brought to court for special occasions and ceremonies, to begin the process of preparing him for the time when he would rule in his own right.

In 1328, the year before his father died and he became king, David was married. The prince was only 4 years old at the time and his bride, Joan, sister of Edward III of England, was just 3 years older than him. This event was a dynastic marriage, to cement a peace agreement between the old rivals and neighbours, England and Scotland.

On and off the throne

David was just 5 years old when, in 1329, he became king. The occasion was a triumph because his father persuaded the Pope to allow his heir to be crowned and anointed. So, for the first time, a Scottish king was crowned in a religious ceremony. David was made king with the backing of the church, an important boost for the young monarch.

David had a powerful Guardian in Thomas Randolph, Earl of Moray, but even he could not prevent the opposition to the young king that gathered around the enemies of the Bruce family. Most important of these enemies was Edward Balliol, son of King John I, who had reigned before Robert I.

Edward Balliol

Edward Balliol was in exile on his family estate in Picardy when David II was crowned. But with an infant on the Scottish throne, he saw the chance to invade, believing that enough nobles in Scotland would support a mature man. And so it proved.

Balliol arrived with an army in 1332, defeated the forces that formed on behalf of David, and was crowned. The English king Edward III supported Edward Balliol's claim on the Scottish throne, in spite of the fact that David was married to Edward's sister, and Balliol soon found that he needed English support to keep him there. The English ruler capitalised on this need,

forcing Balliol to hand over the southern bits of Scotland in return for backing.

In the beginning, Balliol was successful, winning lands and noble supporters in Scotland and forcing young King David into exile in Normandy in 1334. But English backing was a two-edged sword. After 1337, the English were more and more occupied with wars in France, and supporting Balliol became a low priority. With the English gone, the supporters of David attacked Balliol and forced him southwards until his power base disappeared. By 1341, the time was ripe for David to return to Scotland.

After about seven years in exile while the usurper Edward Balliol rampaged across Scotland and then withdrew, David returned in 1341 as a 17 year old ready to grab the reins of power. To begin with, things went well, as by stages the young king built up his authority:

- ✔ David went on a journey around his kingdom, encouraging nobles to support him – and finding out which families had the power to oppose him.

- ✔ Over several years, he gathered support, especially among knights and officials.

- ✔ As he had no son as yet, he put forward his nephew John as heir to the throne.

- ✔ In 1346, he launched an ambitious invasion of England.

But the invasion was a disaster. David was wounded in the head, and most of his key supporters were captured or killed. The king himself was taken prisoner and ended up in the Tower of London.

David in prison

With David out of the way, Edward Balliol reappeared, eager to take over the throne once again. But Balliol found that he still couldn't rely on the all-important support of the English. Although the English were the enemies of David, they were no friends of Balliol either. And an imprisoned Scottish king had enormous value to the English – so long as he *was* a king.

The next few years saw a series of attempts at reaching a deal between David and Edward of England to give Edward something valuable in return for David's freedom. The talks and proposals dragged on for around ten years.

For much of this time, Scotland was under the leadership of Robert Stewart, known in this period as Robert the Steward, a west coast noble who had inherited his title of High Steward of Scotland. The post of High Steward was for the most part an honorary one, but Robert was an astute politician who knew how to wield power. Eventually, his family was to become one of the most important royal dynasties in Scottish – and indeed English – history. But that was all in the future. (For the low-down on Robert and the other Stewarts, see Chapter 12.)

After the protracted negotiations for David's release, during which the king was even allowed out of prison on parole on one occasion to try to persuade the Scots parliament to agree to a deal, the king was finally released in 1357. Scotland agreed to pay a huge ransom to the English, the two countries pledged not to fight, and Edward Balliol was paid a handsome pension and allowed to live quiety out of the way in Yorkshire.

David on the throne

At last David was safely on the throne. He quickly developed a style of rule that owed a lot to his time in England, where he had actually become quite friendly with the man who had kept him prisoner, Edward III. From Edward, he acquired a love of chivalry and jousting, together with an interest in the crusading ideal. He had also discovered that his power depended on his nobles, whom he came to respect, but also, as he grew older, to dominate, too.

But David did have problems with nobles, and the biggest trouble came in the shape of none other than Robert the Steward. Robert thought that David's rule was unfair. The king grabbed taxes to pay the hefty ransom that Edward III had demanded. And, more important still, David, who was still without a son, was manoeuvring to make an English prince his heir, thus ruling the Stewart family out of contention.

So in the early 1360s, Robert the Steward and some of his Scottish noble allies, including the Earls of Douglas and March, launched a rebellion. David moved quickly, on both military and political levels. He gathered an army to crush the rebels and at the same time paid large sums to his allies to make sure that they stayed on his side.

What could have been a disaster for David was averted, and the king continued to rule, levying large taxes to increase royal revenue to its highest ever level, keeping his nobles firmly under his thumb, and attracting able civil servants and courtiers. By the end of his life, the Scottish monarchy was enjoying slightly more prestige than at the start of his reign. But Scotland was still full of rival factions, and the king had to watch his back continuously.

Wife trouble, heir trouble

On a personal level, though, David's life was dogged by difficulties, because he lacked what every medieval king wanted most of all – a direct male heir. Poor David tried several partners in his attempts to have children:

- ✔ **Joan, daughter of Edward II of England and sister of Edward III:** David married her in 1328 and the queen died in 1362; the couple had no children.

- ✔ **Katherine Mortimer:** The daughter of a Scottish knight, she became Edward's mistress in the 1350s, but was murdered in 1360 by a member of the Stewart family. The liaison produced no offspring.

- ✔ **Margaret Logie:** Margaret, a member of a Perthshire family, became David's mistress after the death of Katherine; the couple married in 1363, but again there were no children, and David divorced her in 1370.

- ✔ **Agnes Dunbar:** Agnes was the sister of two of David's key allies. The king was planning to marry her when he died in early 1371.

David seems not to have produced any offspring with any of his partners, one of whom, Margaret, had had a son by a previous husband. In spite of trying, it seems likely that David simply wasn't able to have children.

Because he couldn't produce a direct heir, David's legacy was always in doubt, because rivals could always pop up and allege they had a better claim to the throne than anyone David chose to follow him. And as he passed his mid-40s, David was a sick man. His illness, probably caused by his old war wounds, finally took him in 1371, when he was still only 47. One man had spent much of his life in and around the Scottish royal court, influencing events and watching the political manoeuvres, and that man was ready to take control. He was none other than the High Steward, Robert Stewart (for more about him, see Chapter 12).

Chapter 12

The Stewart Story

*T*he Stewarts were a long-lasting dynasty of Scottish rulers. They first came to prominence in the 14th century and ruled until the beginning of the 18th century. Scotland changed hugely in this long period, developing from a small medieval country at the edge of Europe to a sophisticated state with close ties with its powerful neighbours.

The early Stewart monarchs had to deal with a series of power struggles – for example, king versus barons, Protestant versus Catholic, Scottish versus English – that made life tough at the top and often at the bottom end of society, too. But the Stewarts held tenaciously to power, and some of them greatly increased Scotland's standing in the world.

This chapter tells the Stewart story up to 1603, when a dramatic change in the dynasty's fortunes took place. In 1603, James VI of Scotland took over the throne of England as James I. (For more on the English career of James I, see Chapter 13.)

Trouble with the Barons

In the late 14th century, when the first Stewart kings came to the throne of Scotland, a number of powerful noble families still dominated the country. These nobles had the habit of throwing their weight around, and in order to rule successfully, a Scottish king had to find a way of dealing with them – and preferably getting them on the royal side. The early Stewarts found it tough controlling the Scottish barons, but gradually, they got better at it, becoming stronger rulers and winning Scotland wider respect as a result.

The first two Stewart kings were both called Robert. They seemed a promising, well-liked pair, but both had trouble controlling the noble families around them. Robert II (1371–90) grew up on the west coast of Scotland. He was widely admired – he was good-looking, tall, and, it was said, both generous and honest.

Robert II

When it came to being king, Robert II had a big advantage – he'd already played a huge part in the government of Scotland, acting as Steward of Scotland, holding the office of regent (effectively king) twice during David II's reign (see Chapter 11), and coming to the throne on David's death in 1371, by which time he was already a mature man some 55 years old.

In the early part of his reign, Robert developed a policy of giving his nobles, and his sons, power in their own regions. He didn't travel around the kingdom a great deal, mostly staying at home in Perth and letting his sons (Alexander, John, and Robert) keep control of the more far-flung areas of the kingdom, such as the Highlands. It was a fairly loose style of kingship, and it worked provided that no one rocked the boat. Unfortunately for Robert, after about ten years, the royal boat rocked quite a lot. The 1380s saw two coups:

- ✔ **Coup No. 1 – 1384:** The king's son Alexander had built up his power in the north of Scotland by marching around the Highlands with an army of mercenaries, grabbing land. Alexander's elder brother, John, didn't approve of this approach, nor did he like it when his father failed to deal with the problem. Itching to get on the throne himself, John staged a coup in 1384 and took over power as Lieutenant. Before the Scots knew where they were, they were embroiled in a war France was fighting against England. Robert had allied with France, but did not want to actually fight. John and his noble friends, such as the Earl of Douglas, had other ideas.

- ✔ **Coup No. 2 – 1388:** The war with England brought big trouble for the Scots. The English burned down Edinburgh and forced John to agree to a truce. Even one of the few Scottish successes of the war, the Battle of Otterburn, brought the death of John's friend, the Earl of Douglas. The earl's demise changed the balance of power at court and allowed John's younger brother Robert to take over the Lieutenancy.

Robert II had to spend the last years of his reign under his sons' thumbs. Historians slated him for being cowed by them – and for refusing to join his allies, the French, in their war with England. The medieval chronicler Froissart said he had bleary red eyes, which showed he was a coward. On the other hand, Robert ruled quite successfully in the first years of his reign. He wasn't all bad, but he didn't hold the reins of power tightly enough for a 14th-century monarch.

Robert III

When Robert II died, his first son, John, became king. John took a new name, Robert, and so ruled as Robert III from 1390 to 1406. He probably made the name change to avoid reminding people of the various dodgy kings named John who'd reigned in the past, especially Scotland's John Balliol.

Like his father, Robert III had to try to deal with clashes between powerful noble families and ambitious sons. Most damaging was the ambition of Robert III's son, David, Duke of Rothesay:

- David seized power as Lieutenant in 1399, with the excuse that his father was weak and incompetent in dealing with rebels in the north.

- David himself then fell out with some of his own allies over the Lieutenant's marriage plans and his use of customs money. (He took up with the daughter of one ally, the Earl of Douglas, which alienated another ally, the Duke of Albany.)

- After a vicious propaganda campaign against David, describing him as a moral degenerate who put himself above the law, David was arrested.

The heir to the throne was under arrest and thrown into a dungeon at Falkland Castle, home of his enemy, the Duke of Albany. By March 1402, poor David had starved to death. Robert himself only lived four more years, most of the time under the thumbs of his nobles. There was a new heir to the throne, Robert's son James, but the nobles were trying to use him as a pawn in their manoeuvring for power. Robert decided to send James to France for his protection. In 1406, en route to France, the ship carrying James was attacked by pirates, and the young prince was captured. Robert died soon afterwards, despairing. The kingdom was in crisis.

Jim in a Jam: James I

King James I (1406–37) began his reign a minor who had been captured by English pirates when on a journey to France. The young prince was handed over to the English king, Henry IV. Because relations between England and Scotland were cool, to say the least, the English kept James captive. From an English point of view, James was a priceless bargaining tool in any dispute between the two countries.

The English held on to James for 18 years, but the royal captive wasn't kept in a mouldy dungeon. As a valuable, high-ranking prisoner, James was treated well and educated while he was with the English. In his absence, Scotland was ruled on his behalf by his uncle, Robert, Duke of Albany, and later by Robert's son, Murdac, who held the rank of Governor.

At the end of 1423, the English and Scots came to an agreement that secured the release of James from captivity. The English, who were fighting France at the time, got the Scots to agree not to send any of their soldiers to fight on the side of the French. The Scots were also to pay an enormous ransom of 60,000 marks. In return, James could return to Scotland.

When he finally returned to Scotland in 1424, James was 20 years old and determined to rule with strength. He clearly wanted to avoid the problems previous kings had met when giving nobles too much power in the Scottish regions.

James concentrated on picking up the pieces of Scottish rule by:

- ✔ Removing opponents and potential opponents to his rule, especially the family of Governor Murdac, who threatened to try to hang on to the power they had held before James returned.

- ✔ Raising the money needed to pay the huge ransom the English had demanded for his release.

- ✔ Establishing a royal court on the European model he had seen in England and France.

James knew that it was important to get Scotland taken seriously as a nation by impressing visiting foreign royals and ambassadors. So he embarked on a spending campaign, building a lavish palace at Linlithgow. The palace was kitted out with the latest tapestries, and James's queen, Joan, wore the most expensive jewellery.

It was all very glamorous, but the Scottish Parliament wasn't amused when James tried to raise taxes to pay for all the glitter. The king had to resort to finding money by grabbing land from nobles and raising loans from merchants. Parliament would only give the king money if it was put in a locked box and reserved for spending on things that Parliament thought appropriate.

The big royal spending put a strain on royal relations with the people, especially the rich nobles who resented James's attempts to wrest power and money from their hands. But James was a success in other ways:

- ✔ He was cultured and was one of the few British monarchs to be an accomplished writer – his poem, 'The Kingis Quair' ('The King's Book'), about his love for Joan and his experiences in England, is still read today.

- ✔ He arranged prestigious marriages for his daughters with members of high-ranking European families.

- ✔ He developed a strong style of rule that later members of the Stewart family would build on.

But his lavish spending and his moves toward centralised rule weren't welcome amongst the barons. In 1437, a crisis developed when the interests of powerful families and Parliament came together and tried to arrest the king in Parliament. This attempt failed, and a bunch of opponents rounded on James. An armed group cornered the king in the Dominican monastery at Perth, scuffles broke out, and the king hid in a sewer tunnel. But the other end of the tunnel had been blocked (to prevent tennis balls from the royal court being lost down the drain), and James was trapped. When the attackers found him, they stabbed him to death.

Even poor Queen Joan was injured in the fighting. In fact, her sorry fate garnered her a lot of support as the tragic widow of a king she had loved dearly. As a result, the rebels didn't take over the Scottish crown. After all, killing a king was looked on in Scotland as the most heinous of crimes.

The dead king found some posthumous sympathy, too. His stabbed body was put on display, and many people mourned the man who not so long ago they had lambasted for his habit of taking over people's lands to pay his own growing bills. The murderers were caught, tried, and executed, and Queen Joan prepared to have her small son, another James, crowned as king in his father's place.

Picking Up the Pieces: James II

James II was 6 years old when he was crowned king of Scotland a few months after the murder of his father, James I. During James's minority, the kingdom was governed in the usual way by a Lieutenant, who was traditionally the king's closest male relative. The first Lieutenant was Archibald, Fifth Earl of Douglas, but he died of the plague in 1439, and his heir was a minor. His death left the court prey to squabbles between the nobles and the young king's mother, James I's queen, Joan. The most powerful nobles were members of the Livingston, Crichton, and Douglas families, including James Douglas, who was most famous for being so fat that he was known as James the Gross. These three families dominated Scotland for some ten years.

In 1449, James II picked up the reins of power himself. His first important act was to get married to one of the best-connected women in Europe, Mary of Gueldres, niece of Philip the Good, Duke of Burgundy. His marriage gave James a close link with one of the most powerful families in Europe – and Mary came with a large dowry of £30,000, albeit paid in instalments.

Like his father, James II realised the importance of culture and education. Although he didn't write famous poetry like his father, James II encouraged the arts and Scotland's contribution to the Renaissance, the great renewal of art, science, and culture that was taking place in this period in Europe. A key move was his foundation of Glasgow University.

Deadly Douglases

The courtly manoeuvrings for power didn't end when James was able to act as king in his own right. After a few years, James saw the Douglas family as a major threat to his power. Here's how the issue came to a head in the early 1450s:

- William, 8th Earl of Douglas, built around him an alliance of nobles. Although the earl made the alliance for mutual protection, James seems to have taken it as a threat to royal dominance.

- In 1452, James summoned Douglas to account for what he had done.

- When Douglas came to court, a blazing row ensued, and the earl was set upon by the king and courtiers. Daggers were drawn, and the hapless earl was stabbed to death. His body was said to have 26 stab wounds.

- The new Earl of Douglas gathered an army together and burned down Stirling shortly after James II had left the town.

- By 1455, James II had annexed all the Douglas lands and put an end to the family's power.

James was successful in limiting the power of this noble family, and his work stood the Scottish monarchy in good stead. He stood out as a figure of authority, and people came to respect the king, an imposing figure with a large red birthmark on his face that inspired the nickname James of the fiery face.

Explosive ending

With the Douglases out of the way, James spent much of the rest of his reign attacking England to recover lands that he felt were rightly his. In the 1450s, rival claimants to the English throne were fighting the Wars of the Roses (see Chapter 9), and James was able to score at least one success while they were distracted.

James was an enthusiast for artillery and had acquired a number of big guns, including one affectionately known as Mons Meg from Burgundy. But the big guns led to James's downfall. In 1460, when one of the weapons fired, it broke up, bits of metal flying everywhere. James was standing too close, a fragment pierced his leg, and the king died from blood loss.

People Trouble: James III

When James II was killed in an explosion in 1460, his 9-year-old son, James III (1460–88) became king. When he was a boy, his mother, Queen Mary, was very influential, and not surprisingly, she carried on many of the policies of her late husband. Another important influence on the young king was James Kennedy, Bishop of St Andrews, who took James on a royal tour of Scotland in 1464, encouraging people to state their loyalty to the young king as they went around the country. The third influential noble was Sir Alexander Boyd, who took over control of the king and his government in 1466 by effectively kidnapping James while he was hunting.

Looking to Europe

James took control himself in 1469, soon after marrying Margaret of Denmark, daughter of the ruler of Denmark and Norway, Christian I. This marriage was just one example of a key aspect of James's rule – the way in which he looked to mainland Europe. He had ambitions to give himself the status of emperor and made plans to invade Brittany and take over areas of French territory.

These imperial ambitions came to nothing, but James's policy of making peace with England seemed to make more sense. Even this manoeuvre was doomed, however, because the people of border Scotland were set resolutely against England. The habit of *reiving,* or cross-border raiding, was so ingrained in their way of life that no royal treaty would stop them. There were too many rich pickings, from jewellery to livestock, south of the border.

Nobles versus favourites

James's main failing was in his dealings with people. Like many Scottish kings, he had troubled relations with the country's powerful noble families, and he had a reputation of ignoring the advice of his aristocratic followers and promoting favourites of the lower classes.

James also managed to alienate his relatives. He fell out with his two brothers, Alexander, Duke of Albany, and John, Earl of Mar. Apparently, as a result of their disagreements, John was killed, and Alexander disappeared into exile before the same happened to him. One of the king's sisters, Mary, also fell out with James because he made her marry against her wishes. And the younger sister of the family, Margaret, rebelled against the king's plans for her by having an affair with a nobleman, William, Lord Crichton, and getting herself pregnant in the process.

It wasn't just a dysfunctional family, it was an explosive mixture, and it exploded twice, with dire results for James:

- **Explosion No. 1, 1482:** Mary, Queen Margaret, and a pair of royal uncles staged a rebellion with the backing of English king Edward IV and the involvement of the king's brother, the Duke of Albany. The rebels captured James, and the king was imprisoned in Edinburgh. But Edward died in the spring of 1483, and James recovered his power.

- **Explosion No. 2, 1488:** The problems of 1482 didn't teach James a lesson, and he carried on ruling in a capricious and arbitrary way, dismissing one of his most faithful supporters, Colin Campbell, Earl of Argyll. Another rebellion began, coming to a head in a battle at Sauchieburn near Stirling. James was killed, leaving his 15-year-old son, yet another James, to become king.

Strong-man: James IV

James IV (1488–1513) became king at age 15 and did not take full control until he was 22, in 1495. That was quite old for a late-medieval king, but James wanted to be fully educated when he took up the responsibilities of kingship. When he finally did so, James proved himself to be a strong character who developed an effective way of ruling Scotland, but who got involved in a problematic foreign policy that finally brought him to grief.

James was also a colourful character. He continued the work of his predecessors in bringing the culture of the renaissance to Scotland. And he had an eventful personal life, producing a small tribe of illegitimate children.

Money and government

James had a distinctive take on one old royal problem: how to raise money without getting peoples' backs up. James didn't like calling Parliament. He knew that Parliament could be a meeting point for disagreement and opposition, so he tried as much as possible to rule without it. Because he gathered around him a group of advisers who came from all over Scotland, men who could speak up for the interests of the different Scottish regions, James succeeded in ruling without Parliament most of the time.

But rulers usually called Parliament when they wanted to raise taxes. It could be difficult to get people to pay up without parliamentary sanction. Although James sometimes did get away with raising taxes, he tried other ways of raising money, too – getting control over lands, levying fees in return for charters, increasing rents, and so on.

Sometimes, though, the financial demands of James and his servants got too much to bear. These demands were probably the reason for two rebellions that James had to face in the early years of the 16th century. The two rebels, Donald Dubh and Torquil MacLeod, were eventually defeated in 1506.

But the rebels were the exception. Most people accepted James's kingship, and James made himself more acceptable by putting himself about more than his predecessor, James III, had done. Whereas the earlier James had spent much of his time in Edinburgh, James IV was always travelling around his kingdom, holding courts and settling disputes between his people. These travels made him a more popular king on the whole.

The bed-hopping king

James IV's queen was Margaret, daughter of Henry VII of England. The marriage was politically extremely important to James because it gave him a close alliance with his powerful neighbour, Henry VII. James had always had his eyes on England. As an ally of the French, he had been, in theory, an enemy of England and had supported a usurper, Perkin Warbeck, who had tried to grab the English crown from Henry (see Chapter 13).

But Warbeck failed, and James saw that it made sense to get power over England through subtler means. Marriage to Margaret meant that the Scottish royal family got much nearer the throne of England. In fact, when Henry VII died, and his son Henry VIII became English king, James was actually heir to the English throne until Henry had a son – and it took a long time, and several wives, before Henry's son Edward was born.

All these political considerations meant that the marriage of James IV and Queen Margaret was above all a political one. When it came to having fun in bed, James relied on a string of mistresses, both before and after his marriage. The royal roll-call of mistresses included:

- ✔ Marion Boyd, who bore him two children, a son and a daughter.
- ✔ Margaret Drummond, with whom he had a daughter.
- ✔ Janet Kennedy, with whom he had a son.
- ✔ Isabel Stewart, mother of a daughter.
- ✔ Bessie Bertram, who historians know about because she was the recipient of royal gifts.
- ✔ Another Janet, known as Janet Bare-arse, who leaves nothing to the imagination.

Queen Margaret, incidentally, bore James six children, but all but one of them (a son who became James V) died in infancy.

The Renaissance man

The other side of James's character was his love of learning and his enthusiasm for the developments in Renaissance art that were taking place in Europe during his reign. James presided over a period of excellence in the arts in Scotland, both patronizing important artists and writers himself, and helping to create the kind of society in which they flourished. Here are a few examples:

✔ The king commissioned fine textiles and other decorations for his palaces.

✔ He employed talented artists from continental Europe to make illustrated books, such as a *Book of Hours* (a book containing prayers for the different hours of the day and different days of the religious calendar).

✔ He had his new homes at Holyrood and Linlithgow redecorated in the fashionable French and Italian styles.

✔ He encouraged notable poets, such as William Dunbar, who was awarded a royal pension.

James was also said to speak a large number of languages. He certainly knew Latin, French, some Gaelic, and probably some Danish, from his mother, Margaret of Denmark. He probably knew a few words in several other European languages, too.

Floundering at Flodden

James VI was intelligent and was a capable ruler of Scotland who managed to up royal revenues without offending his people too often. He brought justice to his people with his travelling courts and encouraged the Scottish cities at least to become centres of culture with close links to developments in Europe.

It sounds like a success story, but it all went badly wrong for James. How did it happen? Well, it was to do with his foreign policy and the king's troubled relations with England, the southern neighbour that was nearly always a thorn in the Scottish side.

James knew that Scotland, with its long coastline, was vulnerable to attack from the sea. And his oldest enemy, England, was famed as a nation of seafarers. So James decided that Scotland should have a Navy, too. The king took more than ten years, vast amounts of money, and most of the oak woods of Fife building a mighty fleet. He was proud of his achievement. One ship was named Margaret, after his queen. Another, the Great Michael, took four years to build and was the biggest wooden ship to date.

James's Navy was very impressive and was a clear signal to the English that the Scots weren't to be messed with. Of course, after James married the English princess Margaret in 1503, the English were much less likely to attack

Scotland. But James was still friendly with the French, England's old enemy, so relations were often strained – all the more so because James encouraged *privateers* (pirates, with royal backing) to plunder English ships.

Things got really tense when Scottish privateer Andrew Barton was killed when fighting a ship of Sir Edward Howard, admiral of England, in 1511. It looked as if England and Scotland may go to war – especially because things on the European mainland were getting tense, too.

European politics around 1511 were quite complicated, but to cut a long story short, Pope Julius II (often known as the Warrior Pope – you can see what kind of churchman *he* was) formed an alliance, called the Holy League, against France. The Holy Roman Empire, Venice, Spain, and England (now ruled by Henry VIII) were in the League. James took the side of his old ally, France.

In June 1513, Henry attacked France, and James's ships were sent off to attack Henry's fleet. Bad weather meant the expected fight never took place. But James had an even bigger attack planned. He decided to challenge England on land, and the next month, a vast Scottish army – some say it contained 40,000 men – marched south and were soon taking castles in northern England. It seemed as if James and the Scots were on a roll.

The Scottish attack on England came to a head at Flodden Field, on the edge of the Cheviot Hills, on 9 September 1513. Henry VIII had sent an army north, under the overall command of his wife, Katharine of Aragon, who was in charge because Henry himself was away fighting another war in France. When the English arrived, James was, apparently, ready for them, with his huge army lined up in a good position on the hill.

But then it all went pear-shaped. James sent his massed lines of pikemen through bucketing rain and howling wind to meet the English. But these formally arrayed lines found it impossible to deal with the fast, hand-to-hand fighting of the English. The Scots were soon in a muddy mess and were losing men by the minute.

The Scottish losses were disastrous. As well as thousands of their troops, they lost a host of senior commanders – 14 lords and nine earls. And above all, they lost their leader: James IV himself perished at Flodden. His optimistic reign had come to a sudden, violent end.

King and Queen Mother: Margaret

The sudden death of James IV at the Battle of Flodden Field put his 18-month-old son, James V (1513–42), on to the throne. The boy's mother, Queen Margaret, stepped into the power vacuum and became ruler as Queen-Regent.

Margaret must have known that, as an Englishwoman, she would not be popular as ruler of Scotland. She tried to get around this obstacle by marrying a Scot, Archibald Douglas, 6th Earl of Angus, in 1514.

But Margaret's marriage didn't stop the power struggles that so often dogged a royal minority. Worse still, Margaret found that she didn't get on with her second husband, and James felt he was virtually imprisoned by the Earl of Angus. Finally, Margaret divorced Angus and found herself a third husband, Henry Stewart, Lord Methven, in early 1528.

By this time, James V was 16 years old and sick of being a political pawn, still effectively controlled by his stepfather's family, the Anguses. So in June 1528, James escaped from Edinburgh Castle, reached Stirling, and announced that from then on he would rule in his own right.

Ruthless Ruler: James V

Once he was personally in power, James V had to face a number of the usual problems that beset the Scottish rulers of this period, problems to do with noble opponents, unrest in the Highlands, and raising money. In finding solutions for these challenges, James got himself the reputation of being one of Scotland's most ruthless monarchs:

- **Challenge No. 1 – The nobles:** As soon as he'd assumed personal power, James realised that the noble families who had previously vied with each other to control him wouldn't go away. The Earl of Angus, for example, was ousted by James with the excuse that he had failed to deal with trouble on the English borders. Other opponents and potential opponents were dealt with more violently. Janet Lady Glamis, a supporter of Angus who was rumoured to have tried to poison James, was executed in 1537. So was Sir James Hamilton of Finnart, who was alleged to have plotted against the king.

- **Challenge No. 2 – The Highlands:** The year 1540 saw a royal expedition to the Highlands and islands during which a number of Highlanders were taken prisoner. The king, concerned about unrest in the north of his realm, seems to have been taking these men as hostages to ensure that the Highland lords would behave themselves.

- **Challenge No. 3 – Money:** Raising money when the population doesn't like being taxed is always a problem. Like his father before him, James V looked to other sources of income, especially the church. He rifled church coffers by giving a string of abbeys to his illegitimate children and by putting the screws on the Pope. He made veiled threats that Scotland would not stay loyal to the Catholic Church without a hefty bribe from Rome. Because English king Henry VIII had recently broken from the Roman church, the Pope was worried and paid up: ker-ching!

So did behaviour like this make James exceptionally ruthless? Scottish writers who came after him certainly thought so, and the king had a reputation as a ruthless ruler for centuries afterwards. But more dispassionate historians now think that his actions were par for the 16th-century course. England's Henry VIII had the habit of executing his wives. James just did it to his enemies.

James's other problem was who to marry. He cast around Europe for an eligible bride, and his advisers came up with a long list of possible princesses and nubile nobles in France, Italy, Denmark, and the Holy Roman Empire. In 1536, James settled on Mary of Bourbon, the daughter of a French duke. The Scots were no doubt attracted mainly by her very large dowry. So James set off to France to meet Mary – and was horrified! He said she was a hunch-back.

Undeterred, James found an attractive – and wealthy – bride at the court of the French king, François I. The lucky girl was François' daughter, Madeleine, and James married her on 1 January 1537. But soon after the couple got back to Scotland, poor Madeleine died. James kept her dowry, though.

The death of Queen Madeleine left James free to remarry, and he was soon hitched to Mary of Guise-Lorraine, generally known as Mary of Guise, another Frenchwoman with a big dowry. James was finding out that making good marriages was another way of solving his financial problems!

Mary gave James two sons, but both died in infancy. Their only surviving child was a girl, called Mary after her mother. Mary was born on 8 December 1542 at Linlithgow Palace. The joy of her birth was cut short by tragedy. Just six days after the baby was born, James V died of cholera or dysentry. He left behind a baby girl who was to become probably the most famous of all Scottish monarchs, Mary Queen of Scots.

James V, like any king in this period, wanted a son. There is a story that, just before he died, he made this sententious comment about the Stewart dynasty: 'It cam wi' a lass and it'll gang wi' a lass.' In other words, the dynasty began with a girl, and it was now set to end with one. This saying was made famous by the Scottish writer John Knox, and it's probably a myth. The odd thing was that the prediction came true, but not in the way James meant. The dynasty continued well after Mary's death – but the last of the family's monarchs *was* a woman, Queen Anne, who died at the beginning of the 18th century.

Mary, Queen of Scots

Scotland's most famous ruler, Mary (1542–67) became queen as a baby and spent most of her youth in France. Although she was both attractive and intelligent, she lacked the political skill to navigate her way through the troubles of the mid-16th century.

These troubles centred mainly on two related issues: Scotland's relations with her neighbours, France and England, and the religious disagreements that raged between Protestants and Catholics. There was a personal problem, too. Although Mary's first marriage, to the heir to the French throne, was arranged before she was an adult, Mary later proved to be a disastrous picker of husbands – with explosive results.

Rough wooing, smooth wooing: Young Mary

As queen in her own right, young Mary was hot property. Royals from more than one country were keen for her to marry into their families so that they could get their hands on Scotland. The two most persistent wooers of Mary were the kings of England and France, both of whom had eligible sons.

English king Henry VIII wanted control of Scotland and wanted Mary to marry his son Edward. Eventually, Henry hoped, Edward would become king of both England and Scotland. Henry's way of trying to achieve this goal was to attempt to invade Scotland by attacking the borders. The Scots feared that he would kidnap the small princess and take her away to be married.

This aggressive approach became known as the *rough wooing* of Mary, Queen of Scots. Needless to say, the Scots didn't want their princess kidnapped, so when very small, Mary was hidden away inside the strong walls of Stirling Castle.

Help eventually came from Scotland's old ally, France. French troops helped the Scots fight off Henry's violent advances.

By 1548, the young queen was 5 years old, and the immediate threat from England had been avoided. But the French now pushed for Mary to be taken to France, to become the bride of their prince, François, son of King Henri II. Mary of Guise, the Queen Mother, agreed, so in the summer of 1548, young Mary set off by ship.

Mary settled in France, staying there for 13 years. Surrounded by members of the French court, she soon developed the skills and accomplishments of a European princess:

- She learned French, and the tongue soon became the language with which she was most comfortable.
- She picked up the basics of other languages, such as Latin and Greek.
- She learned how to write poetry.
- She was taught music.

Mary also grew tall, at around six feet, and strikingly attractive. She became a good friend of the French prince, François, and it was no surprise when in 1558 it was announced that the couple were betrothed. They were married in Paris shortly afterwards.

Of course, the royal wedding wasn't just a matter of two young people who liked each other. It had huge political implications, and a group of Scottish diplomats, representing the Scottish Parliament and the interests of Scotland generally, brokered the deal. All kinds of provisions were made for what should happen to the thrones of Scotland and France when the pair died, not to mention what the Scottish people got out of the arrangement. For example:

- ✔ If Mary died first, the relevant Scottish heir to the throne, the Earl of Arran, would become king in Scotland.
- ✔ If François died first, Mary could choose whether to live in France or Scotland.
- ✔ With the crowns of France and Scotland united, dual nationality would be given to the Scottish people.

But, without consulting the commissioners, Mary did another deal, a secret deal with François and Henri, stating that François should continue to reign in Scotland if the queen should die without giving birth. Mary was handing over Scotland on a plate – and, to make matters worse, half of the commissioners who had brokered the official deal died suspiciously before they could return to Scotland.

Catholic versus Protestant

Mary was headstrong, but her life was also deeply touched by sadness. François died in 1560, and Mary's mother died the same year. Mary now had to decide whether to stay in France or return home to Scotland. She decided to go back to the home country, a land she didn't know.

When Mary got back to Scotland, most of her people welcomed her. She was a beautiful young woman who looked every inch a queen. But some people were less enthusiastic. Mary was a Catholic, and Scotland, like many places in Europe at this time, was in the process of turning Protestant. Mary did the sensible thing and said that, while she would not give up the Catholic faith herself, her subjects were free to worship as they pleased.

That suited many, but it didn't please the more fanatical Protestants, who wanted to banish Catholicism from Scotland. Chief among these was John Knox, zealous Protestant reformer and founder of the Church of Scotland.

Even before Mary returned to Scotland, Knox had published a book called *First Blast of the Trumpet Against the Monstrous Regiment of Women*, the women concerned being Catholic queens who tried to make their subjects into Catholics, too.

When Mary returned, Knox objected to her celebration of Mass in the chapel at Holyrood and preached an angry sermon in St Giles High Kirk in Edinburgh. The sermon led to a meeting between Mary and Knox during which the queen insisted that subjects should obey their rulers – to do otherwise was treasonable. Mary didn't have Knox executed for treason, though. The priest withdrew from the front line of public life and concentrated on writing. But the struggles between Protestant and Catholic did not go away.

Too hot to handle

With François dead, the thoughts of Mary, and those near to her, turned to a royal remarriage. Various suitors lined up, and each had his supporters. Catholics, for example, fancied the idea of Mary marrying Don Carlos, son of King Philip II of Spain, and Protestants were relieved when it was announced that Don Carlos had had an accident and was no longer fit to marry.

Husband No. 2: Darnley

Queen Elizabeth, England's Protestant ruler, sent two suitors north to meet Mary. Elizabeth probably doubted that either would succeed, but Mary fell in love with one of them, Henry Lord Darnley, who was actually her second cousin, and the pair were married at six in the morning on 29 July 1565.

Why so early in the day? Well, the Protestant-Catholic enmities still raged on, and Mary's advisers feared that there would be riots if people realised a Catholic marriage ceremony was taking place at Holyrood. Everyone felt it was best to get the ceremony out of the way quickly.

But Mary's troubles had only begun with that ceremony. Darnley turned out to be a disaster as royal consort, for several reasons;

- He turned out to be a repugnant character – self-centred and arrogant.
- He was obsessively jealous, and his jealousy may have led to the murder of Mary's Italian secretary, David Riccio.
- His presence contributed to unrest in Scotland, which came to a head in a rebellion, known as the Chaseabout Raid, in 1565.

Just about the only good thing about Darnley was that he gave Mary a son, James – who had to be locked away in Stirling Castle to prevent rebels from kidnapping him and making him king to replace Mary and the hated Darnley. But hiding away James didn't put off the queen's enemies. In 1566, Mary found herself surrounded by rebels near Musselburgh.

By now, Mary was estranged from Darnley, surrounded by enemies, and her small son was locked away in virtual imprisonment. Then the most dramatic event of her whole reign took place. The house where Darnley was staying blew up in an almighty explosion. Darnley was dead – but not from the blast. His body was found afterwards nearby, lifeless but whole. Everything about Darnley's death was suspicious, but no one knows to this day who killed the hapless consort.

Husband No. 3: Bothwell

Chief suspect in the murder of Darnley was James Hepburn, Earl of Bothwell, a nobleman for whom it was already rumoured that Mary had the hots. What's certain is that Darnley was killed in February 1567, and Bothwell and Mary were married in May the same year. Unfortunate haste or deadly duplicity? Historians will never know.

Bothwell wasn't much better for Mary than Darnley had been. The rebels hadn't gone away. There were now two distinct sides – those who supported the queen, and the so-called King's Men who wanted to put James on the throne. Scotland was in the throes of civil war. But when Mary was surrounded by her enemies at Carberry Hill, a mere month after her wedding, Bothwell was not at her side. Fearing the might of the rebels, he had disappeared and left her in the lurch. Finally, the rebels turned on the pressure still further and forced Mary to give up her throne to her young son. On 24 July 1567, James VI effectively became king of Scotland.

Mary versus Elizabeth

Mary's opponents locked her up in the castle at Lochleven, but her supporters got her free, and Mary fled south to England. The Scottish queen had heard a story that England's queen, Elizabeth, had been sympathetic when she had heard that Mary was in prison. She hoped to be granted asylum in England.

Mary's action posed a problem for Elizabeth. Mary had frequently said that *she* should be queen of England, basing her claim on the fact that she was the great-granddaughter of Henry VII. Elizabeth could not afford to have a claimant to her throne wandering around her country, possibly gathering supporters for a coup, especially as it soon became clear that Mary was indeed a target for any Catholic conspirator who wanted to get rid of Elizabeth.

So Elizabeth did what she had to do. She received her Scottish rival as a guest – and promptly detained her in prison. Being a royal prisoner was often not that much different from being a guest in Elizabethan England. Mary was given quite comfortable accommodation initially. But plotters continued to use Mary as a focus for opposition to Elizabeth, and Mary continued to encourage them.

Finally, after 18 years in captivity, Mary was charged with treason against Elizabeth – an unusual case of one ruler being accused of treason against another. She was executed at Fotheringhay Castle on 8 February 1587. She was initially buried in Peterborough Cathedral, not far away from her place of execution, but later her remains were removed to Westminster Abbey, where she lies in permanent exile amongst the tombs of the rulers of England.

New Hope: James VI

The only son of Mary, Queen of Scots, James VI (1567–1625) became king as an infant and had a long reign, during which the kingdoms of Scotland and England were finally united. After a difficult upbringing, James proved himself an able monarch – an intellectual who wrote several books and who was also a peace-maker.

James's father was murdered and his mother, Mary, Queen of Scots, was executed, so he was brought up as an orphan. He was confined for a long period in Stirling Castle to prevent rivals from kidnapping him, and here his guardians, the Earl and Countess of Mar, brought him up strictly. He was educated by tutors who tried to convince him that his mother was a worthless woman of loose morals.

Meanwhile, Scotland was ruled by a series of regents, dukes, earls, and others, who continuously swapped places in their jockeying for power. During this period, James was given none of the personal support he needed, and the ugly upbringing ended when a group of lords, including Lord Ruthven, kidnapped him in order to grab the advantages of royal power for themselves.

The notorious Ruthven Raid took place in 1582, and by the following year, the teenage James had had enough. He escaped from Ruthven and his cronies, but swiftly found himself dominated instead by James Stewart, Earl of Arran. Finally, in 1585, James announced that he would now rule in his own right.

The late 1580s and 1590s saw the king develop his policy of keeping the peace. Although brought up as a staunch Protestant by his harsh tutors, he resolved to be kind to his Catholic colleagues, letting them off even when coded letters to Spain were discovered – a sure sign that anti-Protestant plotting was afoot.

In 1589, James married a young Danish princess, Anna. Although Anna had a number of miscarriages, the couple produced several children, to the delight of James. Scotland's strict Protestants didn't like the marriage much, however. The king and queen were lambasted for partying, drinking, and dancing. This criticism was too much for James, and he looked for a way to rein in the church. So he brought back senior clergy to the previously bishopless Scottish church, to provide more authority over carping clerics.

Royal paranoia

Although he was a lover of peace, James's difficult upbringing made him a rather jumpy man who often over-reacted to threats. He had a reputation for being paranoid about his safety and was apt to react violently when cornered. A couple of times, his paranoia had dramatic consequences:

✔ **Incident No. 1 – Bothwell's visit:** In 1593, James had trouble with Francis Stewart, Earl of Bothwell (a relative of Mary, Queen of Scots' troublesome husband), who'd had several arguments with the king. Bothwell burst into James's bedchamber, James immediately thought the earl was going to attack him, and he instantly ordered those around him to grab Bothwell. The hapless earl was carted off and banished – even though he insisted that he'd come to make peace with the king.

✔ **Incident No. 2 – The Gowrie plot:** An even more serious incident occurred in 1600 when the Earl of Gowrie and his brother invited James to dinner at their house in Perth. It quickly transpired that those present were going to attack James, who yelled for help. Courtiers dashed to the rescue, and the earl and his brother were soon dead on the floor before anyone could tell how serious their threat had really been.

James the scholar

James was more at home pursuing the peaceful art of scholarship. The king wrote a number of books, was also a poet, translated some of the psalms – and was interested enough to be a patron of other writers. His books include:

✔ *Basilikon Doron*, a book about the best way to govern a country, written for the benefit of his son.

✔ *The True Law of Free Monarchies*, which argues against writers who said that kings should be elected by the people and be responsible to them.

✔ *Demonology*, a book about witchcraft.

✔ *A Counterblast to Tobacco*, which unfashionably said that smoking was a smelly, unpleasant habit.

James was rather ahead of his time in his thinking on tobacco, if nothing else. But he could not have predicted the huge shift in the history of his nation when in 1603, England's Queen Elizabeth died, and he became king of England. (You can find out how he fared as James I of England in Chapter 14.)

Part V

Kingdoms United: Tudors, Stuarts, and Hanoverians

In this part . . .

Three main ruling dynasties – the Tudors, Stuarts, and Hanoverians – held the crown from the 16th to the 19th century. They ruled at a time when the country became the most powerful in the world, exploring the globe's least-known corners, conquering new territories, and building up a vast empire. Closer to home, England and Scotland were united under one ruler in the early 17th century and became fully united as one country about a hundred years later.

These events were very positive ones for the monarchy, but it wasn't all power and success. In the 18th century, Parliament and ministers became much more active in governing the country. Slowly but surely, the Crown was losing its grip on the reins of government as Britain became more democratic.

Chapter 13

The Tudors:
The Monarchy Triumphs

In This Chapter

▶ Checking out the new royal 'brand', the Tudor dynasty

▶ Tracing the disputes between Catholics and Protestants

▶ Understanding the problems faced by married – and unmarried – royals

▶ Exploring the Tudors' difficulties in producing suitable heirs to the throne

*T*his chapter is about one of the most powerful royal dynasties in British history – the Tudors. When the first Tudor king, Henry VII, took over the English throne in 1485, the country was in a right royal mess. During a long civil war between the rival houses of Lancaster and York, many had lost their lives, and royal prestige was at a low ebb. The last Yorkist king, Richard III, had even been accused of murder (see Chapter 9). The Tudors at last brought more peace and stability. Henry VII put the royal finances on a sound footing, Henry VIII tried to increase English influence abroad, and Elizabeth I presided over a period when Britain was producing some of the greatest names in literature and the arts.

But it wasn't all sweetness and light. The Tudors argued constantly over religion, sometimes even putting people to death because of their beliefs. How fanatical was that? And their personal lives were complicated, too, from Queen Mary's absentee husband to Henry VIII's six wives – it's a wonder he found the time or energy to rule at all. But in spite of their marital troubles, the Tudors left the country, and the monarchy, stronger than they found it.

New Broom: Henry VII

The first Tudor king came to the throne after beating Richard III at the Battle of Bosworth in 1485 and ruled until 1509 (see Chapter 9). After years of political ping-pong between the rival houses of Lancaster and York, Henry Tudor seemed to offer the chance of stability. Henry was a Welshman with strong English connections. His mother was Margaret Beaufort, great-great-granddaughter of Edward III. His father was Edmund Tudor, son of a man called Owen Tudor, who had been Henry V's personal attendant, had fallen in love with his boss's wife Queen Catherine of Valois, and married her after Henry V died.

Young Henry VII was tall, strong, and striking, with piercing blue eyes, and he had a reputation as a tough guy who could sort his enemies out. A lot of the English liked him because he seemed a powerful character who could win plenty of support. The Welsh liked him because, well, he was Welsh. But plenty of Yorkist supporters did not want this outsider from the Lancastrian side on the throne. It was not going to be a bed of roses for Henry VII.

But Henry had a cunning plan. He thought he would be safer on the throne if he married a princess from the other side, uniting the houses of Lancaster and York once and for all. It helped that an attractive single woman – Elizabeth of York, daughter of the Yorkist king Edward IV – was available. Henry didn't waste any time. Soon after he was crowned in October 1485, he jumped into bed with Elizabeth. The following January, he made an honest woman of her.

Elizabeth probably didn't have a lot of choice in the matter. She was a well-connected princess caught in a national power struggle. A royal bride in the 15th century knew that she was marrying for political reasons. She would be expected to look good at court occasions, produce lots of children, and make the best of it for the sake of king and country. But by all accounts Henry and Elizabeth's marriage was a happy one. The couple had eight children.

Lancaster and York were united at last. Henry and his advisers came up with a brilliant symbol to advertise this union – the Tudor rose, with its red petals for Lancaster and its white petals for York. It was one of the best bits of royal branding ever.

Bakers and fakers

It wasn't all plain sailing for Henry. Lancaster and York were united in a way, but some people still wanted a real Yorkist king on the throne. Henry had to deal with several rival claimants to power:

- ✔ **The Earl of Warwick:** The earl was the Yorkists's favourite claimant because he was Edward IV's nephew. Henry's response: He had the earl locked safely away in the Tower of London.

✔ **Lambert Simnel:** Simnel was a baker's son, but the Yorkists dressed him up in fine clothes and claimed that he was the real Earl of Warwick. They wanted him to be Edward VI, and no wonder, with a name like Lambert. The fake earl was soon leading an army across England and preparing for an attack. Henry's response: He defeated the attackers, captured Simnel – and gave him a job in the royal kitchens.

✔ **Perkin Warbeck:** He was another fake, who claimed he was the Duke of York – one of a pair of princes who had disappeared a couple of years ago, presumed murdered by Richard III. The Yorkists wanted him to be Richard IV. Henry's response: He captured Perkin and had him executed. At the same time, Henry gave the real Earl of Warwick the chop, too, just to be on the safe side.

New monarchy?

When Henry came to the throne, the royal treasury had very little money. Decades of warfare had seen to that. The king realised he had to tighten the royal purse-strings and find ways of raising money. Quickly. Henry became highly skilled at getting money out of his people. He increased customs duties, raised loans, and squeezed the barons for all they were worth.

Henry was especially good at finding excuses to fine his barons. He took advantage of old laws preventing barons from keeping private armies – and these armies could consist of servants, as well as real armies of soldiers. On one occasion, visiting the Earl of Oxford, Henry casually asked how many servants the earl had in his household. 'Two hundred at least,' boasted the Earl. Henry pounced and extorted a £10,000 fine from the hapless earl. Ouch!

Many barons hated the money-grubbing monarch, but they could do little about it. With every new fine, they got weaker and weaker. Taking power away from the barons seemed like a clever new strategy, but, in fact, Henry was doing what previous rulers had done, too. He was just more efficient about it – and more successful.

Henry had it all – power, riches, and a happy home life. He even prepared well for the next generation by arranging for his eldest son, Arthur, to marry a high-profile princess from Spain, Catherine of Aragon. The monarchy was in better shape than it had been for more than a hundred years. But personal tragedy soured the king's last years. In 1502, Arthur died, leaving the king's second son, also called Henry, as heir to the throne. The following year, the monarch's beloved wife Elizabeth also died. Henry VII spent his last six years sad and lonely.

Punching above His Weight: Henry VIII

The new king, Henry VIII (1509–47), seemed like a great white hope – and a breath of fresh air after dusty Henry VII. He was only 17 years old, fit, and intelligent, and he enjoyed good food, good music, boisterous sports like wrestling and jousting, and female company.

Henry was brave, but rather too reckless for his own good. Three times he nearly lost his life because of his addiction to dangerous sports:

- **Helmet howler:** In 1524, Henry forgot to put his helmet visor down while jousting. The Duke of Suffolk walloped the king on the head with his lance, narrowly missing Henry's face. Henry laughed it off.

- **Lucky leap:** In 1525, Henry pole vaulted over a broad ditch when he was out hawking. The pole broke, sending head-first Henry in the mud. With his head wedged under the sticky goo, he nearly drowned, but a foot-man managed to pull him out – by his foot, presumably!

- **Horse horror:** In 1536, Henry was unhorsed in a joust, and his mount fell on top of him. The king was unconscious for two hours.

The young king was also intelligent and talented. His accomplishments included:

- **A gift for languages** – he knew French, Italian, Spanish, Latin, and some Greek.

- **A grasp of theology** that enabled him to debate with the powerful churchman around his court.

- **A knowledge of the sciences,** especially astronomy, geometry, and maths.

- **A real gift for music** – he could play the lute well, was also good on key-board instruments such as the virginals (no surprises there), and wrote quite a lot of music, including a song called 'Pastime with Good Company'.

Henry was clever, musical, reckless – and rather lucky. But what sort of king would he make? A careful administrator like his father? Or a chivalrous hero like warrior-ancestors Henry V and Edward III? There was no contest. It was the warrior-hero option for Henry, every time. His father's money-grubbing held no interest for young Henry.

Henry started his reign by giving two of his father's hated ministers, Empson and Dudley, the swift heave-ho. They were quickly arrested and bundled off to prison, and the king announced that they would be executed. Henry wanted people to believe that he would have no more extortion or dark threats on his watch. But his father's henchmen weren't actually given the chop for 16 months, because Henry had trouble getting Parliament to agree. It wasn't the last time that Henry made a big gesture that backfired.

With friends like these. . .

If Henry was to be a warrior-king, he would have to go war – and who better to fight than the old enemy, France? Henry was hardly on the throne before he was hinting that he was going to fight France's king, Louis XII, and reclaim some of England's old lands in Europe. On three occasions at the beginning of his reign, Henry planned attacks on France. Each time, it was a disaster.

Here's the lowdown on Henry's French flops:

- **Gascony, 1512:** The English were meant to meet up with Spanish forces and attack the French. But there was a Spaniard in the works. King Ferdinand of Spain didn't show up. Henry's army was left stuck without food and support, in the pouring rain. Result: an expensive, soggy mess.

- **Northern France, 1513:** This time the campaign was planned by Henry's ruthless minister Cardinal Wolsey, and the king led the army himself. The English took many French prisoners and captured the towns of Therouanne and Tournai, but again Henry's allies started to lose interest. Ferdinand of Spain made his own truce with France, while the Pope and Emperor both pulled out of the alliance. Result: Henry was left high and dry.

- **Northern Italy, 1516:** In league with the emperor Maximilian I, Henry employed Swiss mercenaries to attack French forces occupying northern Italy. But Maximilian pulled out, the Swiss demanded more money, and Henry pulled out. Result: Henry lost his bottle – and lost face with France's glamorous new king, François I.

Spend, spend, spend

Henry was well out of the war with France, which was expensive, as well as dangerous. But the power and influence of the French still irked him. Together with his minister Wolsey, Henry hatched a clever plan. Instead of war-mongering, England would play the role of peace-broker in Europe. The trouble was, Europe didn't stay peaceful, and England got broker.

To further his peace mission, in 1520 Henry organised the most lavish summit conference the world had seen. It was called the Field of Cloth of Gold and was a meeting in northern France between Henry and François. The kings, together with thousands of courtiers and followers, met in a lavish temporary town made of wooden buildings and tents. Some 2,000 skilled workers from England and Flanders built Henry a makeshift summer palace.

The French camped in top-of-the-range tents made from glittering golden material. The two kings held a series of tournaments and ate and drank tons of food and oceans of wine and beer. The whole event was so grand and costly that it was called the Eighth Wonder of the World.

The food bill alone came to £8,839 – the equivalent of about £2.6 million today. The food purchased by Henry included:

- 2,200 sheep
- 1,300 chickens
- 800 calves
- 340 'beeves' (that's cattle to you and me)
- 312 herons
- 13 swans
- 17 bucks
- 9,000 plaice
- 7,000 whiting
- 700 conger eels

At this monstrous beanfeast, the two kings tried to outdo each other with displays of swanky clothes, lavish decoration, hoards of attendants, and elaborate settings. The pair were perfectly courteous to each other and challenged each other in different sports. François beat Henry in a wrestling bout, while Henry won an archery contest. But nothing political came of the meeting. The end result was a huge bill – and still no peace. Henry was broke and still lacked the power he wanted.

No hope from the Pope

Henry's biggest problem of all was that he had no male heir. Every king in this period wanted a son to whom he could hand over the crown. But with his wife, Catherine of Aragon, Henry had only one child, a daughter called Mary. In 1527, with Catherine in her 40s, the king felt he had a better chance of producing a boy if he remarried. He had his eyes on a younger woman at court, Anne Boleyn, and was desperate to make her his queen.

In the early 16th century, divorces were hard to come by. You usually had to ask the Pope's permission to get divorced, and the Pope wasn't always keen on the idea, unless you had a good theological argument up your sleeve. Henry thought he had the perfect case for dumping Catherine. Catherine had been married to Henry's elder brother, Arthur, who died, leaving her a widow. Henry married her soon afterwards, but he found a verse in the Bible that seems to condemn such marriages. In the book of Leviticus (chapter 20, verse 21), it says: 'If a man shall take his brother's wife, it is an impurity'. So Henry thought he might have a chance of the Pope granting his wish.

Thomas Wolsey

Even a king as powerful and willful as Henry could not act alone. Henry employed Thomas Wolsey, one of the slickest politicians of the time, as his Lord Chancellor. Wolsey was from a humble background – his father was a butcher, and young Thomas made a career in the church, rising to the rank of Cardinal. So Wolsey had a foot in both camps as a high churchman and a powerful royal minister – he seemed to be in the ideal position to get Henry the divorce he wanted.

In many ways, Wolsey was successful. He controlled Henry's foreign policy and although it sometimes ended in disastrous wars, Wolsey was probably more competent than Henry would have been if left to his own devices. The king rewarded his Chancellor with money, houses, and other gifts, and Wolsey's home at Hampton Court was nearly as large and lavish as a royal palace.

But Wolsey came unstuck. He could not persuade the church to give Henry the divorce he so badly wanted. Suddenly, he found himself out of favour, and even handing Hampton Court to the king did not help him. Both the king and Anne Boleyn's friends wanted him out, and he lost his job. He would have lost his head, too, but he died on his way to London to face a charge of treason.

But Pope Clement was reluctant. He knew that other parts of the Bible support a man who marries his brother's widow. And anyway, he was under the thumb of the Holy Roman Emperor Charles V, who hated Henry because the English had pulled out of their war with his enemy, France. In addition, the queen was Charles's aunt. The Pope sent a representative, Cardinal Campeggio, over to England to hear Henry's case. But the church couldn't come up with a decision, and the affair dragged on for several years.

Then, in late 1532, a crisis occurred. Henry got Anne Boleyn pregnant. He knew he had nine short months to sort things out and make his new child legitimate. The king enlisted the help of Thomas Cranmer, the archbishop of Canterbury. Cranmer agreed to declare Henry's marriage to Catherine invalid, and the poor queen was given the boot and sent into a quiet retirement. She died a few years later. In January 1533, Cranmer married Henry and Anne. It gave Henry a fresh start – and the chance of a son to inherit the English throne.

Head of the church

When Henry ignored the Vatican in his divorce crisis, he knew he was stirring up trouble. He and archbishop Cranmer had overruled the most powerful person in the Catholic Church. Relations with the Pope were breaking down. Henry and his advisers saw that they would have to declare the English church independent from Rome.

Henry pushed a series of laws through Parliament, leading up to a complete break with the Roman church:

- ✔ **1532, Act in Conditional Restraint of Annates:** Put an end to the practice of English clergy paying taxes to Rome.

- ✔ **1533, Act in Restraint of Appeals:** Forbade bishops from appealing to the Pope and declared that England was a sovereign state whose king was responsible only to God.

- ✔ **1534, Act of Supremacy:** Established Henry as the supreme head of the Church of England.

- ✔ **1534, Act for First Fruits and Tenths:** Diverted church taxes into Henry's treasury.

- ✔ **1539, Act of the Six Articles:** Defined the doctrines of the Church of England in law.

Henry now had the new wife he wanted and had freed himself from the influence of the Pope. In this sense at least, Henry was the most powerful English king for centuries.

Bad habits: The monasteries are closed

When he became head of the Church of England in 1534, Henry realised that as well as a source of power, he also had a source of wealth. The church owned lots of land, buildings, and possessions, and Henry quickly commissioned a survey, called the *Valor Ecclesiasticus* (Ecclesiastical Valuation), to find out how much these items were worth.

The valuation showed that a huge amount of wealth was in the hands of the monasteries, which had an income of some £136,000 a year (around £40 million in today's money). Many people were convinced that the monasteries were not the places of piety and goodness that they were meant to be. Many stories of corruption circulated, including monks cutting mass to go hunting and even abbots keeping mistresses. The Act of Supremacy gave Henry power over the monasteries, so he charged his minister Thomas Cromwell to send out inspectors to see whether the rumours were true. If they were true, Henry could close the monasteries and pocket their wealth.

When Cromwell's inspectors came back, they had plenty of tales of sin and abuse for Henry. They reported drunken monks at one abbey, and an abbot profiting from piracy at another. Not all abbeys were corrupt, but Henry had enough evidence to do what he wanted. Between 1536 and 1540, all the monasteries in England and Wales were closed, and Henry was loaded. He could start spending again.

Henry used his new-found wealth in all sorts of ways. He outraged the clergy with some of the uses he found for monastic property:

- The chapel of the London Charterhouse, home of pious Carthusian monks, became a store for garden equipment and tents.

- Stone from the walls of Merton Priory was used for Henry's luxurious palace at Nonsuch.

- God's House, Portsmouth, became an armoury.

- Maison Dieu, Dover, was used to house provisions for the Army.

Henry also sold off about two-thirds of the monastic property to pay for his lavish lifestyle and yet more wars with France.

The six wives

Henry VIII is famous as Britain's most-married king. He changed partners frequently for two reasons – he was trying to produce a son to secure the succession, and he wanted to ally himself at different times with different ruling families in Europe.

Henry's remarriages had a big impact on the royal family. On several occasions, when the king took a new wife, any children from previous marriages were thrown out of the royal household to live with guardians. Only two of Henry's wives, Jane Seymour and Catherine Parr, tried to bring the family back together again. The following section highlight the key details on Henry's six queens.

Catherine of Aragon

Henry married the Spanish princess Catherine, his brother's widow, in 1509, just before he became king. To start with, the partnership was successful. The couple were in love with each other, and Catherine was pleased to have netted a handsome, powerful husband after the sadness of her first spouse's death. Henry wore her initials on his sleeve and called himself Sir Loyal Heart. When he captured some French towns on his campaign of 1513, he gave her the keys to their gates. The couple's happiness was complete when, on New Years' Day 1511, the queen gave birth to a baby boy.

But their happiness was short-lived. Although apparently healthy, the young prince, Henry, died suddenly when only two months old. It was the beginning of years of sadness for Catherine, with a string of pregnancies, stillbirths, and infant deaths until, in 1516, she produced her only sturdy child, a girl called Mary. More stillbirths followed.

Poor Catherine. Unable to produce the son Henry so desperately wanted, she was getting plump and wrinkly, too. The husband she loved and who she had deputised for in his absence no longer wanted her. It was no more Sir Loyal Heart for Henry. In 1533, Henry divorced Catherine and married one of her ladies-in-waiting, Anne Boleyn.

Anne Boleyn

Anne was an attractive temptress who soon had Henry eating out of her hand. Although not conventionally beautiful, she had eyes that a Venetian visiting Henry's court described as 'black and beautiful'. Henry and Anne found each other attractive, but Henry already had mistresses – including Anne's sister, Mary – and Anne did not want to become part of a kind of royal harem. If Henry wanted her, he had to promise to make her his queen.

Henry, hoping that Anne would produce a male heir, promised exactly that. He wrote to her saying that he would marry her, and the couple wed in 1533. Even before they tied the knot, the attraction bore fruit. But Anne's child was a girl, Elizabeth, and Henry was disappointed again. Even so, Anne kept her power over Henry, even influencing the timing of the king's meetings with his advisers.

But Anne's power was eventually her undoing. The queen's enemies at court started to plot against her. They got her charged with adultery – with her brother. Henry could not stand for this betrayal and had her executed in 1536. By then, he had already fallen for another lady-in-waiting, Jane Seymour.

Jane Seymour

Jane Seymour was very different from Anne Boleyn. Quiet and modest, she spurned Henry's advances, which began well before Anne was beheaded. She sent back his letters unopened, refused a present of gold, and would only speak to him when others were present. Of course, this rejection only made Henry more eager to have his way with her, although it was the very opposite of what Jane wanted.

Once Anne was dead, Jane succumbed to the king, and Henry married wife No. 3 in 1536. Jane had a mellowing influence on Henry. She even persuaded him to welcome back to court his first daughter, Mary, who had been estranged from him since the death of her mother Catherine. But best of all for Henry, Jane gave him the son he so desperately wanted – the prince, Edward, was born in 1537.

But the prince came at a terrible price. The queen had been crudely cut open by the Tudor surgeons whose only thought was for the life of her baby son. Jane caught a fever and died 12 days after giving birth, only 18 months after their marriage, leaving Henry with one weak and sickly son, Prince Edward. Henry was bereft, and Jane was the only one of his wives to be buried with all the high ceremony of the Tudor court in St George's Chapel, Windsor.

Anne of Cleves

Henry's fourth wife was a political choice, a Protestant princess from Germany. At the time they married, tensions existed between England and the Holy Roman Emperor, Charles V. Charles was a Catholic, so Henry wanted to strengthen his ties with Protestant royalty. Anne seemed to fit the bill.

Henry's minister Thomas Cromwell inflamed the king's ardour by talking up Anne's beauty. Henry asked for more particulars of the princess's attractions and charged his ambassadors to report back on her looks – and on those of Anne's sister, for good measure. The ambassadors complained that the sisters' clothes did not allow them to inspect the princesses properly, a remark that enraged their host, the Chancellor of Cleves. 'Why? Would you see them naked?' he asked. Fortunately Henry was not there; otherwise, the answer would probably have been an emphatic, 'Yes, please!'

The king solved the problem by sending over his court painter, the renowned Hans Holbein, to do portraits of both sisters – with their clothes on, of course. When the pictures were sent back to England, Henry chose Anne, and the couple married in 1540.

But Henry didn't find Anne attractive when he met her in the flesh – he said she looked like 'a Flanders mare'. When the threat from Charles V receded, Henry divorced Anne – a mere six months after the wedding – and the poor woman went to live in quiet retirement in the country. Henry, meanwhile, went in search of wife No. 5.

Catherine Howard

By now, the king was getting old and was often ill. A problem with his lungs in 1538 had given him breathing difficulties, and he spent a whole week speechless, which was intolerable for noisy Henry. But in 1540, he married teenage Catherine Howard. The new young bride seemed to make Henry feel younger, too. He seemed to have been given a new lease of life.

Catherine had stolen Henry's heart, and he repaid her with lavish gifts – one was a brooch containing 33 diamonds and 60 rubies. But sadly another man, Thomas Culpeper, had stolen hers. After marrying the king, she carried on her relationship with Culpeper. A notorious flirt-about-the-court, Catherine also had relationships with other men in Henry's circle. At first, Henry refused to believe the stories that circulated about his queen's affairs. When he finally accepted the truth, it was the chop for both Catherine and Thomas. They were executed in 1542.

Catherine Parr

Henry's last wife, whom he wed in 1543, was the lucky one. Already twice a widow, she survived him. While married to Henry, Catherine gained power in the court, and, like the king's first wife, sometimes deputised for her husband. She also pulled the royal family back together, reuniting the king's children from his previous marriages and employing good tutors to teach them. Their relationship was much closer to being one of equals. And Catherine was almost Henry's equal in another way. After the king died, she remarried once more, to make her England's most-married queen.

The last years

By the 1540s, Henry's love of good food had got the better of him. He was hugely overweight, with a belly like a barrel and a face like parchment. To make matters worse, he had ulcers on both his legs, which made them swell painfully. For long periods, he also shivered with fevers.

Henry could no longer run, jump, and brandish his sword. He was almost immobile. Servants carried him around on a litter, and special machinery was installed to haul him upstairs. By Christmas 1547, he had drawn up his will, arranged for a council of advisers to help his son Edward when he became king, and prepared for the end. He died on 28 January 1547.

Henry's most important legacy was the break with Rome (see the earlier section, "Head of the Church"). By severing England's links with the Catholic Church and making himself head of the church in England, he created a new connection between monarch and English church, one that that endures today.

His other great legacy was his youngest child. Although Henry spent his life trying to produce a male heir, his daughter Elizabeth was to prove one of the greatest rulers Britain has known. It was the crowning irony of Henry's reign. He would not have been amused.

Boy-King: Edward VI

When Henry VIII died in 1547, he had one surviving son, the boy of nine who became Edward VI. Edward, whose mother was Henry's favourite wife, Jane Seymour, inherited his father's strong will and fierce intelligence, but he did not have Henry's athleticism and rude health. Pale and frail, Edward did not seem likely to live long, and his rule only lasted until 1553.

Prayer Book in . . . Mass out

Henry had Edward educated by some of the greatest scholars of the time. These men, such as the Oxford divine Roger Ascham and Cambridge man John Cheke, gave Edward the most thorough education of any monarch to date. At a time when many princes could hardly read or write, Edward had to do loads of Latin and bags of Greek. Boring? Well, Edward seems to have enjoyed it and been very good at it. He had neat handwriting, too.

Edward's teachers were staunch Protestants who wanted the English church to move still further from the ways of Roman Catholicism. Leading Protestants also acted as Edward's Protectors, advising the boy-king and steering his rule. The first of these Protectors was his uncle, Edward Seymour, Duke of Somerset. Somerset was quite popular amongst ordinary people, because he tried to curb the power of the barons, who had been nicking common land by fencing it off. People needed this land to graze their livestock and were pleased when Somerset put a stop to the barons' foul fences.

Under Edward and Somerset, England became a truly Protestant country. In 1549, they introduced the *Book of Common Prayer*, which contained complete texts for Protestant prayers and services. For the first time, these prayers were in English, not the Latin that the Catholics had used. While many people liked Somerset, not everyone liked the new prayer book. Some people were attached to the old Latin Mass and felt that it was improper to talk to God in common or garden English. The people of Devon and Cornwall even launched a rebellion about it.

Edward and Somerset's troubles got even worse when another rebellion occurred. This time, trouble broke out in East Anglia, because the bumptious barons there were still fencing off common land. It was all too much for Somerset to cope with, and in 1550, he lost his power to a new Protector, John Dudley, Earl of Warwick. Dudley immediately made himself look still more powerful by appointing himself as Duke of Northumberland.

Nine-day wonder

By 1552, things looked bad for Edward. Always pale, he was now thin and spluttering. He had caught tuberculosis, and his doctors could see that he probably only had a short time to live. As usual, thoughts turned to the succession. Protector Northumberland thought he could hang on to power by marrying his son to Lady Jane Grey, a sort of grand-niece of Henry VIII, who had a claim to the throne.

Once the pair were wed, the Protector started to work on Edward, persuading the boy-king to name Jane as his successor. On 6 July 1553, Edward died, and Northumberland had Jane crowned. But Edward's half-sister, Mary, had a better claim to the throne – after just nine days of Queen Jane, Mary entered London and had Jane, her husband, and the scheming Northumberland locked in the Tower. Mary was now queen.

Bloody Mary: Mary 1

Mary Tudor, who ruled from 1553–58, had Spanish blood in her veins, and it showed. She was the daughter of Henry VIII and his first wife, Catherine of Aragon, and, like her mother, she was a devout Catholic. Today, Mary has a bad reputation because of the way she persecuted Protestants, but at the time, most of her subjects liked her.

Mary had had a hard time of it as a girl. When Henry VIII turned against Catherine of Aragon in favour of his second wife, Anne Boleyn, he turned against Mary, too. He referred to her as illegitimate and, like the royal bully he was, tried to cow Mary into submission. But Mary was feisty and stood her ground – she refused to accept that her mother should be denounced.

Some time after Catherine died, Henry accepted Mary back into court life, but she did not fit in easily. It probably didn't help that she was not conventionally pretty and felt herself to be an outsider. She also knew her father could easily throw her out again. The one constant thing in Mary's existence was her passionate devotion to her Catholic faith. Her faith was the main influence on her entire life and on her short reign as England's queen.

The Spanish question

Less than a year after coming to the throne, Mary announced her marriage plans. And they were a bombshell. Mary had decided to wed the king of Spain – the most powerful Catholic ruler in Europe. Most English people were amazed. They were going to be ruled not only by a Catholic but by a foreign Catholic. Philip, the Spanish king, was to be joint ruler with Mary – his head was even put on the coinage, which was not a popular measure. Trouble was brewing for England's Protestants.

The Protestants' fears were justified. Mary brought Catholicism back to England, and she did so with a ruthlessness that looked far from Christian. As soon as she was on the throne, she began to act:

✔ She ordered the church to celebrate the Catholic Mass in Latin once more.

✔ She repealed all the anti-Catholic laws passed by Henry VIII.

✔ Around 1,000 Protestants left England for friendlier countries in Europe.

✔ More than 300 Protestants who would not give up their faith were burned at the stake.

Long-distance loving

While all this was going on, Mary was also getting to know her new husband. After a few months of marriage, Mary believed herself to be pregnant. After another few months, it turned out to be wishful thinking. Philip, who didn't find his new wife very attractive, had high-tailed it back to Spain, leaving Mary high and dry. Mary was upset, lonely, and left with only her religion to console her.

Mary threw herself into her work, spending hours on state business and engagements, and then sitting up half the night writing letters to Philip. She was often heard crying when alone in her room, and one ambassador reported a rumour that the queen was tortured by dreams of love and passion.

But they were just dreams. It was two whole years before Philip returned to England, and this time he was more interested in organizing England's Navy for his planned war with France than in the pleasures of the marriage bed. In any case, Mary was now in her late 30s, which in Tudor times was very late to be planning a family. Even so, there was hope when the queen once more seemed to be pregnant.

Meanwhile, Philip's war in France seemed at first to be going well, but a blow came for the English in January 1558 when the French counter-attacked and took Calais, the one part of France that had remained in English hands since the Hundred Years War (see Chapter 8) in the 15th century. Mary was devastated, and political defeat was replaced by personal tragedy when her second pregnancy turned out to be cancer. She fell ill and died, of a mixture of grief and physical illness, aged only 42.

Gloriana: Elizabeth 1

When Mary died in 1558, the way was left clear for her half-sister, Elizabeth, to be crowned queen. Elizabeth, the daughter of Henry VIII and his second wife, Anne Boleyn, is one of the most famous British monarchs, and understandably so. She reigned for 45 years, presided over a time of English success in all sorts of fields from exploration to the arts, sent her enemies packing, and did all this work without what every woman at the time would have expected as her right – the support of a husband.

Elizabeth could manage all these responsibilities because she was highly intelligent. She could speak and write Latin, Greek, French, and Italian, wrote poetry, and could play keyboard instruments as well. But she wasn't a swot. She liked big banquets and lavish state occasions, and she was especially partial to court ceremony – all her officials and courtiers had to line up in strict order of rank when waiting to speak to her.

Elizabeth adored clothes and jewellery. Her dresses were studded with gems, and one of her most prized possessions was a ruby the size of a tennis ball. She also had a passion for dancing, which all the eligible young men at court were very willing to indulge. Historians remember Elizabeth as the Virgin Queen, but her contemporaries had a more impressive-sounding nickname for her: Gloriana. However, her glorious life started with setbacks and trauma.

Troubled childhood

Before Princess Elizabeth was 3 years old, her father had her mother beheaded for adultery. As a child, she had her own household and visited court occasionally. When her father died, she lived with his last wife, Catherine Parr, and Catherine's second husband, Sir Thomas Seymour.

Seymour meant trouble for Elizabeth. Big trouble. He planned to marry her when Catherine died, hoping that the young princess would become queen, and he would worm his way on to the throne beside her. Seymour also fancied his teenage ward and was always making up to her sexually. Stories went around that Seymour would try to fondle Elizabeth, that he had romps in bed with her, and that on one occasion he ripped off one of her dresses because he said the colour didn't suit her.

Elizabeth managed to ward off Seymour's advances, but they left her psychologically damaged. Her experience with Seymour, plus her father's troubled marriage history and her mother's violent death, made Elizabeth suspicious of marriage. She saw sex as a threat – but she also saw that her sexuality could give her power, so long as she kept control.

High-maintenance monarch

When Elizabeth was crowned queen she was already popular. She had the Tudor red-headed, fair-skinned good looks, a ready wit, and lots of glamour. People were so obsessed with her that on coronation day, they ripped up the blue carpet that was laid to the door of Westminster Abbey because they wanted a piece of the material on which she had walked. The souvenir-hunters nearly tripped up several of Elizabeth's attendants. Who said celebrity was a modern invention?

Elizabeth quickly turned out to be very demanding. She expected expensive gifts from her courtiers at least three times a year – every New Year, on her birthday, and on her *accession day,* the anniversary of the day she came to the throne. One New Year, she got from various favourites:

✔ A purse and brooch encrusted with jewels from the Earl of Leicester.

✔ A golden jewel from the Earl of Essex.

> ✔ A gold pomander and a chain set with pearls from Sir Thomas Heneage.
>
> ✔ A coronet and collar of gold, diamonds, and jewels from Sir Christopher Hatton.
>
> ✔ A jewelled fan that opened to show her portrait from Sir Francis Drake.

Jewels rule. Elizabeth loved gifts like these, especially if they had her own portrait on them as well. It wasn't just vanity – she needed to convince people that she was a powerful ruler who would not be overthrown.

The queen put the generosity of her courtiers to another, more cunning use. Most monarchs splashed out lots of money building palaces, but not Elizabeth. She spent a lot of time staying in her courtiers' houses instead. Some courtiers forked out a fortune doing up their houses, just in case she came to stay. They had to foot the bill, so she lived the high life and saved money at the same time – a royal double whammy.

Like a virgin?

The people were hysterical and her courtiers vied with each to get their houses made over, but Elizabeth was determined to keep her head. She pledged that she would be a good queen. She was also determined to stay single. She knew that if she gave in and got married, it would be the end of her personal power in male-dominated Tudor England. She quickly realised that any man who asked to marry her would want one thing – a seat on the English throne.

And another thing. Nearly all the eligible princes in Europe were from Catholic families. Elizabeth was a Protestant, so the last thing she wanted was some European Catholic ruler taking the country back to Rome again. One Catholic king who was interested in Elizabeth was none other than Queen Mary's widower, Philip of Spain. If he got his hands on Elizabeth, not only would England be Catholic again, but it would become a distant outpost of Spain. So Elizabeth gave suitors the brush-off.

But the problem was that Elizabeth actually rather liked male company, and she got really jealous when any of her maids married – especially if they didn't ask her permission. One got her ears boxed for this mistake; another had her husband thrown into prison. Talk about a green-eyed monster! State business meant that Elizabeth met men all the time, and all those palace dances threw her into the arms of many courtiers – literally. Many of these courtiers were men who helped Elizabeth rule. They weren't royals, so they weren't really serious suitors, but the queen flirted with them to make them do what she wanted.

Elizabeth even gave them nicknames:

- ✔ Sir William Cecil, Lord Burghley, Secretary of State and Lord High Treasurer, was Spirit.
- ✔ Sir Francis Walsingham, Privy Councillor and spy-master, was Moor.
- ✔ Robert Dudley, Earl of Leicester, military commander, was Eyes.
- ✔ Sir Christopher Hatton, eventually Lord Chancellor, was Lids.
- ✔ Sir Walter Raleigh, seaman and explorer, punning on his first name, was Water.

Most of the men were seriously interested in Elizabeth and fantasised about marrying her. Raleigh wrote poetry about her, and a jealous looker-on said that Hatton, 'had more recourse to Her Majesty in her Privy Chamber than reason could suffice'. Phew! Hanky panky in the Privy Chamber? It's unlikely. Elizabeth knew how to flirt, but she only went so far. She knew she had to be in control.

Even so, two courtiers got very close to the queen, and their closeness to her was more than fantasy:

- ✔ **Robert Dudley, Earl of Leicester:** Elizabeth and Eyes had the hots for each other and were even rumoured to have had a child. But really, Elizabeth kept her distance. Leicester was most important to her as a military man when England joined the Dutch in going to war against the dreaded Spanish.
- ✔ **Robert Devereux, Earl of Essex:** The Earl of Essex was Leicester's step-son. Another military commander, he led English forces in Europe and rose in favour at court. But he and Elizabeth had a quarrel when he turned his back on her – oops! – and she boxed his ears. As a punishment, Essex was sent to fight for Elizabeth in Ireland, but he made an unauthorised peace deal with the Irish – big mistake! When he got back to England, Elizabeth put him under house arrest. Finally, Essex, miffed at his treatment but still eager for power, plotted a rebellion against the queen, but was discovered and found guilty of high treason. There was only one thing for it: off with his head.

Rivals and spies

Life wasn't easy for Elizabeth, as the story of Essex (see preceding section) makes clear. She was surrounded by ambitious men, who either wanted to marry her or overthrow her. What's more, she had a serious rival for the throne in her cousin Mary, Queen of Scots (see Chapter 12 for more about Mary). Elizabeth and Mary were strong personal rivals. Once, when visited by Mary's envoy, Elizabeth jealously asked him whether she or the Scottish queen was the more beautiful. The envoy replied that Elizabeth was 'whiter', but that Mary was also 'very lovesome'. White was beautiful in Tudor times, so it was a good answer.

But the trouble between the two queens was more serious than this personal rivalry. Assuming that Elizabeth had no children, Mary was next in line to the English throne. She was also a Catholic, so the Scottish queen became a focus for anyone who wanted a Catholic on the throne in England. When Mary was in trouble at home and fled to England, Elizabeth pounced and put her dangerous rival straight in prison.

Many Catholics in England and Europe were desperate to rescue Mary and put her on the throne. In 1569, a pair of northern noblemen, the Earls of Northumberland and Westmorland, organised a revolt in the north with the aim of rescuing Mary. The revolt was defeated, but Elizabeth knew there would be other attempts to sweep her off the throne.

But Elizabeth had a secret weapon. She had one of the most efficient networks of spies in Europe, all under the watchful eyes of shady operator Moor Walsingham. He and his spies rooted out several Catholic plots against the queen:

- ✔ **The Ridolfi Plot:** In 1571, a banker from Florence teamed up with the Duke of Norfolk to dethrone Elizabeth. They were backed by the Pope and the Spanish. Result: Plot discovered, and plotters beheaded.

- ✔ **Jesuit Plot:** In 1580, two Jesuit priests, newly landed in England, were accused of plotting against the queen. Result: One, Edmund Campion, beheaded; the other, Robert Parsons, escaped back to Europe.

- ✔ **Throckmorton Plot:** In 1584, Catholic conspirator Francis Throckmorton was plotting to kill the queen and follow the murder with a French invasion. Again, the Spanish were involved. Result: Throckmorton arrested and beheaded.

- ✔ **Babington Plot:** In 1586, another Catholic, Anthony Babington, plotted to kill the queen, this time with Mary's backing. Walsingham, however, had been intercepting Mary's letters. Result: Babington executed, and Mary beheaded.

Blown away: The Spanish Armada

Elizabeth's other problem was King Philip of Spain. He was involved in several of the Catholic plots against the queen (see preceding section), and it was clear that if he could not get England by marrying Elizabeth, he would try to take the country by force. Elizabeth didn't make it any better by encouraging her seamen to attack Spanish ships. To do so, the queen turned pirate. Not literally, of course. She got her best sea captains to attack Spanish ships and bring the booty back home. It helped the treasury, too.

Sir Francis Drake

Several old English salts collected Spanish gold and silver from the high seas. Sir Francis Drake was probably the most famous. A notable navigator, he was the first Englishman to see the Pacific and the first from his country to sail all the way around the world. He brought home tobacco and potatoes from America – and a load of gold from the Spanish ships he plundered. Elizabeth knighted him and encouraged his expeditions pillaging Spanish ports, such as Cadiz. Drake also played a key part in the defeat of the Spanish Armada.

Philip got miffed that his ships were being robbed – and that the English queen was encouraging the thieving by giving her captains licences to take booty and knighting them when they did. In 1588, Philip decided to retaliate. Big time. He put together the biggest collection of ships anyone had ever seen and planned to attack England. The great Spanish Armada was gathering.

But Philip hit problems before the Armada even set off. Drake sailed into Cadiz harbour and set fire to lots of the Spanish ships moored there, 'singeing the King of Spain's beard,' as he put it. As if that attack wasn't a big enough pain in the face for Philip, his best naval commander died, and he had to put an inexperienced man, the Duke of Medina Sidonia, in charge of the fleet. Even so, when it did set off, the Armada looked impressive – 141 ships sailing in a crescent formation up the English Channel. But the Spanish hadn't reckoned on two English secret weapons:

✔ **Secret weapon No. 1 – Sir Francis Drake:** Well, he wasn't really much of a secret, but Drake turned out to be a better naval tactician than Elizabeth dared hope. He kept the Spanish ships moving so that they couldn't land in England. He attacked the Armada with flaming fire ships, setting many of them alight. These attacks panicked the Spanish and broke up their formation, so the English fleet could attack individual enemy ships. The Armada was on the back foot.

✔ **Secret weapon No. 2 – The weather:** A great storm got up, sending the Spanish fleet further up the Channel and then northwards, along the east coast, around Scotland, and, eventually, Ireland. Lots of them sank, leaving surviving sailors to crawl up the Irish beaches. Only a few made it back to Spain.

The great Armada was blown away and Elizabeth was safe.

Past and future

Elizabeth was in her mid-50s when the Armada was defeated. She reigned for another 15 years, turning into a formidable old woman who kept her spirit almost to the end. Desperate to keep up appearances, she coated her face with white makeup to hide her wrinkles, wore an auburn wig, and had herself painted in bigger, richer dresses than ever.

The queen loved her country and was proud of its achievements. Her explorers, such as Sir Francis Drake and Martin Frobisher, sailed all over the world. Writers, such as William Shakespeare, were world class – Elizabeth adored his plays. And so were some of the musicians, like composers Thomas Tallis and William Byrd.

Elizabeth herself had shown that England could stand up against the most powerful countries in Europe. But she had no children. As she lay dying, she realised she had to name an heir. Perhaps reluctantly, Elizabeth ordered that James of Scotland, the son of Mary, Queen of Scots, should be the next English king.

Chapter 14

The Stuarts

The most lasting change that occurred under the Stuart monarchs of the 17th century had to do with the relationship between England and Scotland. In 1603, King James of Scotland added England to his domains, and just 100 years later, under Queen Anne, the last Stuart ruler, England and Scotland were formally united as one kingdom. It was at last possible to speak of Great Britain as a political concept.

The other big issue for the Stuart rulers of the 17th century was that the relationship between king and Parliament finally deteriorated beyond repair. In the 1640s, England was torn by a civil war between royalists and parliamentarians. When the parliamentarians won the war, the king, Charles I, was executed, and England became a republic.

But England's republican rulers held to an uncompromising brand of religious Puritanism that didn't suit most people, so eventually the Stuart monarchs were welcomed back to the throne. But in the late 17th century, Parliament put in place a Bill of Rights to restrict the power of the monarch, confirming Parliament's control over laws, taxes, and other issues. Britain's constitutional monarchy, with strictly limited royal power, was born.

The Stewart family had had close connections with France for much of the 16th century, and by the time James VI of Scotland became James I of England, it was quite common for the family name to be spelled in the French way, as Stuart. As a result, it has become customary to use this later, French-style spelling when referring to the family as rulers of the two realms of England and Scotland, after 1603.

The Wisest Fool: James 1

James I of England had reigned for more than 30 years as James VI of Scotland before he became king of the English. He was a highly intelligent man who wrote several books and had a lot of good ideas – for example, he wanted to keep Europe peaceful and to bring his two kingdoms closer together politically. But James was hampered in his ambitions because he was not a very practical ruler. He didn't manage Parliament very well, and he was not a very good judge of character. He was once referred to as 'the wisest fool in Christendom', and this strange description certainly sums up his intellectual ability and the difficulty that he had putting some of his ideas into practise. (You can find details of James's early years as king of Scotland in Chapter 12.)

A Scotsman in England

James was a direct descendent of Henry VII, the first Tudor king (see Chapter 13), so he had a very good claim to the English throne. But as ruler of Scotland, big obstacles were in the way of his taking up the crown of England. Henry VIII had banned the ruler of Scotland from also being king of England. James got around this problem by asserting that a higher authority had allowed him to rule England – James insisted that he had God's approval.

As well as this divine sanction, James brought a number of more worldly advantages that made him an attractive king of England:

- ✔ He had long experience of being king in Scotland.

- ✔ He was a Protestant, so his religion was compatible with the way the church had gone under Elizabeth I.

- ✔ He had the support of key courtiers of the last Tudor queen, Elizabeth, who had named him as her heir (see Chapter 13).

- ✔ He already had several children, providing a secure, straightforward succession.

To begin with, James's rule was quite successful. He had good advisers, and they worked to bring England and Scotland closer, with a common monetary system and a flag, the *union flag*, which has formed the basis of the British flag ever since – even though it wasn't officially adopted until 1707. James also worked for peace in Europe by allying himself through the marriages of his children to both the Elector Palatine (ruler of part of Germany) and the king of Spain, who had been sworn enemies.

The King James Bible

One important event for which King James I is remembered happened near the beginning of his English reign. In 1604, he commissioned a group of theologians from England and Scotland to put together a definitive English translation of the Bible.

It was a visionary move by the Protestant king. A number of English versions of the Bible, or parts of the Bible, already existed. But by bringing together a large team of churchmen, including leading scholars in Oxford and Cambridge, to produce a new one, James was creating a translation that became popular immediately and was the standard one for centuries. In fact, many people still prefer the King James Bible. Even though it is, of course, written in 17th-century English, its language has a beauty and poetry that few modern versions match.

Fall guy: The gunpowder plot

In 1605, English Catholics were fuming because the Protestant king would not recognise their faith. They wanted the freedom to worship as they saw fit, and some thought the best way to achieve this goal was to replace James as ruler. Accordingly, a group of Catholics led by Warwickshire knight Sir Robert Catesby decided to take the law into their own hands and blow up the king at the state opening of Parliament on 5 November 1605.

The conspirators got as far as filling a room under the building where Parliament met with gunpowder when one of their number told a relative, who was a member of the House of Lords, to stay away. The news passed to the authorities, who found the gunpowder, saving the king and the assembled dignitaries the day before the explosion was due to take place.

One conspirator, Guy Fawkes, was found in the cellar with the gunpowder. The others were rounded up, and all were executed. Ever since, Fawkes has been the best-known of the conspirators, and images of 'the Guy' are still burned every year on bonfires to commemorate the discovery of the conspiracy.

Ruling without Parliament

James's notion that he ruled through the authority of God meant that he had little regard for Parliament when it tried to put the brakes on his rule. And Parliament turned out to be opposed to a number of James's ideas. For example, the king wanted to bring England and Scotland closer, to create something akin to a single unified realm. But Parliament wouldn't have this unity, fearing that the proposed changes would limit their rights.

As a result of this tension, James preferred to rule without the involvement of Parliament. The one problem with doing so, as previous monarchs had found, was that the king needed Parliament in order to raise taxes. And Parliament could be obstructive to this measure, as James found, for example, in 1614, when Parliament was called, and the session broke up amid fierce disputes without any laws being passed. This disastrous session became known as the *Addled Parliament*. Consequently, James preferred to raise money by other means – for example, through increasing customs duties – that did not require parliamentary consent.

A moral maze

In 1612, disasters started to assail James, and he seems to have lost direction as a ruler. His favourite son, Henry, Prince of Wales, died of typhoid, and the king's two key advisers, Robert Cecil, Earl of Salisbury, and George Home, Earl of Dunbar, also both died. James was never so competent or so well advised as a ruler after this time.

The royal mess got worse when James became involved in what is known as the *Overbury scandal*. It began when one of James's favourites, Robert Carr, Earl of Somerset, was pursuing a married woman, the Countess of Essex. James didn't discourage the liaison, as he should have done, but actively encouraged it by helping the Countess get her marriage annulled on the grounds that her husband was impotent.

So far, so bad. But things got worse. A friend of the Countess who had helped her get the marriage dissolved, a character called Sir Robert Overbury, was murdered (someone fed him powdered glass). In the ensuing row, the story of the scandal became public knowledge – including the fact that James himself reputedly had the hots for Robert Carr. So much for James as an upright Christian monarch.

A powerful partner

James's closest and most enduring favourite was George Villiers, a gentleman from Leicestershire who came to the king's notice in 1614. He was swiftly knighted by James, who in subsequent years raised him through the various rungs of the peerage until he became Earl of Buckingham.

James's personal relations with Buckingham went as far as the bedroom. Writings from the king survive, and they describe Buckingham as his 'wife' and James as the 'husband' of the pair. Buckingham's hold over James was so great that the favourite became one of the richest men in the country.

Buckingham had an enormous influence on the way James ruled, and he took a direct part in the affairs of state. For example, in 1623, he went to Spain to try to negotiate a marriage for the king's son Charles. The expedition failed, but Buckingham survived to make friends with the prince – something that stood him in good stead when Charles later became king.

Henry, Prince of Wales

James's favourite son Henry was born in Stirling Castle in 1594 and became Prince of Wales in 1610. He was everything James wanted in a son – intelligent, athletic, and wide-ranging in his interests. Henry read deeply in science, was knowledgeable about the Navy and the sea, and was a patron of the arts. He seemed to represent real hope both for the royal family and the country. And, as a devout Protestant, he was also dear to the church. But in 1612, Henry died, apparently of typhoid, although it was rumoured that he had been poisoned. James was heartbroken, and England and Scotland lost a remarkable potential ruler.

A loyal wife

James's real wife was Anne of Denmark, whom he married in 1589 when he was ruler of Scotland. She bore the king nine children, although sadly most of them died in infancy. Those who survived into adult life were:

- ✔ **Henry Frederick (1594–1612),** who was Prince of Wales and seemed set to be an ideal king before dying at the age of 18.

- ✔ **Elizabeth (1596–1662),** who married Frederick Henry of Wittelsbach, Elector Palatine of the Rhine, a marriage that was to produce a line that would inherit the throne in the 18th century.

- ✔ **Charles (1600–49),** who was to become King Charles I.

Anne seems to have been a good and long-suffering partner of her husband, bringing a breath of European sophistication to his court by patronizing artists from the European mainland. She put on an outward show of being a Protestant, but was privately Catholic.

A wife and a war

James's daughter Elizabeth married Frederick Henry of Wittelsbach, Elector Palatine of the Rhine, in 1613. The couple settled down to what should have been a quiet life as rulers of one of the more powerful princedoms of Germany. In 1618, their fortunes improved further when Frederick was chosen to be king of Bohemia, a territory right in the middle of Europe that is now a large chunk of the Czech Republic.

But Frederick was stepping into a hornets' nest. Many Bohemians wanted this new Protestant ruler; but the family who had ruled in the area previously, the powerful Hapsburgs, were Catholics and wanted Frederick out. The result was the Thirty Years' War, Europe's last major war of religion.

The Winter Queen

Elizabeth, daughter of James VI and Anne of Denmark, was an intelligent woman who, with her husband Frederick, presided over a cultured court in Heidelberg, where they ruled over the Palatinate of the Rhine. The Palatinate was a Protestant state, and under Frederick's father, it had become the heart of a union of Protestant lands in Europe. When Frederick was offered the throne of Bohemia, one of the heartlands of Protestanism, his Protestant advisers encouraged him to accept. But Frederick and Elizabeth remained in Prague, Bohemia's capital, only for the winter of 1619–20, after which the Catholic forces of the Hapsburg family defeated the Protestants at the Battle of White Mountain (near Prague), and the Winter King and Queen were forced into exile. They lived out their lives in The Hague, Holland, and Elizabeth died in London when visiting the English royal family.

Soon Catholic Spanish troops were moving into Frederick's homeland, the Palatinate, and many English Protestants were demanding that England should get involved in the war, too. But James wanted to make peace. He tried to arrange a marriage between his son Charles and the Infanta, or Princess, of Spain, including in the deal an agreement that the Spaniards would withdraw from the Palatinate.

The proposed marriage deal between Charles and the Infanta fell through, and after 1620, an increasing tide of opinion in England wanted to go to Europe and fight in the war. But James held out for peace, and his reign ended in disagreements between the king, on the one hand, and the Prince of Wales and Buckingham on the other. In 1625, James died after a long illness, leaving his son Charles to pick up the pieces left by these divisions – and leaving Buckingham still the most powerful man in the kingdom. (See the section "A powerful partner," earlier in this chapter, for more on Buckingham.)

Losing Your Head: Charles 1

Charles I (1625–49) tried to follow in the footsteps of his father, James I. He therefore attempted to rule as an absolute monarch, where possible ignoring Parliament and raising revenues independently, as James had tried to do. He was a buttoned-up, difficult character, who loved order and believed that if everyone obeyed him in the proper way, he would have a harmonious kingdom.

But things didn't turn out the way Charles planned. After he had been on the throne for about 15 years, the kingdom began to lurch from crisis to crisis until the country was launched into a terrible civil war in which the king and his followers fought against Parliament. After years of fighting, Charles was captured, charged with treason against the people, and beheaded. England became a republic.

Right royal mess

Things kept going wrong under Charles I, which was surprising in a way because when the king came to the throne in 1625, he had quite a lot going for him. Sadly, each plus point had a corresponding minus point that landed Charles in trouble:

- Charles's father, James I, had left behind him a book, describing exactly how a monarch should rule, so Charles had some instruction in the job. But James's views were so set on absolute monarchy that they were destined to fail in an era in which people would not accept royal authority alone.

- Charles inherited James's key minister, Buckingham, so the country had continuity. But Buckingham was disliked, messed up foreign policy, and alienated Parliament.

- Charles gathered a number of other loyal advisers around him. But these men had an uphill struggle, given Charles's views of how monarchy should work.

- The king was happily married to Henrietta Maria of France. But Henrietta was a Catholic, which made her unpopular among many, and had a downer on England – she always thought things were better in France.

And this, surprise, surprise, wasn't all. Charles began to mess up badly when it came to a number of key issues. He was soon alienating people left, right, and centre.

- **Mess-up No. 1 – Religion:** One of Charles's key gurus was the archbishop of Canterbury, William Laud. Laud's brand of Churchmanship was highly centralised – in other words, people were expected to obey the bishops. It was rather like Charles's view of kingship, in fact. Also, although Protestant, some rituals had a rather Catholic flavour. Many didn't like it, and Charles got some of the blame.

- **Mess-up No. 2 – Scotland:** This mess-up was partly to do with religion, too, because one of the ways Charles offended the Scots was by introducing a new prayer book into their churches without consulting anyone. When not offending the Scottish church, Charles was offending Scottish landholders by taking back lands previously granted by the crown and then regranting them on new terms – terms more advantageous to the king, of course. When the Scots objected to his changes, Charles sent in the troops to try and sort them out – but the Scots preempted him by invading northern England.

✔ **Mess-up No. 3 – Ireland:** Charles appointed Thomas Wentworth, a member of an old Yorkshire family, as governor of Ireland. The aim of both governor and king was to bring Ireland more closely under royal control and save money while they were about it. Part of their policy involved playing the old-established population, known as the Old English (who were mainly Catholic), and the more recently settled New English (the Protestants) against each other – a tactic, in the long run, guaranteed to alienate people on a grand scale. And they certainly didn't seem to care who they offended. The Old English were threatened by a proposal for more new settlers in Connaught, while the New English were badly affected when Charles seized Londonderry, their most important town. And as in Scotland, the king also tried to bring the church – the Protestant Church of Ireland – into line with the church in England. Things didn't look good for Ireland under Charles.

King versus Parliament

Charles's royal mess-ups had a pattern – a monarch who believed he had absolute powers trying to impose those powers on people and places that didn't want interference. Charles could throw his weight about because the Stuarts had increased the personal power of the monarch. They could raise money through lands and duties without going through Parliament, and they used hand-picked personal friends and ministers to help them rule. But this kind of government meant abusing royal power – for example by changing tenancy deals to extract more cash from landholders. It couldn't go on for ever.

After more than ten years of this tyrannical personal rule, many people had had enough. They especially resented the way Wentworth grabbed lands in Ireland and Charles's sweeping religious changes. People in northern England weren't amused either, when the Scots, who had beaten Charles in battle, forced Charles to agree to a treaty that allowed them to occupy Newcastle on Tyne and forced Charles to pay them an indemnity as well.

The events in the north showed that Charles's tyrannical authority had evaporated, and he would no longer be able to rule and raise revenue on his own. Charles was forced to call Parliament and make concessions, including the dismissal of many of his key advisers and supporters. Charles fought a battle over Wentworth, but Parliament had it in for Charles's most ruthless henchman. They used their powers of *attainder* – basically convicting him of treason without the need for a proper trial – and Wentworth was executed in 1641.

Crisis: The Five Members

After Wentworth's execution and Charles's diminished power (see preceding section), that ought to have been that. Parliament had more power, Charles's power was controlled, and life for most people was simpler. But that didn't account for Charles. He simply couldn't live without his absolutist powers and was soon trying to flex his muscles again. When five Members of Parliament made moves against the king, Charles tried to have them rounded up and arrested. The Five Members were:

- **John Hampden,** who had resisted paying some of Charles's taxes and was agitating to get royal power limited more severely.

- **John Pym,** a scathing critic of Charles's tyrannical rule.

- **Arthur Haselrig,** another of Charles's critics and a leading independent Member of Parliament.

- **Denzil Holles,** a member of an aristocratic family and a long-standing opponent of over-powerful ministers, from the time of Buckingham onwards.

- **William Strode,** another key opponent of Charles and Wentworth.

When Charles came to Parliament in January 1642 to have these five arrested, he found that they'd been tipped off and were not present. Charles was humiliated, and many moderate Members of Parliament who were in the chamber turned against him because of his actions. Parliament was further angered by Charles's refusal to let them choose his ministers and by his objections when they wanted to put the militia – England's only army – under Parliamentary control.

War breaks out

The crisis over the Five Members (see preceding section) was a signal that crown and Parliament were on collision course. On 20 August 1642, Charles raised his *standard* (royal flag) at Nottingham, which was the signal that civil war had begun.

The fighting lasted four years. To begin with, things did not go too badly for Charles. The king showed himself to be a competent leader in a crisis and a brave man on the battlefield, leading his army in many of the major battles in the conflict. This side of his character must have come as quite a surprise to many. And the royalist side had another surprise up its sleeve in the shape of Prince Rupert, the king's nephew, who also showed himself to be a strong leader.

Charles had some cause for hope early on in the war. After an indecisive battle at Edgehill in Warwickshire (1642), the Royalists scored victories at Atherton Moor (1643), Roundway Down (1643), Bristol (1643), Winceby (1643), and Cropredy Bridge (1644).

But soon after came major Parliamentarian victories at Marston Moor, Yorkshire (1644), and Naseby, Northamptonshire (1645). After suffering those kind of big defeats, the Royalists found it impossible to regroup, and in 1646, after a rapid ride northwards, Charles surrendered to the Scots, who eventually handed him over to Parliament.

Prince Rupert

Prince Rupert of the Rhine was the son of James I's daughter Elizabeth and her husband Frederick, Elector Palatine. When Frederick lost his power in the Thirty Years' War, Rupert came to England. With his experience in fighting in the European war, Rupert was seen as a valuable military leader, and Charles made him General of Horse and then Commander in Chief. Rupert made his mark as a brave cavalry commander, winning several battles before suffering defeats at the hands of the Parliamentarian leader, Oliver Cromwell. His last defeat as a land commander was at Bristol, the final stronghold of the Royalists, in 1645.

The Parliamentary turn-around in 1645 and 1646 came about largely because of the rise of Oliver Cromwell, a new commander on the anti-Royalist side. Cromwell had been a Member of Parliament since 1628, and when war started, he built up and led a powerful cavalry unit. He realised the importance of proper training and discipline, and after the Parliamentary forces suffered their string of defeats at the start of the war, he was one of the leaders who made their army more professional. The result was the New Model Army, a well-trained unit with new commanders (who kept their positions only if they proved to be competent), paid troops, and good discipline.

Head under heels

Once Charles was in their hands, many men in the Parliamentarian army wanted to put him on trial. They saw the king as a bloodthirsty war-monger who had caused the death of many innocent people. But not everyone saw it this way. Many Members of Parliament baulked at the idea of putting the king on trial – and so did Parliamentarian leaders, such as Cromwell. If Charles was found guilty of treason, they'd have to execute him – and what then?

Men like Cromwell hoped to put pressure on Charles to give up the throne in favour of one of his less absolutist relatives, but it wasn't going to happen. Charles wouldn't give in, and neither would the army. In December 1648, the army surrounded the Palace of Westminster where Parliament met, and only let in those who were prepared to put the king on trial.

The trial took place in front of some 50 Members of Parliament. Throughout the trial, Charles refused to accept that the court was a legal one and would not enter a plea. With a crowning irony, he claimed that he was resisting the tyranny of those around him. The trial lasted several days, from 20 to 27 January 1649, during which time the king conducted himself with dignity but refused to back down. On 30 January 1649, Charles II was beheaded for treason against the people, and England faced a future as a republic.

England as a Republic

With no monarch after the execution of Charles I in 1649, England was governed by a Council of State under the chairmanship of the dynamic Parliamentary leader, Oliver Cromwell. The Council governed in conjunction with the Members of Parliament who had gone along with the trial of Charles I and who were the remnant, or rump, of the full Parliament. They have been known ever since as the *Rump Parliament.*

England's period as a republic lasted from 1649 to 1660, and it had two main phases, the *Commonwealth* (1649–53), during which the Council ruled through Parliament, and the *Protectorate,* during which Cromwell (and later his son, Richard) ruled in a much more personal way, trying to develop new institutions of government but becoming more dictatorial in the process.

Oliver Cromwell, England's Chairman of the Council, was a bundle of energy and a good leader. He was also very ruthless, as he had to be to achieve what he did. As leader of the notorious Puritan New Model Army, he had a reputation for being rather austere, but actually he enjoyed hunting and music – the kind of recreations that many a royal had liked, in fact. He was also famous for being ugly and told one artist to paint his portrait, 'warts and all'. That comment showed, of course, that he was rigorously honest, too.

Cromwell was also a religious Puritan, a strict Protestant with a rigid moral code who tried to impose these values on England. During the Cromwellian period, people were fined for swearing, drunkenness, gambling, and even playing sports. The Puritans closed the theatres and limited the number of pubs and inns. Eventually, this kind of moral extremism turned people against Cromwell and made them long for the return of a more relaxed form of government.

Commonwealth

The first phase of Cromwell's leadership saw more fighting in what has become known as the *Second Civil War,* in which Cromwell's forces defeated Royalists who remained loyal to the king in Ireland and Scotland. And there weren't just Royalists to defeat, but also royals – Charles I's son, another Charles, emerged as leader of the Scottish Royalists. Young Charles was actually crowned as Charles II in Scotland, enduring in the process a long sermon that reminded him of all the sins of his ancestors.

In 1651, Charles II and his followers marched south to confront Cromwell's forces at Worcester. The republicans were the winners of the battle, and Charles, after a spell hiding in an oak tree to avoid capture, fled. Disguised as a servant, he crossed England and was helped away in a fishing boat. No one betrayed the escaping would-be king, in spite of an offer of a 1,000-pound reward for his deliverance. With the departure of Charles, the Royalist opposition was over, and Cromwell could set about trying to govern the country.

Protectorate

Cromwell and his close allies eventually lost patience with the Rump Parliament. They longed for a Parliament that was more representative and when the members of the Rump Parliament refused to go, they took measures to throw them out. Along with the MPs went the mace, the symbol of the power of the Speaker of the House of Commons – 'Take away that bauble,' ordered Cromwell.

Cromwell then embarked on a series of measures to try to create a fairer form of government:

- ✔ Cromwell's first attempt at Parliamentary reform consisted of a Parliament of men selected by local churches. The resulting body of almost 140 MPs met in1653, but turned out to be Puritans who were even more uncompromising than Cromwell and wanted to abolish everything in sight. Cromwell dismissed them.

- ✔ The next attempt, known as the *First Protectorate Parliament,* was a more representative body of 400 MPs in one House of Commons. But the Members, who met in 1654, objected to being bossed about by the Lord Protector Cromwell. Cromwell dismissed them, too.

- ✔ The Second Protectorate Parliament met in 1656–58, and in an atmosphere in which people were fed up of the prevailing Puritan restrictions on their liberty, its members offered Cromwell the crown. Cromwell refused and re-established the two-house Parliament with Cromwell continuing as Protector.

In 1568, Cromwell died, and his son took over as Protector. In 1659–60, the Rump Parliament returned, Richard Cromwell resigned, and negotiations began to bring back Charles II. In May 1660, Parliament finally voted to bring back the monarchy.

Cromwell fell foul of similar problems to Charles I, the monarch he replaced. (See the section 'Losing Your Head,' earlier in this chapter, for more on Charles's problems.) He found dealing with Parliament difficult; its members found his rule too autocratic and obstructed many of the measures he wanted to introduce. Many in Ireland had even better reasons to dislike Cromwell, because he imposed English rule there ruthlessly, rewarding his soldiers and supporters with land grabbed from the local Catholic population and thus fuelling divisions that have existed there ever since. On the other hand, Cromwell was in a lot of ways an effective leader who greatly improved

England's standing in the world, fighting successful wars against the Dutch and Spanish, making treaties with other nations, and allowing the Jews back to England after a long period of banishment.

Merry Monarch: Charles II

After England's experiment in republicanism fell apart in 1660 (see preceding section), Charles II (1660–85) was welcomed as king. A libertine, famous for multiple mistresses and friendships with aristocratic ne'er-do-wells, Charles certainly seemed a breath of fresh air after Oliver Cromwell.

But Charles brought with him some of the same problems his father and other predecessors had had – how to deal with Parliament and how to plan the succession, especially when it turned out that his queen, Portuguese princess Catherine of Braganza, was unable to produce a living child – her story was a sad one of stillbirths and miscarriages. This misfortune produced a succession problem that was made still worse because the next person in line to the throne was Charles's brother James, a convert to Roman Catholicism.

Bed, bawd, and the finer things in life

People used to call Charles II the Merry Monarch because his main interest seemed to be in having a good time. He seems to have been an amoral character who swayed this way and that, both in politics and in bed. It's easy to lose count of how many mistresses the king had – he had at least eight, all of whom bore him children. A number of these women were elevated to the aristocracy as duchesses. Others, like actresses Nelly Gwynne and Moll Davies, were part of the low-life theatrical scene that Charles liked to have contact with.

Arts and sports

Royal patronage of the arts made a comeback, and Charles was especially keen on the portrait painter Sir Peter Lely, who did a good line in portraits of the duchesses that Charles got on so well with. More music was around too, including in church – something that Puritans such as Cromwell had looked down on.

Charles enjoyed himself in other ways, too. His attachment to actresses extended to a more general love of the theatre and opera, which flourished when the playhouses reopened after closure under the Puritans. The king was also a keen and skilful yachtsman, an enthusiastic follower of horse-racing, and a dog-lover famous for the small spaniels that now bear his name. He was an accessible ruler, too, who liked to be out and about and didn't see himself above waving to his subjects or talking to jockeys.

London's burning

Charles's reign wasn't all enjoyment. For all the gaiety of his life in London, the capital was blighted in the 1660s, first by disease and then by fire.

First, the bubonic plague: This grim disease had been terrorizing England – especially London – for decades. Even in Shakespeare's time, the theatres had often had to close during outbreaks of plague. But the outbreak in 1665 was particularly severe. Some 70,000 people perished, and many religious people viewed the disaster as God's judgment on a loose-living people.

In 1666, the second disaster, the great fire, scorched its way across London. It lasted for five days. Though the timber-framed buildings of London had seen fires before, none had been quite as bad as this one. While Puritans were muttering darkly about the possibility that the fire was started deliberately by Catholics, it was, in fact, a disastrous accident. The flames destroyed around half the city and felled 89 parish churches. The royal family even played a part in stopping the fire in its tracks, with the Duke of York bringing in explosives to remove houses, deprive the fire of its fuel, and prevent it from spreading further.

Gimme the money!

Charles didn't trust Parliament, and that's hardly surprising – they had his father killed, after all. When it came to raising money, Charles, like many another ruler before him, looked for another source of cash that didn't involve him begging to the people's representatives.

Charles hit upon a rather clever, if also rather devious, scheme. His aide Thomas, Earl of Danby, was engaged in preparations for a war in France. Charles wasn't so keen on the idea, especially when he realised that he could secretly go to the French king, Louis XIV, and do a deal whereby he would call off the war in return for a hefty subsidy.

Charles wheedled an annual payment out of the French, avoided war, and kept himself free from the indignities of begging for money from Parliament. The manoeuver seemed like a triumph, but it did help to lead Charles into some deeper waters.

No popery!

When people realised that Charles was sympathetic to the Catholic French, they started to think he was too much under the thumb of the Church of Rome, especially when they saw how easy-going he was with his Catholic brother, James.

In 1678, an ugly rumour started that a group of Catholics were plotting to kill the king. The people who were scare-mongering about this *Popish plot,* which didn't actually exist, were a bunch of liars, chief amongst whom was a certain Titus Oates. It was fairly widely known that Oates was a liar and scandal-monger, but innocent Catholics were arrested and even put to death on his dodgy evidence.

Parliament also tried to get James banned from becoming king after Charles, and all kinds of schemes were hatched to create more acceptable heirs to the throne:

- Some people wanted Charles to divorce his queen and find another consort who could bear him a son and heir.
- Others wanted to make the Duke of Monmouth, the oldest of the king's illegitimate sons, legitimate, and so eligible as heir to the throne.
- Still others promoted James's daughter, Mary, as an heir, because she was a Protestant.

Charles stood out against these schemes and, with his French income, was able to ignore the wishes of doubters in Parliament and go his own sweet way.

A final triumph

A few years later, in 1683, a real attempt to remove Charles occurred. A group of plotters intended to put the king to death as he rode past an inn called Rye House on his way between London and Newmarket. This so-called *Rye House Plot* was the work of a group, most of whom had been soldiers in Cromwell's army and were now supporters of the Whig political party. Charles, by contrast, favoured the Tories.

During Charles's reign, two political parties developed that were to go on being influential for several centuries to come. The Tories believed that the king's right to rule was sanctioned by God; they were also implacable supporters of the Church of England. The Whigs, by contrast, had a more down-to-earth view of the power of the king and were in favour of greater toleration for members of churches other than the C of E.

The Rye House Plot was discovered, and Charles survived. What's more, the king took advantage of the plot to remove prominent Whigs – irrespective of whether they were actually involved in the plot or not. At least two key Whigs – Lord Russell and Algernon Sidney – were executed on flimsy grounds after the Rye House Plot was discovered.

With his enemies out of the way, Charles ruled securely and successfully for the next couple of years, but in February 1685, he had a stroke. Charles didn't die straight away, joking with those around him that he was 'an unconscionable time dying'. But after a few days, he slipped away, leaving the kingdom to his brother James.

Trouble Ahead: James II

James II (1685–88) was the only surviving son of Charles I and was 51 years old when he came to the throne. He lived through the trauma of the English Civil War, spent much of his life in exile, and converted to Catholicism. Much of his energy during his short reign was spent trying to secure religious freedom for Catholics, but he faced huge opposition and was forced off the throne, returning to mainland Europe to spend his last years in exile once more.

Zeal of the converted

James was born in 1633. By 1649, England was a republic, and in the following decade, the young prince was in exile on the European mainland, serving as a general in the armies of France and Spain. In 1660, James's brother, Charles II, came to the throne, and things started to look up for the monarchy.

But James threw a spanner into the works – rather more than a spanner, actually. He got Anne Hyde, daughter of the Lord Chancellor, pregnant. It was said that the pair had been married in secret on Christmas Eve 1659, but no one knows for sure whether this marriage actually took place. The couple tied the knot publicly in September 1660, when Anne was heavily pregnant with their first child.

Things didn't go well for the couple. Anne bore James eight children, but all except two girls, Mary and Anne, died in infancy. Anne Hyde herself died, of cancer, in 1671. She had been a convert to Catholicism and probably influenced her husband who gradually, during the years they spent together, moved towards the Roman church. James formally announced his conversion a couple of years after Anne died, but had probably been a Catholic for some time already.

Rebellion and revenge

Another setback came in the shape of a rebellion, organised by the Duke of Monmouth only a few months after James became king. Monmouth was the illegitimate son of Charles II, and in Charles's reign, there had been a movement to legitimise him and present him as a viable heir to the throne.

Monmouth, who had been living in Holland until James came to the throne, landed on the south coast, made a proclamation stating his claim to the throne, and attracted a gathering of several thousand men, mostly dissenters who wanted James out. They took the town of Taunton, but were defeated by royal troops at the Battle of Sedgemoor. Monmouth went into hiding, but was found and executed. Other conspirators were captured and tried, and these hearings became known as the *Bloody Assizes* because some 320 rebels were executed. More still were sent to America as slaves.

Toleration and intolerance

James worked hard to try to win religious toleration in the Protestant realm that he inherited. In 1687, he issued a Declaration of Indulgence, which, as well as pledging to protect the Church of England, also allowed Catholics to worship in public. (Previously, they had been forced to worship privately, in their own homes.)

The king also made moves to make life fairer for Catholics in Ireland, by giving them control over the government and army. But James stopped short of dealing with the issue of land ownership – in an island where more than three-quarters of the people were Catholic, more than three-quarters of the land was owned by Protestants.

Religious toleration looks a good thing from a modern perspective. But a large and powerful establishment in England was offended by it. Dozens of officials were sacked because they wouldn't sign up to James's reforms.

Then James tried to get the Anglican clergy to agree to support toleration. Archbishop Sancroft and six bishops refused – and promptly found themselves under arrest. They were put on trial for seditious libel, and James had the jury packed with men who he thought would support him. But the jury let the bishops off, and few in the Church of England now thought much of James.

The king in exile

It wasn't just the Church of England that disliked James. Many nobles who were supporters of the church and the establishment also opposed the Catholic king. To make matters worse for them, the widower James remarried, and his new bride, Mary of Modena, was another Catholic. The nobles saw a Catholic dynasty ahead.

This dynasty came closer to developing when it was announced that Mary had given birth to a baby boy. At last, James had a son, and an English Catholic dynasty was in the making. Or did James have a son? A lot of rumours said that the child wasn't James's at all and had been smuggled into the queen's bedroom in a warming pan, a kind of 17th-century hot-water bottle. But real prince or not, there this baby was, threatening to one day take over the throne for the Catholics.

The Protestant nobles were already plotting to get rid of James II, and they had a secret weapon: the Dutch leader, William of Orange, who was married to James's eldest surviving child, Mary. William was a Dutchman. He wasn't actually king of the Netherlands – his title was *Stadtholder*, which means he was the leader of the Dutch provinces and head of their army. For the plotters, William had a number of advantages as a potential saviour, and indeed ruler, of England:

- ✔ He was a Protestant.
- ✔ He was an experienced soldier.
- ✔ He was fighting a war with France and wanted England's support in that war.
- ✔ His wife Mary was a prominent member of the English ruling family, so she had a clear claim to the throne, even if William didn't.

In late June 1688, a group of Englishmen invited William to come to England and liberate the country from the Catholic rule of James. By November, William had landed at Brixham on the south coast, and his support swelled as he marched to London. James, his army officers deserting him, left England on 11 December.

James lived in French exile until he died in 1701. He was a broken man, convinced that he had messed things up – which he had – and that his fate was God's judgment on him.

Joint Rule: William and Mary

William of Orange and his wife Mary, daughter of James II, ruled as joint monarchs in a unique arrangement that was devised because of the unusual way they came to power. William was invited to England to rid the country of James II, who was widely disliked because of his Catholicism. But his wife, as the old king's daughter, had the better claim to the throne, although William was actually part of her family, too, since the couple were cousins.

So the dual-rule arrangement came into being. The transfer of power was peaceful in England, but it was a very different matter in Catholic Ireland, where William had to fight for power. Ironically, William was never much liked in England – it soon became clear that his main interest was in his French wars. Mary, on the other hand, was a likeable personality who loved her husband and was much loved by her people.

Glorious revolution?

William and Mary were crowned joint king and queen in a double ceremony. But all the real power was in the hands of William. For the first time in a long time, Parliament limited the monarch's power. The English were turning their backs on the absolutist ideas of the earlier Stuart rulers and creating the basis for the constitutional monarchy that still exists today.

Royal power was limited by a Declaration of Rights, which was accepted by William and Mary before Parliament made it fully official as a Bill of Rights. It contained a number of key provisions:

- ✔ Parliaments must be held frequently.

- ✔ Elections must be free.

- ✔ Laws cannot be suspended without the consent of Parliament.

- ✔ Parliamentary consent is needed before taxes can be levied.

- ✔ The royal *dispensing power,* by which the king could permit acts that were otherwise illegal, is itself illegal.

- ✔ No Catholic can become king or queen.

Supporters of William reckoned that the joint monarchs' takeover, with their power curbed by the Bill of Rights, amounted to a Glorious Revolution, in which a new, fairer regime was ushered in by means of a bloodless coup.

The Irish couldn't see William's takeover as bloodless, though. The Catholic majority, not surprisingly, sided with their coreligionist, James, while the Protestants supported William, or King Billy as they affectionately called him.

In 1690, William had to fight to control Ireland. His army met James's troops at the Battle of the Boyne. William, who could draw on troops from Holland, Denmark, England, and Ulster, had a bigger and better-equipped army than James. As a result, James was overwhelmed. The old king fled to France, but many of his men were slaughtered. The aftermath was nearly as bad for the Catholics, who were made second-class citizens under the thumb of the Protestants who dominated the Irish Parliament. Ever since, Irish Catholics have decried the Battle of the Boyne, while the more militant Irish Protestants have celebrated it and King Billy's role in bolstering their power.

English kings in Ireland

The kings of England had claimed to be overlords of Ireland since the 12th century, but their power was very limited and mostly restricted to the area around Dublin. Under the Tudors and Stuarts, the English tried to increase their influence in Ireland. The most effective, and also the most disruptive, way in which they did so was by encouraging Protestant settlers to move to Ulster. These settlements became known as *plantations,* and *planting* settlers was a policy pursued by both Elizabeth I and James I. The imbalance of power created by this system, in which the Protestant minority were given influence out of all proportion to their numbers, is at the root of the conflicts that still exist between Catholics and Protestants in Ireland today.

Going Dutch

In 1694, Queen Mary caught the smallpox and died. The sweet-natured queen was widely mourned, and even William, who doesn't seem to have loved the wife he married for dynastic reasons, said that he had never known her to have a single fault.

After Mary's death, William ruled alone. According to the terms of his takeover of the English throne, the next in line to the throne should actually be the children of William and Mary. But the couple had no children – Mary had had a series of stillbirths. Next came Mary's sister, Anne. And finally came any children William might have if he remarried.

William never remarried, and Anne delayed her claim to the throne while William was alive, so the Dutch king ruled alone for the next eight years. In the last years of his reign, he continued with his wars. William's conflict with the French cost the country dearly – the expense marked the beginning of the National Debt and also the foundation of the Bank of England. Then came preparations for another war when Carlos II of Spain died, leaving his realm to the French.

Seeing a chance to gain more power and land through fighting, William got ready to go to war again. But in September 1702, he fell from his horse in Hyde Park, broke his collar bone, caught pneumonia, and died. The throne was left for Mary's sister, Anne, who also inherited the National Debt and William's plans for war.

All Together Now: Anne

The 12 years of Queen Anne's reign (1702–14) were marked by almost continuous illness and personal sadness for the monarch and almost continuous war for the country. It was a fairly grim time, but it wasn't really the queen's fault. She spent most of her reign in pain and had to rely on others for advice. But one positive development, on the whole, occurred. The joint kingdoms of England and Scotland were properly unified, and under Anne's rule, the kingdom of Great Britain came into being.

My hero

Anne was the daughter of James II and his first wife, Anne Hyde. She suffered terrible health for most of her life. Rheumatism, gout, and dropsy gave her constant pain. She had horrendous abscesses and was overweight. She married

George, son of the king of Denmark, and then more troubles began – a string of no fewer than 18 pregnancies that led to a series of miscarriages and still-births. Two children lived for a few months; one, William Henry, Duke of Gloucester, lived to age 11. By 1708, her husband was dead, too.

To take away some of the pain caused by her ill-health, Anne took the drug laudanum. This drug may have made it difficult for her to think or act coherently, and she relied on guidance from a couple who were her best friends, Sarah Churchill, who had known Anne since the two were girls, and Sarah's husband John, a military leader who in 1702 became Duke of Marlborough.

Anne saw Sarah as her social equal – the pair even wrote letters to each other as Mrs Morley and Mrs Freeman – and saw John as a hero. He was one of the leaders of the army that had defeated the Monmouth rebellion against James II and then became a prominent supporter of King William. In Anne's reign, John scored a number of key victories in England's wars against the French.

As a unique reward for his generalship – especially the victory at Blenheim in 1704 – Anne gave John Churchill a vast royal estate near Woodstock in Oxfordshire, and Parliament paid for the building of an enormous house, Blenheim Palace, for the Duke and his wife. Well, it didn't pay the whole cost. Building costs spiralled, and the Churchills ended up paying some of the bill themselves.

Britain: A United Kingdom at last

Since the time of James I (who was also James VI of Scotland), the two kingdoms of England and Scotland had been ruled by the same monarch, but in other ways, they were separate countries. Each had its own Parliament and its own laws. In difficult times, there was always the worry that Scotland might make a break for it and declare itself independent of England. Many in Britain were especially scared of this possibility because of the support in Scotland for James Francis Edward, the surviving son of James II and his second wife, Mary of Modena, as a rival for the throne. In Anne's reign, the two kingdoms were united, in the hope that this split would never happen.

In 1707, the Act of Union was passed. This act abolished the Scottish Parliament and made London's Westminster Parliament represent Britain. Scottish MPs sat in the House of Commons and Scottish peers in the Lords, but Scotland kept its own laws, church, and educational system.

This situation lasted for almost 200 years, until the devolution movement, campaigning for more separate government for Scotland, prevailed, and Scotland was given its own Parliament again after the passing of the Scotland Act in 1998. But the two countries remain united and are still part of Great Britain.

By 1714, Anne was worn out. Because she had no children, she had to find a way of securing the succession. The choice was between her half-brother James, the hope of the Catholics, and the House of Hanover, the German Protestant family who were connected to the Stuarts through Sophia, Electress of Hanover, who was a granddaughter of James I. In 1714, both Queen Anne and the Electress Sophia died, and the British throne passed to Sophia's son, George I.

Chapter 15

The House of Hanover

. . . .

In This Chapter

▶ Revealing how a German family came to Britain to rule

▶ Developing the role of the Prime Minister

▶ Ruling a vast empire, stretching all the way around the globe

▶ Evolving a less powerful, more ceremonial monarchy

. . . .

After the death of the last Stuart ruler, Queen Anne, in 1714 (see Chapter 14), George I, the first Hanoverian ruler, came from Germany to become king. A German king of Britain – what a weird idea! Although George traced his ancestry back to the Stuart line, he was a non-English-speaker who seemed foreign to Britain. He had quite a few problems, most of them stemming from the fact that he was an alien ruler. But George's descendents became more and more British and presided over a time during which Britain's power in the world grew dramatically.

Under the Hanoverians, industry developed, agriculture became more efficient, and the empire grew by leaps and bounds. But if Britain became more prosperous and powerful as a nation, the monarchy wasn't always a success. Big dips in its fortunes occurred when Britons watched with horror the extravagant and dissolute antics of George, the Prince Regent (later George IV). And another drop in popularity developed when Queen Victoria cut herself off from her people and went into deep and lengthy mourning after the death of her beloved husband, Albert. It was a surprise, and a relief in royal circles, when Victoria recovered her popularity, and her son Edward VII developed a less political, more symbolic role for the monarchy.

Fish Out of Water: George I

George I (1714–27) came to Britain from his native Germany and never properly learned to speak English. By the time he came to the throne, he was 54 years old and an experienced ruler and military leader. But George never really fitted in his new country, preferring to spend a large part of the year back home in Hanover.

If George disliked Britain, the Brits didn't think much of him either. He had to cope with a rebellion in Scotland and at least one plot at home. Much of the responsibility of government was not even in royal hands, because one of the most notable developments of the monarchy during George's reign was that of the role of the Prime Minister.

The power of the monarchy had been severely limited by the Bill of Rights brought in under William and Mary in 1688, when Parliament's powers were defined clearly (see Chapter 14). But the Stuart monarchs still played a prominent role in the government of the country. With the arrival of the Prime Minister, a dominant politician who could make policy and get it implemented, the monarch was beginning to become much more of a figure-head than in the past.

The German king

George I inherited the British throne after the death of Queen Anne, who had no surviving children. Under Anne, Parliament had passed an Act of Settlement which laid down who should rule when she died. The choice fell upon Sophia, the daughter of Frederick, Elector Palatine of the Rhine. Sophia was the granddaughter of the first Stuart king of England, James I. This ancestry gave her a good claim to the throne, and, most importantly to Queen Anne and her government, Sophia was a Protestant.

But Sophia died shortly before Queen Anne herself passed away, so her eldest son, George, who was Duke and Elector of Hanover, became king of Great Britain. The 54-year-old George was a rather dour, unsmiling character who spoke only German. His Dukedom was part of the Germanic Holy Roman Empire, and George was prominent in imperial politics, becoming Arch-Treasurer of the Empire in 1710. He had also been successful on the battle-field, commanding the Imperial Army during the War of Spanish Succession in 1707 to 1709.

Scandal with Sophia

By the time he came to the throne, George was divorced from his wife, Sophia Dorothea of Celle. The couple had children, but Sophia was unfaithful to George, and rumours about her affair and its fallout abounded. Sophia took up with a Swedish Colonel called Philip von Königsmark. When George found out, he locked up Sophia and divorced her – and Königsmark disappeared. Then the rumours started:

- According to one version, George ordered the murder of Königsmark.
- Another rumour blamed Clara, Countess von Platten, who'd previously had an affair with Königsmark, for doing away with him.

> ✔ George was said to be having an affair with Sophia Charlotte, the daughter
> of Clara, who had also been the mistress of George's father, Ernst. In other
> words, George was said to be sleeping with his half-sister.
>
> ✔ George and Sophia Charlotte were both rather overweight, and gossips
> who saw them together took to calling them Elephant and Castle.

All this was hearsay, mind you. What was certain was that the king had
another mistress.

Messing with Melusine

Ehrengard Melusine von Schulenberg was known to be the mistress of the
king – and had been even before George divorced his wife. The pair had children, and people at court and in government knew about Melusine and saw
her as a kind of unofficial consort, but without the power of a true queen. She
even had a title, Duchess of Kendal.

Unlike Sophia Charlotte, Melusine was extremely thin, and her nickname was
the maypole. There was a story that she and the king had married in secret –
but this tale is, again, a rumour.

Up he rises: The Old Pretender

The Act of Settlement had put George in line for the throne because his
family were Protestants. Needless to say, some Catholics didn't want a
Protestant king, and some of them still revered the memory of the last
Catholic king, James II. These supporters of James, known as Jacobites,
wanted James II's son, James Edward Stuart, to become king. Some even
took to calling him James III, although Protestant supporters of the
Hanoverians referred to him as the Old Pretender.

Just under a year after George I was crowned, in September 1715, the first
Jacobite rebellion began at Braemar. Fortunately for George, the rising was
not hard to crush. In November 1715, 10,000 Highland supporters of James
stood up to some 35,000 government troops at the Battle of Sheriffmuir. After
this battle, the outnumbered Highlanders broke up, but the battle served to
remind the Hanoverians that their hold on the throne could be challenged.

Yes, Prime Minister!

Because he spoke very little English, George I needed a lot of help with the work
of ruling his English-speaking people. For the first couple of years of his reign,
the king's son, George Augustus, came to cabinet meetings and translated for
his father. But young George fell out with his father, largely over the king's treatment of Sophia, and after 1717, George I was in dire need of practical help.

Because the monarchy was restored after the Commonwealth period, the Stuart rulers had gathered around them a small group of ministers who acted as advisers. These people met in a private chamber called the *cabinet* (a cabinet was a small room), and by the reign of Queen Anne, the word cabinet was used for the people themselves. The members of the cabinet came from the political party that held the majority in the House of Commons.

In 1715, and again in 1721, an experienced Member of Parliament called Robert Walpole was appointed First Lord of the Treasury. This position was the most senior post in the cabinet, and when Walpole was given this job the second time, in 1721, he was in effect the king's special adviser and the first Prime Minister of Britain. This time, he stayed in the post permanently for more than 20 years, from 1721 to 1742.

In 1720, a major royal scandal hit the headlines. The problem surrounded the South Sea Company, which had been set up to trade with Spanish colonies in the South Seas. Thousands of people invested their savings in the company, expecting to make their fortunes, and even George I was involved – he became Governor of the company.

By 1720, lots of people still wanted to invest in the company, and so some officials in the company began to issue worthless false stock. In 1720, the bubble burst. The scam was discovered, lots of people realised their investments were worth nothing, and there was anger when they found out that senior people at court were involved in the dodgy deals.

As a senior member of the company, George was tarred with the same brush as the criminals, and it took Walpole's clever politicking to help him through the crisis, which ever since has been known as the South Sea Bubble.

The problems over the South Sea Bubble encouraged George to take a back seat for the last few years of his life. In any case, he was in the habit of spending summer and autumn in his native Hanover. All these things gave Walpole still more power, setting the style for the kind of arm's-length government that was to mark the British monarchy in later reigns, too. George was making one of his visits to Hanover in 1727 when he had a stroke and died. He left one son, George Augustus, who became King George II.

Selfish but Successful: George II

When George II (1727–60) came to the throne, he was in his 40s and in many ways well-prepared for his new job. He had helped his non-English-speaking father in cabinet meetings in the early years of his reign and as a young man showed himself brave in battle during the War of the Spanish Succession. But George also had a stubborn, selfish streak that made him enemies.

This curious combination of qualities brought George some success as king. His generals helped him make territorial gains that marked the real beginnings of the British empire. Closer to home, he was able to fight off the challenge of the Jacobite claimants to the English throne. All these achievements came, of course, at the expense of a lot of bloodshed. But they meant that George could pass on a relatively secure throne to his son, together with vast territories around the world.

King and consort

George II was a rather pompous character – he liked to get things right and had a great respect for etiquette and protocol. Although he was born in his father's home town of Hanover, he had been brought to England, and by the time he became king, he knew its people and its language well.

When he was 21, George married Caroline of Ansbach, daughter of the Margrave (ruler) of Brandenburg-Ansbach. Caroline was intelligent and played an important public part in the royal family even before her husband became king. Caroline was influential in several ways:

- ✔ In George I's time, when he had no queen because he had divorced his wife, Sophia, Caroline often played the role of first lady.

- ✔ Again in George I's reign, Caroline and young George were at the heart of the Leicester House Set. This political group, named for George and Caroline's residence in London, enabled the pair to influence important politicians. They could use this influence against the king, demonstrating one of the least likeable character traits of the Hanoverian family – they mostly hated each other!

- ✔ Once George II became king, Caroline continued to use her intelligence and influence as the power behind the throne.

Caroline seems to have been very supportive to her husband, and she was also a keen supporter of Robert Walpole, the Prime Minister who had come to power during the reign of George I. Caroline died in 1737, and her husband seemed to be genuinely upset – even though he'd had mistresses when she was alive. For her part, Caroline seems to have tolerated the mistresses, valuing her companionship with George and the power she exercised as queen.

When Caroline approached death, she tried to encourage George to remarry. But he said he would not. Instead, he lived more publicly with his mistress, Amalia von Walmoden. He said that he had known many women, but none of them was fit to buckle Caroline's shoe.

War, war, and more war

Prime Minister Robert Walpole pursued peaceful policies during his time in power under George II. But after his great supporter, Queen Caroline, died in 1737, Walpole lost his power. With the main influences for peace gone, George became involved in a series of wars. Here's a list of some of the key European conflicts in the latter part of George's reign:

- ✔ **War of Jenkins's Ear, 1739:** Britain goes to war with Spain over the ear of a Captain Jenkins, which was said to have been cut off in a fight at sea.

- ✔ **War of Austrian Succession, 1740–48:** Various European powers fight over who should rule parts of the Holy Roman Empire; Britain and France are also at loggerheads for control of North America and India.

- ✔ **Seven Years' War, 1756–63:** Europe is again in turmoil as the Austrian Hapsburg family try to win back Silesia, a territory they lost in the previous conflict.

George was personally involved in the War of Austrian Succession, because it was the last war in which a British monarch actually led his own troops into battle. This event happened at Dettingen in Bavaria in 1743 and showed that George, for all his arrogance, was also a brave leader.

A proper Charlie: The Jacobite Rising

The Jacobites, the people who supported the claim to the throne of the descendents of James II, kept their cause alive throughout the time of George I and into the reign of his son. After the Old Pretender, James Edward Stuart, who had led the 1715 rising, came his son, Charles Edward Stuart, known to his followers as Bonnie Prince Charlie and to others as the Young Pretender.

Charles lived in exile in France, but had put together plans for an invasion of England by 1745. Knowing that he would have plenty of support in Scotland, birthplace of the Stuart dynasty, he decided to travel there and then invade England from the north. He started impressively, but his campaign went seriously pear-shaped:

- ✔ In July 1745, Charles and a few supporters landed in Scotland.

- ✔ Charles attracted an army of some 3,000 men from the Highlands and arrived outside Edinburgh on 17 September. The city surrendered.

- ✔ The Jacobites scored a further victory over England at Prestonpans, about 10 miles from Edinburgh, a few days later.

> ✔ Charles delayed after Prestonpans, waiting until November to cross the
>   border into England.
>
> ✔ A huge English force under the king's son, William, Duke of Cumberland,
>   defeated Charles at Culloden Moor on 15 April 1746, forcing Charles to
>   flee to the Highlands. Cumberland unmercifully had Jacobite supporters
>   and troops pursued and killed after the battle, and the Young
>   Pretender's invasion attempt was over.

Charles Stuart's fatal error was to hesitate after winning the Battle of
Prestonpans. If he had gone south more quickly, he could have done big
damage in England and may even have forced George off the throne. Instead,
he thought that a delay might give more and more English time to come
around to his cause.

The English didn't see it Charles's way, however. One symptom of their reac-
tion was a famous occasion in September 1745 when the national anthem,
'God save the king', was sung for the first time. Charles didn't calculate for
English patriotism, a sign that his claim to the throne on behalf of his father
was hopeless.

After his defeat, Charles fled, dressed as a woman, to the island of Skye,
before making his way to mainland Europe. After a long life in relative
obscurity, he died in Rome in 1788.

Meanwhile, many of his supporters were put to death, some languished in
prison, ill-treated and starving, and others were sent as slaves to plantations
in America. Oppressive policies were introduced in Highland Scotland, where
so much of Charles's support had originated. These measures ranged from
political ones (such as taking the power from the chiefs of the clans) to symbolic ones (such as banning kilts, tartans, and other symbols of clan identity).

Poor Fred

George II's eldest son was Prince Frederick, who was born in 1707. Frederick
spent his early life in Hanover, but came to England in 1728 and was made
Prince of Wales the following year. Frederick did not get on with his parents.
Queen Caroline was reported to have called him an ass, and the king and
queen sidelined him, preferring their younger children. They even delayed
allowing him to marry, implying that they didn't trust him to carry on the
succession.

As a result of his poor treatment, Frederick became a focus for those who
opposed the king and his minister Walpole. The prince supported Walpole's
political opponents and even used his interest in the arts against George, setting up an Opera of the Nobility as a rival to the opera company sponsored
by the king.

Prince Frederick obviously hoped to become king after his father. But the prince died suddenly in 1751, while George was still alive. He succumbed to a burst abscess on one of his lungs. The unfulfilled prince has been known ever since as poor Fred.

Building an empire

George was a German king, and, like the English, the Germans were old enemies of the French. In the early 18th century, France was a major power with interests all over the world, including India and North America. Being at war with France from the 1740s onwards gave George a reason to attack French outposts around the world. A string of victories under able leaders gave the king huge territorial gains amounting to a vast empire.

Britain had had interests in India since the British East India Company began to set up trading posts there in 1600. But India is a vast and diverse subcontinent, home to many peoples with many religions, spread far and wide. War with France gave George, and his talented and adventurous Indian governor Robert Clive, the chance to push out the French. Clive – a soldier as well as an administrator – won a serious of victories against France (Madras, Arcot, Cacutta, Chandernagore, and Plassey) between 1746 and 1757 that cemented British power in India, opening up a vast source of raw materials, such as cotton, and a ready market for British manufactured goods.

In addition, Prime Minister William Pitt wanted to remove the French from Canada and increase British power and influence there, too. The chance came in September 1759 with a British force under General James Wolfe, a soldier who, although a mere 32 years of age, already had a good record of fighting for George. Wolfe triumphantly took Quebec from the French. The victory entailed the dramatic ascent of the high cliffs along the city's river frontage to take the French by surprise.

In terms of the power of the monarch and the area of the globe ruled from Britain, George II was a resounding success. It was an impressive achievement for a rather pompous and not very intelligent man. But George was helped by an able Prime Minister and an intelligent consort in the first part of his reign. Toward the end of his life, he was served by men who won him rewards on the battlefield.

But fate had a final, deflating trick to play on pompous George – he died of a heart attack while sitting on the lavatory. His grandson, another George, was ready to take his place on the throne.

Farmer George: George III

George III (1760–1820) was the grandson of George II and the son of Frederick Louis, the second George's son who died in 1751 when only 44. When he came to the throne, George III was a young man. He was well educated, religious, and had wide interests. But he was also rather stubborn and lacked the good judgement that an effective ruler needs.

George's reign was dominated by foreign policy. Britain lost its North American colonies when the United States became independent in 1776, but he also had successes, such as notable victories in the wars against the French emperor, Napoleon.

The king, however, was more at ease pursuing personal interests, such as agriculture. He toured the country finding out about new farming techniques and improved the royal farms at Windsor and Richmond, increasing their profits by a factor of ten. George even wrote articles about agriculture, using the pen-name of Ralph Robinson. His success in this field and his ease when talking to country people earned him the nickname Farmer George.

The end of George's long reign was marked by illness. He suffered bouts of instability, and his contemporaries thought him insane. But he suffered from a physical illness, porphyria, that brought on these symptoms, which got so bad that his son, yet another George, had to rule as Prince Regent in the last decade of his reign.

Right and proper?

By the standards of the 18th century, George III lived a very moral life. He had one affair when a young man, with a woman called Hannah Lightfoot who was the daughter of a London shoemaker, and there was a rumour that the couple had married in secret. The affair doesn't seem to have been long lasting, and it was small beer compared to the loose living of most of the Hanoverian rulers.

When he knew that he had inherited the throne, George did the rounds of the courts of Europe and quickly found his bride, Charlotte of Mecklenburg. Charlotte was not George's first choice, coming from a fairly low-profile Germanic princely family. But the couple were married in September 1761 and two weeks later were crowned as king and queen.

George and Charlotte seem to have been a faithful couple, and they had 15 children. Their ordered family lifestyle was in stark contrast to the antics of some of their offspring, who became famous for loose and lavish living. Their eldest son, George, was the most notorious. Young George had a string of mistresses as well as entering into a marriage that was illegal because his bride, a commoner called Maria Fitzherbert, was a Catholic – an English king or heir to the throne wasn't allowed to marry a member of the church of Rome.

Losing America

George III is famous for the biggest crisis of his reign, the loss of Britain's colonies in the part of North America that became the United States.

The problem across the Atlantic was that British kings and their Prime Ministers tried to impose unpopular taxes, but offered the colonists no representation in the British Parliament.

George's ministers imposed a series of taxes on America, and the colonists were not amused. Here's the dirt on some of these money-grubbing measures:

✔ **Cider tax, 1763:** Caused an uproar and was subsequently repealed.

✔ **Molasses tax, 1764:** Also later repealed.

✔ **Stamp duty, 1765:** Imposed on legal documents and newspapers. Caused a big outcry and was quickly repealed, in spite of the king's misgivings.

✔ **Tea tax, 1773:** Led to the famous Boston Tea Party, when colonists tossed tea on board ships in Boston Harbour into the water and the British sent in the troops.

The king's ministers were blamed for these disasters, but the general influence of the king was attacked, too. And things got worse for Britain when war broke out between Britain and America. The colonists were victorious, and the United States of America was created. It was a disaster for George, but the beginning of great things for the United States.

Ruling the waves

George's reign is also famous as the period in which Britain ruled the waves, scoring notable victories over the French in the Napoleonic Wars.

To match the American debacle, the Brits had a resounding success in the 1790s and early 1800s in a series of battles against the old enemy, the French. The French leader at the time was Napoleon Bonaparte. By the end of the 19th century, Napoleon was busy extending his power all over mainland Europe, and the Brits were in constant fear that he would cross the Channel and invade Britain, too.

Napoleon was all too good at winning land battles. But the British had a secret weapon in Admiral Horatio Nelson, the hero of the British navy. Nelson scored a series of victories over the French navy that eventually put to rest to any invasion plans that Napoleon may have had. His most famous victories were

- ✔ **The Battle of the Nile, 1798:** Nelson smashes most of the French navy to pieces in Aboukir Bay in Egypt.

- ✔ **The Battle of Copenhagen, 1801:** The British fleet destroy the Danish navy in Copenhagen harbour when it seemed that the Danes were going to enter the war. Nelson, second in command on this occasion, was ordered not to attack but ignored the command.

- ✔ **The Battle of Trafalgar, 1805:** Nelson defeats both the French and the Spanish fleets as they were sailing from Cadiz, Spain, towards the Mediterranean. Nelson was killed in the battle, but French and Spanish naval powers were destroyed.

Britain ruled the waves. It wasn't just the naval battles that defeated Napoleon. The army leader the Duke of Wellington helped give him the boot, too. At the Battle of Waterloo in 1815, Wellington struggled to hold off the French, but when Britain's Prussian allies arrived, Napoleon was finally defeated.

Mad or sad?

King George III is well known for being Britain's mad king. In fact, his health was a problem early on in his reign, when he had a physical collapse in 1765. Parliament passed a Regency Act, to allow a relative to rule in his stead when he was ill, but he seemed to recover.

Then, later in life, the king had a series of debilitating attacks – the worst ones were in 1788, 1801, and 1804 – each time giving the impression that he was losing his mind. In the 1788 episode, for example, he grew violent, attacking the Prince of Wales. He also talked continuously. In the 1801 and 1804 episodes, the symptoms got worse, but were followed by periods of recovery. To onlookers at the time, it seemed that the king was steadily succumbing to mental illness.

Things got even worse for George in November 1810, when his youngest daughter, Amelia, died. Soon afterwards, the king had a still worse bout of illness, talking incoherently, failing to recognise people, and baffling a number of eminent doctors who the royal family consulted. It became clear that he would be unable to rule, and his son George was appointed Prince Regent, king in all but name.

George III, meanwhile, was packed off to Windsor Castle, where he was kept for the rest of his life. Here, he spent nine years, deranged and also blind. He seems to have been badly neglected, his hair and beard allowed to grow long.

Modern medical experts who have studied George's case history believe that he was not suffering from mental illness in the strict sense of the phrase. The most likely diagnosis of the king's illness is a blood disease called *porphyria,* which can cause symptoms similar to mental illness. Historians suspect that a number of English kings had porphyria. The line of sufferers may even go as far back as Henry VI, who had periods of apparent mental collapse.

If Britain's mad king was not mad, he certainly had a sad end. One person, though, was happy at George's decline in health. That was the Prince Regent, who had been waiting for years to get his seat on the throne. He could barely conceal his happiness at being made Prince Regent in 1811, ten years before becoming king in his own right when his father finally died, a broken man of 81, in 1821.

Prince of Pleasure: George IV

When George III became so ill he could not rule, his son, also George, ruled in his stead as Prince Regent. When the prince became king as George IV in 1820, his character was already very well known. George IV (1820–30) was notorious as a libertine who was devoted to a life of luxury and enjoyment. He ran up huge debts on everything from grand houses to lavish parties, enjoying the benefits of kingship without attending to its responsibilities.

Lord of luxury

As both Prince Regent and king, George spent a fortune on his lifestyle. He was obsessed with having the best of the latest fashions in everything from clothes to houses and ran up enormous debts in the process. In 1802, the Prince's debts were calculated at £146,000 and included:

- £20,000 spent on a regimental band.
- £17,000 on jewellers' bills.
- More than £9,000 owed to the Prince's tailors.
- About £7,500 owed to lacemakers.

At this period, the Prince's annual income was around £108,000 per year, but out of it he had to pay for essentials, staff, and the expenses of the Princess of Wales, so his debts were way more than he could afford.

The main surviving monument to this life of luxury is Brighton Pavilion, the extraordinary house he built near England's south coast, an architectural extravaganza with Indian-style onion-shaped domes on the roof and rich decoration inside. George even sent a representative to China to buy various things for the rooms inside the Pavilion. Wallpaper, tables, gongs, pottery, swords, and garden seats were all brought back from China for the Royal Pavilion.

George's patronage of artists, architects, and decorators, influenced a whole new style of architecture, called Regency. Not all of it was as exotic as Brighton Pavilion, but it was all elegant, and it went with new fashions in dress and a vogue for glamorous parties. It was all the kind of thing that rich people in London liked, and as a result, George was quite a popular figure when young. But George's hedonistic lifestyle also had its down side. It wasn't just the money. George also had a string of mistresses. The prince's first mistress set the tone. She was an actress called Mary Robinson, known as Perdita after the character she was playing in Shakespeare's *The Winter's Tale* when George first saw her. The couple were together for a while, and then George found another mistress – and discovered that Mary expected to be paid off in return for keeping quiet about their liaison.

This pattern went on for several years, with each jilted mistress extracting a hefty payment, and with the king – who had always spoiled his son when the prince was a child – forking out the money.

The secret wife

The sequence of royal mistresses was interrupted when George married a young widow called Maria Fitzherbert. Mrs Fitzherbert was an inappropriate wife for an 18th-century heir to the throne, in several ways:

- ✔ She was a commoner, and kings were usually married to other royals or members of the aristocracy.

- ✔ She was twice a widow, which meant she came with the kind of historical baggage (not to mention sexual experience) that was not normal for royal wives.

- ✔ She was a Catholic in an era when the law forbade the king from being a Catholic. In effect, marrying Maria barred George from the throne.

- ✔ She did not have the approval of the king even though the 1772 Royal Marriages Act made it necessary for all matches of royal family members under age 25.

George would have been content to get around this problem by maintaining Maria as a mistress. But Maria refused to live in sin with George and insisted on marriage. So George and Maria married in secret, in the full knowledge that their match was illegal under English law, even though it was accepted by the Catholic Church.

The coronation scandal

In the period after George married Mrs Fitzherbert, he was overeating, drinking like a fish, and satisfying his sexual cravings with yet more mistresses. His rather more moral father, George III, with the backing of Parliament, insisted that the prince should take a wife who was acceptable in English law. There would be no trouble about George's marriage to Mrs Fitzherbert because it was seen in law as void, so George wouldn't be committing bigamy by marrying a second time.

The king found a bride for George in Caroline of Brunswick, a relative of the Hanoverians who, though somewhat unattractive, was at least Protestant, previously unmarried, and royal. King and Parliament also produced a tempting bribe for George – if he would marry Caroline, Parliament would help pay off a chunk of his debts.

George duly accepted this bribe, and a meeting was arranged between him and Caroline, just three days before they were due to be married. George was disappointed with his bride, who was said to have a personal hygiene problem, was rather plain, and had a reputation for temper tantrums. The prince asked for a stiff brandy on meeting her and was still drunk when they got married three days later.

George and Caroline stayed together just long enough for the queen to produce a child, Princess Charlotte Augusta, but then separated. The king was soon back with Mrs Fitzherbert, while the queen was shunted out and spent her spare time setting up an orphanage.

By the time George III died, Caroline was in exile in Italy, where there was a rumour that she was having an affair with a courtier called Bartolomeo Pergami. However, when she heard that George was about to be crowned, she shocked king and court alike by demanding to take her rightful place at his side.

George offered to pay his estranged queen £50,000 a year to stay out of the country, but she refused. Instead, she came to England and faced up to an inquiry into her conduct. A kind of trial was held in the House of Lords, and Caroline was found not guilty of any misconduct, but George *still* managed to keep her away from the coronation. Poor Caroline died of some kind of intestinal illness a few weeks afterwards.

King and public

What did the people of Britain think of the dissolute George? Most people disapproved of him, and many even hated him. It was not just his dissolute lifestyle. He reigned at a time of high unemployment and widespread poverty, and he had close links with reactionary politicians who did nothing to alleviate these social ills. He was especially detested in London, where Parliament had to cope with his mounting debts and carry on running the country while he was partying with his mistresses.

Britain was fortunate that for the first seven years of his reign, the government was steered along by a strong and able Prime Minister, Lord Liverpool. Later, another powerful minister, the Duke of Wellington, took over the government. A notable feature of his period in office was the Catholic Emancipation Act of 1829, which allowed Catholics to take public office, a right they had previously been denied. George, meanwhile, tended to keep away from the London limelight, preferring to stay in Windsor and Brighton while his ministers ran the government.

One reason for the king keeping out of the public eye was simply that he had lost all his glamour. George's health was in serious decline:

- He was virtually blind, with cataracts in both eyes.

- His gout was so bad that he couldn't sign official documents.

- He was grossly overweight – one contemporary described him as looking like a feather bed.

- He had bladder trouble and breathing difficulties.

- He dosed himself with laudanum and cherry brandy.

The king lived out his last years in rather pathetic seclusion, dying in 1830 of respiratory disease. He had had one legitimate child, Princess Charlotte, who became a much more popular figure than her father. She married Prince Leopold of Saxe-Coburg-Saalfield in 1816, but died in childbirth the following year. As a result of this tragedy, George had no direct heir, and his brothers realised that they were in line for the throne. The throne passed to George's eldest surviving brother, William IV.

All Change: William IV

The daughter of George IV, Princess Charlotte, died before her father, and the king's first brother, Frederick, died before him, so his younger brother, William IV (1830–37) became king at the ripe old age of 64. His reign was short, and its main achievements, the passing of some important reforming laws that made Britain more democratic, went through Parliament in spite of the king's conservative opinions.

Sailor Bill

As a younger son, William did not expect to become king, and as a young man, he embarked on a career in the Navy. Amazingly, in a time of power and privilege for royals, he did not ask for special treatment when he joined the Navy and began as an ordinary able seaman, working his way steadily through the ranks until he was given command of his own ship and was finally, in 1811, made Admiral of the Fleet.

Apart from his naval career, William was known, like most of his family, for being highly sexed. He had a number of mistresses, but in his mid-20s, he had a long-term relationship with one of them, an actress called Dorothea Jordan. Dorothea and William had ten children. Because his main title was Duke of Clarence, the children were given the surname Fitzclarence.

The illegitimate sons of royalty were often given surnames beginning with the prefix *Fitz*. This term comes from the French word for son, *fils*. So a surname beginning with Fitz was a two-edged sword, enabling the bearer to show his connection with the royal family, but also indicating that he was not part of the legitimate royal line.

The Fitzclarence family seemed happy, but William ditched Dorothea in 1811, after they'd spent more than 20 years together. The split is a bit of a mystery, but it's thought that the reason was that Dorothea, by then an alcoholic, had gone to seed, and William was looking for a more attractive partner.

When it became clear that he was in line for the throne, William decided to marry. His chosen bride was Adelaide, daughter of the German Duke of Saxe-Meiningen. She was just under half the age of the 52-year-old William, but the pair got on well together and settled down happily. Adelaide even brought up William's illegitimate children, although sadly none of her own babies lived beyond infancy.

Vote, vote, vote: Electoral reform

During William's reign, there was a movement to make the electoral system fairer by giving more people the right to vote. Lord Grey, the leader of the Whig government that came in when William became king, was keen on reform; the other side, the Tories, opposed it. In 1831, the Whig-dominated House of Commons passed a Reform Bill, but the House of Lords, which included a majority of Tories, threw it out.

With the chance of reform snatched away, a lot of popular resentment developed over what the Lords had done – riots even occurred in some places, such as Bristol, Nottingham, and South Wales. To get the Reform Bill through the House of Lords, the Prime Minister put pressure on William to create 50 new Whig peers – enough to outvote the Tories and get the bill passed. William was not keen on using his power to create lords politically in this way and refused. The government resigned, William appointed a new Prime Minister, the Duke of Wellington, and an election occurred, which the Whigs won. With a Whig majority in the House of Commons, the king had to agree to appoint the new peers, but in the end, he didn't have to appoint them – the House of Lords agreed to the Reform Bill after all.

This wasn't the only time when William intervened dramatically in government affairs. In 1834, he sacked the government out of the blue – while he was having dinner at Windsor Castle! The result of William's hasty action was another election, which was also won by the side the king didn't support. William's heavy-handed involvement in government made him a far-from-perfect constitutional monarch.

One way of looking at William is to see him as a caretaker ruler, a man who was already middle-aged when he became king and whose main function was to keep the throne warm for the next ruler, Queen Victoria. In this view, he was just muddling along. But a more positive view sees him as a reforming king, showing how the limited powers of the monarchy can be used to bring about beneficial change.

Whichever view of William is true, he was never likely to reign for long. He died in 1837, aged 71, of pneumonia and cirrhosis of the liver. Because he and his queen, Adelaide, produced no surviving heirs, the throne passed to the king's niece Victoria, daughter of the Duke of Kent, one of the brothers of George IV, and his wife Mary Louise Victoria, who came from one of the noble Germanic families from whom the Hanoverians often chose their marriage partners.

Loathed and Then Loved: Victoria

When Victoria was named as William IV's heir, she was shown a family tree to help explain her relationship to the British king. When she realised how close she was to becoming queen, she said, 'I will be good'. And good she was, a pillar of rectitude, for all of her long reign.

Queen Victoria (1837–1901) reigned longer than any other British monarch. She presided over the period when Britain was at its most prosperous, at the centre of a worldwide empire and in the forefront of technology and industry. To begin with, Victoria was not much liked, but in partnership with her consort, Prince Albert, she won people over. Unlike so many royal couples, the queen and consort were actually in love, and the public saw their large family as an ideal they could look up to. In addition, many benefited directly from the reforms Albert pressed for in fields such as education and public health.

Trying to be good

Victoria was in a difficult position when she came to the throne. She was a young single woman of 18 who, as far as most British people were concerned, was related to the Hanoverians and therefore stood for the dodgy morals, German outlook, and extravagance of the dynasty. She had had a tough childhood because her father died when she was a baby. Her first couple of years on the throne were difficult, too, as shown by two episodes that happened in the early years of her reign.

Falsely accused: Lady Flora Hastings

It was not surprising that politicians and courtiers tried to control and influence the apparently weak young queen. One of these men was Sir John Conroy, a close friend of Victoria's mother. Victoria disliked Conroy and believed he was trying to influence her through one of her ladies-in-waiting, Lady Flora Hastings, who Victoria thought was having an affair with Conroy.

When Lady Flora's stomach began to swell, Victoria jumped to the conclusion that Conroy had got her pregnant. Lady Flora denied the charge, and Victoria made her undergo a humiliating medical examination. Result: Lady Flora was still a virgin. The swelling turned out to be the result of cancer of the liver. Lady Flora died soon afterwards, and Victoria was reviled and jeered at in public.

Ministerial mayhem

In 1839, the Prime Minister, Lord Melbourne, resigned. Victoria had relied heavily on his guidance and missed him deeply. The incoming Prime Minister, Robert Peel, was worried that the queen would be unduly influenced by the ladies-in-waiting at her court, who had been appointed by the previous Whig government. He demanded Tory replacements.

Victoria put her foot down and refused. Peel, in turn, refused to be Prime Minister, and Lord Melbourne returned, much to the queen's relief. Victoria got some stick for her liking of Melbourne, who had been tainted with scandal in the public mind since his wife had had an affair with the poet Lord Byron years ago. People called the queen Mrs Melbourne, but at least she got her way over her ladies-in-waiting.

King without a crown: Prince Albert

Albert, the son of Germanic nobleman Ernst, Duke of Saxe-Coburg-Gotha, first met Victoria in 1836. The queen's parents thought he would be a good match for their daughter, and she was attracted to him, too. When the couple met again three years later, the queen proposed marriage. The couple were wed in February 1840, and their marriage was happy, fulfilling, and fertile – Victoria had nine children.

Albert didn't become king when he married Victoria. He took the title of Prince Consort. In other words, Victoria remained the reigning monarch, while Albert's role, in theory, was mainly ceremonial, just like that of a queen when a king was on the throne.

But in practice, Albert was much more than a ceremonial royal. He had a huge influence over his wife, shaping not just the life of the royal family, but influencing new policies and laws that affected everyone in the kingdom. Perhaps his greatest achievement of all was the 1851 Great Exhibition, an enormous display of the products of the entire British empire, held in the Crystal Palace, a specially built glass-and-iron building of vast proportions, erected in London's Hyde Park. Albert was such an important figure that he has been called a king without a crown.

With their large brood of children and their loving relationship, Victoria and Albert headed up that rare thing, a happy royal family. The image they created, of a happy family at the head of the nation, was highly influential, and ever since, people have expected the royal family to be a picture of domestic bliss – even when it has fallen far short of this ideal.

The queen and consort had other ideals, too. They were all too aware of the scandalous history of the House of Hanover, in which it was normal for kings to have strings of mistresses, and many of Victoria's relations were born out of wedlock. Albert, too, grew up with a father and brother who jumped in and out of bed with different women.

Victoria and Albert wanted to be different from their predecessors. They believed that if they set a good example, the moral climate of the whole country would improve, too, which happened, up to a point. Courtiers and politicians realised that 'unofficial' liaisons would be frowned upon. Many of them still had their mistresses – but they were more discreet about it.

Families and peace

One other consequence of Victoria's family values was that she saw her family as extending right across Europe. This view was true, literally, because she was related through her huge family to most of the crowned heads of the continent.

This extended family came into being mainly because of Victoria herself. She had nine children and arranged marriages for them with royals on the European mainland. Some of her children married members of the royal families of Prussia and Russia; others wed princes and princesses of the ruling houses of the various smaller states that existed before Germany became a single united country.

Victoria wanted to keep her European family, so on the whole, she worked for peace in Europe – and indeed in the lands beyond Europe over which she had power or influence. Here are a few examples of Victorian peace initiatives:

- ✔ **1857:** In the war between Austria and Sardinia, she persuaded her government to stay neutral.

- ✔ **1858:** She appealed for leniency and calm after the bloodshed during the Indian Mutiny.

- ✔ **1877–8:** She and Prime Minister Disraeli kept out of the way when Turkey was fighting – and massacring – in Bulgaria, although Disraeli did intervene in the war between Russia and Turkey.

Ministerial manoeuvres

In 1861, Prince Albert died. His death was due to several assaults on his health:

- ✔ He caught a bad cold, which turned to pneumonia, after a visit to Cambridge to take his son Bertie to task about his debts, mistresses, and other misdemeanours.

- ✔ He caught typhoid fever because of the unhygienic state of the drains at Windsor Castle.

- ✔ He had become exhausted after sitting up all night amending a letter from the British government to Abraham Lincoln – if Albert hadn't changed the letter, Britain would probably have entered the American Civil War on the side of the South.

As a result of Albert's death, the whole complexion of the monarchy changed. Victoria went into deep mourning and lost the close contact with her people that she had achieved through her husband. After a while, people got tired of Victoria's grief – widows were expected to mourn, but the queen's grief seemed to go on for ever.

Victoria kept in touch with the business of government through a succession of Prime Ministers. Here are some of the most important:

- ✔ **Robert Peel (PM 1834–5, 1841–6):** Peel was famous as a supporter of free trade, reducing taxes and repealing duties to encourage commerce. In 1839, the Tory Peel was on the point of becoming Prime Minister, but realised that his government would be weak because it would have a minority in the House of Commons. To strengthen his position, Peel wanted Victoria to appoint Tory ladies in her household. Victoria refused, effectively preventing Peel from taking office.

✔ **Benjamin Disraeli (PM 1868, 1874–80):** Disraeli brought in social reforms (in housing, safety at work, and other areas) and promoted the British empire. Disraeli handled Queen Victoria by flattering her and by making her Empress of India in 1877. Disraeli's flattery ensured that he was the queen's favourite Prime Minister.

✔ **William Ewart Gladstone (PM 1868–74, 1880–5, 1886, 1892–4):** Gladstone was a supporter of the working classes and introduced reforms in a wide range of areas, from local government to the law, which were designed to make the lives of ordinary people easier. Queen Victoria didn't get on with Gladstone because she didn't like his way of preaching at her. She also disliked his policy of removing state support from the Irish church and was upset when he did not support British general Charles George Gordon when Gordon was besieged in Khartoum, capital of Sudan.

✔ **Viscount Palmerston (PM 1855–8, 1859–65):** Palmerston was a very popular Prime Minister, but the queen didn't take to him at all. She disapproved of his habit of seducing her ladies-in-waiting and disliked the way he made changes to diplomatic communications after she'd seen them, undermining her role in foreign policy.

Jubilee!

Victoria snapped out of her mourning when she found an unlikely male confidant in John Brown, one of her servants from the Scottish Highlands. Brown seemed able to break through the queen's grief and was prepared to answer her bluntly, without a lot of the false deference with which people normally approached royalty.

The queen got some flak for her relationship with Brown. Rumours circulated that it went beyond a mere friendship, and that Victoria had reverted to the Hanoverian type and jumped into bed with a commoner. This rumour was almost certainly untrue, but the queen's popularity took a nose-dive. Victorians, who were quite prepared to accept that a man might have any number of mistresses, couldn't countenance any hint of sexual freedom amongst their womenfolk. In the early 1870s, some even called for the monarchy to be abolished. This reform didn't happen, of course, and the criticism died away and was forgotten after Brown died in 1883.

One event that helped make royalty popular gains was the Golden Jubilee, held in 1887 to celebrate Victoria's 50th year on the throne. It was a major royal occasion, with kings and queens from all over Europe attending. The main events were a banquet attended by 50 European kings and princes, and a memorial service in Westminster Abbey.

Ten years later, a Diamond Jubilee marked the 60th anniversary of the queen's accession. This time, the emphasis was on the British empire, with troops and others from Britain's various colonies in attendance. As the century drew to a close, Britain enjoyed a feeling of optimism and affection for the queen. She died in 1901, the head of the world's largest empire and the longest reigning monarch in British history.

Unlikely Success: Edward VII

Edward VII (1901–10) was the eldest son of Queen Victoria and her consort Prince Albert. Because his mother had such a long reign, Edward was almost 60 years old when he came to the throne. He spent most of his life as Prince of Wales, enjoying all the pleasures life could offer him, from the embraces of numerous mistresses to slap-up meals in top Parisian restaurants. When he finally became king, Edward was rather poorly prepared for his new role, but he made a surprisingly good job of it, developing the ceremonial aspect of the monarchy and becoming a popular national figurehead.

As the son of Prince Albert, Edward took his father's surname of Saxe-Coburg, so, technically, he was not strictly a member of the royal House of Hanover. But because of anti-German feelings in the first World War, Edward's descendents changed their Teutonic name to a more English-friendly one, Windsor. As a result, Edward was the only king of the house of Saxe-Coburg, so in this book he's included with his Hanoverian relatives for convenience.

Playboy prince

Prince Albert Edward was born in 1841. His parents, Queen Victoria and Prince Albert, brought him up in an atmosphere of moral seriousness, in the hope that he would not turn out like the previous Prince of Wales – the Prince Regent, who became George IV – who was infamous for a dissolute life of overspending.

But Bertie rebelled against his parents' strict values. The prince was a party animal who loved big occasions, good food, and foreign travel. A keen sportsman, he was a lover of yachting, shooting, hunting, and horse-racing. Another passionate interest was the newly invented motor car. Bertie owned several cars, all of which were adorned with the royal coat of arms.

The prince's greatest love of all was for the opposite sex. He soon notched up a list of mistresses that included many actresses, and this trend continued after he had married the beautiful Princess Alexandra, elder daughter of the king of Denmark, in 1863.

Queen Victoria, of course, did not approve of her son's behaviour, especially when he told her that her lengthy mourning after the death of Albert was making her unpopular. The queen's attitude toward Bertie amounted to one of distrust, and she wouldn't let him anywhere near the governmental side of her duties – in other words, he wasn't allowed to play any part in meetings with ministers or to see any of the official papers she had to sign. It was not surprising, then, that Bertie devoted more and more of his life to the pursuit of pleasure.

The king as ambassador

When he became king, Edward VII had had little experience of politics, but he had a genuine love of the ceremony surrounding the monarchy. He liked going on tours around the country so that his subjects could see him in the flesh. He established the custom that the monarch is the one who ceremonially 'opens' Parliament each year. And he made sure that ceremonial occasions, from receptions to visits by foreign rulers, were held with all the appropriate pomp.

As a prince, Edward had been keen on foreign travel and he had a special affection for France. When he became king, he continued to travel for pleasure. But his good personal relations with the French had important consequences for his country, too. The king's French connections brought Britain and France closer together politically. In 1904, an Anglo-French agreement settled various disputes between the two countries about their colonial interests. Edward's good relations with France encouraged this *entente cordiale*.

The other side of the diplomatic coin was England's relations with Germany. Edward and his nephew, the German ruler Kaiser Wilhelm II, simply did not get on, in spite of the fact that Wilhelm had been very fond of Queen Victoria, who had died in his arms. The personal coldness between the two men pushed their countries apart, too.

Edward's social skills made him a popular ruler. He saw how well people responded to seeing the royal family in public and gave them what they wanted with lots of public appearances. And in spite of his habit of 'playing away' with his many mistresses, his marriage to Queen Alexandra seems to have been affectionate, and the couple surrounded themselves with a loving family of princes and princesses.

When Edward died in 1910, he was widely mourned. A 7-mile queue stretched through London as people waited to pay their last respects. Vast crowds, perhaps up to 2 million strong, took to the streets to watch his funeral procession. Edward's mourners respected a king who had made the monarchy more symbolic and less political as it entered the 20th century. They did not know that this trend was set to continue.

Part VI

Modern Royals: The House of Windsor

In this part . . .

In the 20th century, the British monarchy faced a number of crises. Some of these, such as the two World Wars, were devastating for everyone but posed a special challenge to the monarchy – what was the role for the ruler now that he was no longer his country's military leader?

More personal crises became national ones, too, because the monarch is a public figure. The most famous crises were the abdication of King Edward VIII in 1936 and the death of Princess Diana in 1997. On both occasions, people questioned the future of the monarchy, but both times the institution survived – because of the dedication of the individual members of the royal family and because of the gradual adjustments they made to their outlook and role.

Chapter 16

Monarchs at War

. . . .

In This Chapter

▶ Investigating the first three kings of the House of Windsor

▶ Discovering how the monarchy coped with two World Wars

▶ Understanding the 'abdication crisis'

▶ Watching the royal family become less remote and closer to the people

. . . .

*I*n the first half of the 20th century, two kings called George dominated the royal history of Britain. They were both shy, rather private men who were in many ways ill-suited to the public role of monarchy. But both George V and his son George VI managed to overcome their hang-ups to become leaders who were respected and, in the end, loved by their people.

Between the two Georges came Edward VIII, who reigned only for a few months, was never crowned, and gave up the throne in order to marry a woman whom the establishment deemed unacceptable to be queen.

These unlikely rulers presided over difficult times. George V led his country through World War I and the political upheavals that followed it. The Britain of George VI's reign had to face the even greater devastation of World War II. In the 20th century, it was no longer acceptable for a king to be a military leader in any real sense, so both monarchs had to find ways of being a war leader without going into battle.

By the end of George VI's reign, therefore, the monarchy had transformed itself. During World War II, the king met ordinary people regularly, developed a common touch, and was at the centre of a royal family that was featured widely in the press and on the news.

What's in a Name: George V

George V (1910–36) never expected to become king. He was the second son of Edward, Prince of Wales (later Edward VII – for more about him, see Chapter 15) and Queen Alexandra, but in 1892, his elder brother Albert Victor died.

Suddenly, George found himself next in line to the throne after his father. After the reign of Edward VII, George became king.

George V had expected to have a career in the Navy, and he spent about 15 years in the service, rising to the rank of Commander. On the death of his brother, George was forced to do extra studies in politics and languages to prepare himself for kingship, and he didn't like these lessons. Neither was the prince very well suited to the public role of a monarch – he was shy and disliked parties and royal receptions. He preferred solitary pursuits, such as fishing and adding to his enormous stamp collection.

In his political and social outlook, George was a conservative. He rejected his father's libertine lifestyle, preferring the high moral tone of his grandmother and grandfather, Victoria and Albert. He disliked new and showy fashions and turned his nose up at tarty makeup and the other trappings of the Jazz Age, which began in the 1920s, right in the middle of his reign.

As if coping with modern fashions and the role of king wasn't enough, George was expected to marry his late brother's fiancée, Princess May (also known as Mary) of Teck, which he did, with good grace. As an innately conservative character, George realised that he had to fit in with the demands of his new role.

In the end, George proved a competent monarch, who played his part in steering his country through the horrors of World War I and various political crises both before the war and in the decades afterwards.

Crisis in the Lords

George V came to the throne smack in the middle of a political crisis. In 1909, the governing Liberal Party had produced a budget that included a tax on the rich to pay for old-age pensions. The wealthy ranks of the House of Lords mounted a huge opposition to this measure, and the Prime Minister, Herbert Asquith, had asked King Edward VII to create lots of new peers who would approve of the tax and vote for it in the House of Lords. Edward died before making up his mind, so the problem was left with George.

George gave way to Asquith's demands, and the situation was eased after a general election brought more Liberals into the Commons – making it more difficult for the Lords to defy them. George had got through his first political crisis by the end of 1910, some six months before he was even crowned king. But he didn't like what he'd been expected to do. He said that if the king was meant to stay out of party politics, 'it was equally the duty of politicians to avoid dragging him in'.

War and the monarchy

World War I lasted from 1914 to 1918 and was the most terrible human conflict to date. Britain and Germany were the key combatants, and since the royal family had close ties to both countries, they were deeply involved in the war and the suffering it caused. George V did not like war-mongering, but once Britain was at war, he supported the men who fought 'for king and country', making numerous visits to troops on the battlefield.

War with Germany produced a wave of anti-German feeling in Britain. This sentiment went to absurd extremes, and anyone with a German-sounding name was apt to be treated as an enemy. This prejudice put the royal family, with their German roots, in a tough position. King George had inherited the family name of Saxe-Coburg from his father, and the name reminded everyone of the royal family's Germanic roots. The writer H G Wells criticised George for heading a court that was 'uninspiring' and 'alien'. George, who regarded himself as British through and through, responded that he may be uninspiring, but 'I'll be damned if I'm an alien'.

But the government put George under pressure to do something, and in 1917, he changed his family name to Windsor. The king's secretary suggested the new name, which was also taken by the rest of the king's family. With its links to the ancient castle where the royal family had lived since the Middle Ages, Windsor seemed the quintessence of Britishness.

The name change was a success. It seemed to signal to the people that the royal family were solidly behind Britain. And when other branches of the royal family also changed their names (the Battenbergs, for example, became the Mountbattens), the impression was reinforced. The British royal family really *were* British.

George had never liked the aggressive military stance of his cousin, Kaiser Wilhelm II of Germany. He warned the Kaiser several times that if Germany invaded France or Russia, Britain would come to the aid of the country that Germany attacked.

But the Germans thought they knew better and that, when push came to shove, Britain would stay neutral. In the summer of 1914, Germany declared war on Russia and France – and marched through Belgium on the way to attack France. As a result, Britain declared war on Germany.

British monarchs were no longer expected to lead their troops into battle – the last ruler to do that had been George II in 1743. The monarch was still the leader of the armed forces, but only nominally – the generals and admirals were the real leaders. However, George V used the symbolic power of the monarchy to help the war effort. He raised morale by making frequent visits to the troops – he averaged more than 100 visits per year during the four years of the war – and by handing out medals for bravery.

The royal family also refused to be treated specially. When food was rationed, they kept to their share of the rationed items along with everyone else. When hostilities ended, the king took a leading role in commemorating those who had been killed, beginning in 1920 the tradition of remembering the dead on 11 November, the day on which the armistice was signed.

Turbulent times

While the fighting went on in mainland Europe, there was trouble at home, too. A rebellion in Ireland was followed by a clutch of political crises involving the monarch. George V had a hard time, but his popularity didn't suffer in these turbulent times.

The Easter Rising

In the famous Irish Easter Rising of 1916, a group of nationalists seized the General Post Office and other buildings in Dublin and proclaimed an Irish Republic. For five days, heavy fighting occurred before British troops captured the leaders and put an end to the rising.

Quickly 14 of the leaders of the rising were tried and executed. This retaliation proved a bad move on the part of the British, because it rallied support for the nationalists, who before had not been widely popular. King George was on the side of conciliation, and a Government of Ireland Act in 1920 introduced new parliaments for Northern and Southern Ireland in Belfast and Dublin respectively.

The Northern Irish parliament went ahead, but Republicans objected to the proposals for a Dublin parliament, holding out for a completely independent southern Ireland. Their ambitions were realised in 1921, with the foundation of the Irish Free State, covering all of Ireland except for Ulster. The Free State had *Dominion status* – in other words, it was a kind of halfway house toward independence, a separate state that still owed allegiance to the British crown. Southern Ireland would not be totally independent until the 1930s.

More upheavals

George continued to try to stay out of politics, but he was forced to intervene on several further occasions. The 1920s and early 1930s were a time of political change. For decades, the British political system had been dominated by two parties, the Liberals and Conservatives. But in this period, a new party was increasing in strength. The Labour Party was a party of the left, eager to improve the lives of ordinary working people. Its rise created political uncertainty and made conservatives like the king anxious. Meanwhile, George had to negotiate his way through three political crises:

- ✔ **1923, The PM resigns:** Prime Minister Andrew Bonar Law delivered his resignation, and George had to ask a new Conservative Minister to form a government. Faced with the choice between two main candidates, Lord Curzon and Stanley Baldwin, the king chose Baldwin.

- ✔ **1923, Hung Parliament:** A general election at the end of the year delivered a Parliament in which there was no overall majority. Labour was the largest party, but the Liberals and Conservatives together had more MPs, but wouldn't work together. George invited Labour leader Ramsay MacDonald to form a government.

- ✔ **1931, National Government:** Ramsay MacDonald resigned, but the king persuaded him to form a *National Government,* a coalition between Labour, Conservative, and Liberal politicians that many members of his own Labour Party opposed.

In the second and third of these crises, George had to go against his innate conservatism and invite the Labour leader to become Prime Minister. It went against the grain, but in the end, the two men got on well.

All in the family

In spite of the fact that George's marriage to Princess May of Teck was an arranged one over which the couple had no control, the king and his queen – who became known as Queen Mary – got on well and became genuinely affectionate.

The royal couple had a large brood of six children and, like the family of Queen Victoria (see Chapter 15), were the image of an ideal first family. But the reality wasn't as happy as it seemed. George, stiff, shy, and morally strict, didn't get on well with his offspring. He was very critical of their failings and rather fearsome.

Things changed, though, when the boys got married, because the king warmed to his various daughters-in-law and the grandchildren they produced. George's children were:

- ✔ **David,** who, after becoming Prince of Wales, was later briefly king as Edward VIII. Edward upset his father because of his private life, especially when he fell in love with a twice-divorced American, Mrs Wallis Simpson. A divorcée was then held to be an unsuitable partner for a future king and head of the Church of England.

- ✔ **Albert,** later king as George VI. Shy like his father, Albert felt himself poorly suited for public life, but later had to adapt to the demands of kingship.

✔ **Victoria Alexandra Alice,** known as Mary. Mary married an English earl and was given the title Princess Royal.

✔ **Henry, Duke of Gloucester,** who was briefly Governor-General of Australia.

✔ **George, Duke of Kent,** the husband of Princess Marina of Greece. He was the only one of George's children to wed a member of a foreign royal family.

✔ **John,** who suffered from epilepsy. He was kept out of the public eye and died in his teens.

Health worries

In 1928, George V fell ill – very publicly in front of an audience at Buckingham Palace. When the royal doctors diagnosed septicaemia on one of the king's lungs, things looked grim. The Prince of Wales was called home from a trip to Africa, and an operation followed to remove the infected blood from the king's lung.

The operation was successful, but the king was still weak – for several days, it looked as if he may die. But George V pulled through, even though he needed a lengthy period of convalescence to get over the illness and the operation. The convalescence began with several months in a house in Bognor on England's south coast.

The wider world

George inherited the vast empire built up under the Hanoverian rulers of the past two centuries (see Chapter 15). Like Queen Victoria and Edward VII before him, he took the title Emperor of India, and at the beginning of his reign, he showed how important the title was to him by being crowned twice – once in Westminster Abbey and once, as emperor, in Delhi.

George's reign also saw the beginning of the end of the vast British empire. In 1931, Parliament formulated the Statute of Westminster, which created the idea of a *Commonwealth of Nations* – a network of countries that could talk to each other as equals. It was not the end of the empire, of course. However, it paved the way for the period in the 1940s when many nations of the empire were granted independence while still keeping a special relationship with Britain through the Commonwealth.

'Bugger Bognor!'

George wasn't fond of his convalescent home in Bognor and went back to Windsor Castle in May 1929. During the following months, his health deteriorated on a couple of occasions and his doctors suggested a return to Bognor. 'Bugger Bognor!' was the king's spirited reply. He stayed at Windsor and was better by the autumn of 1929.

King on the air

In spite of George's traditional outlook, he took the monarchy into the modern world in one important way. George V was the first British ruler to make regular broadcasts. By doing so, he brought the royal family into people's homes in a way that hadn't happened in the past and paved the way for today's modern media-conscious monarchy.

The royal broadcasts began at Christmas 1932 and, because television was in its infancy at this time, took place on the radio. The king's first broadcast was scripted by the famous writer Rudyard Kipling. The king expressed the desire that the communication offered by the radio (or the *wireless,* as it was then known) would bring the empire closer together and explained that his task, as he saw it, was 'to arrive at a reasoned tranquillity within our borders, to regain prosperity without self-seeking, and to carry with us those whom the burden of past years has disheartened or overbore.'

The royal talk was very successful and was even available as a recording. George – and his writer Kipling – realised the power of broadcasting to enhance understanding and communication between the diverse nations of the British empire. Ever since, British rulers have broadcast to the nation at Christmas, although today the sovereign appears on television, as well as radio.

A popular king

The good feeling encouraged by the radio broadcasts was enhanced in 1935 when George celebrated 25 years on the throne with his Silver Jubilee. The Silver Jubilee was a hugely popular event, and evidence indicates that even George himself was surprised at how well it went. He never deliberately sought popularity, and when he saw the people's loyalty and enthusiasm expressed at the Jubilee he's reported to have said, 'I never knew they felt like that about me'.

People liked George because he managed to combine the virtues of an upright moral figurehead with the image of a family man, while also making genuine efforts to understand the needs of his country and his empire. He tried to be a safe pair of hands as a king, and most people were sad when he died in 1936. Little did they know how hard his doctors had worked to ensure that the king died during the night. That way, the news first appeared in the 'quality' newspapers that came out the following morning, rather than in the more downmarket evening newspapers.

George had been deeply worried in his last years that his eldest son and heir, the glamorous but vulnerable Edward, Prince of Wales, would not make a good king. 'After I am dead the boy will ruin himself in 12 months', the king said to Prime Minister Stanley Baldwin. And he was right.

Love or Monarchy: Edward VIII

Edward VIII, eldest son of George V and Queen Mary, reigned between January and December 1936. He is famous as the king who gave up his throne for love. Edward wanted to marry an American woman, Wallis Simpson, who was twice divorced, whereas the British establishment (that's Parliament, mainly) couldn't stomach a king – who would also be leader of the Church of England – married to a divorced woman.

A long apprenticeship

George and Mary's eldest son was called Edward Albert Christian George Andrew Patrick David. His last four names were those of the patron saints of the four nations of Britain (England, Scotland, Ireland, and Wales respectively), while his first three names were those of other members of the Windsor family. At home, he was called David.

Troubled beginnings

At the beginning of his life, David didn't expect to become king – his father was a younger son and only inherited the crown because of the death of his elder brother. David's early life was typical for a son of his family – he was brought up by a nanny, educated at home by a private tutor, and then went to naval college as preparation for a career at sea.

This upbringing was a mess. The nanny abused her royal charges, treating them sadistically, but, of course, hiding the fact. This abuse went on for three years until David's parents found out. The tutor was dull and put David off academic work for life. The naval college was better, but he had to leave when his father became king, and David became heir to the throne.

Prince of Wales

When George V became king in 1910, David was made Prince of Wales in a ceremony in Caernarfon Castle that was meant to look medieval, even though it wasn't. The ceremony, called an *investiture,* was actually an elaborate piece of play-acting that was meant to conjure up the rituals of the medieval royal family. Amongst the stone ruins of the great North Welsh castle, David had to do homage and swear loyalty to his father the king. From now on, he took his official name – he was known as Prince Edward.

Edward was fairly scathing about the mock-medieval ceremony. He had to wear a surcoat made of purple velvet, which didn't go down very well with a young man who liked the latest modern fashions. Even so, he was a handsome young man who played his part well, and he won the hearts of the public. It seemed as if Edward was going to be the glamorous member of the royal family.

But the reality of Edward's life was far from glamorous. He was made to travel to Europe to improve his French and learn some German. A spell as a student at Magdalen College, Oxford, left him decidedly underwhelmed. He thought things were looking up when World War I began in 1914, and he went into the army. But as heir to the throne, Edward wasn't allowed to actually fight. Edward had to be content with a desk job – though at least that job was near the front, not back home in England, a fact that helped the prince's credibility with the troops.

Trouble and strife

Things looked good for Edward after the war. In the 1920s, he was allowed to pursue the glamorous lifestyle he liked so much, indulging his love of everything modern, from learning to fly an aeroplane to drinking the latest cocktails and wearing the most fashionable clothes. The up-to-the-minute pattern on his suits soon spawned imitators, and 'Prince of Wales check' became popular. Edward was good-looking, fashionable, and young, and seemed to represent a new direction for the monarchy.

But the prince also had his problems. Edward found getting along with his father difficult. His father criticised him over his modern dress and his modern ideas. This rebellion, if that's what it was, went deeper – Edward began to neglect his royal duties, skipping engagements and ignoring palace procedures. People close to the royal family feared that he would make a poor king if he did not pull himself together.

More seriously still, the prince showed no inclination to marry. Marrying a suitable partner was something that was expected of the heir to the throne, because it was still his duty to produce heirs for the future. Edward, by contrast, was regularly seen in the company of other men's wives.

The British royal family had a long history of adultery, and mistresses had been a fact of life for centuries. Probably if Edward had kept his sex life and his married life separate, like so many of his ancestors, he would have had little trouble. But Edward found himself in love with one of these unsuitable partners, the American divorcée Wallis Simpson.

Edward met Wallis when another of the prince's women friends, Thelma Furness, introduced them. Wallis had one divorce under her belt when she met the prince and was on her way to a second, but at this point, she was still married to British shipping broker Ernest Simpson. Edward and Wallis were soon in love, and the British establishment was seriously worried.

The abdication crisis

In January 1936, George V died, and the Prince of Wales became king as Edward VIII. It didn't take long for people to realise that the new king's heart was not in his job. Dispatch boxes full of official papers lay around unopened, and it was clear that Wallis Simpson was taking up much of the king's attention.

Edward wanted Wallis to become his queen. But the establishment – the archbishop of Canterbury, the Prime Minister, much of Parliament, and Edward's mother – thought that a royal marriage to a twice-divorced American was unconstitutional, especially because as king, Edward was Supreme Governor of the Church of England. Nevertheless, Edward, whose success with the media as Prince of Wales made him feel that the public would accept his actions, carried on seeing Wallis. The controversy came to a head in the late summer of 1936:

- ✔ In August, the couple went for a cruise. The newspapers in America and Continental Europe ran articles about their holiday, but the British press suppressed the fact that the couple were travelling together, for fear of a scandal.

- ✔ In September, Wallis stayed with the king at the royal Scottish home, Balmoral.

- ✔ In October, Wallis's divorce came through. The court granted her a *degree nisi,* which meant that she would be free to marry Edward the following April, shortly before the coronation was planned.

- ✔ On 16 November, the Prime Minister, Stanley Baldwin, told the king that his proposed marriage to Wallis would not be acceptable to the government. The king responded that he would abdicate if he was not allowed to marry Wallis.

- ✔ On 1 December, the Bishop of Bradford gave a speech in which news of the planned abdication was made public for the first time.

- ✔ On 10 December, Edward signed the *instrument of abdication,* a document in which he gave up the throne and renounced any claim to the throne on the part of any of his future heirs.

Looking back, the abdication seems inevitable: Edward and the authorities were on a collision course, and neither side seemed able to move. But the abdication wasn't the only possible outcome. More than one compromise had been discussed. Wallis could have continued as the king's mistress, living with him unofficially, but neither of them were keen on this arrangement. A *morganatic marriage,* in which Wallis married Edward but did not become queen, could have taken place, but the government did not like this solution and the governments of Britain's dominions made it clear that they wouldn't accept it. But Edward held out for kingship on his terms, with the woman he loved at his side, and in 1936, this love was simply unacceptable to the establishment.

The day after Edward signed the instrument of abdication, he made a now-famous broadcast to the nation, explaining that, because he had not been able to be king with Wallis beside him, he had decided to stand down. The country was stunned – especially as the public had been shielded from many of the details of Edward's relationship with Wallis because they'd been reported only in the foreign press, not in Britain.

Aftermath of abdication

Edward's brother, Albert, became king as George VI on 11 December 1936, the day after the instrument of abdication was signed. Edward, meanwhile, crossed the English Channel to France, where he married Wallis the following year. For Edward, it was the beginning of decades of isolation from his family and his country.

Edward had assumed that the abdication would be the start of a new chapter in his life as a member of the royal family who could still take part in royal occasions and royal duties. But it didn't turn out like that. He soon realised that the other royals resented what he had done, and that all kinds of restrictions were put on his life. For example:

- When Edward and Wallis got married in 1937, no member of the royal family came to the wedding. It was a clear signal that the couple were on their own as far as the royal family went.

- Edward was given a title, Duke of Windsor, and Wallis therefore became Duchess of Windsor. But although Edward, as a senior royal, was allowed to be called His Royal Highness the Duke of Windsor, Wallis was not supposed to use the style Her Royal Highness. It was a signal that Wallis would never be accepted as a member of the royal family.

- Edward was paid a financial allowance, but the payment was made on the condition that he would not return to Britain without permission.

In effect, the couple were isolated from the royal family. Although they had many society friends and a big house in Paris, they must have felt out on a limb.

The Duke of Windsor was probably treated poorly for several reasons. For one thing, the new queen, George VI's wife, Elizabeth, knew how much her shy, withdrawn husband hated the idea of becoming king. She greatly resented the way in which, as she saw it, his brother had forced the issue and left George with a job he profoundly disliked.

Another reason was that Edward was a loose cannon. The authorities felt he had already brought the royal family into disrepute and didn't want him to be closely associated with them. And you can see their point when it emerged that the Duke had decided in October 1937 to go to Germany and visit the country's Nazi leaders. This was the period of the gathering storm before World War II. It's likely that the Duke's main reason for his German visit was to try to stave off war, but ever since, it's been hinted that the former king had Nazi sympathies.

A further ruffle of official feathers occurred when the Duke and Duchess left Paris (travelling to Spain and Portugal) just when France was on the point of falling in May 1940. This departure was in huge contrast to the courage of King George and Queen Elizabeth, who stayed bravely in London during the bombing. People felt that the Duke of Windsor simply was not 'sound'.

In the end, the Duke was spirited away from Europe and given the job of Governor of the Bahamas until the end of the war in 1945. He then returned to Paris where he lived with Wallis until he died in 1972. Queen Elizabeth II, no doubt keen to bring reconciliation, visited him shortly before his death. Wallis lived on until 1986.

Reluctant King: George VI

When King Edward VIII gave up the throne before even being crowned, his brother Albert took over and ruled as George VI (1936–52). His brother's swift abdication meant that he was ill-prepared for the job, and, as a man who deeply disliked appearing in public, he did not want to be king. But George had a strong sense of duty and so stepped into his brother's shoes.

From these unlikely beginnings, George VI became one of the most popular monarchs in British history. In this achievement, he was helped by his wife, Queen Elizabeth, who stood by him, helped him overcome his shyness when appearing in public, and radiated a personal charm that helped the image of the monarchy to no end. The couple needed all the strength they could muster, because the terrible years of World War II and its aftermath dominated virtually the entire reign.

A personal problem

King George VI was christened Albert Frederick Arthur George. His parents were the Duke and Duchess of York, who later became George V and Queen Mary, and at home, the boy was known as Albert or Bertie. Like his elder brother David, who later became Edward VIII, Bertie had a distant relationship with his parents and was brought up by a nanny who treated him cruelly.

In the royal nursery, the princes were treated affectionately one moment and cruelly the next, and the meals were as irregular as the affection. As a result, young Bertie developed digestive problems that were to stay with him for the rest of his life.

Bertie's father added to the prince's problems by insisting that his legs were fitted with splints every night in an attempt to cure his knock-knees. In addition, like many left-handed children in the early 20th century, Bertie was forced to write with his right hand. This catalogue of emotional and physical problems must have caused deep psychological damage, and the damage was revealed in one striking outward symptom. From the age of eight, Bertie had a marked stammer, and, like his gastritis, it lasted into adulthood.

A prince at war

Like many royal sons before him, Bertie headed for a career in the Royal Navy. When he took his exams at the Royal Naval College, Osborne, he came in at the bottom of the class, but he went on to the next stage of his naval career anyway, eventually becoming a midshipman on HMS *Collingwood*. Although not an academic, the prince at least shone athletically as a good rider and talented tennis player. At last, Bertie had found things he was good at – and, as an extra bonus, his left-handedness was accepted on the tennis court, too.

But the prince's naval career was cut short by illness. His stomach problems had flared up, and his doctors ordered an operation for appendicitis. Sadly, however, this surgery didn't cure his problems, and he spent most of the next three years in medical care – which still didn't improve his health.

May 1916 saw Prince Albert back on board his ship, eager to play his part in World War I. He was still suffering bouts of sickness, but at the end of the month, HMS *Collingwood* took part in the Battle of Jutland, and the prince took his place at one of the gun turrets.

The following year saw an upturn in the prince's health after another operation, this time for a duodenal ulcer. He transferred to the airborne branch of the armed forces (first the Royal Naval Air Service and then the Royal Air Service) and learned to fly. He was the first member of the royal family to do so.

Finding a role

After the war, the prince continued in what became the Royal Air Force. He honed his tennis skills as well, becoming RAF doubles champion with his partner Louis Greig. In 1920, he was made Duke of York, and the thoughts of the royal family and its advisers turned to the question of the role of the second in line to the throne.

What was a prince *for* in the early 20th century? Albert's elder brother David, the future King Edward VIII, had his own answer – having a good time, mostly. But Albert was made of sterner stuff. His strong sense of duty – and no doubt the realization that he would never cut such a dashing figure as his brother – made him convinced that he should do something more worthwhile. As a result, he travelled the country and made it his mission to seek out ordinary people and try to understand their lives.

The 1920s were a time of social and industrial unrest. Bosses were cutting wages, and many people were out of work. And there was a huge social and economic gulf between rich and poor, upper and working classes. The prince tried to bridge this gap by becoming patron of the Industrial Welfare Society and by setting up the Duke of York's camps, which were meeting places for boys from the working classes and from Britain's upper-class fee-paying schools.

The prince's activities were small beer by modern standards. British society needed more than boys' camps, where the main event was sitting around the fire singing songs, to make life fairer and more equal. But the camps proved popular and carried on until the beginning of World War II in 1939. They also helped the image of the monarchy. The royal family was starting to become less remote and more interested in the lives of ordinary people. It was an indication of how the monarchy would develop in the future.

Queen Elizabeth

In 1923, Prince Albert took the most important step in his life when he married Lady Elizabeth Bowes-Lyon. Elizabeth was born in England, but was the daughter of Scottish aristocrats who could trace their lineage back to the 14th-century Scottish king, Robert Bruce (see Chapter 11). She spent much of her early life at one of her family's Scottish homes, Glamis Castle, where she developed a lasting love of the countryside and of outdoor pursuits such as fishing.

The ideal couple

The prince and Elizabeth met and courted much like most couples – theirs was not an old-fashioned arranged royal marriage. And the pair had a lot in common. They were both devoted to country pursuits, and they shared common values. But they were very different characters. Whereas Albert was shy and withdrawn, Elizabeth was outgoing and vivacious. But these differences made her an ideal partner for the prince, because she was able to help him through the difficulties of public appearances and the horrors of speech-making.

The partnership gave the public something, too. With its history of arranged marriages and extramarital affairs, the royal family hadn't been very good at romantic love. And in the king's eldest son David, who had a preference for seemingly unsuitable partners, married women especially, this tradition seemed set to continued.

With Albert and Elizabeth, the people got a genuine royal romance, a couple who were both devoted to each other and made a good working partnership. And the marriage was an all-British romance, too, in contrast to those of past generations, when there had been a tradition of British royals marrying members of overseas royal families.

 World War I had shown the dangers of marrying members of a foreign royal family. You could very easily end up fighting the family you'd married into. A thoroughly British marriage seemed the best solution – and helped bolster patriotism, too.

The perfect family

This loving relationship soon produced children, two daughters – Elizabeth, the future queen, who was born in 1926, and Margaret Rose, born in 1930. Now the House of Windsor had a perfect royal family. Not since the heyday of Queen Victoria, Prince Albert, and their brood had the royals produced such an obviously happy and loving family that people were encouraged to look up to (see Chapter 15). But whereas Victoria's family had been large and, well, Victorian, the family of Albert and Elizabeth was small, like the nuclear families that would become the norm in the mid- to late 20th century. It wasn't just in flying aeroplanes that the royal family were moving with the times.

This royal good news story went down very well with the media, and it wasn't long before the royal family was defining itself in terms of family values. It gave the monarchy a strong, positive image. But it also made the royal family vulnerable, because when later generations suffered broken marriages, the public were more surprised than they should have been. But that was in the future.

Adjusting to kingship

Prince Albert became King George VI when his brother, Edward VIII, abdicated in 1936. The abdication was a blow to the royal family and a profound shock to the prince, who had no time to prepare himself. He felt unsuited to be king, but also felt that it was his duty to do the job his brother had given up.

King George had to steel himself for a number of tough tasks:

- ✔ He had to gather his strength to play a public role that he disliked.

- ✔ He had to decide what his relationship would be with his brother Edward and with Edward's wife, Wallis, who, in the eyes of the royal family, had caused all the trouble.

- ✔ He had to try to restore some of the prestige of the monarchy, which everyone felt had been thoroughly tarnished by the abdication episode.

- ✔ He had to hastily prepare for a coronation for which the date was already set.

The king would have found all these tasks virtually impossible without the support of his wife. But in some ways, Elizabeth was part of the problem. She was deeply critical of Edward for giving up the throne and of Wallis for coming between Edward and his duty. She insisted that Wallis not be allowed the prestigious title Her Royal Highness and encouraged the rest of the royals to keep their distance from the Duke and Duchess of Windsor. Queen Mary, the widow of George V and the mother of Edward and the new king, encouraged this line, too. And so George VI faced a further challenge: to live his life cut off from the brother who'd been so close to him and whom he'd looked up to.

George VI's coronation was, of course, a big state occasion – if anything, even bigger than usual, with leaders from all the countries of the British empire filling Westminster Abbey. Afterwards, the press wrote nearly as much about the royal princesses as about the king and queen, as if to remind everyone that a proper family now resided in Buckingham Palace, not a playboy prince and some American divorcée as so nearly might have been the case.

Once crowned, George and Elizabeth set off on a series of visits abroad. This trip was no holiday. Britain's allies – France, Canada, and the United States – were targeted. George, as much as anyone, knew that these friendly nations had to be cultivated, because Hitler was already in power in Germany, and the threat of war was looming large.

Wartime

George VI was a former naval officer who had fought bravely in World War I. But he did not like war and did not want another world conflict. He supported Prime Minister Neville Chamberlain, who attempted to secure peace by making concessions to Hitler, and George offered to make a personal appeal to the German leader. But the foreign office, well aware that such appeals could land the king in hot water, quashed the idea.

War broke out between Britain and Germany in 1939, and by the following year, Hitler had invaded France, and Neville Chamberlain had resigned as Prime Minister. His replacement was Winston Churchill. George didn't get on well with Churchill, mainly because the new leader had been a supporter of his brother. But both men knew that the current crisis was deeper than the one surrounding the abdication – they had to work together, and they did. Soon, Churchill's flair as a wartime leader impressed the king, just as it won over most Britons.

The year of 1940 was also the year of the *Blitz,* the ruthless German bombing campaign that devastated many British cities, London above all. The king and queen went to visit bombed-out working-class communities in London's East End (especially badly hit because of the nearby docks). Although they went to sympathise and raise morale, the royal couple were greeted with boos and jeers.

What had happened? From the royal point of view, the king and queen were trying to help by raising morale on the streets of London. But the Londoners' attitude seemed to be that it was easy for a king and queen to go slumming it in the East End when they could retreat at a moment's notice to the safety of their palatial homes. The princesses had already been sent off to the relative safety of Windsor Castle.

However, the royals didn't make the war years as easy for themselves as they could have done. As the Blitz continued, it became clear that the king and queen were determined to stay in London, bombers or no bombers. Then Buckingham Palace itself was struck, and the royals narrowly escaped death. They came out fighting, and the queen said defiantly, 'I'm glad we've been bombed. Now we can look the East End in the face.'

In the end, their dogged refusal not to retreat to the safety of the country or abroad did the king and queen a favour. They gradually won the respect of their people, and George's popularity as a ruler went from strength to strength. Even though he was not allowed to see active service as he had done in World War I, George could visit troops and bombed-out civilians, and his visits began to raise morale, not to destroy it.

Helping Britain recover

When World War II ended in 1945, Britain had to recover both from the damage caused by the enemy and six years in which every aspect of life – politics, industry, home life, the lot – had been dedicated to winning the war. In the July 1945 general election, Britons voted out the wartime leader Winston Churchill, the Conservative who had led Britain's politically multi-coloured wartime government of national unity.

The election brought a new Labour government to power under Prime Minister Clement Atlee. The new government unfolded a programme of change with huge improvements in a range of services, from education and the health service to the pensions system, all run by the state.

George VI was shocked and disappointed by the way in which the people booted out Churchill, the man who had led the country to victory in the war. For the royals, the Labour government was hard to cope with in a number of ways:

- ✔ With its policy of redistribution of wealth, the Labour party seemed to attack the system of property and privilege, which the monarchy headed up.

- ✔ The monarchy was simply on a different wavelength than the socialists – George was a conservative character who couldn't understand why people should be given their false teeth for free.

- ✔ With their notion that the state should provide, the Labour government seemed to threaten even the tradition of charity and good works that the royal family stood for.

The king and queen buckled down and worked with the Labour Prime Minister as best they could. The royal family carried on its charitable work, for it was soon clear that there was still a need for it – the state couldn't do everything. They supported events such as the Festival of Britain, the national celebration of all that was best about Britain that took place in 1951. And they came to respect the members of the government as individuals.

For seven years after 1945, George VI and Queen Elizabeth played their full part in helping Britain recover from the horrors of World War II. But the king's post-war years were dogged with poor health. He had treatment for circulation problems, and then lung cancer was diagnosed in 1951. George survived an operation to remove his left lung, but was weakened. In February 1952, the king died in his sleep. His eldest daughter, Elizabeth, who had already been carrying out some of her father's work because of his ill-health, became queen.

Chapter 17

Thoroughly Modern Monarch: Elizabeth II

*E*lizabeth II (1952–present) came to the throne after the death of her father, George VI, when Britain was still recovering from World War II. She has steered the monarchy through more than half a century of change, during which the royal family has been exposed to some of the most searching publicity in its history.

As a modern constitutional monarch, Elizabeth II has little power to make policy or change the way her country is governed. She's proud to be above party politics, and when she opens Parliament every year, she makes a speech in which she presents the policies of her government, whatever its political colour. But her weekly audiences with the Prime Minister can be very influential. Every premier of her reign has said how much they value her advice, based as it is on the kind of long experience of many governments that no politician can ever hope to have.

Queen Elizabeth's experience, together with her devotion to her work, are the unchanging features of her reign. But the monarchy has also seen new developments since the queen has been on the throne. On a worldwide scale, the most important has been the final disappearance of the British empire and its replacement with the looser Commonwealth of Nations.

On a more intimate level, the most significant change has been the monarchy's relationship with the media. Elizabeth and her family have had to cope with the regular intrusion of television cameras into their lives, the development of a dedicated team of royal photographers who follow the royal family wherever they go, and a series of former royal staff members who have published behind-the-scenes stories about the royal family.

The family life of the queen and her children has been scrutinised most closely of all. Under George VI, the monarchy had come to define itself as a family – the king and queen with their two daughters seemed a perfect and happy family unit. Queen Elizabeth, Prince Philip, and their four children seemed to follow suit – until the children grew up and experienced a series of hurtful marital breakups. The resulting scandals damaged the monarchy's image and gave ammunition to those who wanted to abolish the monarchy altogether. But the queen herself has remained aloof from the scandal. No one questions her dedication to her work, her country, and her people.

Education of a Princess

Princess Elizabeth was educated at home, by a governess, just as any upper-class girl of the Victorian or Edwardian era would have been. Her governess, Marion Crawford, had planned to work with deprived children, but ended up teaching Elizabeth and her sister Margaret the subjects (English, history, geography, maths, Bible study, drama, and music) that they would need for a rounded, if basic, education. A specialist tutor came in to give them French lessons, too.

As heir to the throne, Elizabeth also had instruction in the history and structure of the British constitution. For these lessons, she travelled from Windsor Castle to nearby Eton College – the public school that she may well have attended full-time had she been a boy – to be taught by the vice-provost, Sir Henry Marten.

From Marten, Elizabeth learned the harsh truth of modern monarchy: Parliament rules the country, and the sovereign is a largely symbolic figure who has to take his or her place in the complex web of activities that brings new laws from their first conception to the statute book. She was taught all about the roles of the civil service, of Members of Parliament, and of the Prime Minister.

Elizabeth also found out how the monarchy had changed over the years. Her ancestor Queen Victoria had ruled over a world empire. Elizabeth's grandfather, George V, saw this empire beginning to dissolve and countries such as Canada and Australia winning their independence while also keeping the sovereign as head of state.

In addition to these formal lessons, the future queen also learned by watching her father, George VI. The king influenced his daughter in a number of ways:

 ✔ **Sense of duty:** George did not want to become king, but he accepted that it was his duty to do so. Unlike his brother, Edward VIII, he would never give up the throne.

✔ **Work ethic:** George put his all into the job of kingship. He did the paperwork thoroughly, spent long hours on charitable work, and sacrificed months of his life on royal visits and tours. Again, this work ethic was in contrast to his brother, who had neglected many of his duties, especially the regular briefings from government.

✔ **Devotion to service:** Both George and his daughter saw monarchy in terms of serving their country.

✔ **Charitable work:** George was devoted to helping his chosen causes, and Elizabeth, too, felt that charitable work was an important part of the role of both the monarch and the royal family.

Elizabeth saw her father spending hours reading the boxes of documents that came from the Cabinet for his attention. And she saw a man who, though he had little real power, was immensely well informed about everything that was going on in what was still called His Majesty's Government. And Elizabeth saw another thing, too. This accumulated knowledge gave the king a unique insight into everything the government did. And so, when the Prime Minister of the day came for his weekly meeting with the king, the premier went away feeling that he'd had a well-informed conversation with a respected adviser. When she became queen, Elizabeth, too, would strive to be a valued confidant to a succession of Prime Ministers.

Prince Philip

Elizabeth's young life wasn't all constitutional history and preparation for rule. For one thing, she fell in love. She first met Prince Philip of Greece in 1939, when he was 18 years old and she was a mere 13. They were related because they both shared a great-great grandmother in Queen Victoria. They hit it off at once, at their first meeting, but the age gap between them and Philip's naval service in World War II kept them apart. They exchanged letters, though, as cousins might, and as the years passed, they grew closer. By 1944, they were in love.

Philip's background

Prince Philip's grandfather was William of Denmark, who had become king of Greece in 1863. He had relatives in virtually every European royal family and had Danish, German, and Russian blood in his veins. He needed all the royal connections he could muster; when he was still a baby, his father, brother to King Constantine of Greece, was kicked out of his country because he was implicated in some military defeats, and the family had to rely on the support of relatives. Philip spent his childhood in various places – Paris and then schools in London and Germany – and saw little of his family for much of this time.

Isolation from his family gave the young prince a self-sufficient character that helped him on the way to a successful career in the Navy. In 1941, Philip was mentioned in dispatches for his part in the Battle of Cape Matapan, and the following year, he began to take part in the dangerous work of escorting convoys of merchant ships along Britain's east coast – a stretch frequently under attack from fast German torpedo boats.

The royal couple

Elizabeth's parents liked Philip, but were keen that Elizabeth should wait until she was older before marrying. The royal betrothal was not announced until July 1947, eight years after the couple first met. The wedding took place in November of the same year.

The royal marriage was a success because of the differences between the partners, as well as their similarities. Elizabeth, for all her experience of meeting people around the world, was and is a shy person, someone who keeps her emotions to herself and prefers to avoid argument and confrontation. Philip, by contrast, liked to speak his mind and didn't mind offending people in the process.

Soon after they were married, Elizabeth's father, George VI, became ill. From 1949 onwards, it was known that the king's illness was related to his smoking, and in 1951, lung cancer was confirmed. Against this sad backdrop, Elizabeth, with Philip at her side, began to take over some of the work that the king would have done in younger and healthier times – for example, touring Canada in 1951.

Another tour was planned for 1952, and Elizabeth and Philip flew to East Africa on their way to Australia and New Zealand. But they never got further than Kenya because on 6 February 1952, the news reached them that the king had died. Philip's support was invaluable to Elizabeth as the couple and their party returned to London to begin the preparations for the king's funeral and the start of the new reign.

In the years immediately after their marriage, the loving couple produced two children, Prince Charles and Princess Anne. From early on, the two children spent several periods apart from their parents – Elizabeth's royal duties and Philip's naval command often dividing up the family. As a result, Charles and Anne saw a lot of their grandparents, George VI and Queen Elizabeth. Their closeness to their grandmother was to continue for the whole of that lady's long life. Two further sons, Princes Andrew and Edward, arrived a few years later.

✔ **Prince Charles:** The queen's eldest son was born on 14 November 1948, a few days before his parents' first wedding anniversary. Prince Charles has developed his role as Prince of Wales, building up his princely estate, the Duchy of Cornwall, and founding charities in his areas of special interest, including architecture, the environment, and education. (For more about his life and work, see Chapter 18, The Prince of Wales.)

✔ **Princess Anne:** The royal daughter was born on 15 August 1950. In her teens and 20s, Anne was a prize-winning horsewoman, representing her country as a three-day-eventer in the Olympic Games. Later, she devoted herself to a range of charitable work. Anne is widely seen as one of the most hard-working members of the royal family.

✔ **Prince Andrew:** The queen's second son was born on 19 February 1960. Prince Andrew pursued a career as an officer in the Royal Navy, seeing active service as a helicopter pilot during the Falklands War of 1982.

✔ **Prince Edward:** The youngest son of the queen and Prince Philip was born in 1964. Prince Edward broke with royal tradition by resigning his commission in the Royal Marines and working in the arts, at first in the theatre and later in television.

The New Elizabethan Age

In the 16th century, Elizabeth I had been one of the most successful of all British monarchs (see Chapter 13). She had defended her island nation against invaders, developed its influence around the world, and presided over a period of great artistic and literary achievement. When Elizabeth II became queen in 1952, everyone had high hopes that she preside over another great reign.

In a way, it seems absurd to compare the 20th century with the 16th century. The role of the monarch had changed hugely, from personal ruler to constitutional monarch. Britain had also gained and lost a huge empire in the intervening years, giving the nation a very different role in the world. Yet some similarities existed. Not so long ago, Britain had fought off invasion threats during World War II. Although Elizabeth II's empire had diminished, she was still one of the world's leading powers. And the recent Festival of Britain had shown what Britain had to offer culturally. It was a time of hope and optimism, symbolised by the coronation of Britain's young new queen.

The coronation

To prepare adequately for the ceremony and make sure that all invited heads of state and representatives of nations could attend, Elizabeth II's coronation was not scheduled until June 1953. The royal family had more than a year to get ready for the event, and Elizabeth's coronation was one of the most carefully planned in history.

There was one sticking point, though. Elizabeth herself did not want the ceremony to appear on live television. Film cameras could record the event for showing in cinemas around the world. A radio commentary could describe the coronation to millions. Film can be edited, and radio allows the ceremony to be described at one remove. Live television, on the other hand, reveals any small error as it happened and would make public the queen's taking of Holy Communion, something she saw as a private moment.

When it was announced that the TV cameras would not be allowed into Westminster Abbey, a national outcry in the press and questions in Parliament occurred. Few knew that it was the queen herself who was so opposed to TV coverage. Behind the scenes, though, Elizabeth was persuaded to change her mind – provided that the cameras were kept away at the private moments, such as her anointing and taking of Holy Communion.

In the end, therefore, the TV cameras were allowed in. TV ownership was still a rarity in 1953, but many bought sets especially for the occasion, and many more crowded into their neighbours' living rooms to see the coverage. As a result, more people felt that they were closer to the queen than before, and the televised coronation was a triumph.

The episode also revealed more than one important thing about Elizabeth II. Her initial unwillingness to appear on TV showed her shy side and her suspicion of the new. But the young queen also demonstrated that when she had to, she could compromise and take the monarchy, whose traditions she regarded so highly, on to new ground. This adaptability was to help the Windsor dynasty survive upheavals much more severe than the one surrounding the coronation.

The beginning of the reign

The start of any reign experiences defining moments and decisions that show what kind of ruler the new monarch will be. Queen Elizabeth's reign began with an argument about the royal dynastic name and an international tour that in their different ways showed her priorities as ruler. A few years later, these arguments were followed by a disaster that revealed a lot about the queen's character and how she saw her public role.

The royal name

One of the knotty problems that the royal family faced when Elizabeth became queen was exactly what it should call itself. Because Elizabeth had married Philip, she should in theory take his name, Mountbatten, and the name of the dynasty should change, too.

But the government of the day didn't see things this way. They were strongly convinced that the royal family should keep the name of Windsor. It wasn't hard to see why. The name Windsor had been adopted by George V at the time of World War I as a replacement for his Germanic family name (Saxe-Coburg) because it felt wrong for the king of Britain to have a German name when the country was at war with Germany. So Windsor had a patriotic ring. In addition Windsor was the name of Windsor Castle, the royal family's oldest and most romantic residence. The Castle, with its 1,000 or so years of history, seemed to stand for royal tradition at its strongest.

So Windsor it was. Philip, for one, wasn't pleased. Like most men of his generation, he wanted to give his name to his children. Custom was on his side, after all. And in the 1950s, a child's name indicated its paternity. If your children had a different name, people would think they weren't actually your children. Philip was hurt and angry and tried to get the royal name changed to Mountbatten. In spite of his forceful arguments, the government and the queen's Windsor relatives prevailed.

Things improved for Philip a few years later. First, in 1957, it was announced that the consort, known to date as the Duke of Edinburgh, would be given the title of Prince. Second, in 1960, the queen reached a compromise about the family name. Princes and princesses in the line of succession would still be known as Windsor, but any grandchildren outside the direct line of succession would be called Mountbatten-Windsor. Prince Philip's family name would continue.

The Commonwealth tour

Shortly after the coronation, Queen Elizabeth and her consort set off on a tour of the British Commonwealth. It was an epic journey, taking six months and allowing the queen to visit Australia, New Zealand, Africa, and numerous South Sea islands.

The Commonwealth tour introduced millions of people around the world to 'their' queen. Many of these citizens were the people of the colonies that still formed part of the shrinking British empire. But there were also many dominions, countries that had been granted independence but which still chose to recognise Queen Elizabeth as their head of state.

The tour was a success. It introduced the Commonwealth to the new queen and showed the queen's affection for the countries of which she was head. As her reign continued, it became clear that the family of nations that made up the Commonwealth was something that the queen held especially dear. Ever since this landmark tour, Elizabeth has tirelessly promoted the Commonwealth and regularly meets with the leaders of its countries, many of whom have come to respect her advice, just as British Prime Ministers have done.

Staying out of politics

Another defining moment of the beginning of Queen Elizabeth's reign was the Suez crisis of 1956. The Suez Canal in Egypt had been controlled by England since the 1870s, when the then Prime Minister Benjamin Disraeli bought about half the shares. The Canal became valuable to Britain because it gave easier access by sea to her colonies in the east, especially India.

But in 1956, Egypt seized the canal, robbing Britain of its sea link with India. Britain's Prime Minister, Sir Anthony Eden, did a secret deal with Israel and France to send in troops and recapture the canal. International pressure, however, forced Britain and her allies to withdraw. The crisis brought Britain into disrepute and damaged the economy. Eden resigned the following year.

The repercussions left Britain without a Prime Minister and in a fix, for the following reasons:

- ✔ No election was due, so a new Prime Minister had to be chosen from amongst the leaders of the ruling Conservative party.
- ✔ Most Conservatives wanted Harold Macmillan.
- ✔ Many political pundits wanted R A Butler.
- ✔ In a situation like this one, the queen was meant to select a new Prime Minister. However, she was also meant to be above politics.
- ✔ In practise, the queen listened to Conservative bigwig Lord Salisbury, who asked his colleagues and put forward Macmillan as the preferred candidate.

The queen went with the flow and plumped for Macmillan, but was accused by the press, who mostly preferred Butler, as taking part in a stitch-up. But now that historians know the whole story, they know that what Elizabeth was really doing was staying as far outside politics as she could, and letting the politicians make up their own mind.

Around the same time as she was coping with the aftermath of the Suez crisis, the queen also had to face some severe criticism from the press about her style. Lord Altrincham, who owned and edited a magazine called the *National and English Review*, described her speeches as 'prim little sermons'. He said the impression given by Elizabeth was like 'a priggish schoolgirl'. His criticisms were directed mainly at the speeches the queen made, not at her personality, but Altrincham was denounced in the popular press as unpatriotic. Both people and newspapers rallied behind Elizabeth.

The Aberfan disaster

Crises and problems test the monarchy like nothing else, and one of the biggest tests for the young Elizabeth II came with the Aberfan disaster in 1966. On 21 October that year, one of the vast heaps of mining spoil that dotted the landscape of South Wales collapsed, burying much of the village of Aberfan. The avalanche engulfed the village school, and 116 children were killed, as well as 28 adults.

How should a monarch respond to this kind of tragedy? King George VI and his wife, Queen Elizabeth, had had no doubts. They saw it as part of their duty to visit the scene of a tragedy and to talk to the survivors. They had seen that their presence usually helped people who were coping with a tragedy – if the king and queen were grieving with them, then, in a sense, the whole country was sharing their grief.

The response of their daughter was rather different. She was all too aware that the presence of royals anywhere created extra work for their hosts, and she was concerned that her presence would distract people from the important tasks of searching for survivors or treating the injured. What good would the rather theatrical gesture of visiting the survivors do?

The queen did not rush down to South Wales, and some people criticised her for staying away. So, eight days after the disaster, she made the trip to Wales and saw the devastation for herself. Newspaper photographs of her sad face showed that she was grieving along with everyone else. People appreciated the visit, and the queen saw the difference it made.

Public Monarch

Episodes such as the Aberfan disaster (see preceding section) showed the importance of the queen's public role. People were fascinated by seeing her, as if some of the magic associated with medieval kings and queens was still attached to her person. If they couldn't see her in the flesh, people increasingly had the opportunity to see her in the papers and on television. The media were becoming more and more interested in the monarchy, and the late 1960s and 1970s saw a number of episodes – the investiture of Prince Charles as Prince of Wales, a ground-breaking television programme about the royal family, and the queen's Silver Jubilee – where the media gave the monarch and her family closer scrutiny. The royal family came into the living rooms of the nation as they never had before.

The Royal Family programme

In 1969, Prince Charles reached 21 and came of age. Media coverage of the prince – who was by now a student at Cambridge University – reached fever pitch, as newspapers and television companies strove to tell people what kind of life he was leading, how he was being prepared for his future role as king, and what they thought his character was like.

By now, Queen Elizabeth and her family were used to the media. They knew what it was like to be filmed on state occasions and royal visits, to be written about in the press, and to have photographs of themselves relaxing at home published in magazines. But most of this coverage was of public events and even the at-home pictures were carefully selected. The royal family had no sense in which people knew about life inside Buckingham Palace or could overhear the conversations that the queen had with the people she met at receptions or state occasions.

The BBC's film *Royal Family* was designed to fill these gaps. Directed by prominent BBC documentary maker Richard Cawston, it presented an intimate portrait of the royal family, including such sequences as:

- ✔ Footage showing the queen and her children enjoying a family meal at home, in which all the conversation could be heard.

- ✔ Scenes showing the royal children relaxing and at play, including a famous sequence in which the string of a cello played by Prince Charles broke, hurting Prince Edward and reducing him to tears.

- ✔ Eavesdropping scenes in which the viewer could hear conversations between the queen and her guests.

- ✔ Scenes of the royals at work, talking to staff and dealing with paperwork.

A committee consisting of palace staff, BBC people, and Prince Philip oversaw the whole production. The committee came up with ideas and vetted the film that was shot. Anything unacceptable to the royals wasn't included – and some of the royals' favourite activities (taking part in blood sports, for example) were omitted, because many viewers would have found them offensive.

Not surprisingly, the result was rather bland by modern standards. However, in 1969, it set the world on fire. Never had people got so close to the ruling monarch. Never, they felt, had they come so near to understanding their characters. And that was the real revelation. The queen had previously come over in public as a rather distant personality, lacking her father's common touch or her mother's flair. Now her subjects realised that she wasn't a cold fish. In private, she enjoyed a joke with the best of them. She was human, like everyone else, and *Royal Family* did a good job in helping people to appreciate this fact. The film became an instant hit, was repeated several times, and was popular on foreign television, too. The media monarchy had made a great leap forward.

The new Prince of Wales

The year 1969 was a big one for the monarchy in the media, because it was also the year in which Prince Charles was made Prince of Wales, in a high-profile ceremony that was broadcast on live television. The title Prince of Wales dated back to the beginning of the 14th century, when Edward I gave his son, also Edward, the title (see Chapter 8).

Since then, many, but not all, elder sons of the monarch have been made Prince of Wales, and a special prince-making ceremony, called the investiture, was developed. Prince Charles's investiture took place in July 1969. In spite of the rather odd false-medieval ceremony, threats from extreme Welsh nationalists, and concerns about how the young prince would perform, the event was another media success for the monarchy, watched on live television by millions of people.

The Silver Jubilee

In 1977, Elizabeth II had been queen for 25 years. She had slowly developed her approach to the monarchy, honing her media skills and supporting good causes from local charities to the queen's beloved Commonwealth family of nations. The queen was a generally popular figure and the authorities decided to celebrate her 25-year stint on the throne with a Silver Jubilee like the one that marked 25 years of George V's reign in 1935.

Many Britons felt that there wasn't much to celebrate. Inflation, an industrial slump, and high unemployment had made the 1970s a tough time for many. Some were doubtful about the tact of holding a royal celebration. The doubts ranged widely:

- ✔ **What was it for anyway?** Many people were unsure what a Jubilee was and thought it was marking 25 years of the royal marriage or some other event.

- ✔ **Was it too extravagant?** With many people unemployed, spending lots of money on a gigantic party seemed frivolous or even immoral. Couldn't the money be spent some other way?

- ✔ **What about democracy?** Left-wing groups, such as the Socialist Workers' Party, campaigned against the Jubilee, and even moderates doubted whether the monarchy should be celebrated so extravagantly in a country that was meant to be a democracy.

- ✔ **Did anyone really care?** In the face of the arguments for and against the Silver Jubilee, some simply didn't care whether it was held or not.

In spite of all the misgivings, the Jubilee was a popular success. The monarchy owed its triumph to several different factors:

- ✔ **Support on the ground:** Support for the queen at a grass-roots level emerged in a series of around 12,000 street parties held up and down the country to celebrate 25 years of the reign. These parties, organised by bodies such as local Women's Institutes, brought communities together. As a result, when people felt good about their communities, they felt good about the monarchy, too.

- ✔ **Personal respect for the queen:** Britons are very good at distinguishing between the monarch and the monarchy. Even many republicans have enormous personal respect for Elizabeth II, because they admire her dedication and hard work. They may not like the job she does, but they can see that she does it well.

- ✔ **Royal accessibility:** After the Jubilee service in St Paul's Cathedral, the queen walked to the celebration in the Mansion House. It was her first London *walkabout,* in which she chatted with many of the people who had come to watch. The walkabout, which was widely reported, gave people real, tangible contact with the sovereign, showing her to be accessible and friendly.

Despite all the anti-royal murmurings, the Jubilee came off well and confirmed the personal popularity of the queen. The monarchy prepared to enter the 1980s on a high, and the high seemed to get still higher when it was announced in 1981 that Prince Charles was at last to get married, to Lady Diana Spencer. Britain prepared itself for the most high-profile and glamorous royal occasion since the coronation.

Annus Horribilis: A Truly Horrible Year

The wedding of Prince Charles and Lady Diana Spencer, or Princess Diana as she became, was a high point in the royal fortunes. When the royal couple walked out of Westminster Abbey on 29 July 1981, they did so to the cheers of the nation and the adulation of the media. The event was portrayed as a fairytale wedding, the culmination of a romance, and the climax of a Cinderella story.

But the good news was short-lived. Very soon, the marriage of Charles and Diana was proving fragile, and before much longer, it had turned into a battle between the prince and the princess (and their various supporters) for control of their stories in the media. (For more information about this marriage, see Chapter 18.)

For the queen – and the rest of her family – this media battle was a sad spectacle. Other people once again questioned the purpose and relevance of the monarchy. And the situation was made worse because two of the queen's other children had also suffered marital breakdown. This chapter of disasters came to a head in 1992, which Queen Elizabeth dubbed the royal family's 'annus horribilis', a truly horrible year. As well as the royal marital breakdowns, the queen also had to cope with a terrible fire at Windsor Castle and a new call to reform the royal finances.

Royal splits

The year 1992 was a crisis point in the lives of the queen's three married children. Princess Anne got divorced, Prince Andrew formally separated from his wife, and the breakdown of Prince Charles's marriage was publicly confirmed in a particularly lurid way. The monarchy, having defined itself as a family, found itself having to cope with family breakdown.

Princess Anne and Mark Phillips

The Windsors' family troubles had begun several years earlier. The first solid news of these tribulations came out in 1989, when Princess Anne separated from her husband, Mark Phillips. The Phillips's marital breakdown hit the headlines when the press printed stolen love letters to Princess Anne from Commander Tim Laurence, an equerry to the queen.

The tabloid newspapers had a field day with the split. They had never warmed to Princess Anne, who had often shown her annoyance with intrusive reporters and whose horsey and hard-working personality didn't give them the glamour they wanted. But the queen herself was unfazed by her daughter's relationship with Laurence – she recognised that Anne's marriage had broken down and was rather pleased that she had found happiness with someone else.

Prince Andrew and Sarah, Duchess of York

In January 1992, a series of photographs were published showing Prince Andrew's wife, Sarah, Duchess of York, in embarrassing poses with an American friend, Steve Wyatt. By March, Sarah and Andrew were legally separated, but the breakdown wasn't the quick conclusion to an unfortunate episode that the royals must have hoped for.

Sarah continued to embarrass the royal family – most notably by appearing in another set of scandalous photographs in August. This time, the Duchess was pictured with another male admirer, a man called John Bryan who had been described as her financial adviser. But it was a good deal more than financial advice that was being administered in the pictures, which showed the Duchess, poolside in the South of France, topless, and apparently enjoying have her toes sucked by Bryan. How much worse could things get? It took a few years out of the limelight for the Duchess to return to respectability.

Prince Charles and Princess Diana

The way in which Prince Charles and Princess Diana split was chronicled not through stolen letters or long-lens photographs, but through intercepted phone calls. In the 1980s and early 1990s, snoopers often used radio equipment to listen in to mobile phone calls, and both Charles and Diana were victims of this voyeurism. Two bouts of this eavesdropping were published at around this time, one from Diana's mobile and one from Charles's. For the royal family, they made the most depressing reading of all.

- ✔ **Phone tap No. 1 – Squidgygate:** The tape from Diana's mobile appeared in 1992, though it was a record of a call made back in 1989. It was published in the *Sun,* whose editor chose to make it public because the paper's rival, the *Daily Mirror,* had had such a boost in sales when it published the pictures of the Duchess of York and John Bryan. The Squidgygate tape, as it became known, recorded a conversation between Diana and James Gilbey, a member of a well-known family of gin manufacturers who himself worked as a car salesman. The conversation, in which Gilbey called Diana 'Squidgy', implied that the pair were having a sexual relationship.

- ✔ **Phone tap No. 2 – Camillagate:** The second recording came from a conversation between Charles and his mistress, Camilla Parker Bowles. It was published in 1993 and relayed a highly intimate conversation between the couple, culminating in Charles's admission to Camilla that his ambition was 'just to live inside your trousers'.

But even before the Camillagate scandal broke, the public had raw evidence of the marital breakdown of the fairytale marriage of the heir to the throne and the Princess of Wales. At the end of November 1992, the couple met at Kensington Palace and agreed that they should separate formally. The Prime Minister officially announced the separation in the House of Commons early the following month.

With its overtones of scandal, the breakdown of Charles and Diana's marriage was a mess, one that would take more than a decade to resolve. For more on the story, see Chapter 18.

The Windsor fire

In November 1992 came a disaster that was in some ways just as hurtful to Queen Elizabeth as her family problems. At Windsor Castle, an overheating spotlight set fire to a curtain. Flames spread swiftly through the building, and 100 rooms, including nine of the castle's lavish state apartments, were either destroyed or seriously damaged.

The damage was more than physical. The Windsor family, named for their most ancient home, held this place dear. The castle, a royal residence for around 1,000 years, represented hundreds of years of royal heritage, had hosted countless state occasions, and was also a private home with fond memories. The queen was devastated by the fire.

The fire only affected one corner of the vast castle, but it was still a large part of the building, and the damage was awesome:

- At the heart of the fire, roofs were destroyed, and panelling was burned off the walls.

- Elsewhere, the flames travelled through roof spaces, scorching away ceilings but doing less damage to the walls.

- Priceless objects, from chandeliers to carpets, were ruined.

- The building was further threatened because firefighters had to play their hoses on the structure for hours, saturating it.

But there were upsides, too. Most of the paintings were saved – largely through a rescue operation led by Prince Andrew. And most of the major damage was to the upper floors – brick and stone vaults stopped the flames from spreading further down.

Repairing the castle would take years and cost millions of pounds. But the castle was uninsured – how do you value priceless treasures for insurance, after all? An argument began about who should pay the repair bill.

Many people, including Britain's Conservative government, believed that the castle was a national asset, so the nation should pay. So Heritage Secretary Peter Brooke announced that the government would find the money, which could be as much as £40 million.

But the backlash was huge. People and press – partly fed up with the royal family after all the publicity about their marital breakdowns and affairs – objected en masse. The fire was the royals' problem, and they should sort it out. The government backtracked, and the royal family had to pay up. Not only that, but a complete review of royal finances was ordered.

Paying for royalty

Questions had always surrounded the royal finances. Back in 1971, when Queen Elizabeth had been on the throne for nearly 20 years, she negotiated a rise in the *Civil List,* the money paid by the government to the royal family, and during the negotiating process, the royal finances were made public as never before.

The Civil List dates back to the 18th century, when George III made a deal with Parliament. He gave up his income from the royal lands in return for a regular income from the state. In Queen Elizabeth's reign, the Civil List has included payments to give several other members of the royal family, from Prince Philip downwards, an income. The state has also paid for other essential royal expenses (including the various forms of transport that get the family around the world). In addition, the family enjoy income from other estates that weren't included in George III's deal.

The 1971 negotiations revealed the true cost of the monarchy to Britain. They showed that the annual cost of the aircraft of the Queen's Flight, for example, came on its own to more than the whole Civil List payment. So did the cost of the royal yacht, *Britannia*. The royal family cost the nation much more than most people realised. And unlike the rest of the country, the royal family didn't pay income tax.

Back in 1971, when widespread sympathy abounded for the monarchy and everyone had to cope with high inflation, the royals didn't find it too difficult to persuade Parliament to increase the Civil List payments.

But in 1992, things were different. People had had enough bad news from the royal family and weren't willing to foot the bill for Windsor. What was more, the question of the royals' nonpayment of income tax came up again. The time was ripe for a new look at the royal finances.

Early in 1993, as a result of the review of royal finances the previous year, Britain announced a raft of changes in the way it pays for its monarchy. Here's the gist of the changes:

- The government continued to fund the queen, Prince Philip, and the Queen Mother.

- The Prince of Wales continued to receive no money from the Civil List. His expenses were and are met from the considerable income generated by the Duchy of Cornwall.

- Other royals, such as the queen's other children and her sister, Princess Margaret, had their Civil List payments paid back each year by the queen.

- The queen agreed to pay tax on her income and capital gains.

- Inheritance tax would be paid on all the queen's bequests, except those to the heir to the throne. The exception was to ensure that key crown properties, such as Sandringham and Balmoral, would not have to be sold off to pay inheritance tax.

These reforms did a lot to make the royal finances more acceptable, even though some critics still objected to the exemption from inheritance tax on the ruler's bequests to her heir.

Tragedy and Change

The royal separations and the other events of 1992 were thrown into sharp perspective by the still more terrible news that came on 31 August 1997, the death of Diana, Princess of Wales, in a car crash in Paris (see Chapter 18). This deep personal tragedy profoundly affected Diana's two sons, Princes William and Harry, the Princess's family, the Spencers, and, of course, her former husband and in-laws.

In addition to coping with the personal grief, the monarchy had the task of responding appropriately to the death of a very popular member of the family who had become estranged from them. The royal family has traditionally relied on protocol and precedent to guide them through difficult situations. But nothing like Diana's death had ever happened, so the family had to make up the rules as it went along, trying to satisfy media expectations, to respond to the extraordinary public sadness at Diana's passing, and to cope with their own grief at the same time.

Getting through this tough time, though, eventually helped the royal family. The queen and those around her have learned to adjust and respond to the challenges of life in the 21st century.

Media and monarchy

After the death of Princess Diana, the nation mourned. But the press looked in vain for signs of grief from the royal family. The queen and some of her close family were at Balmoral, where they were coping with their own sadness – and no doubt trying to comfort Charles and Diana's two sons. Meanwhile, at Buckingham Palace, not even a flag was flying at half-mast.

The reason for the lack of a flag was clear to the palace authorities, who were just following the rules about when to fly flags at the palace. The royal standard flies at Buckingham Palace to indicate that the monarch is in residence. No monarch, no flag. Simple. But the press didn't see it this way. No flag looked like a deliberate act of disrespect, and they objected.

The complaints about the flag seem trivial in retrospect, but at the time, they highlighted the apparent remoteness of the queen and the rest of her family. The queen and her staff realised that they had to make the royal grief more public, and a number of measures brought the monarch closer to the people:

- ✔ A special service was held at the church near Balmoral, mentioning the Princess's death. On their way back from the service, the royals stopped to look at the memorial flowers that had been left at the gates of Balmoral.

- ✔ Princes Andrew and Edward, who were in London, made a public visit to the Chapel Royal, where Diana's body was lying in rest, to pay their last respects. (Prince Edward had already visited the chapel privately.)

- ✔ The queen and the rest of the family who were at Balmoral were flown quickly to London. The queen and Duke of Edinburgh stopped to look at the flowers on their way through the gates of Buckingham Palace.

- ✔ The queen made a live broadcast to the nation paying tribute to Diana and saying how she made 'many, many people happy'.

These changes showed how the monarchy could adjust to difficult circumstances. When the need arose, the monarchy could cast off old protocols, and the queen and her staff could invent new ways of dealing with situations.

Threats and tensions

In the 21st century, people are just as fascinated by the monarchy as they have ever been. Many media stories cover the monarchy, recounting everything from official visits to exposés of the private lives of royal family members.

But fascination also brings its problems. The royals are news, and a number of people have tried to exploit this fact by breaching royal security in various ways. There's nothing new about this type of betrayal. For example, the queen was disturbed by an intruder in Buckingham Palace in 1982. But a rash of incidents hit the headlines between 2001 and 2004:

- **The fake sheikh:** In April 2001, a reporter from the *News of the World* newspaper, disguised as a sheikh, arranged a meeting with Sophie, Countess of Wessex. The Countess promised that if the sheikh employed her PR company, he'd get all sorts of advantages from her royal connections.

- **The gatecrasher:** In June 2003, comedian Aaron Barschak dressed himself as Osama Bin Laden and gate-crashed the 21st birthday party of Prince William at Windsor Castle.

- **The fake footman:** In November 2003, it emerged that a journalist, Ryan Parry from the *Daily Mirror* newspaper, got a job as a royal footman at Buckingham Palace. He took photographs of private areas of the palace and was in post when President Bush was visiting the queen.

- **Batman:** In September 2004, Jason Hatch, a protester from the group Fathers for Justice, dressed as Batman and scaled one of the walls of Buckingham Palace.

No one came to any harm during these stunts, but one thing became clear. The royal household had to improve its security. The monarch, more than ever accessible to the people, also had to be protected. And so the old tension, between the ruler as public figure and private person, continues to occupy the minds of the royals and their staff into the 21st century.

Chapter 18

The Prince of Wales

· ·

In This Chapter

▶ Finding out about a prince's education

▶ Understanding the role of the Prince of Wales

▶ Revealing the marriage of Prince Charles and Princess Diana

▶ Describing the prince's fortunes after Diana's death

· ·

*P*rince Charles is the eldest son of Queen Elizabeth and Prince Philip. He was born in 1948 and has therefore spent all his adult years as heir to the throne. His whole life has been shaped by this fact and by the fact that the heir has no clearly defined role.

Like several other members of the current British royal family, Prince Charles has developed his role in two ways: supporting the queen in her official duties and helping others, especially by carrying out an impressive list of charitable works.

The prince would certainly see these day-to-day activities as the most important part of his role in today's royal family. But the media have been attracted more to the sensational side of Charles's life – especially by the story of his marriage to Diana, Princess of Wales, the breakdown of their relationship, and the princess's tragic early death in a car accident in Paris. Charles's second marriage has also attracted a lot of attention from reporters and broadcasters.

The Young Prince: Prince Charles

Prince Charles's education and early life were shaped by the fact that he is heir to a crown that values tradition but is also moving into the modern world. His early life was dominated by public school, Cambridge University, and a spell in the armed forces – all unsurprising fare. His life also has some unusual twists – his boarding school was a very unusual one, and his later education included a spell learning Welsh.

Schooldays

In the past, royal children traditionally received their education at home. Queen Elizabeth II, for example, was taught by a governess, and, to begin with, so was her young son. Charles's governess, Catherine Peebles, had already taught the offspring of George VI's brother, the Duke of Kent. She taught Charles to read and write, introduced him to history and geography, and gave him the basics of French.

Miss Peebles was a success, but Charles's parents realised that education at home, while nurturing their son, wasn't bringing him out of his shell. They decided that he should be educated among other boys, and after three years with his governess, Charles started school.

Hill House

Charles's first school was Hill House, a small day school in West London just a few minutes from Buckingham Palace. Previous royal children, if they had gone to school at all, had gone to boarding school. Charles was the first to attend a day school, arriving every day in a chauffeur-driven car, but otherwise being treated very much like the other pupils. The prince went to Hill House for a year and didn't do badly. His teachers reported that the 8-year-old Charles was good at reading and writing, but below average in maths. He had started Latin and showed a strong interest in both music and art.

Cheam

Hill House wasn't the main event in Charles's education. He was expected to go to boarding school, and the first step on that road was *prep school,* the kind of English boarding school that prepares you for public school and that you attend between the ages of 8 and 13. Just before he was 9 years old, Charles was sent to Cheam, the prep school that his father had attended some 25 years earlier.

Cheam was very much the traditional English boarding school, which meant a lot of things that Charles didn't much like – cold showers, runs in the rain, rugby, and corporal punishment, for example. But toward the end of his five years there, Charles made a success of it and was head boy in his final year.

Gordonstoun

When the time came, at age 13, for Charles to go to public school, he again followed his father's footsteps, this time to Gordonstoun in Scotland. Gordonstoun wasn't a typical public school. Its founder, Kurt Hahn, who had been a Jewish refugee from Nazi Germany, believed that Spartan conditions were good for the young. As well as the usual public school diet of wet runs and cold showers, pupils at Gordonstoun were expected to sleep with the windows open, even in winter. Those with beds near the windows often woke up with damp or snowy sheets.

Charles didn't enjoy Gordonstoun. He remembers it as a place where he was bullied. He was also lonely because other pupils shied away from befriending him because they were scared of being accused of 'sucking up to royalty'.

The place had its good side, though. The prince was able to take part in activities that he liked, including sailing, music, and drama, and his interest in art was encouraged. At age 16, he received five O Levels (English Language, English Literature, French, History, and Latin) and at 18 two A Levels (Grade B in History and Grade C in French). Charles ended his career at Gordonstoun as school *Guardian* (the equivalent of head boy).

After school

The education of a prince involves far more than just school. The royal family has a tradition that its young male members should spend time in the armed services. In addition, Charles got an opportunity that was quite unusual for a member of the royal family – he went to university.

Trinity

After Gordonstoun, Charles went to Trinity College, Cambridge, where he began three years as an undergraduate, initially reading Archaeology and Anthropology. The palace authorities insisted that he should be treated as a normal undergraduate – as normal, that is, as you can be when you're constantly accompanied by a detective and your every public move is liable to be reported in the press.

On the whole, Charles responded well to the challenges of trying to read for a degree while the nation watched. At the end of his first year, he passed his Part One exams, and he also found time to take part in university drama and play polo.

Charles switched subjects to history after his first year and went on to get a Lower Second in his final exams – an average degree, in other words, but a good achievement for someone who was working under public scrutiny and had found school heavy weather.

Aberystwyth

Charles had one other experience of university life. In 1969, he spent three months at the University College of Wales at Aberystwyth. He was there as part of his preparation for his role as Prince of Wales, and one of his most important tasks was to learn Welsh – or at least to pick up enough of it to make the occasional speech.

Tension has existed between England and Wales for hundreds of years, as one English king after another tried to conquer and rule their western neighbour. By 1969, when Charles went to Aberystwyth, many people thought Wales should be independent once more. Most of these people were men and women who wanted peaceful change. However, a few extremists were prepared to use violence against the British.

The week Charles arrived in Wales, an explosion occurred outside the police headquarters in Cardiff. Would the extremists try to blow up Charles, too? They didn't – partly thanks to an enormous security operation around the prince. Gradually, most Welsh people warmed to Charles. At the end of May 1969, he spoke at an *Eisteddfod* (a Welsh festival of the arts). Speaking in Welsh, he was well received. It was a good preparation for the ceremony in which Charles officially became Prince of Wales.

The investiture

Charles was made Prince of Wales in a special ceremony called an *investiture* at Caernarfon Castle in July 1969. The investiture, a kind of coronation, wasn't an ancient ceremony. It was devised in 1911 when the son of George V, the future King Edward VIII, was made Prince of Wales.

Lord Snowdon, photographer, designer, and the husband of Princess Margaret, oversaw the 1969 ceremony. Snowdon specified the costumes, seating, and three thrones of Welsh slate beneath a canopy of Perspex (transparent so that the TV cameras could record what was going on). Snowdon's visual flair and the stunning setting – the grandest of the castles built by Edward I – ensured that the ceremony looked good, both live and on television.

In July 1969, the royal family and various dignitaries assembled in Caernarfon Castle, together with the television cameras, to record the ritual in which Charles swore allegiance to his mother and was crowned Prince of Wales. Quite a few anxieties surrounded the ceremony:

- **Would it work on television?** No ceremony like this one had ever been televised before, but the broadcast was well received. Each stage of the proceedings was planned carefully to allow good camera angles. It worked.

- **Would there be a terrorist attack?** In spite of threats from extreme nationalists, the investiture was completed safely.

- **How would the prince himself shape up?** Prince Charles had had training in handling the media, but was inexperienced. Charles did well, though, even learning enough of the Welsh language to give a speech in the tongue of his new principality. The new prince was a success.

The investiture was a triumph. Millions watched it on television, and most people in Wales accepted their prince warmly. Charles topped the ceremony by setting off on a week's tour of Wales. Again, officials were worried about the possibility of terrorism, but no attack came, and the young prince was welcomed widely. It was his first major media event, and he acquitted himself well.

In the services

Following tradition, Charles went into the armed services after university. He began in 1971 in the Royal Air Force, but after six months moved to the Royal Navy, beginning at the Royal Naval College, Dartmouth. Charles spent five years as a naval officer.

Charles became an accomplished officer in the Navy. He was praised for his leadership abilities, determination, physical courage, and his flair for handling a ship. He also learned to fly helicopters, overcame his problems with maths enough to navigate, and coped with seasickness.

In other areas of his life – such as his emotional outbursts and his complaints about his lot – Prince Charles has sometimes been accused of wimpishness. But he wasn't a wimp in the Navy. Most of the men in his family had been soldiers or sailors at one time or another, and the services were in his blood. Charles could see the job he needed to do and got on with it. However, when he came out of the Navy in 1976, the prince faced a different challenge. He now had no defined job and had to find out for himself what his role was to be.

King-in-Waiting

There is no official role attached to the title of Prince of Wales. Each Prince knows he is heir to the throne and is, in one sense, waiting for his parent to die in order to be allowed to get on with his destined role – that of monarch. But Princes of Wales have rarely been allowed just to sit around and wait to be crowned king. In the Middle Ages, the first Prince of Wales won himself a notable reputation as a soldier. Today, a Prince of Wales is expected to make himself useful, too.

Each holder of the title Prince of Wales has to define his role for himself, and that was Prince Charles's first task after he left the Navy. He carved out a role in three main areas – by carrying out the long list of public duties that a senior member of the royal family was expected to perform, by running the Duchy of Cornwall, and by supporting charities that reflected his wide-ranging interests.

This working life has continued from the mid-1970s until today, a 30-year period during which the personal fortunes of Prince Charles have varied, and his public popularity has plunged – and, latterly, made something of a recovery. The public duties, the charitable work, and the involvement in the Duchy of Cornwall have been constants in a changeable world.

Public duties

The Prince of Wales undertakes a bewildering array of public duties – visits, openings, inaugurations, celebrations, meetings, tours, and so on. These duties are designed to support the similar work of the queen, as well as reflecting the specific interests of the prince himself in fields from education to architecture, organic farming to healthcare. Altogether, the prince might attend some 500 events in a year, mostly in Britain but including a large number overseas.

Summarising this diverse work is tough, but in one month, May 2006, the prince:

- ✔ Hosted various events, including a dinner for supporters of the Prince's Trust and a reception for the Kathmandu Valley Preservation Trust.
- ✔ Opened the restored royal palace at Kew, West London.
- ✔ Gave a number of speeches, including one on young people at the Scottish Parliament, one to the World Health Assembly, and another on preserving the buildings of Edinburgh.
- ✔ Led the celebrations of the 30th anniversary of the Prince's Trust.
- ✔ Went on numerous visits across the United Kingdom.
- ✔ Attended celebrations of the work of the Royal Shakespeare Company.

Other months saw receptions for war veterans, events relating to health charities, tree plantings, and conferences. The prince has a full diary and is a very active representative both of the monarchy and the numerous good causes he supports.

The Prince's Charities

During the 30-odd years he has been Prince of Wales, Prince Charles has given his name, and a large amount of his time, to a growing list of charities that work in the fields where he has a special interest.

Sixteen charities are currently grouped under the overall name The Prince's Charities, and the Prince is President of all 16 and founder of 14. Together, the group makes up the UK's largest multicharity enterprise, and it raises more than £100 million annually.

The charities are arranged in six main groups. Here's the low-down on some of the best-known charities in each group and the work they do:

✔ **Opportunity and enterprise:** *The Prince's Trust* is probably Charles's best-known charity. It offers training, mentoring, financial assistance, and other help to young people, especially those who have struggled at school, have been in long-term care, or have had other social problems. In 30 years, the trust has helped over half a million young people.

✔ **Education:** *The Prince's Drawing School* was set up to provide a centre of excellence in observational drawing. The School runs life-drawing classes, as well as courses in painting, sculpture, calligraphy, and print-making. Around 400 students attend each week.

✔ **Health:** *The Prince's Foundation for Integrated Health* exists to encourage the development of integrated healthcare – in other words, enabling conventional and complementary health practitioners to work together.

✔ **The built environment:** *The Prince's Regeneration Trust* promotes the rescue and regeneration of historic buildings so that they become assets to their local area. Particular successes have involved the restoration of industrial buildings to provide places where people can live, work, or enjoy themselves. The aim is to make each restored building 'work for its living' and to encourage others to regenerate historic buildings in a similar way.

✔ **Business:** *Business in the Community* encourages businesses to improve their impact on society. It helps companies tackle social disadvantage, poverty, and crime, and to improve the impact they have on the environment. More than 750 companies work together as members of Business in the Community.

✔ **The Arts:** *Arts and Business* helps businesses support the arts and the arts to inspire business. It builds creative partnerships between companies and artists with the aim that these links are beneficial to both sides. Arts and Business has been in existence for almost 30 years, and the Prince became its President in 1988.

Prince Charles is the President of all these charities, and his role is more than just a figurehead. Many of the projects and schemes that they promote were originated by the prince himself, or during discussions in which he played a key part. He is passionate about these good causes, and his passion has sometimes led him into controversy. His views on architecture have resulted in some scathing attacks on the work of modern architects, including a famous remark about a proposal for a new wing on London's National Gallery, which Charles described as a 'monstrous carbuncle'. His ideas about education have also led to some critical remarks about the quality of English teaching in the schools.

Prince Charles's charitable involvement commits him to a lot of work, from hosting formal events to attending meetings and reading briefing papers. Much of this important work is done behind the scenes, beyond the glare of TV cameras and the lenses of press photographers. The public is used to seeing images of Prince Charles on the ski slopes or reports of his lavish dinners and receptions. It's easy to forget that much of the prince's life is taken up with the hard work that helps his charities function.

The Duchy of Cornwall

As heir to the throne, as well as being Prince of Wales, Prince Charles is also Duke of Cornwall. The Duchy of Cornwall is a vast private estate established in 1337 by Edward III for his son, Prince Edward. The idea behind the Duchy was – and still is – to provide the Prince with an income with which his public, charitable, and private activities can be funded. Prince Charles also funds the activities of his two sons and the Duchess of Cornwall from his Duchy income. The Duchy consists of some 54,000 hectares of land, mostly in southwestern England – in short, it is a big business.

The Duchy is the prince's business – up to a point. Prince Charles is entitled to the large income (£13.2 million in 2005) from the estate. However, he isn't allowed to take the proceeds from any of its assets that are sold. The proceeds from any sale are invested back in the Duchy to ensure that the estate is preserved to hand on to the next heir to the throne.

Most of the vast property holding of the Duchy of Cornwall is let to tenants. It is made up of a diverse collection of farms, houses, and commercial properties and includes a big chunk of the London district of Kennington, as well as vast tracts of countryside. A lot of the income comes from rents, but Prince Charles is not a hands-off landlord who takes his money and runs. He has used the Duchy estates to put his money where his mouth is and put into practice his views on many subjects, from agriculture to architecture. Here are a few examples:

- ✔ Poundbury, a new settlement in Dorset adjoining the town of Dorchester, was built on Duchy land. Its architecture and planning were based on the principles that Prince Charles has developed over the years, especially the use of traditional architectural styles and familiar local building materials.

- ✔ The home farm at Prince Charles's house, Highgrove, was converted to organic farming around 20 years ago. It is now one of Britain's premier organic farms.

- ✔ Building conservation projects throughout the Duchy estate pay testimony to the prince's interest in the built environment, especially in respecting and learning from the architecture of the past.

- ✔ The Duchy's woodlands are sustainably managed in line with the prince's environmental views, and the quality of this management is recognised by the Forestry Stewardship Council.

The interest in conservation and the environment is typical of Prince Charles's long view of the Duchy of Cornwall. The prince sees his role as one of enhancing the assets of the Duchy so that he can pass the estate on to his heir in a healthier state than he found it when he inherited it.

Charles and Diana

Prince Charles married in 1981, when he was 33. By this time, Charles had been linked with a number of different young women, but by late 1980, he was convinced that Lady Diana Spencer, daughter of Earl Spencer, the queen's *equerry* (an officer of the royal household who attends a member of the royal family), was the woman he would marry. The wedding was lavish, and the media portrayed it as a 'fairytale' event. Diana quickly blossomed into a media star. But the marriage did not last, and as the royal relationship fell apart, the prince fell out of sympathy with media and public alike.

Charles before Diana

As Britain's most eligible bachelor, Prince Charles found plenty of eager young female companions. In the 1970s, the prince's girlfriends formed a favourite topic in the media, and photographers vied to get pictures of Charles with his latest conquest.

It's now public knowledge that Charles was encouraged, by his favourite great-uncle and mentor Earl Mountbatten of Burma, Prince Philip's uncle, to play the field. In 1974, Mountbatten wrote a now-famous letter to Charles, in which he said, 'I believe, in a case like yours, the man should sow his wild oats and have as many affairs as he can before settling down but for a wife he should choose a suitable, attractive and sweet-charactered girl *before* she met anyone she might fall for.'

Among the young women who were linked romantically with Prince Charles in his early years, a number stand out:

- Lucia Santa Cruz, daughter of the Chilean Ambassador to Britain, who got to know Charles when he was at Cambridge.

- Camilla Shand, later Camilla Parker Bowles, daughter of a former cavalry officer and great-granddaughter of one of Edward VII's mistresses, who eventually became *the* woman in Charles's life. (See the upcoming section 'Charles and Camilla'.)

- Jane Ward, who worked at the Guards Polo Club.

- Sabrina Guinness, of the brewing family.

- Lady Jane Wellesley, daughter of the Duke of Wellington.

- Amanda Knatchbull, granddaughter of Earl Mountbatten.

These attachments weren't all equally serious. Charles remained good friends with Lucia, for example, and proposed to – and was refused by – Amanda. Camilla, though, was different from them all, an attachment to whom Charles would return.

But, because of the values of the royal family at the time, Charles could not marry Camilla. Camilla had had affairs, and the view of both the royal family and palace officials during the 1960s and 1970s was that the heir to the throne should not marry a woman 'with a past'. And in 1973, Camilla was ruled out as royal bride for another reason – she married army officer Andrew Parker Bowles.

Fairytale gone sour

Prince Charles had known Diana Spencer for some years before they became engaged. Diana belonged to a prominent upper-class British family, and it was inevitable that the pair should have crossed paths. For example, Diana was a guest at the ball held at Buckingham Palace to celebrate Charles's 30th birthday in 1978.

Charles and Diana, though, first got to know each other in 1980, when she was just 19 and he was 31. Soon the couple were seen together often, Diana had been to stay at Balmoral, and the press were talking enthusiastically about the relationship. Diana appealed to the media as an 'ideal' princess in several ways:

- She came from a noble family and was the daughter of an earl.
- She had had no past relationships to sully her reputation.
- She was young.
- She was attractive.

By November 1980, Charles was 32. He'd previously said that he thought 30 was a good age to settle down and marry, and press speculation was increasing that Diana would be his chosen bride. Charles seemed to find it difficult to make up his mind, and his father wrote him a letter reminding him that it was unfair to subject Diana to media pressure – if he was serious, he should propose. In February 1981, Charles asked Diana to marry him, she accepted, and plans began for the wedding.

The big event

The royal family doesn't go in for long engagements, so Charles and Diana were married on 29 July 1981, in full splendour, at St Paul's Cathedral. The event combined tradition and glamour – the traditional splendour of a religious service in one of Europe's biggest and most beautiful churches with the glamour of the couple, Charles in full-dress naval uniform, Diana in a taffeta and lace dress featuring a 25-foot-long train. Not surprisingly, the interest in the wedding was vast:

> ✔ A congregation of 3,500 were invited to attend in St Paul's Cathedral.
>
> ✔ Some 600,000 lined the streets of London to try to get a glimpse of the couple.
>
> ✔ An international television audience of around 750 million people is said to have tuned in to view the event.

Few spectators were disappointed. The British royal family does ceremony very well, and at the centre of the ceremony was a young woman, both shy and beautiful, who the media were happy to portray as a fairytale princess. Everyone looked forward to a happily-ever-after ending to the story.

The promise of Charles and Diana's wedding seemed fulfilled when, less than a year after the ceremony, Diana gave birth to a baby boy. Prince William was born on 21 June 1982. A couple of years later, on 15 September 1984, the couple's second son, Prince Harry, arrived.

The fairytale couple had turned into the ideal family, and Charles and Diana had provided the monarchy with what it always wants – a secure succession or, 'an heir and a spare'.

Splitting up

The fairytale marriage of Prince Charles and Princess Diana went wrong, however. The problems began very soon after the wedding. They sprang from the fact that the couple had very little in common and that both had emotional needs that the other could not satisfy. It was painful for Diana:

> ✔ She felt that she didn't fit in with the royals' way of life and disliked the 'hunting and fishing' lifestyle that Charles enjoyed so much.
>
> ✔ She didn't get on with her husband's friends.
>
> ✔ She developed the serious eating disorder bulimia nervosa and began to lose weight drastically.
>
> ✔ Charles seemed unable to comfort her.
>
> ✔ She began to be convinced that Charles was cheating on her.

Charles found it hard to cope with Diana and her problems or to help her out of them. He tried, but was repaid with suspicion and rebuff, with the result that he felt rejected, too. Meanwhile, Charles was also resentful that Diana was proving so popular with the public. No one seemed to care about the decades of work that he'd put in as Prince of Wales. Diana's power over the media could throw all that into shadow. Frozen out, Charles turned to his old love, Camilla Shand, now Mrs Camilla Parker Bowles.

The media war

In past centuries, the British royal family had taken this kind of marital infidelity for granted. Kings and queens married for dynastic reasons, produced heirs, and then went their separate emotional ways. And for a while, for much of the 1980s, in fact, Charles and Diana tried to live in this way, keeping up a united front while Charles spent as much time as he could with Camilla, who had been married to Andrew Parker Bowles since 1973.

By the early 1990s, the mutual resentment developed into a virtual war between Charles and Diana, and it was a very public war, fought in the pages of books and in television interviews.

Diana's 'True story'

The first big blow in the war came from Diana. In 1992, a book, *Diana: Her True Story,* by journalist Andrew Morton (published by Michael O'Mara) appeared. It described Diana's plight as a woman who had been wronged, who could not escape from a loveless marriage, and whose husband was unfeeling and cold toward her. The book was a depressing story of a young woman who had thought she'd entered into the perfect marriage and was now suffering from depression and near despair.

According to Morton, the book was based on accounts supplied to him by 'Diana's friends'. It later emerged that things weren't quite that simple. What actually happened was that Diana supplied the information herself – not through direct contact with Morton, but through her friend James Colthurst, a doctor who taped his conversations with the princess.

Diana: Her True Story was a bombshell. The marital breakdown of Charles and Diana was now public knowledge. Charles tried to patch things up by taking his wife on holiday on a friend's yacht. But the couple spent most of the holiday apart, Diana waterskiing and Charles painting. It certainly wasn't the second honeymoon that had been mentioned in some newspapers.

Separation – and Camillagate

In December 1992, Charles and Diana announced that they were to separate. This separation wasn't a shock after the Morton revelations, but it instantly had people asking questions about the future of the monarchy:

- ✔ What would happen to Diana if and when Charles became king?

- ✔ Would Charles eventually want to remarry?

- ✔ Could a self-confessed adulterer become king at all when the ruler was also head of the Church of England?

These questions were all difficult, but they were overshadowed by another media revelation early the following year. An Australian magazine published a transcript of a private telephone conversation between Charles and Camilla Parker Bowles.

The *Camillagate* tape was seized on by the media – even those who wouldn't print the pillow talk of the heir to the throne and his mistress were fascinated by it and talked about it. The event only served to emphasise the mess Charles was in. Every new report or revelation reduced his popularity further and seemed to enhance the reputation of Diana.

Charles retaliates

Charles's response to the media onslaught from Diana came in 1994. The broadcaster Jonathan Dimbleby approached Charles with a proposal to make a television documentary and to publish a book to mark the 25th anniversary of his becoming Prince of Wales. Charles responded with enthusiasm, opening up his papers, letters, and diaries to Dimbleby – and opening up emotionally, too.

In the resulting programme, Charles was brutally honest. He talked about the fact that he'd had a difficult childhood and frankly admitted his adultery with Camilla. If the prince thought that honesty would do him credit, he miscalculated badly. Most of the vast 15 million-strong viewership of the programme deplored his confession of adultery and his remark that Mrs Parker Bowles would remain his friend. Many people also looked down on the prince's tendency to blame his difficult upbringing for his troubles, too.

The Dimbleby programme and book didn't help Charles. The public revelations it brought to light also hastened the split of Camilla and her husband, Andrew Parker Bowles – their plans to divorce were announced in January 1995.

The crowded marriage

Diana made her own bid for media sympathy in 1995. Her interview with the broadcaster Martin Bashir was aired on BBC's current-affairs programme *Panorama* and attracted even more viewers than the Dimbleby programme about Charles. Diana made it clear that she held Charles and Camilla completely to blame for the breakdown of the royal marriage. One of her most famous remarks was that the marriage contained three people and was 'a bit crowded'.

During the course of the interview, Diana also made it clear that she thought Charles would never be king. She confessed to her own adultery, but managed to blame Charles and Camilla for it. Her status as victim or wronged woman gained her widespread sympathy. Diana had won another battle in the media war.

Death of a princess

After Diana's devastating comments to Martin Bashir (see the preceding section) she and the Prince of Wales moved swiftly to a divorce. After some wrangling, Diana agreed to let go of the coveted title Her Royal Highness and to accept a financial settlement, made up of a payment of £17 million, as well as an annual allowance for her office and staff. The divorce became absolute on 28 August 1996.

Diana continued to fascinate the media after the divorce, and the press soon began to report her new romantic attachments. One was to a heart surgeon, Hasnat Khan. Another was with Dodi al-Fayed, son of the Egyptian owners of Harrods department store in London. Diana was with Dodi in Paris on the night of 30-31 August 1997, when their car, moving at speed to escape pursuing paparazzi, crashed into a concrete pillar in the Place de l'Alma tunnel. Both Diana and Dodi perished in the crash.

Since Diana's death, some have speculated that the accident wasn't all it seemed – or even wasn't an accident at all. But the evidence, and the fact that the death took place under the noses of a group of press photographers, makes this conspiracy theory highly unlikely.

The period immediately after Diana's death was a low-point for the royal family. They were widely attacked in the media for seeming distant and not grieving publicly for the princess. (For more about this topic, see Chapter 17.)

Prince Charles described himself as 'numb with shock' when he heard about Diana's death. After a trip to Paris to bring back the princess's body, he concentrated on being with his sons and trying to give them the feeling of security they acutely needed. Some commentators had previously accused Charles of being rather distant from his sons. However, this aloofness certainly wasn't the case now, and those who know him say that they have always shared, and still do, a close bond.

Diana's funeral saw Charles, his two sons, and the Duke of Edinburgh, together with Diana's brother Charles Spencer, walking behind the gun carriage that carried her coffin to Westminster Abbey. It was a scene of dignified mourning and suggested that in the months to come, the royal family could leave behind the strife and start to rebuild the credibility of the monarchy. For now, they were part of a scene of national grief, during which thousands left floral tributes in memory of Diana or threw flowers at the hearse as it passed.

Charles and Camilla

In the years after Princess Diana's death, Camilla Parker Bowles became an almost constant companion of the Prince of Wales. To begin with, a large part of the public, revering Diana's memory, found this arrangement hard to take. But gradually, Camilla became more widely accepted, and she and Charles married. Charles finally achieved the personal happiness he wanted, and the couple have developed mutually supportive public roles.

Non-negotiable relationship

After the divorce of Charles and Diana, Charles went on record as saying that he would not give up Camilla, even though he could not marry her. His relationship with her was 'non-negotiable'. After the divorce, Charles and Camilla were often seen together, and Camilla soon began to make public appearances. But there was a lot of public doubt about whether they could marry. For those who admired Diana deeply, Charles's liaison with Camilla looked liked a betrayal of her memory. In addition, many people still felt that a man who would one day become Supreme Governor of the Church of England should not marry a divorced woman.

After the death of Diana, Charles and Camilla attended many of the same events, but did so separately, arriving and leaving at different times to make the point that they weren't appearing as a couple, while also getting people used to seeing them together. But in January 1999, they made a point of going to a party together, and telling the press that they were doing so. Their relationship was headline news again – and it was clear that Camilla was a central and public part of Charles's life.

The following year, the Queen, who did not approve of out-of-wedlock relationships like her son's with Camilla, finally yielded to the inevitable and accepted the pair as a couple. The way was open for the couple to live together openly and to move toward becoming man and wife.

Marriage

In February 2005, the marriage of Charles and Camilla was announced. The marriage was to be a small civil ceremony in Windsor the following April, followed by a blessing in St George's Chapel. In the event, the run-up to the wedding wasn't easy. The newspapers portrayed several minor hitches as major disasters:

- ✔ **Hitch No. 1 – The venue problem:** The plan was for the civil marriage ceremony to be held in Windsor Castle. But the royal household realised too late that if the Castle was to be licensed for weddings, everyone would be queuing up to be married there – you can't just licence a place for *one* wedding. The plans changed, and the ceremony was arranged for Windsor's Guildhall, where civil weddings are normally held in the town.

- ✔ **Hitch No. 2 – The Queen declines to attend:** When it became clear that Charles and Camilla would have to get married in the Guildhall, the queen said she wouldn't go, but would come to the blessing in the chapel afterwards. The press portrayed this refusal as a snub, but it wasn't – she just didn't want to go to a 'public' ceremony in the High Street. She was still going to the blessing, which for her, a religious woman and head of the Church of England, was the important thing.

- ✔ **Hitch No. 3 – The Pope dies:** Pope John Paul II died a few days before the wedding, and the funeral was arranged for Friday 8 April, the planned wedding day. To allow key participants to go to the funeral, the wedding had to be rescheduled for Saturday 9 April.

The wedding passed off successfully, and the press generally covered it with warmth. Even the Prince's popularity rating, at an all-time low around the time of Diana's death, was beginning to inch upwards.

Since the wedding, the Prince of Wales and Camilla, Duchess of Cornwall, have been able to 'go public' as a working royal couple who both love each other and get on with the work their role commits them to. The future of the Windsor monarchy seems more secure, and its main players seem more content than they have been for years.

Part VII
The Part of Tens

The 5th Wave — By Rich Tennant

WELCOME TO THE BRITISH ISLES INVASION HOURS
M-W 8 - 4 PM
T-S 12 - 6 PM
SUNDAY - CLOSED

"Who knows what day it is?"

In this part . . .

*H*ere are some interesting snippets of information about the monarchy that didn't fit into the other parts of this book. You can find information about some of the most interesting people who have been close to the monarch at various points in history – the royal consorts (the wives of the kings and husbands of the ruling queens) and some of the men who have held the title Prince of Wales. In addition, this part contains details of many of the most interesting places – both royal homes and other sites – where visitors can experience royal history at first hand.

Chapter 19

Ten Royal Homes

The British monarch has several houses, and they're all large historical piles. One, Windsor Castle, has been in the family for around 1,000 years. Several houses are *official residences,* buildings that go with the job and play a part in the work of the sovereign – holding receptions and banquets, for example, and housing the offices of key members of royal staff.

Others are private houses, personally owned by the monarch and used by the royal family as homes. Many official residences are often open to the public, so you can visit Windsor Castle, Buckingham Palace, or the Palace of Holyroodhouse and see for yourself the settings of state banquets and royal rituals. The royal homes, like Sandringham and Balmoral, contain exhibition rooms that are regularly opened to the public.

This chapter also includes Highgrove in Gloucestershire, the country house of the heir to the throne, Prince Charles, where the Prince has created a garden that is now famous throughout the world.

Buckingham Palace

The most famous royal house is the sovereign's official London residence, Buckingham Palace. It became a royal home in 1761, when George III bought it for his wife, Queen Charlotte. At the time of the purchase, it was known as Buckingham House because it had been the London home of the Dukes of Buckingham.

George IV had the builders in and upgraded the palace in the 1820s, employing his favourite architect, John Nash, to double the size of the main block. Many of the state rooms date from this time. Another upgrade occurred during Victoria's reign, when more private rooms, such as nurseries, were added to accommodate the queen's large family. Victoria also added the Ballroom, the palace's biggest room – at nearly 37 metres long, it was the largest room in London when it was built. The palace's famous front, where red-uniformed soldiers stand on guard, dates from a still later remodelling from the time of George V.

Many visitors are attracted to the palace by the ceremony of changing the guard. It's a kind of ritual hand-over when one bunch of guards departs, and the next contingent take over. The new guard arrives, complete with military band. After a certain amount of marching and music, the old guard departs, and the new one takes its place. The men who perform this ritual are real soldiers and come from some of the most prestigious regiments in the British Army.

As well as being the sovereign's London home, Buckingham Palace is a working building, housing all kinds of offices for royal staff. It's also the setting for countless royal occasions – receptions, dinners, investitures, and the famous royal garden parties that take place in the grounds. More than 50,000 people a year visit the palace to attend all these events.

For years, Buckingham Palace was a private building – only the monarch's invited guests got to look inside. But Queen Elizabeth II now opens the palace to the public at times during the summer months when the royal family isn't in residence. Now tourists can see the grand state rooms and marvel at the gilded furniture and the stunning paintings by the likes of Rembrandt, Rubens, and Poussin. Visitors can also look at part of the palace garden, a vast green oasis in the middle of London.

One of the other big attractions at Buckingham Palace is the Queen's Gallery, which displays many important items from the royal collections. The gallery was originally built in 1962 on the site of the palace chapel, which was destroyed when London was bombed during World War II. The gallery has hosted many exhibitions highlighting areas where the royal collection is especially strong – paintings by Canaletto, drawings by Leonardo da Vinci, and glorious jewelled items made by Fabergé.

Buckingham Palace is also home to the Royal Mews, a large stable block that houses extraordinary state vehicles like the Gold State Coach (used for coronations) and the other coaches that are used during important royal events. The limousines used by the queen on state occasions are also kept here. Some garage!

Windsor Castle

The oldest royal residence is Windsor Castle. It was originally built by William the Conqueror in the 11th century and has been expanded, modified, and made over many times. It is now a fortress-palace and the largest occupied castle in the world.

Several monarchs contributed to making Windsor Castle the truly spectacular place it is today:

- Henry II rebuilt the large Round Tower and many of the castle walls in the 1170s.

- Edward III built the vast St George's Hall for the use of the Knights of the Garter.

- Edward IV and Henry VIII built the magnificent St George's Chapel in the 15th and 16th centuries.

- George IV, in the 1820s, rebuilt many of the state rooms and added the large Waterloo Chamber, designed to hold portraits of the characters involved in the defeat of the French emperor Napoleon at the Battle of Waterloo in 1815.

- Elizabeth II had to restore nine main rooms and around 100 smaller rooms after the castle caught fire in 1992.

All that investment and involvement has made Windsor a very special place, and it's a favourite of the royal family. Queen Victoria spent much of her time there, and Queen Elizabeth II spends a month over Easter and most weekends throughout the year at the castle.

As well as being a much-loved family home, the castle is also the venue for all kinds of state occasions. St George's Hall (55.5 metres long) is a good room for big banquets – it houses a table that can seat 160! Many foreign rulers, heads of state, and dignitaries have enjoyed visits to Windsor.

St George's Chapel is one of the main attractions in the castle. This large late-medieval building is stunning, its soaring windows and stone vault making it the equal of many cathedrals. Services are held there regularly, but it has also been the scene of major royal occasions, notably weddings (like that of Prince Edward and Sophie Rhys-Jones) and funerals (such as that of the current queen's late sister, Princess Margaret). The chapel, dedicated to the chivalrous Saint George, is the setting for the annual celebration of the Order of the Garter. Every year, the queen, the Duke of Edinburgh, and their fellow Knights of the Garter process through Windsor Castle wearing the badge of the order, the Garter Star. Their destination is St George's Chapel, where the annual service takes place.

Visitors to Windsor Castle can also see the Drawings Gallery, which stages exhibitions from the unrivalled royal collection of prints and drawings, Queen Mary's Dolls' House, a perfect miniature designed by the major architect Edwin Lutyens, and, of course, the lavish state apartments.

The Palace of Holyroodhouse

The official royal residence in Scotland is the Palace of Holyroodhouse, in Edinburgh. The palace is at one end of Edinburgh's famous royal mile, the long street that connects Edinburgh Castle at one end with Holyroodhouse and the new Scottish Parliament building at the other. The Palace of Holyroodhouse is big, imposing, and very Scottish – with its round towers and conical roofs, it looks like an even grander version of many Scots baronial halls and tower houses. Holyroodhouse looks the part, and it has the history, too. Scottish kings and queens lived there before Scotland and England were united under one ruler in the 17th century.

The weird name, *Holyroodhouse,* comes from the palace's early history. The story goes that it was first founded as a monastery by David I in 1128. David had a vision of the cross, also known as the Holy Rood, and took it as a signal to found the monastery – hence the strange name.

In the 16th century, James IV began the palace next to the monastery, and a few decades later, the palace became the home of Mary, Queen of Scots. One of the most dramatic events of her reign, the murder of her secretary, Rizzio, took place in the queen's apartments at Holyroodhouse.

Charles II made a lot of improvements to the palace in the late 17th century, but for a couple of hundred years, the royal family didn't use Holyroodhouse very much, although George IV visited it and ordered that Queen Mary's rooms should be preserved. But Queen Victoria, who loved Scotland, stayed there quite a lot on her way to and from her beloved Scottish country house, Balmoral.

The present queen stays at Holyroodhouse quite regularly, whenever she's busy with royal engagements in Scotland and especially at the end of June or in early July, when she usually spends a week in Edinburgh. This week sees a large garden party with some 8,000 guests and sometimes visits from world leaders.

Visitors to Holyroodhouse can see the state apartments, with their memories of Mary, Queen of Scots, their fine series of portraits of the kings of Scotland, and some of the best tapestries in the world. The Queen's Gallery houses items from the royal collections.

Sandringham

Prince Albert Edward (the future King Edward VII) bought this country house in Norfolk in 1862. He rebuilt the house completely so that it was big enough to house the large gatherings he regularly hosted as heir to the throne, and he also made many changes on the surrounding estate, building new roads and cottages and relandscaping the garden, for example.

Sandringham became a much-loved family home and was the base for the shooting parties that were a favourite royal pastime. During the time of Edward VII and George V, Sandringham clocks were moved on an extra half an hour during the winter so that the royals and their guests could have more daylight hours shooting. When people on the estate asked the time at midday, for example, the reply would be 12.30 ST – in other words 12.30 Sandringham Time. Edward VIII abolished Sandringham Time, but the house remained a favourite country retreat for the royal family. It's the house where the royals spend Christmas.

Because it was bought privately, Sandringham is still held by the monarch as a private house – it doesn't belong to the nation. It's attached to a large country estate, which is run by a land agent on behalf of the sovereign. More than half the land is let to tenant farmers; the rest is farmed or used for forestry on behalf of the monarch.

As well as the farmland, the estate includes the Sandringham Country Park, 600 acres of woods and heathland, which is permanently open to the public. The Country Park's facilities include nature trails, caravan sites, a shop, and a restaurant. At some times of the year, Sandringham House and its gardens are open to the public. The house also has a museum that houses royal memorabilia and an impressive collection of vintage royal vehicles, from a 1900 Daimler car to a bright red fire engine of 1939 once used on the estate.

Balmoral Castle

The Balmoral estate in Aberdeenshire, Scotland, was bought for Queen Victoria by her beloved consort, Prince Albert, in the mid-19th century. The existing 15th-century castle was too small for Albert, Victoria, and their family, so Albert quickly set about building a new castle. Albert himself contributed to the design of the new building, which is very grand, and very Scottish, with an impressive tower at one end. Like Sandringham, Balmoral is a private house of the monarch and is not owned by the state.

The estate at Balmoral is enormous – there are around 50,000 acres in total and the scenery, from mountain to moorland, is spectacular. Part of the estate is farmed, but there's not that much good farmland as the royal land contains seven mountains that rise to more than 3,000 feet above sea level. But a large area of the estate is forested, including a 2,500-acre forest that Queen Victoria bought when she heard a timber merchant was going to chop it down. There are also thousands of acres of land given over to game resources, especially deer and grouse. Conservation is a high priority for the royal family, and measures are in place to protect the area's important wildlife and to plant native species of trees.

The grounds, gardens, and exhibitions of Balmoral Castle are open to the public for several months each year.

St James's Palace

Although it's not very well known, St James's Palace, tucked away in central London, is actually the sovereign's main official residence. It was mainly built in the 1530s and was a royal home for some 300 years. The monarch doesn't actually live there any more, but it's still the official residence of the queen. Foreign diplomats are always referred to as Ambassadors to the Court of St James.

Henry VIII built St James's Palace, and quite a bit of his red-brick building survives. Later rulers added to the palace, producing the complex of buildings and courtyards that survives today. Visitors can only see these from the street, though, because St James's Palace isn't open to the public.

The palace is now used for lots of different functions. It's the London residence of the Princess Royal and Princess Alexandra. It contains numerous offices of royal staff, housing the Royal Collection Department, the Yeomen of the Guard, and the Queen's Watermen, amongst others.

St James's Palace is the place where the accession council meet whenever a reigning monarch dies. After the meeting, the reign of the new monarch is announced from the Proclamation Gallery, which overlooks one of the palace courtyards.

Clarence House

Clarence House is in the middle of London near the street called Pall Mall. It's right next to St James's Palace. The house was built in the 1820s and was first of all the home of Prince William Henry, Duke of Clarence, which is how it got its name. The Duke of Clarence eventually came to the throne as William IV, and he continued to live there when he was king.

But Clarence House is well known today because, for nearly 50 years, from 1953 until 2002, it was the home of one of the most popular members of the royal family, Queen Elizabeth the Queen Mother. After the Queen Mother died in 2002, the house became the official residence of the Prince of Wales, his sons, Princes William and Harry, and Prince Charles's second wife, the Duchess of Cornwall.

The house accommodates offices for the staff of the Prince of Wales and is the nerve centre from which the Prince's charitable work is coordinated. As the residence of the Prince of Wales, Clarence House is the last royal home in London to be used for the purpose for which it was originally designed. Part of the building is opened to the public during the summer months. The public rooms, where the Prince of Wales holds receptions and other events, are still largely furnished as they were in the time of the Queen Mother and contain pieces from her large collection, including numerous works by 20th-century British artists.

Kensington Palace

The royal family first had a palace on this site in west London when in 1689 William IV bought a building called Nottingham House and employed the architect Christopher Wren to extend it. The result was Kensington Palace, and this elegant house was the favourite home of every ruler from William III until George II.

Kensington Palace is best known today because Diana, Princess of Wales made it her official home and had her office there. The palace now contains the London residences of a number of royal family members, notably the Duke and Duchess of Gloucester, the Duke and Duchess of Kent, and Prince and Princess Michael of Kent. The state apartments, together with a number of rooms housing royal exhibitions, are open to the public.

Highgrove House

The country home of the Prince of Wales is at Highgrove, near the small Cotswold town of Tetbury in Gloucestershire. Highgrove was built from 1796–98 and altered about 100 years later. The house was bought by the prince's estate, the Duchy of Cornwall, in 1980. It attracted the prince because it is in southwest England, near to many of the Duchy's other properties.

Since then, the prince has altered the house, adding decorative touches to the exterior and making other changes, such as building a function suite in the grounds where he can hold meetings and other events.

But perhaps the biggest changes the prince has made at Highgrove have been in the gardens. When he took over the house, the garden was rather run down and windswept, but Prince Charles redeveloped it, adding new sections year by year and doing a lot of the planting himself. From the rose garden to the kitchen garden, it is now widely admired.

Frogmore House

Frogmore is a little-known house near Windsor Castle on land that came into royal ownership in the time of Henry VIII. Frogmore House itself was used by George III's queen, Charlotte, as a retreat away from London. It was also a favourite residence of George V and Queen Mary. Today, the elegant white house is occasionally used by the royal family for receptions and is open to the public on a few days each year.

Nearby is one of the great monuments of Victorian Britain, the Royal Mausoleum. It was built in the time of Queen Victoria after the death of Prince Albert. When she died, her body, too, was placed there beside her beloved husband's.

Chapter 20

Ten or So Royal Places

In This Chapter

▶ Checking out buildings that were once royal homes and palaces

▶ Discovering sites that bring military history to life

▶ Locating great architectural monuments with royal associations

*M*any places in Britain have close and enduring links with the royal family and are interesting to visit. Quite a lot of these places are *Historic Royal Palaces* – in other words, buildings that were once royal homes but are now open to the public as visitor attractions. They vary immensely, from the vast complex of the Tower of London to smaller buildings like Kew Palace. Many other places have royal associations, from the sites of bloody battles to peaceful churches such as Westminster Abbey. This chapter contains ten of the best royal places. They all have fascinating stories to tell.

The Tower of London

The Tower of London, by the River Thames in the heart of the capital, is one of Britain's largest medieval castles. It was first built in the late 11th century by King William I and was at the heart of royal life for hundreds of years afterwards. The Tower has played lots of roles in its time – royal home, fortress, prison, mint, jewel house, and place of execution. Today, it's a fabulous tourist attraction with displays and exhibitions on all sorts of aspects of royal history. It's also the place where the *Crown Jewels* – the royal collection of crowns, orbs, sceptres, and other priceless ceremonial rocks – is shown to the public.

Like lots of ancient buildings, the Tower of London has changed a lot over the years. It began as, surprise, surprise, a big tower. The large square structure, called the White Tower, is still at the heart of the building. Over the centuries, more and more bits were added until loads of extra buildings housed everything from servants to horses, two concentric sets of outer defensive walls, and a big moat around the whole lot.

During the Middle Ages, the Tower was a key asset for the royal family, especially in times of war. But it was perhaps most famous of all as a prison. During the Wars of the Roses (see Chapter 9), the civil wars between the rival royal families of York and Lancaster in the 15th century, the young King Edward V and his brother Richard were imprisoned in the Tower and mysteriously disappeared. They were probably murdered.

In Tudor times (see Chapter 13), the Tower's history got even bloodier. It was home to political and religious prisoners, men such as Sir Thomas More, who refused to acknowledge Henry VIII as head of the English church after the king broke away from the Roman Catholic Church. Henry also had two of his wives, Anne Boleyn and Catherine Howard, executed in the Tower. Henry's children, Queens Mary and Elizabeth I, continued to use the fortress as a favourite place for having their opponents' heads chopped off, and Elizabeth herself was held there when her half-sister Mary was on the throne.

In the 17th and 18th centuries, the Tower became the base of the Office of Ordnance, the people who supplied the Army and Navy with their equipment. In other words it was a large arms dump. The big fortress also had room for the Royal Mint, the Records Office, and the Royal Menagerie (housed in the Lion Tower). In the Victorian period, most of these functions moved out to various buildings around London, and the menagerie became the core of London Zoo. The arms stores were knocked down, and the Tower took on much of the look it has today, a historic medieval castle on a truly awesome scale.

Today, you can find loads to see at the Tower. Here are some highlights:

- The White Tower houses arms and armour from the royal armouries, plus gruesome instruments of torture.
- The Jewel House shows the royal crowns and regalia, including some of the world's biggest diamonds.
- Several towers, including the Bloody Tower, include displays about the building's famous prisoners.
- The Tower Ravens wander around the site – according to legend, if the ravens leave, both the fortress and the kingdom will fall, so the ravens are very well looked after.
- The Yeoman Warders in their striking black and red uniforms were once the Tower's guards; now they show visitors around on guided tours.

The Tower of London is also the home of one of the most famous royal rituals, the *Ceremony of the Keys*. This ritual, which consists of the ceremonial locking up of the Tower, has taken place every night for at least 700 years. The Tower's Chief Warder processes around the building, carrying the keys and locking important gates. He is accompanied by an escort made up of a group of soldiers because security is still vital at the Tower. The monarch no longer lives there, but the Tower's contents, which include the Crown Jewels, are priceless.

Hampton Court Palace

The enormous palace at Hampton Court, in west London, started life as the home of Cardinal Wolsey, powerful churchman and minister to Henry VIII. But when Wolsey got too powerful, he handed the palace to Henry in an attempt to get back into favour. It's been a royal property ever since and was a favourite royal home of many 16th- and 17th-century monarchs.

Hampton Court is mostly built of brick. Its buildings are arranged around several big courtyards. Some buildings date from the time of Henry VIII and Wolsey, while others were built in the time of William III and his queen, Mary, who employed the ace architect Christopher Wren to design enormous extensions.

A visit to Hampton Court is like a walk through Tudor and Stuart history (see Chapters 13 and 14), with evocative old bits like Henry VIII's big banqueting hall and state rooms, and not-quite-so-old bits like the dozens of rooms that make up the royal apartments of William III and Mary, some of the best interiors of their period anywhere in the world. The Tudor kitchens are a big attraction, with 16th-century-style cooking smells and roaring roasting fires.

Hampton Court has 60 acres of lovely gardens, too, with loads of flowers, a famous grape vine, and a big hedge maze to get lost in. It's no accident that one of Britain's foremost garden festivals takes place here every year.

The Banqueting House

One of the most important British royal palaces has almost completely disappeared: Whitehall Palace, which was situated, as its name suggests, in Whitehall, the street in the middle of London that now connects Trafalgar Square with the Houses of Parliament and contains lots of government offices. Between 1530 and 1698, Whitehall Palace was the monarch's main London residence, but in 1698, it was destroyed by fire.

All, that is, except for the Banqueting House, a lovely elegant building that faces on to Whitehall. The Banqueting House was built for James I. The king wanted a really big room, not just for banquets but for all kinds of state occasions and entertainment, such as plays and masques. The king brought in Inigo Jones, the most famous architect of the time. Inigo had been to Italy and was fired up by all the Roman ruins and Renaissance palaces he'd seen. So he designed a building for James in the Classical style, with lots of columns and other details he copied from the buildings of Italy.

When the Banqueting House was built, in 1619–22, most buildings in London were timber-framed and very higgeldy-piggeldy. The Banqueting House, with its straight lines and Classical columns, was something new – and the new fashion caught on. Soon everyone wanted Classical-style buildings, and British architecture was never the same again.

But it wasn't just high fashion. The Banqueting House became a celebration of monarchy, too. When Charles I took over the throne from his father, James I, the new king commissioned the artist Rubens to paint a series of pictures for the Banqueting House ceiling. These pictures show James as a wise king, making the room into a kind of memorial of good Stuart government.

And that memorial was very ironic indeed. When Charles I lost the civil war and his enemies decided to execute him, where did they stage the beheading? Right outside the Banqueting House! 'How are the mighty fallen,' – that was the message the king's opponents were putting across.

Today, the Banqueting House has been beautifully restored, and visitors can marvel at its gilded interior decoration and Rubens's marvellous ceiling paintings, and reflect on one of the most dramatic stories in the history of the monarchy, when King Charles I lost his head and England lost its king.

Westminster Abbey

Westminster Abbey is a huge church in the middle of London, right next to the Houses of Parliament. The church has a very long history, and for most of this time, it has been linked in one way or another with members of the royal family. It has been the setting for every English coronation since 1066 and many other royal events, from weddings to funerals, have been held here, too.

King Edgar (see Chapter 4) founded the original monastery at Westminster around 960. A few decades later, another Saxon king, Edward the Confessor (see Chapter 5), decided to give the abbey a further endowment, and it was rebuilt. The new church was consecrated in 1065, and the saintly king Edward was buried there after he died shortly afterwards.

Since then, a number of rulers made gifts to improve and extend the magnificent abbey still further. Two of the main builders were Henry III, who rebuilt the church in the 13th century in the new Gothic style of architecture, and Henry VII, who added a lavish chapel to the building in the 16th century.

In 1540, the monks left Westminster when Henry VIII closed all the monasteries, but the magnificent church was allowed to remain. It contains the memorials of many of Britain's kings and queens. Other highlights of the abbey include poets' corner, with its memorials to many of Britain's greatest writers; the shrine of the saintly king Edward the Confessor; the chapter house, a beautiful octagonal room of about 1250; and the museum, with its many royal statues and relics.

Kew Palace

This lovely little palace is in the Royal Botanic Gardens at Kew – themselves one of the great attractions of Britain with their fabulous trees, flower beds, and vast greenhouses full of palms, tropical plants, and temperate specimens. The palace was originally built by a Flemish merchant and for years was known as the Dutch House. It became a royal home in 1728 when three of George II's daughters came to live there.

For much of the 18th century, the palace was one of number of royal homes in Kew, including a couple of larger palaces that have since been demolished. But what makes Kew Palace fascinating today is that it has recently undergone a ten-year restoration, so visitors can see the building in better condition than it has been for over 200 years. And they can also find out all kinds of fascinating facts about the building that have come to light as a result of the work.

Kew's restorers made some amazing finds about the palace and its decoration. Here's just a selection:

- A patch of red pigment on an outer wall showed that the walls were once colour-washed bright red. So the glowing colour has been put back, and the palace is now very red indeed!

- Research into 19th-century decorators' bills enabled conservators to commission fabrics and carpets to reproduce the way some of the rooms looked in the time of George III.

- Analysis of layers of paintwork has allowed workers to restore early paint finishes.

- Some smaller upper rooms have been left as they were abandoned in the 18th century, so that the structure is revealed – in some places, you can even see the plasterers' thumbprints.

Add to all this fascinating exhibits bringing to life George III's many interests – including science, music, astronomy, and the arts – and Kew is one of the most fascinating, as well as one of the least known, of all the former royal homes.

Horse Guards Parade

Horse Guards Parade is a parade ground in central London, which is the site of one of the most vivid and spectacular royal ceremonies, Trooping the Colour. Trooping the Colour takes places in June to celebrate the monarch's official birthday. The monarch's official birthday is the day on which her birthday is celebrated publicly. British rulers developed the idea of a summer official birthday so that events, such as parades in honour of the monarch, could be held in good weather.

The ceremony of Trooping the Colour consists of a military parade and march-past involving some 1,400 troops, 200 horses, and about 10 military bands. The 'Colour' is the flag of one of the regiments that does the job of guarding the monarch, and the idea of parading the flag dates back to the time when it was essential for all soldiers to be able to recognise their own flag because it formed a vital rallying point in battle.

The ceremony of Trooping the Colour involves the monarch inspecting the troops. Then various elaborate displays of marching follow, during which the Colour is *trooped,* or marched, in front of the guards. The whole ceremony, featuring ranks of soldiers in bright red uniforms, is very colourful and is a highlight of the royal calendar.

Caernarfon Castle

Caernarfon Castle is one of the massive castles that Edward I built in North Wales as part of his campaign to take over Wales and rule it with a rod of iron. Actually there's a whole group of castles built in Wales by Edward at the end of the 13th century (see Chapter 8). Harlech, Conwy, and Beaumaris are three outstanding ones. But Caernarfon is the best of them all. It's known today not only as an awesome medieval fortress but as the backdrop to the ceremony in which Prince Charles was made Prince of Wales in 1969.

Caernarfon Castle is enormous – it's well over 500 feet in length, and many of the walls are ten feet thick. The building was planned and supervised by Edward's top master mason, a man called Master James of St George, who originally came from the Savoy area of France but worked on several of Edward's castle-building projects in Wales.

The castle was a state-of-the art fortress, with nine big towers and two enormous gatehouses that both protected the inhabitants and gave them positions from which to fire arrows at attackers. But it also had a huge symbolic role. Master James designed the walls with polygonal towers and bands of coloured masonry. This design directly imitated the great city walls at Constantinople (modern Istanbul), the great eastern capital of the Roman empire. It was as if Edward was saying to the Welsh, 'I have the might of a Roman emperor – challenge me at your peril.'

For much of the period, from its construction to the beginning of the Tudor dynasty in 1485, Caernarfon Castle played its role as the key base of the English kings in Wales. Caernarfon was virtually a second capital city from which English troops could march out if the Welsh showed signs of rebelling against their English kings.

But Henry VII, the first Tudor king, was a Welshman, and from his time on, the kingdoms of Wales and England were united fairly peacefully. So the old castle was neglected. In the 20th century, though, its historical interest was recognised, and it was preserved as a historic building.

Stirling Castle

Set on top of a tall cliff above an extinct volcano, Stirling has one of the most stunning locations of any British castle. The building was prominent in Scottish chronicles and played an important part in Scotland's military history, especially in the wars of the 13th and 14th centuries. It was also the scene of the murder of the Earl of Douglas by James II in 1452 and, later still, was the childhood home of Mary, Queen of Scots, and the place where she was crowned.

Stirling Castle has stunning architectural remains from the time of three notable Scottish kings – James IV, James V, and James VI. Amongst the best bits are the enormous medieval Great Hall, James III's massive gatehouse, the 16th-century kitchens, and the ornate 16th-century Renaissance royal palace.

One of the biggest and most stunning buildings in Scotland, Stirling Castle brings many episodes in Scottish history to life, both through its ancient stones and its modern interactive displays. It's also the scene of many popular entertainments – the esplanade or parade ground has staged concerts by major stars such as Bob Dylan.

Osborne House

Queen Victoria and Prince Albert (see Chapter 15) took over Osborne, on the Isle of Wight, in 1845, because the queen wanted a quiet country house where she could spend time with her family away from the cares and duties of state. Albert worked closely with his architect and builder, Thomas Cubitt, to rebuild the existing house, producing an Italian-looking design with a pair of tall, flat-topped towers, rather like the bell towers of Mediterranean churches.

Inside, the royal couple packed the house with works of art, from marble sculptures to dozens of portraits of their relations from the various royal families of Europe. Prince and architect also worked together on the gardens, again designed along Italianate lines and now restored to their Victorian glory. After Albert died, Victoria continued to improve the house, adding the Durbar Room, a huge banqueting hall with an ornate plaster ceiling full of symbols of India, paying homage to Victoria's rule as Empress of India over the subcontinent.

Visitors to Osborne today can really breathe in the atmosphere of Victorian England. From the grand drawing room, with its gilded furniture, to the more homely nursery, with its intricately patterned carpets, bed linen, and drapes, the house conjures up the kind of life the queen and her family led when they were out of the public eye.

Runnymede

Runnymede is in southern England, a few miles from the great royal castle at Windsor. It isn't a royal home or a battle site – it's just a field near the River Thames. But it's one of the most important places in British history because it was here in 1215 that King John set his seal on Magna Carta, the document in which he gave up absolute royal power and promised to consult the barons about key aspects of government (see Chapter 7). In other words, Runnymede could be called the place where British democracy began to develop.

Today, the meadows at Runnymede, partly wooded with both broad-leaved and coniferous trees, are a pleasant place to walk, admire the scenery, and look across the river to parkland containing the remains of a medieval priory and a yew tree said to be 2,000 years old. Visitors can also see the Magna Carta memorial, built by the American Bar Association and paid for with donations from some 9,000 American lawyers. Nearby are two other memorials: one to the airmen and women who died during World War II and another, erected in 1965, to President John F Kennedy.

Bosworth Field

One of the most important royal battles was fought in a field in the parish of Sutton Cheney, in Leicestershire in the English Midlands. The Battle of Bosworth Field took place in 1485. The opponents were Richard III, England's last king from the house of York, and Henry Tudor, the Welshman who won the battle and became Henry VII, the first Tudor ruler.

The battle was important for several reasons:

- It ended the years of strife known as the Wars of the Roses.
- It put on the English throne the Tudors, who produced influential rulers such as Henry VIII and Elizabeth I.
- It marked the end of the long period now known as the Middle Ages.

If you go to Bosworth Field today, you can walk across the terrain where the fighting took place. A visitor centre provides details of the battle and displays about the life of the period. Every year, on the weekend closest to the date of the battle (22 August), re-enactors wielding longbows, pikes, and swords recreate the battle.

Chapter 21

Ten Princes of Wales

In This Chapter

▶ Hanging on to power in Wales

▶ Preparing for life as king

▶ Jockeying for power and influence

*T*he title *Prince of Wales* was originally used to refer to native Welshmen who ruled their own country. In the Welsh language, the title was *Tywysog,* which literally means leader. But at the end of the 13th century, the English king, Edward I, began a campaign to conquer Wales, and by 1301, he had control of much of the country. So he gave his own son, also called Edward, the title of Prince of Wales. Ever since then, the title has been given to the eldest son of the English or British ruler.

This chapter looks at the lives of ten of the most famous Princes of Wales – three Welsh ones and seven of the 21 English princes who have had the title. The two most famous English Princes of Wales, George, who later become King George IV, and Charles, the current Prince, are covered in detail in their own chapters (Chapters 15 and 18 respectively).

Llywelyn ap Iorweth

This great Welsh leader was from Gwynedd in North Wales, and by about 1195, when he was in his 20s, he was ruler of this area. He developed good relations with the English king, John, and married one of John's illegitimate daughters, Joan. In 1208, he annexed Powys, in mid-Wales, after the ruler of this area, Gwenwynwyn, fell out with King John. Gwenwynwyn was the second most powerful man in Wales after Llywelyn, so taking over Powys in effect made Llywelyn ruler of the whole of Wales.

But Llywelyn's good relations with his father-in-law didn't last, because John invaded Gwynedd in 1211. Soon Llywelyn made an alliance with some other Welsh lords and fought back, throwing out the English. To get his own back, when the English barons turned on John and forced him to agree to Magna Carta, limiting his powers, Llywelyn joined them. That taught the English king not to mess with Llywelyn.

The next English king, Henry III, made a treaty with Llywelyn. Although fighting still sometimes occurred along the borders of England and Wales, the prince kept his power over Wales until he died in 1240. The Welsh respected this mighty ruler and often referred to him as Llywelyn the Great.

Llywelyn ap Gruffydd

Llywelyn came to power in Wales because he was the son of a nobleman called Gruffydd, who was an illegitimate son of Llywelyn ap Iorweth. After struggles against the English king Henry III and against other powerful lords in Wales, Llywelyn was eventually recognised by the English as ruler of Wales in the 1260s. He ruled until 1282, and so was the last undisputed prince of independent Wales before Edward I began to conquer the country – the Welsh sometimes refer to him as Llywelyn Our Last Leader.

As well as being a powerful military leader who could quell opposition in Wales, Llywelyn had to be a skilled politician to get recognition by England. The 1260s were a period when the English king, Henry III, was dealing with heavy opposition from his barons. The barons' leader, Simon de Montfort, became so powerful that by 1264 he was virtually ruler of England. So to get recognition from England, and to ensure that the English wouldn't attack Wales, Llywelyn first had to make a treaty with de Montfort. He managed this in 1265, but shortly afterwards, de Montfort was killed, and Llywelyn had to start all over again, reaching agreement with Henry himself in 1267.

That was the peak of Llywelyn's power because the next English king, Edward I, was determined to conquer Wales. Llywelyn and his Welsh relatives fought valiantly, but Edward threw huge resources into his campaign. Edward even gave Llywelyn an easy way out, offering him a big estate in England in return for giving up Gwynedd to the English. But Llywelyn refused to give in. He was finally separated from his army by a trick and killed – his severed head was later displayed with gruesome glee by the English in the streets of London.

Edward

In April 1284, the English queen, Eleanor of Castile, wife of King Edward I, gave birth to a baby son. He was born in Caernarfon Castle, the greatest of King Edward's huge fortresses in Wales, the land he'd just conquered. The king was undoubtedly pleased that his son was born in Wales – in fact, he seems to have made sure that Eleanor was in Caernarfon in time for the birth because he wanted his son to be made the first English Prince of Wales.

In 1301, it was formally announced that the young boy was Prince of Wales. There's a story that the king held up the infant Edward and 'offered' him to the Welsh as 'your new prince', but it's untrue – it was made up by a 16th-century writer. But in effect, that's what Edward was doing – giving the Welsh a new prince, not a native ruler but one who would stand for English domination of their country.

Edward didn't know a lot about the politics of this event when he became Prince of Wales, as he was only 7 years old at the time. And he had a short reign as Prince of Wales because in 1307, his father died, and he became king of England. For more information about his reign as King Edward II, see Chapter 8.

Edward, the Black Prince

The Black Prince was the son of King Edward III and his queen, Philippa of Hainault. He was born in 1330 and became Prince of Wales in 1343. Young Edward liked fine clothes, tournaments, gambling, and big spending. He was a founding member of the knightly Order of the Garter and established himself as one of the most glamorous of all the Princes of Wales.

But Edward wasn't all velvet cloaks and showy hats. By the time he was 16 years old, he'd won huge respect as a soldier, too. In the 14th century, Britain was deeply embroiled in the Hundred Years' War against France (see Chapter 8). The prince played a leading role in several key battles:

- **Crécy (1346),** when England beat France. The 16-year-old prince commanded a division (roughly one third) of the English army and fought bravely.

- **Poitiers (1356),** which was another major English victory. The prince kept a reserve cavalry unit hidden in some woods; these men were able to attack the French from the rear, causing grave damage.

- **Najera (1367),** a battle in Spain between the English and their ally, Pedro Castille, against the French and their ally, Pedro's brother Henry. The English and Pedro won, but Edward and Pedro fell out over money afterwards.

Edward was England's great hope, a brilliant leader and a talented soldier who seemed likely to make the ideal medieval king. But after his military campaign in Spain, he fell ill and died in 1376 before his father.

No one is quite sure why Edward became known as the Black Prince. The nickname wasn't used in the prince's lifetime and seems to have begun to be used about 200 years after his death. One possible reason is that he wore distinctive black armour. Another explanation is that it was a name coined by the French, who saw him as a figure of doom because of the defeats he inflicted on them.

Owain Glyndwr

Owain Glyndwr (his name is sometimes given in the English form, Owen Glendower) was a nobleman from Powys who led a revolt against King Henry IV from 1400 to around 1412. He was briefly successful in returning Wales to Welsh rule, but had to fight almost continuously to keep his power. Owain became the last Welsh leader of Wales and has therefore become a figure with a mythology all his own. Shakespeare portrayed him as a kind of royal magician and later Welsh nationalists made him into a hero. He is remembered as one of the most remarkable guerrilla leaders Britain has known.

Owain was born in 1359, but his father died when he was still a child, and he was brought up by foster parents. Later, it's thought that he studied law in London before returning to Wales. In the 1390s, Owain had a dispute with a Welsh neighbour, and when there was an appeal to Parliament, judgment was given against him. As a result, Owain rebelled against English rule and was proclaimed ruler of Wales in the year 1400. Henry IV turned his army on the rebel, but bad weather and Welsh guerrilla tactics defeated the English while support for Owain spread through Wales.

The Welsh and English fought for years for control of Wales. In 1405, the French, Henry's arch-enemies, came to Wales to fight on Owain's side. But the following year, the French pulled out, and Henry himself fought with more vigour. From then on, the Welsh lost ground, but continued to fight a desperate guerrilla war against the English. The struggle went on until Owain disappeared in 1412. No one knows what happened to Owain, but by 1421, his son had negotiated a pardon with the new English king, Henry V, and the English kings were confirmed as rulers of Wales once more.

Edward of Westminster

The only son of Henry VI and Queen Margaret of Anjou, Edward of Westminster was born in 1453 and was made Prince of Wales a year later at a ceremony in Windsor Castle. He became famous as the only holder of the title to die in battle, and his life and career were perhaps the saddest of all the Princes of Wales.

Edward had a troubled youth. His father disinherited him, and the Yorkist Edward IV seized the crown. Queen Margaret responded by getting support together for an attack on the Yorkists, to put Henry VI back on the throne with her son Edward as the rightful heir (see Chapter 9). She enlisted the powerful Earl of Warwick as her supporter, and, as part of the deal, Edward was married to Warwick's daughter, Anne. The campaign was only intermittently successful – they got Henry back on the throne, but he was soon replaced by Edward IV again. And poor prince Edward was killed at the Battle of Tewkesbury in 1471, fighting for his inheritance.

Arthur, Duke of Cornwall

Remember the story of King Arthur, the great legendary king who will return to rule England one day? Well, in the 16th century, England nearly had a King Arthur. Arthur, Duke of Cornwall, was the eldest son of King Henry VII and his queen, Elizabeth of York (see Chapter 13). He was born in 1486, was made Duke of Cornwall at birth, and became Prince of Wales in 1489. His father, who had won his crown in the Battle of Bosworth the year before Arthur was born, was keen to arrange a good marriage for the prince to secure the future of the Tudor dynasty, so Arthur was betrothed to the Spanish princess Catherine of Aragon when he was just 2 years old. They were married in 1501, when Arthur was still in his teens.

All the hopes of Henry VII rested on his young son, but tragedy struck. Soon after the wedding, Arthur caught a fever, and he died in spring 1502. His parents were distraught. But one young man did rather well out of the tragedy. Arthur's younger brother Henry inherited his titles – and, amazingly, his wife, Catherine. In 1509, he became one of England's most famous rulers, Henry VIII.

Henry Frederick, Duke of Cornwall

The first son of King James VI of Scotland (who was also James I of England) and his queen, Anne of Denmark, was born in 1594 at Stirling Castle. At this time, his father was king of Scotland. When James became King of England as well, in 1603 (see Chapter 14), Henry was made Duke of Cornwall. He was invested as Prince of Wales in 1610.

Henry was one of the most remarkable Princes of Wales. He was highly intelligent and very interested in the arts, building up contacts with notable artists and writers, collecting Flemish and Italian paintings, and turning his court into one of the most cultured England has ever seen. He was also physically attractive – tall, handsome, and good at all kinds of sports, from riding to fencing. There were hopes that he would make an outstanding king, but in 1612, when he was 18, he caught a disease and died. The era's greatest poets, including John Donne and George Herbert, wrote tributes to him. Modern historians are virtually certain from the descriptions of his illness and the post mortem examination that he died from typhoid. His titles passed to his younger brother, Charles.

James Francis Edward Stuart

In 1688, a baby was born to Mary of Modena, second wife of King James II (see Chapter 14). Both the king and his wife were Catholics, and there were widespread fears that the country would be landed with another Catholic ruler when James II died – he had two Protestant daughters by his first wife, but a male heir took precedence. The opposition to James II, his religion, and his still tiny male heir quickly gathered pace, and in a matter of months, King James fled the country.

After James's flight, William III and his wife Mary (eldest daughter of James II) took over as joint monarchs. Technically, baby James's time as Prince of Wales lasted only a few months. But to his Catholic supporters, it lasted years. They saw James as the rightful king once his father died in 1701, and young James spent much of the rest of his life raising support for his claim to the throne. He became known as the Old Pretender and had a substantial following in Scotland and France.

James tried to take over the throne in 1715, but his invasion plan was a failure, and soon after, his supporters turned to his son, Charles (known as Bonnie Prince Charlie) as their leader. In James's sad life of exile, his title of Prince of Wales did him little good, and he remained yet another bearer of the title not to make it on to the throne.

Frederick, Duke of Cornwall

The son of King George II, Frederick was born in 1707, when his father was still Prince George and his mother Princess Caroline of Ansbach (see Chapter 15). As a child and young man, he lived in the family home of Hanover and so spent most of his young life away from his parents, who lived in England. When his father became king in 1727, Frederick was made Prince of Wales and was finally allowed to come to England to take up his new position. But his parents rejected him, lavishing all their affections on their younger children who had been born in England.

Cut off from family affection – and also from family power – Prince Frederick set up a rival court at his London home, Leicester House, where he lived in splendour. He ran up big debts, but settled down when he got married to Augusta of Saxe-Gotha in 1736. The pair had a large brood of children and lived, isolated from the court, mostly at their country house at Cliveden in Buckinghamshire. Frederick died in 1751 at the young age of 44, frustrated at his lack of political power but proud of his family.

Chapter 22

Ten or So Charismatic Consorts

. . . .

In This Chapter

▶ Finding roles for royal spouses

▶ Wielding an influence from the sidelines

▶ Marching into battle and being frogmarched into jail

. . . .

*T*he position of royal spouse has meant playing many different roles, from mother to deputy monarch. Many royal consorts remained deeply in the shadow of their powerful spouses. But a few stand out as powerful personalities, and some have had a profound effect on British history. A few, like Eleanor of Aquitaine, were powerful politicians; some, like Eleanor of Castile, increased the wealth of the crown; and one, Margaret of Anjou, even led troops into battle.

Because the majority of British rulers have been kings, most of these consorts have been women and have had to cope with the demands of politics and dynastic power while also bringing up children. It's a tough task, but a few of the most charismatic consorts have thrived on this kind of royal multi-tasking. A couple of the more successful ones are covered elsewhere in this book – Queen Victoria's husband, Albert, in Chapter 15, and George VI's consort, Queen Elizabeth, in Chapter 16.

Eleanor of Aquitaine

A high-ranking noblewoman from southern France, Eleanor (c. 1122–1204) rose to be one of the most famous and influential women of the 12th century. She was the daughter of Guillaume, Duke of Aquitaine, and when her father died, Eleanor, still only a teenager, inherited his huge southern French lands – basically the area between the River Loire and the Pyrenees. She married Louis VII, king of France, in 1137, but in 1152, Louis divorced Eleanor. In the Middle Ages, a divorce, which was quite unusual, had to be approved by the church. The official grounds for the divorce of Louis and Eleanor were that the couple were too closely related, but the real reason probably had more to do with Louis's jealousy. Eleanor, who had two daughters with Louis, became the wife of Count Henry of Anjou, who later became King Henry II of England, shortly after the divorce.

Eleanor was fiery, intelligent, passionate, and devoted to her southern French homeland. She bore Henry eight children, including two future kings of England (Richard I and John). In addition to all this child-bearing, Eleanor played a major part in the government of her husband's large empire, which stretched from northern England to southern France, often deputising for him in one region while he was in another. But she seems to have turned against her husband and was involved in a plot in which the couple's sons revolted against Henry. No one knows for sure why, but in 1174, Eleanor was captured, taken to England, and thrown in prison for at least ten years.

But in 1189, Eleanor made an amazing political comeback. Her favourite son Richard inherited the English throne, and his mother became his deputy, wielding even more power than she'd done in the early years of her marriage to King Henry. This responsibility was a major task because Richard was absent from England for most of his reign, pursuing military campaigns in Europe and the Holy Land, and he even got captured by his enemies. By this time, Eleanor was 67 years old (an age that most medieval people saw only in their dreams), and she was amazingly active, holding courts all over England, making governmental decisions, and playing a part in the measures to get Richard released from captivity.

Eleanor was a superstar of the Middle Ages and one of the most influential women of the period. Some medieval writers criticised her because she was said to have had several affairs, but most of these writers were monks who couldn't cope with a woman wielding power in a man's world, and a lot of what they wrote was malicious gossip. She was one of the most powerful royal consorts in British history.

Eleanor of Castile

Eleanor of Castile (1241–90) was the daughter of King Ferdinand III of Castile in Spain and his second wife, French noblewoman Jeanne de Dammartin. She married the English prince Edward, who was to become King Edward I, in 1254.

Eleanor was not the kind of medieval wife who stood aside and let her husband make all the running. During the baronial wars of Henry III's reign she was suspected of helping Henry's opponents hire Spanish mercenaries, and when the wars ended, she acquired many lands that had been held by the rebels, building up her already considerable wealth. After the wars, she joined Edward on a different kind of military campaign – she travelled with him on Crusade (see Chapter 8). On the way home, Edward discovered that his father had died and that he and Eleanor were king and queen.

As queen, Eleanor carried on building her wealth. She grabbed lands that were held as security for English knights' debts to Jewish moneylenders and then began to build up yet more property by buying land where she could. No previous queen had actively gone out and acquired landed estates, and many contemporaries were shocked that a woman should be involved in this kind of business. But the income from the land brought in much-needed cash for the royal family, and Eleanor spent some of it founding monasteries and encouraging English writers.

Eleanor and Edward seem to have been a devoted couple, and when the queen caught a fever and died in 1290, he was distraught. Eleanor was away from the court, near Lincoln, when she died, and Edward organised a big funeral procession to bring her body back to London. Ornate stone crosses were built at the procession's 12 stopping places, and the surviving crosses, beautifully carved, are among the glories of medieval art. They're a fitting tribute to a rich, powerful queen who was also a generous patron of the church.

Isabella

Queen Isabella (1292–1358) was the daughter of Philip IV of France and his wife Joan of Navarre. In 1308, she married Edward II at Boulogne and was crowned queen in Westminster Abbey the same year. The young queen seems to have found life difficult with Edward. Her husband was not an easy character to get on with – because of his devotion to his favourites, courtiers such as Piers Gaveston, he had little time for his wife. The couple had four children, but they came slowly and with long intervals in between, which was quite unusual in the Middle Ages when kings and queens usually wanted to produce heirs as quickly as possible.

In 1325, Isabella's brother, French king Charles IV, seized Edward's lands in France, and the queen returned to France. Estranged from her husband, Isabella fell in love with Roger Mortimer, one of Edward's nobles who had fallen out of favour. The following year, Isabella and Mortimer invaded England and forced Edward II off the throne. In January 1327, they replaced him with Isabella and Edward's teenage son, Edward III. Isabella and Mortimer ruled the country as regents.

A few years later, Edward III took over power in his own right. Mortimer was executed, and Isabella was sidelined – she spent the last 30 years of her life in seclusion at Castle Rising in Norfolk.

Margaret of Anjou

Margaret (1430–82) was the French-born wife of Rene I of Naples (he was also Duke of Anjou in France) and Isabella, Duchess of Lorraine. She married the English king Henry VI in 1445. From the start, Margaret had a difficult time as Henry's wife. The king was more interested in religion than either his kingdom or, probably, his queen, and suffered terrible periods of mental breakdown. But Margaret stuck by her man when it mattered, like when his rival Richard, Duke of York, tried to take over the kingdom.

Henry and Margaret were captured by Richard, but Margaret managed to escape – and straightaway raised an army. She scored some major victories, including the Battle of Wakefield in 1460, when she had rebel leaders, the Duke of York and the Earl of Salisbury, executed. Their heads were later hung on the gates of the city of York as a terrible warning to their supporters. Another victory, at St Albans, enabled Margaret to free Henry from captivity. But further battles ended in defeats for the queen, even when she led her own troops into battle at Tewkesbury in 1471. After this defeat, Margaret was imprisoned in the Tower of London, until the King of France took pity on her and paid her ransom. She lived out her final few years in her native Anjou.

Margaret's career was an amazing one. It was very unusual for a woman to play a major part in planning military campaigns, let alone to lead troops in the actual fighting. Margaret did so, bravely, and she's remembered as a remarkable leader, even if, in the end, she was defeated.

Elizabeth of York

The father of Elizabeth of York (1466–1503) was King Edward IV, and her mother was Elizabeth Woodville, Edward's queen. This made Elizabeth a princess of the House of York in the period when the Yorkists were fighting with the House of Lancaster for the English throne.

As a Yorkist princess, Elizabeth made an attractive wife for anyone who wanted to strengthen their claim to the throne – or to weaken a rival's claim. When Edward IV died and his brother Richard III became king, there were rumours that Richard wanted to marry Elizabeth for these reasons, even though he was married already. Richard failed to pull off this trick, and Elizabeth was finally married to the next king, Henry VII, the first Tudor.

By taking a Yorkist queen, Henry was making his hold on the crown stronger by allying himself with the House of York. But it seems likely that the marriage was more than a political convenience. The couple had seven or eight children. Elizabeth also played an important role at court, helping to plan new buildings for the royal palace at Greenwich, for example. And everybody seemed to like her – she was described as both handsome and able: not only Henry was saddened when she died, after the difficult birth of her daughter, Katherine, in 1503. Henry had her buried in his magnificent new Lady Chapel at Westminster Abbey.

Philip II of Spain

Britain has been ruled by women only on a few occasions, but when kings and queens had real political power, having a woman on the throne posed a dynastic challenge – foreign kings turning up wanting to marry the queen and hoping to take over the country, too. Queen Victoria sidestepped the issue by marrying a relatively minor royal who was content to be Prince Consort rather than king. Queen Elizabeth I got around the problem by refusing to marry at all. But Elizabeth's sister, Mary, married one of the most powerful kings in Europe, Philip II of Spain.

Philip must have been overjoyed. England was a big prize. The wedding took place in 1554, by which time Mary was already queen in her own right, and the deal was that Philip would have a big role to play in decisions about ruling Britain. But Philip wasn't actually made king of England, even though there were moves in that direction. (His head was put with Mary's on coins, for example.)

Philip had a lot on his plate. He had a huge realm on mainland Europe, as well as England. So governing England was mostly left to native English advisers. But, as both he and Mary were devout Catholics, he played a major part in restoring the links with the Roman church that had been broken by Mary's father, Henry VIII. But Philip's influence on England was curtailed. He had to spend a lot of time away from the country, looking after his European interests and fighting wars on the mainland. In 1558, Mary died, her Protestant sister Elizabeth became queen, and Philip's role in England came to an end.

Henrietta Maria

Queen Henrietta Maria (1609–69) was born Henriette-Marie de Bourbon, daughter of Henri IV of France and his wife Maria de Medici. She was married to King Charles I in 1625, shortly after Charles became king. This was a proxy wedding, and the couple were married in person the following year. To begin with, Henrietta Maria found her relationship with her new husband difficult.

A lot of Charles's time was spent with his favourite, the Duke of Buckingham, and the queen, who had been an orphan, missed France greatly. But after Buckingham died in 1628, Charles and his queen became closer and warmer and seem to have grown to love each other dearly.

As well as bearing nine children, Henrietta Maria took an active part in politics, especially when her husband's power was threatened by Parliament and the country moved toward the civil war of the 1640s. She rallied support for Charles, raising both money and troops for his cause. And she was devastated when the royalists finally lost the war, and Charles was led to the scaffold to be executed.

After the beheading of her husband, Henrietta Maria retired to France, where she lived for most of the rest of her life apart from a few years when she returned as Dowager Queen when the monarchy was restored in 1660. Henrietta Maria was in many ways a good queen who gave her husband children and supported him loyally in the monarchy's darkest years. But she was also an outsider, a Frenchwoman and Catholic in Protestant England, and a wife who had to stand by when her husband was executed.

Catherine of Braganza

The Portuguese princess Catherine of Braganza (1638–1705) married Charles II in 1662. In many ways, she had the most difficult time of any British queen because the king was an addicted womaniser who had a string of mistresses. Catherine, meanwhile, was unable to produce a living heir for Charles, in spite of a number of pregnancies.

Catherine coped as best she could with her husband's unfaithfulness, and Charles, for his part, tried to ensure that his mistresses treated the queen with respect (one was even ditched for not doing so). When Charles died in 1685, Catherine stayed in England for a while, but eventually returned to Portugal. She's remembered as a long-suffering consort who gave England one lasting legacy – she made tea popular, and it's been the national drink ever since.

George of Denmark

The husband of Queen Anne was George of Denmark. They were married in 1683, when he was Prince Jørgen of Denmark, and she had no thought of becoming queen. After the marriage, he became a British citizen and was known in Britain as George. He was a rather staid character, not really the most charismatic consort – in fact, Charles II said of him, 'I have tried him drunk and I have tried him sober; and there is nothing in him.'

But George's life proved that there was more to being a consort than having a good time with the more dissolute members of the royal family. He was an able administrator, a leader of the Navy, and a good husband to Anne – the poor queen got pregnant many times, but none of their children survived into adulthood. George died in 1708, and the queen was deeply upset. He wasn't glamorous, but he was a dutiful partner who didn't want to use his position as royal husband to carve out more power for himself.

Adelaide of Saxe-Meiningen

Adelaide of Saxe-Meiningen (1792–1849) was the daughter of Georg, Duke of Saxe-Meingingen and his duchess, Luise Eleonore. She married the future King William IV in 1818. It was an unusual wedding in several ways. First, it was a double ceremony at which William's brother, Edward, also married. Second, the bridegroom, William, had shown no inclination to get married for decades, even though he'd had a mistress for years and had several children by her. What changed William's mind was that he suddenly realised he was in line for the throne, and he needed a proper wife and legitimate heirs to secure the succession.

This put Adelaide in a peculiar situation. It was her job both to produce an heir and to fit in somehow with her husband's existing domestic situation. Sadly, Adelaide and William didn't succeed in producing an heir who survived infancy. But she did accept and accommodate her husband's past, getting to know his illegitimate children and helping to bring them up.

All this brought Queen Adelaide a lot of public sympathy, which she encouraged by being generally good-tempered and devoting a lot of her time and money to charitable causes. She was also kind to her niece, Victoria, the future queen, even though Victoria's mother didn't like her very much. So Adelaide was in many ways a model for later rulers, sacrificing her personal life for good works and to support the monarchy, and she remained popular in her later life, surviving her husband by 12 years.

Alexandra of Denmark

Like Queen Adelaide (see preceding section), Alexandra of Denmark (1844–1925) married a British royal with a colourful past. Her husband was Queen Victoria's eldest son, the Prince of Wales and future King Edward VII. Edward was famous for his affairs and his love of lavish living. The fact that both of these preoccupations were often pursued in Paris didn't make them much less public, or less potentially difficult, for a wife to handle.

The royal couple married in 1863 and spent the next 38 years as Prince and Princess of Wales while Queen Victoria ruled her vast empire. Alexandra was beautiful, and Edward liked her, in spite of his wayward ways. During the first decade of their marriage, the queen had six children.

Alexandra grew to tolerate Edward's mistresses and made a worthwhile public life for herself by supporting many charities, gaining the respect and love of the British people in the process. Perhaps the most famous of her charities was Queen Alexandra's Royal Army Nursing Corps, founded to look after wounded soldiers during the Boer War. She survived King Edward by 15 years.

Index

Notes

Notes

FOR DUMMIES®

Do Anything. Just Add Dummies

HOME

UK editions

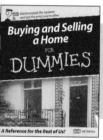

Buying and Selling a Home
FOR DUMMIES
0-7645-7027-7

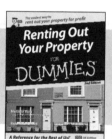

Renting Out Your Property
FOR DUMMIES
2nd Edition
0-470-02921-8

DIY & Home Maintenance
ALL-IN-ONE
FOR DUMMIES
0-7645-7054-4

PERSONAL FINANCE

Investing
FOR DUMMIES
0-7645-7023-4

Paying Less Tax 2006/2007
FOR DUMMIES
0-470-02860-2

Sorting Out Your Finances
FOR DUMMIES
0-7645-7039-0

BUSINESS

Starting a Business
FOR DUMMIES
0-7645-7018-8

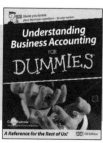

Understanding Business Accounting
FOR DUMMIES
0-7645-7025-0

Business Plans
FOR DUMMIES
0-7645-7026-9

Answering Tough Interview
Questions For Dummies
(0-470-01903-4)

Arthritis For Dummies
(0-470-02582-4)

Being the Best Man
For Dummies
(0-470-02657-X)

British History
For Dummies
(0-470-03536-6)

Building Confidence
For Dummies
(0-470-01669-8)

Buying a Home on a Budget
For Dummies
(0-7645-7035-8)

Buying a Property in Eastern
Europe For Dummies
(0-7645-7047-1)

Children's Health
For Dummies
(0-470-02735-5)

Cognitive Behavioural Therapy
For Dummies
(0-470-01838-0)

CVs For Dummies
(0-7645-7017-X)

Diabetes For Dummies
(0-7645-7019-6)

Divorce For Dummies
(0-7645-7030-7)

eBay.co.uk For Dummies
(0-7645-7059-5)

European History
For Dummies
(0-7645-7060-9)

Gardening For Dummies
(0-470-01843-7)

Genealogy Online
For Dummies
(0-7645-7061-7)

Golf For Dummies
(0-470-01811-9)

Hypnotherapy For Dummies
(0-470-01930-1)

Irish History For Dummies
(0-7645-7040-4)

Marketing For Dummies
(0-7645-7056-0)

Neuro-linguistic Programming
For Dummies
(0-7645-7028-5)

Nutrition For Dummies
(0-7645-7058-7)

Parenting For Dummies
(0-470-02714-2)

Pregnancy For Dummies
(0-7645-7042-0)

Retiring Wealthy For Dummies
(0-470-02632-4)

Rugby Union For Dummies
(0-470-03537-4)

Small Business Employment
Law For Dummies
(0-7645-7052-8)

Starting a Business on
eBay.co.uk For Dummies
(0-470-02666-9)

Su Doku For Dummies
(0-470-01892-5)

The GL Diet For Dummies
(0-470-02753-3)

Thyroid For Dummies
(0-470-03172-7)

UK Law and Your Rights
For Dummies
(0-470-02796-7)

Wills, Probate and Inheritance
Tax For Dummies
(0-7645-7055-2)

Winning on Betfair
For Dummies
(0-470-02856-4)

FOR DUMMIES®

Do Anything. Just Add Dummies

HOBBIES

Poker
0-7645-5232-5

Sewing
0-7645-6847-7

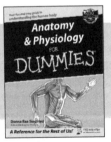

Drawing
0-7645-5476-X

Also available:

Art For Dummies
(0-7645-5104-3)

Aromatherapy For Dummies
(0-7645-5171-X)

Bridge For Dummies
(0-471-92426-1)

Card Games For Dummies
(0-7645-9910-0)

Chess For Dummies
(0-7645-8404-9)

Improving Your Memory
For Dummies
(0-7645-5435-2)

Massage For Dummies
(0-7645-5172-8)

Meditation For Dummies
(0-471-77774-9)

Photography For Dummies
(0-7645-4116-1)

Quilting For Dummies
(0-7645-9799-X)

EDUCATION

Cooking Basics
0-7645-7206-7

The Koran
0-7645-5581-2

Anatomy & Physiology
0-7645-5422-0

Also available:

Algebra For Dummies
(0-7645-5325-9)

Algebra II For Dummies
(0-471-77581-9)

Astronomy For Dummies
(0-7645-8465-0)

Buddhism For Dummies
(0-7645-5359-3)

Calculus For Dummies
(0-7645-2498-4)

Forensics For Dummies
(0-7645-5580-4)

Islam For Dummies
(0-7645-5503-0)

Philosophy For Dummies
(0-7645-5153-1)

Religion For Dummies
(0-7645-5264-3)

Trigonometry For Dummie
(0-7645-6903-1)

PETS

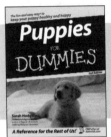

Puppies
0-470-03717-2

Dog Training
0-7645-8418-9

Cats
0-7645-5275-9

Also available:

Labrador Retrievers
For Dummies
(0-7645-5281-3)

Aquariums For Dummies
(0-7645-5156-6)

Birds For Dummies
(0-7645-5139-6)

Dogs For Dummies
(0-7645-5274-0)

Ferrets For Dummies
(0-7645-5259-7)

Golden Retrievers
For Dummies
(0-7645-5267-8)

Horses For Dummies
(0-7645-9797-3)

Jack Russell Terriers
For Dummies
(0-7645-5268-6)

Puppies Raising & Training
Diary For Dummies
(0-7645-0876-8)

Available wherever books are sold. For more information or to order direct go to www.wiley.com or call 0800 243407 (Non UK call +44 1243 843296)

FOR DUMMIES®

The easy way to get more done and have more fun

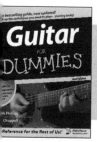

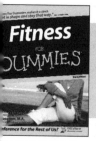
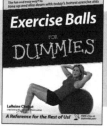

DISCARD FOR DUMMIES®

Helping you expand your horizons and achieve your potential

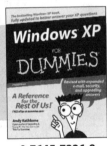